# GERMAN ▾ MYTHS
# AND ▾ LEGENDS

*A Teutonic warrior, by Gustave Doré.*

# GERMAN·MYTHS AND·LEGENDS

*By*

## DONALD A. MACKENZIE

*Illustrated by Gustave Doré*
*and*
*Other Artists*
*of the Nineteenth Century*

## AVENEL BOOKS
New York

Previously titled *Teutonic Myth and Legend*.

Copyright © 1985 by Crown Publishers, Inc.
All rights reserved.

Published 1985 by Avenel Books,
distributed by Crown Publishers, Inc.
225 Park Avenue South, New York, New York 10003

Manufactured in the United States of America

*All line illustrations without attribution are by Gustave Doré.*

Library of Congress Cataloging in Publication Data

Mackenzie, Donald Alexander, 1873–1936.
    German myths and legends.

    Reprint. Originally published: Teutonic myth and
legend. With new foreword.
    Includes index.
    1. Mythology, Germanic.    2. Legends, Germanic.
I. Title.
BL860.M3   1985       293'.13       84–28353
ISBN: 0–517–46299–0

h g f e d c

*To My Wife*

# CONTENTS

FOREWORD . . . . . . . ix

PREFACE . . . . . . . . xiii

INTRODUCTION . . . . . . xvii

I. STORY OF CREATION . . . . . 1

II. THE NINE WORLDS . . . . . 11

III. THE DEEDS OF ODIN . . . . . 21

IV. HOW EVIL ENTERED ASGARD . . . 29

V. THE WINTER WAR . . . . . 44

VI. TRIUMPH OF LOVE . . . . . 53

VII. THE LOST SWORD OF VICTORY . . . 64

VIII. FALL OF ASGARD . . . . . 72

IX. THE GODS RECONCILED . . . . 82

X. LOKE'S EVIL PROGENY . . . . 90

XI. THOR'S GREAT FISHING . . . . 98

XII. THE CITY OF ENCHANTMENTS . . . 112

XIII. THOR IN PERIL . . . . . . 126

XIV. THE GREAT STONE GIANT . . . . 137

XV. BALDER THE BEAUTIFUL . . . . 146

XVI. THE BINDING OF LOKE . . . . 165

XVII. THE DUSK OF THE GODS . . . . 177

XVIII. THE COMING OF BEOWULF . . . 187

XIX. CONFLICT WITH DEMONS . . . . 197

XX. BEOWULF AND THE DRAGON . . . 210

XXI. HOTHER AND BALDER . . . . 221

XXII. THE TRADITIONAL HAMLET . . . 232

# CONTENTS

| XXIII. | HAMLET'S STORM-MILL | . . . . | 246 |
| XXIV. | LAND OF THE NOT-DEAD AND MANY MARVELS . | 254 |
| XXV. | THE DOOM OF THE VOLSUNGS | . . . | 282 |
| XXVI. | HOW SIGMUND WAS AVENGED | . . . | 292 |
| XXVII. | HELGI HUNDINGSBANE . | . . . . | 299 |
| XXVIII. | SIGURD THE DRAGON SLAYER | . . . | 309 |
| XXIX. | BRYNHILD AND GUDRUN | . . . . | 322 |
| XXX. | THE LAST OF THE VOLSUNGS | . . . | 338 |
| XXXI. | GUDRUN'S VENGEANCE . | . . . . | 343 |
| XXXII. | SIEGFRIED AND THE NIBELUNGS | . . . | 354 |
| XXXIII. | THE PROMISE OF KRIEMHILD | . . . | 362 |
| XXXIV. | HOW BRUNHILD AND KRIEMHILD WERE WON | 372 |
| XXXV. | THE BETRAYAL OF SIEGFRIED | . . . | 382 |
| XXXVI. | THE NIBELUNGEN TRAGEDY | . . . | 391 |
| XXXVII. | DIETRICH OF BERN | . . . . | 404 |
| XXXVIII. | THE LAND OF GIANTS | . . . . | 415 |
| XXXIX. | THE WONDERFUL ROSE GARDEN | . . | 424 |
| XL. | VIRGINAL, QUEEN OF THE MOUNTAINS . | . | 434 |
| XLI. | DIETRICH IN EXILE | . . . . | 439 |
| XLII. | THE KING'S HOMECOMING | . . . | 448 |
| | INDEX · . . . . . . . | 455 |

# FOREWORD

---

Donald A. MacKenzie's intensive and complete collection of the myths and legends of the German peoples draws the reader into a sombre and violent world, a spiritual terrain which mirrors the severity of the northern climate from which they sprang. These are the myths of the Teutonic, or Germanic, peoples, but they come down to us through the renditions of the Norse poet-storytellers because the Scandinavians were the only group of Teutonic tribes to save and record the early pre-Christian beliefs and legends. The ancient Teutons were divided into three major groups: the Goths, who at first settled in central Europe, and then migrated toward the East; the Teutons, who settled throughout the Scandinavian countries; and the West Germans, ancestors of the present Germans and the Anglo-Saxons, who lived at first in North Germany and then gradually migrated toward the Rhine and the Danube, while some of their tribes later crossed the Channel to Britain.

In the very creation myth of the Norse people an inherent cruelty and harshness is revealed. A giant, Ymer, lumbers through the vastness of the cosmic void. He is captured by an early family of gods, who grind his body in a mill to form the universe. His bones become the mountains, his blood the sea, his skull the heavens.

The primitive gods eventually give birth to the Norse pantheon, the Asa-gods, who live in the celestial city of Asgard. These deities are powerful, the creators and rulers of mankind, but, unlike the Greco-Roman gods, they are neither omnipotent nor immortal. They, like mankind, are subject to the inexorable decrees of the spinning sisters, the Norns, or Fates. The Asa-gods are doomed to an end which is as violent as the origin of the cosmos; they will be defeated in battle by the rebellious progeny of Ymer, the evil giants known as the Jotuns. The universe will return to primal chaos following the "Ragnarik," or "Twilight of the Gods."

The vulnerability of the gods is a salient characteristic of Norse mythology, highlighted in many of the tales recounted by Mr. MacKenzie. Odin, chief of the gods, must sacrifice his right eye in order to drink from the fountain of wisdom. In another interesting example, the gods, in order to remain forever young, must daily eat of the golden fruit guarded by the dawn goddess, Idun. When she is abducted by a giant, the gods begin to wrinkle and turn grey. In yet another example of the god's curious lack of omnipotence, Balder, the deity who repre-sents the joy inspired by sunlight, is murdered with an arrow carved from mistletoe. The death of Balder is, of course, an expression of the gloom of the Scandinavian winter. It also illustrates a fundamental pessimism: the most resplendent and virtuous deity is the first of the Asa to be defeated.

The murder of Balder is committed by a god unique to Norse mythology, Loke. He is sometimes portrayed as a mis-chievous prankster and sometimes as a deceitful and malevolent Satan figure, sower of discord among the gods and an ally of the Jotuns. The subtle Loke is a master of transformation, taking the form of swiftly moving animals such as the salmon or eagle. He is the father of the frightful ogress, Hela, ruler of the underworld.

Norse beliefs concerning the afterlife reveal the central importance of warfare and the dominance of the warrior in pagan Scandinavia. Warriors who die bravely are carried from the battlefield by Odin's daughters, the Valkyries. They are brought to a paradise, feasting with Odin and Freyja, the beautiful goddess of fertility; while those who die of illness or old age must go to the underworld, Hel, where they are judged and set to expiate their sins. The evil are confined to Nifel-hel, the region of torture, where they lose the power of speech and are transformed into monsters.

The importance of the warrior is also evident in the heroic legends retold by Mr. MacKenzie. These all revolve around the theme of vengeance, central to the Norse moral code. The hero, Beowolf, slays the man-eating monster, Grendl, and then must battle Grendl's mother, who seeks revenge for her son's death. MacKenzie includes in his volume an ancient version of the Hamlet legend, in which the Danish prince succeeds in wreaking vengeance on his father's usurper. MacKenzie's prose rendition of the *Nibelungenlied* (the *Song of the Nibelungs*), tells of the mutual vengeance of Kriemhild and Brynhild, two women in love with the dragon slayer, Siegfried.

Donald A. MacKenzie's narrative retelling of Norse mythology is interspersed with excerpts from British poetry inspired by the legendary atmosphere. The extremely thorough collection is also a convenient reference work, which may be read sequentially or by chapters concerning a specific god or hero. The work is richly illustrated with works by artists of the nineteenth century, including delightfully irreverent drawings by the French master, Gustave Doré.

DONALD FLANELL FRIEDMAN
New York City
1985

# PREFACE

This volume deals with the myths and legends of the Teutonic peoples. These evolved from primitive beliefs, and have been handed down from generation to generation and from century to century in the folk literature of oral tradition. They survive to us in folk tales, divine and heroic lays, and in sagas and epic narratives. In the north the myths about the gods persisted longest and had fullest growth, owing to the slow advance of Christianity, which met with obstinate resistance for over two centuries after the conversion of the southern Teutons. The myths about the old tribal heroes continued to flourish meantime all over the Teutonic area. In Central Europe, however, the folk lays were influenced by the higher and milder civilization which prevailed, and special interest attaches to their stray references to the gods, because these are of distinctly archaic character, as a result, it would appear, of the arrested growth of pagan ideas. The division of the Teutonic peoples, and their development under different conditions, caused the ancient folk literature to be subjected to varied treatment. In Central Europe the tribal songs were welded into detailed narratives, and each had for a central figure a popular hero like, for instance, Dietrich of Bern. A similar

process subsequently prevailed in the north. Thus had
origin the " saga cycles ", which link one with another,
for they were distributed over a wide area by wandering
minstrels, who altered and adapted them to meet the
requirements of time and locality. The highest literary
development occurred when educated poets made still
freer use of the subject matter of tribal lays and produced
epic narratives, which were not sung, but recited before
cultured audiences. These were subsequently revised
and committed to manuscripts for perusal. To this class
belong two of outstanding merit—the Germanic *Nibelungenlied*, with its significant although confused historical
setting, and the distinctive Anglo-Saxon *Beowulf*, which is
interspersed with fragments of old hero songs, and bears
evidence of alterations and additions by the copyists.

In the following pages our readers are afforded a
comprehensive survey of the divine and heroic literature
of the Teutonic peoples, which grew up at various periods
and in different districts under the inspiring influence
of common tribal traditions. The drama of Northern
Mythology is reconstructed, so far as such has been
found possible of accomplishment, in continuous narrative form, with the inclusion of the old Svipdag myth,
which exercised so marked an influence on Middle Age
romance. We have grouped together the various tales
regarding adventurous journeys made by heroes to Hela,
so that our readers may be familiarized with Teutonic
conceptions of the Other World. The prose renderings
of heroic narratives include the Beowulf epic, the Balder-
Hother romance, the Hamlet legend, the saga of the
Volsungs, the lay of the Nibelungs, and the less familiar
Dietrich legends, in which the deeds of the primitive

Thor are attached to the memory of the Gothic Emperor of Rome. In all these literary productions the development of early myths can be traced, and their internal evidences regarding beliefs and customs and habits of life are of undoubted historical interest.

The folk tales and folk beliefs of the Teutons have not a few points of contact with those of the Celts. On that account Vigfusson suggested that the comparative study of Celtic lore "might throw light on the origin of much so-called Norse mythology", for Iceland, which has given us the Eddas, was partly colonized by the mixed peoples from the Scandinavian settlements in these islands. We have, therefore, dealt in our Introduction with the archaic giant lore of Scotland, which links with that of Cornwall, and drawn attention to the "Seven Sleepers" legends of the Highlands which have hitherto been overlooked. The conclusion suggested, however, is that some of the striking resemblances which are found must be traced to remoter influences than those prevailing in the Viking Age. Both Celts and Teutons were blends of the same ancient races—the Alpine "broad heads" and the Northern "long heads". They had therefore a common heritage of fused tribal beliefs, which must have varied, of course, in different districts. It may be that the westward-moving Celts, who absorbed the Mediterranean peoples of the late Stone Age, were, in turn, strongly influenced by their intellectual life, and that the Teutons came more directly under the spell of Asiatic modes of thought. At any rate it is evident that predominating fundamental conceptions of divergent origin exercised supreme control over the mental habits of the separated sub-races. Teutonic lore is mainly "father-kin" in character, while Celtic is mainly "mother-kin". The deities of the Teutons are controlled by a Great Father, and their elves by a king. The deities of the Celts are children of a Great Mother, and their fairies are ruled over by a queen.

Sometimes we find indications of late fusion of the characteristic folklores of the two great sub-races, which are highly suggestive and of historic significance. In the Teutonic epic *Beowulf*, the story regarding Grendel and his mother is of special interest in this connection, because it is "mother-kin" lore of British character. It is not found in the North German cycle of romance, and is of a type still surviving in these islands, which closely resembles the monster lore of early Greece. The inference is that the poet who gave the epic its final shape in England had a British mother, or, at any rate, came under the influence of British intellectual life. Like Shakespeare, who utilized old plays, he may have refashioned an earlier Anglian poem, appropriated its geographical setting, and infused the whole with the fire of his genius.

It may be suggested that in the material dealt with in this and Squire's Celtic volume there is much inspiration for the poets of the future. The fusion of peoples in these islands has produced a virile blend, and the combined influence of their myths and legends, and their fairy songs and hero songs, may yet, happily, stir to life a great Romantic revival which will be productive of a new and virile literature truly national in character.

DONALD A. M'KENZIE.

# INTRODUCTION

"Teutonic Myth and Legend"*applies to the ancient religious conceptions and traditional tales of the "non-Celtic" northern peoples, whom Continental scholars prefer to call "Germanic" in the widest sense of the term. The myths varied in different districts and at different periods. It is doubtful if there ever was in any particular age complete uniformity of religious belief over a wide area of separated States. In fact, there are indications that sects and creeds were at least as numerous among Teutonic peoples in early times as at the present day. Stories repeated orally were also subject to change; they were influenced by popular taste, and rendered more effective by the introduction of local colouring.

Teutonic Mythology survives in its most concrete form in Scandinavian literature. On that account it has to be considered from the northern point of view, although much of it is clearly not of northern origin. Our principal sources of knowledge of this great Pagan religious system are the two Eddas of Iceland.

These Eddas are collections of mythical and heroic poems and stories. One is called the Elder or Poetic Edda; the other, Snorri's or the Prose Edda. The latter was discovered first; it came into the possession of appreciative scholars in the seventeenth century, by whom it was studied and carefully preserved.

*The original title of this book.

The Prose Edda is a synopsis of Northern Mythology, with poetic quotations from lost poems and references to an earlier work. It was partly written and partly compiled by the great Icelandic scholar, Snorri Sturlason. He was born some time between 1179 and 1181, and was the son of a chief. Adopted by the learned Jon Loptsson, grandson of Saemund the Wise, he passed his early years at Oddi, where his literary tendencies were fostered and cultivated. He married a wealthy heiress, and settled in 1206 at Reykjaholt, where he lived in comparative luxury. Nominally a Christian, he was in reality an educated Pagan. He was a poet and historian, a lawyer and a politician; he combined great ambition with want of courage, and avarice with "aversion from effort"; he was also of loose morals. In 1215 he became President of Iceland, and afterwards resided for a time in Norway, where he was a Court poet. In 1222 he was again President of his native island. He held office for about ten years, and exercised his influence at every opportunity to enrich himself. He obtained a divorce from his wife, after living with her for twenty-five years, and married an heiress. It is not surprising, therefore, to find him involved in serious quarrels with his kinsmen. There were also political complications which had a tragic sequel. He was murdered by his son-in-law in 1241, at the instigation of the King of Norway.

In addition to the Prose Edda, Snorri's works included Heimskringla, or Sagas of Norse Kings, which opens with Ynglinga Saga, and the History of Olaf.

The discovery of Snorri's Edda in the seventeenth century caused a search to be made for the older collection to which it referred. Happily the quest was fruitful, and the lost manuscript came into the hands of an Icelandic bishop, who called it for the first time the "Edda of Saemund".

Saemund was a scion of the royal house of Norway, who was born in 1056 and died in 1133. He studied in France and Germany, and was afterwards parish priest of Oddi in Iceland. According to tradition, he was the author of a prose work on mythology which unfortunately perished. It is probable, however, that Snorri was acquainted with the lost manuscript while resident at Oddi, and he may have used it when compiling the Prose Edda. At any rate, scholars are now agreed that Saemund was neither the author nor compiler of the particular Edda which was long associated with his name.

The Elder Edda is a collection of mythical and heroic poems—lays of the gods and lays of the Volsung and other heroes—by various unknown authors. They are valuable treasures of antiquity, for they throw great light on northern beliefs and manners and customs. Some survive in fragments; others are fairly complete, and are introduced by brief prose summaries. A portion of them were evidently of pre-Christian origin.

As literary productions they are of unequal merit. They are all ear-poems, composed to be sung or recited, and therefore melodious, musically vowelled, and clear, as compared with the eye-poems of many modern authors, which have more harmony than melody, and are composed for the reader. A particular group of these Eddic poems are more dramatic and imaginative than the others, and certain critics are inclined to hold that their high development was caused by Celtic influence. Iceland was peopled not only from Norway, but also from the Hebrides, where the Vikings mingled with the people and married the island maidens. Many settlers were also of mixed Irish descent. Nor was the old English element absent, as certain borrowed words show clearly. But, when these facts are given adequate consideration, it must be borne in mind that literature, and especially poetry, owes usually more to the individual than to the race. If we knew as little of Keats as we do of the author of *Beowulf*, it might be held that he was a son of Greek parents who settled in England.

The survival of these Pagan Eddic poems in Christian times is suggestive of the slow extinction of old beliefs. Christianity was adopted in Iceland in 1000, a century after it had spread throughout Norway, and two hundred years before the people of Sweden can be said to have abandoned their ancient religion. It must not be inferred, however, that the Icelanders were exemplary Christians in Saemund's day or even in Snorri's. The bulk of them were, no doubt, half-Pagan, like those Ross-shire Highlanders in the vicinity of Loch Maree, who, as late as the seventeenth century, offered up sacrifices of bulls and performed other heathenish rites, to the horror of the Presbytery of Dingwall. The Icelanders must have clung, long after the introduction of Christianity, to the Pagan beliefs and practices of the great sea kings. They continued, we know, to chant the lays and recite the old traditional tales about the gods and ocean heroes of the mother country. The collectors may, indeed, have had more than a literary appreciation of oral song and haunting tradition.

When Snorri was a boy, a Danish priest named Saxo was engaged writing a history of his native land. The first nine books are like the *Histories of the Kings of Britain* by Geoffrey of Monmouth, for they are founded on the traditional poems and tales of the time. Saxo Grammaticus ("the Lettered") writes of Odin and the

other gods as if they were men, and when he refers
to them as "gods" he takes occasion to scorn the
hollowness of the claim, rarely failing to comment on
the absurdity of the beliefs entertained by ignorant
people. His history is a quarry of folklore and romance.
To it we owe our Shakespeare's *Hamlet*, for the story
which is retold in these pages from the Danish priest's
immortal work, was the original source of our great
poet's inspiration.

This "history" is indispensable to students of
Scandinavian religion. Rydberg, the poet and folk-
lorist of Sweden, is the author of a monumental work
on *Teutonic Mythology*,[1] in which he made exhaustive and
critical examination of the tales embedded in Saxo's
works, showing their relation to the Eddas and Sagas
and existing oral poems of the north, and making
masterly endeavour by their aid to reconstruct the great
mythological drama of the northern peoples. He has
not escaped criticism, but his reputation has withstood
much of it. On every point he has raised he cannot
be regarded as conclusive, but no scholar before or
since has shown greater aptitude for restoring form
from mythological chaos. His intimate knowledge of
his native lore gave him special equipment for his work.
Not infrequently scholars, by a process of detached
reasoning, miss the mark when dealing with folklore,
because their early years, unlike Rydberg's, were not
passed in its strange atmosphere. The theorist is never
as reliable as he who was aforetime a faithful believer
in giants and elves, spirit voices and awesome omens.

"No one," wrote Frederick York Powell,[2] "has

---

[1] An English translation by R. B. Anderson was published in London in 1889,
but is out of print.

[2] Introduction to English translation of Saxo Grammaticus.—Nutt.

commented upon Saxo's mythology with such brilliancy, such minute consideration, and such success as the Swedish scholar, Victor Rydberg. . . . Sometimes he stumbles badly, but he has placed the whole subject on a fresh footing, and much that is to follow will be drawn from his *Teutonic Mythology*."

To Rydberg the writer owns his indebtedness in the present work, a portion of which is constructed according to his conclusions.

Edda is a word of uncertain origin. In a twelfth-century poem it is used to mean "great grandmother", and it is suggested that late sceptical compilers applied it to signify "old wives' tales". The theory has a somewhat modern note, for in legends, especially those of Scotland, the "old wife" is either feared or respected. The Hag, who is the terrible mother of giants, is called Cailleach Mor, "the big old wife", and the wise witch who imparts secrets and powers to men is simply "old wife".

Edda became associated in Iceland with the technical rules of verse. "Never to have seen Edda" signified a complete ignorance of poetic art, so it may be that among a mingled people the "great grandmother" was an imported Muse of a Matriarchal tribe. Saga, we know, was individualized as a maiden, and was wooed by Odin. A recent theory[1] is that Edda is derived from "Oddi", the place where Saemund preached and Snorri studied.

The Eddas are, of course, the collected folk-songs and folk-tales of the northern peoples. In addition we have also available, for purposes of study, other old manuscripts and a considerable mass of valuable lore gleaned in recent years from oral sources, as well as the renowned surviving Sagas and minor poems of the skalds (song-smiths), which abound with mythological references.

[1] Eirikr Magnusson's.

Some folk-tales are fragments of forgotten mythologies; others are part of the floating material from which mythologies were made. The two classes should therefore be studied together for purposes of elucidation, while consideration must ever be given to folk-customs which also enshrine ancient religious beliefs. The gods evolved from beliefs, and these loomed vast and vague on man's mental horizon ere they were given definite and symbolic expression. Indeed, detached stories of gods, especially Nature-gods, must have existed for indefinite periods ere they were subjected to a unifying process and embraced in a complete philosophy of life. A Mythology, therefore, must not be regarded as a spontaneous creation of a particular Age, but rather as a growth which had of necessity a history like, for instance, the Art of a finely sculptured stone, or that of the shapely and decorated Celtic bronze shield found embedded in Thames mud.

Matthew Arnold regarded poetry as a "criticism of life". That definition may, in a restricted sense, be applied to a Mythology, especially one of highly developed and complicated construction. We can conclude that it evolved from a school of thought which made critical selection of existing material when the work was undertaken of systematizing religious beliefs to suit the needs of a particular Age. As religion and law had in ancient times most intimate association, an official religion was ever a necessity in a well-organized State, and especially in one composed of mingled peoples. A Mythology, therefore, was probably the product of a national movement, and closely connected with the process of adjusting laws and uniting tribes under a central government. In the union and classification of gods we have suggested the union of peoples and the probable political relations of one tribe with another. No deity could be overlooked, if the interests of all sections were to be embraced, because the destinies of each were controlled by a particular god or group of gods of immemorial import. The gods of subject peoples would, of course, become subject to those of their rulers.

A Mythology was therefore not only a criticism; it was also a compromise. The lesser gods were accepted by those who imposed the greater, and new tales had to be invented to adjust their relationships one to another. Contradictory elements were thus introduced. The gods differed greatly. Some had evolved from natural phenomena; others were deified heroes. A seaside tribe showed reverence to gods which had origin in their own particular experiences and ideals, which differed to a marked degree from those, for instance, of an inland, forest-dwelling people. Settled communities and nomadic peoples professed beliefs in accordance with their particular modes of life. Between the various classes of a single social organization, even, there would exist religious conceptions which were fundamentally opposed. Invaders who formed a military aristocracy would import and perpetuate their own particular beliefs and rites, while those of the conquered people continued as aforetime. Indeed, archæological remains demonstrate to the full that different burial customs were practised simultaneously in the same district, although each had origin in religious conceptions of divergent character. Two examples may be cited—(1) the crouched burial with food vessel, associated with the belief that the spirits of the dead haunted the place of interment and had to be propitiated, and (2) the cremation burial which ensured that the spirit, like that of Patroklos, would never again return from Hades when it had received its meed of fire

(*Iliad* xxiii. 75). In our northern tales there are evidences of various burial customs. Balder is cremated in Asgard, but he is interred in a barrow in the heroic story from Saxo. Beowulf and Sigurd are burned, Helgi is given sepulture in a mound, and Sigmund and his son are enclosed in a chambered grave when buried alive.

But while peoples who were mingled together practised different religious rites, invaders ever showed reverence, as did the Romans, to local gods and local beliefs. In the process of time one section would be influenced by the other. A fusion of religions would result from a fusion of peoples, but every district and every community would not be similarly affected. The clash of ideas would also be productive of speculative thought, and each Age would contribute something new from its accumulated ideas and experiences. Yet in the midst of the mass of floating lore there would ever survive beliefs of remote conception, for a folk-religion is conservative in essence. A people's inherited super-stitions are not readily eradicated. The past endures in the present. Even in our own day folk-beliefs and folk-customs of Pagan origin have tardy survival after many long centuries of Christian influence.

When, therefore, the thinkers and teachers of Scandi-navia framed their great Mythological system, they had to select and compromise; they were not only critics but diplomatists as well. New tales had to be invented, and old tales adjusted, to instruct and convert and unite all sections. Social relationships were given a religious bearing; the gods of the common people were shown to be subject to those of their rulers. All outstanding popular beliefs had to be accounted for, with the result that heroic tales were mingled with Nature myths, and the whole was infused with ethical and political purpose.

The Mythology was thus coloured by the thought of the times and the conditions and character of the people, while it was given, of course, appropriate setting amidst local scenery.

Northern Teutonic Mythology must have had gradual growth. It appears to have attained its highest development in the Viking Age, when a united and masterful people, stirred, no doubt by well-organized political conditions, to a great awakening, spread far and wide to impose their rule and their culture upon alien peoples. When earlier migrations took place, amidst the battle storms of violent tribal fusion, the new religious system was in process of formation. The Angles and Saxons, for instance, were not greatly influenced by the Odin cult when they reached these island shores. Their deified tribal heroes were still predominant. That has been made abundantly clear by Stopford Brooke in his masterly study, *History of Early English Literature*.

So far as we are able to reconstruct the Mythology —nor can we expect complete agreement among the experts in this regard—it appears to have been highly developed and adjusted to the minutest detail. The official religion, of course, may not have been accepted in its completeness by all classes; sections may have still clung to favoured deities, while they recognized others unknown to their ancestors. Odin, we know, was esteemed more highly by scholarly skalds than by fighting men, who continued to exalt and worship Thor as chief or most influential god, and to repose their trust in the magical influence exercised in battle by the shadowy but ancient war-god Tyr. No doubt the teachers remained the while serenely confident that ultimately the spirit-god would be held in greater regard by thinking men than gods of physical might. But the growth of

*Odin, from the design by Burne-Jones.*

*Odin overseeing navigation.*

this great Pagan mythology was arrested by the gradual advance of Christianity, and it is given popular reconstruction in these pages as it possibly existed, especially in the north, when the influence of the new and greater religion coloured the Balder story, and the idea was interpolated of a greater All-father than Odin. The Saxo stories are drawn upon to fill gaps, although gaps may have ever existed. We may add that we call the Mythology Northern Teutonic in preference to "Germanic", because of its geographical setting, and for the pregnant reason that it has survived mainly in the form given to it by the mingled peoples of the North.

The local character of this particular mythological system is strongly emphasized in "the story of creation". Only a Northern people living in close proximity to Arctic ice-fields could have conceived of a chaos-gulf bounded on the north by a cold and darksome Nifelheim, and on the south by a warm and bright Muspelheim. Life begins to be when and where the ice-blocks are thawed. The gods and their doings are also coloured by their Scandinavian environment. "Light-battles" and fierce Nature-wars are emphasized in a land of pronounced seasonal changes. No matter whence certain deities were imported, here in the land of long winter nights they are acclimatized and naturalized. They contend against indigenous frost-giants; they fight and then become the allies of indigenous Vana-gods; they visit a sea-folk's terrible storm-god Æger in his hall at the sea bottom; they acquire northern temperaments and become fatalists like all seafarers, ancient and modern.

Teutonic gloom overspreads Teutonic Mythology. Odin and his Asa clan live ever under the shadow of Ragnarok, "The Dusk of the gods". This gloom hangs heavily as northern storm-clouds over early "Teutonic" literature. It haunts the Eddas and Sagas; it permeates Anglo-Saxon poetry. Dr. Clark Hall says of *Beowulf*, "There is undoubtedly less colour about the second part than the first, and more gloom. The habit of fore-boding which is noticeable in Part I is so prominent in Part II as to give a general tone of fatalistic hopeless-ness to it. Sunshine and shadow no longer alternate— shadow is over all." The same comment might be applied with equal force to the Nibelungenlied. Al-though "gloomy" and "Celtic" have become synony-mous terms of late years, yet Celtic (Irish) Mythology and old Gaelic literature both in Scotland and in Ire-land strike, in comparison with what is termed Teutonic, a brighter and more cheerful note. It may be that the gloom is aboriginal—pre-Celtic and pre-Teutonic—a shadow of primitive but persistent mental habits.

In Teutonic Mythology, as in Greek, there are evi-dences of remote race-memories. The Asiatic "broad-heads" who crossed Europe in "waves", which began to arrive in the vast periods of the late Stone Age, must have imported not only new customs and new weapons, but also fragments of immemorial myths. Superstitions survive longer than stone monuments, and they pass through language to language, and from land to land, with the buoyancy of American timber which drifts across the Atlantic to Hebridean shores. An instance may be noted in the northern "Story of Creation". The body of Ymer, the chaos-giant, is cut to pieces; his flesh and bones become soil and rocks; his skull is the sky dome; his progeny is engulfed in his blood, which is the sea. Babylonian tablets relate a similar story. In the begin ning Bel-Merodach slew the chaos-giantess Tiawath; he cut up her body, and with one part he framed the earth and with the other the heavens. Her blood was forced

to flow southward by a strong north wind—it became the
river which filled the sea.

Comparisons may also be drawn between Teutonic
and Greek Mythologies. But these will be found to be
of slighter character. Those elements, common to both,
which are not Asiatic may be of early Mediterranean
origin, for as ancient cities lie below ancient cities, so do
ancient mythologies rest upon the wrecks of others of
still greater antiquity. As Jubainville has shown in *Le
Cycle Mythologique Irlândais et la Mythologie Celtique*,
Greek and Celtic are closely related and mainly of common origin. They are children of one mother; but
Scandinavian Mythology cannot be regarded as other
than a distant relation.

In all three Mythologies there is a central Nature-
myth tragedy. In Greek it is the slaying of Night by
Dawn. Hermes, surnamed Argeiphontes, in his character
as Dawn-god, slays Argus, the many-eyed, who is Night,
with a round stone, which is the Sun. In Celtic (Irish)
Mythology the Dawn-god, Lugh, kills Balor of the Evil-
eye, who is Night, with the same round sun-stone. The
myth also applies to the slaying of Winter by Summer
and of Evil by Good. The tragedy of Scandinavian
Mythology, on the other hand, is the slaying of Day
(or Summer) by Night (or Winter). Blind Hoder shoots
Balder (in his Edda character as Summer Sun-god) with
the wintry mistletoe-arrow. He is prompted by Loke,
the Scandinavian Mephistopheles, who plots to hasten
the downfall of the gods. Light is thus overcome by
Darkness, Summer by Winter, and Good by Evil.

Another broad and fundamental contrast is afforded
by the conceptions of Night in the Northern and other
European Mythologies. Instead of the tyrannical Balor
of Ireland, or the monstrous Argus of Greece, we have

the beneficent northern Night-goddess Nat, daughter of Mimer (Wisdom) and sister of Urd (Fate). She brings to mankind refreshment and inspiration. Her lover is Delling, the red elf of dawn, and their son is Dag (Day).

Nat is evidently of eastern origin. In the Rig-veda the goddess of night (dark daughter of day) is, like Nat, both noble of aspect and character; she "increases riches". In the tenth Mandala she is thus addressed :—

> Kind goddess, be propitious to thy servants
> Who at thy coming straightway seek repose.
>
> .    .    .    .    .    .
>
> Drive thou away from us, O Night, the wolf,
> Drive thou away the thief, and bear us safely
> Across thy borders. . . .

In Teutonic Mythology, Evil is not necessarily associated with Darkness. The tempter and plotter is handsome Loke in his character as a fire-god; he is evidently an ally of Surtur, who burns up the world at Ragnarok. Loke is corrupted by the Hag of Ironwood, the "Mother of Evil", whose evil progeny includes the fierce wolves— one of which swallows the moon, while the other devours Odin — the great Midgard Serpent, and the repulsive, torture-loving Hel. Her Babylonian counterpart is Tiawath, among whose offspring are immense serpents, fiery dragons, raging hounds, fish-men, &c. The Northern Hag's husband, Gymer, is keeper of her flock, as is also the husband, Kingu, of Tiawath's.

The World, according to northern belief, is supported by a great tree which is ever green. This conception is not peculiar to Scandinavia, but nowhere else is an ash-tree similarly exalted in dignity. At its roots are three wells, and in one is a gnawing dragon or serpent. The gods dwell under its branches; they sit in judgment upon the dead beneath the ash in the Underworld. It trembles when Ragnarok is at hand; it is the oracle. Evidently the worship of trees and wells was so prevalent in the north, that no more popular idea could be conceived than that of a tree-supported universe. Even in our own day the superstitious reverence shown for "wishing-wells" is not uncommon, and the trees connected with them still flutter with prayer-rags. In Celtic Mythology, Dagda, the oak-god, has for wife Boann, the River Boyne. The well at the river source is one of the many celebrated in dragon-myth story. Finn Magnusen would have us regard "the world-tree" as the symbol of universal nature, but it was more probably a concession to popular belief, and dignified to accord with the general mythological scheme.

Odin would appear to have been originally an isolated tribal god—a deified martial chief, who became associated with a Nature Myth. He is a war-god and a magician; he controls battles and is the inventor of runes; he hangs on the world-ash, which bears one of his names, " Ygg's-gallows " (Ygdrasil), as if he were, as he probably was, a king who was sacrificed. Yet his universal character is emphasized by his sky-dome hat and sky cloak flecked with cloud-spots. He is a one-eyed giant, a Cyclops; his lost eye sinks in Mimer's well as the sun sinks in the sea. He is also the wind-god—the Wild Huntsman in the Raging Host. As wind-god he is the " spirit-god " in accordance with the widespread association of " wind " and " breath " and " soul " (spirit, for instance, is derived from *spiro*, I breathe). He gives "soul" to the logs of ash and alder which become the first man and the first woman. He is All-father, the framer of the world. Odin was probably exalted, because he was the spirit-god, by the wise men of Scandinavia, and made chief ruler in their Asgard, but his connection with the other gods is slight and arbitrary. Thor, his son, was originally an oak-god, and, like Jupiter, is wielder of the thunderbolt. It is, however, in keeping with the sublime character of Northern Teutonic Mythology that the "spirit-god" should be supreme, and the constant friend of his kinsman Mimer (Wisdom), whose daughter is Urd (Fate).

The giant stories were constructed on a lower plane of thought. A single exception is Thor's adventure in the palace of Utgard-Loki, where he wrestles in vain with the Hag, who is Old Age, and endeavours to drink up the ocean. The mythical interpretations of the others cannot be pressed too closely, lest more be read into them than was ever intended. It is evident that the reciter's imagination was allowed to run riot, and that the narratives assumed their extended form as popular wonder-tales.

When the tribal heroes of northern peoples were glorified by story-tellers, they were invariably depicted as giant-killers. In the half-mythical history of Geoffrey of Monmouth, Corineus contended successfully against the giants of Cornwall—he slew them in dozens—and after wrestling with the greatest, Goemagot, he cast him over a cliff. Siegfried, in the Nibelungenlied, and Dietrich, in his Thunor (Thor) character, are also slayers of giants. In Highland giant-lore there are several similar heroes who, like Thor, are friends of the agricultural people. The hunting-folks had their own hunting-giants, like the Highland Finn and his warrior band, who are not militiamen as in Ireland.

It has been remarked that the Northern Teutonic frost-giants are indigenous. But there is another class of giants who are as widely scattered as the drinking-cup urns of the ancient and mysterious people that settled in the fertile districts of these islands and of Scandinavia, and have been traced through mid-Europe. These are the Mountain-giants. In the neglected archaic lore of Scotland they are called Fomors[1], but they are not the Fomors of Ireland, nor have they a necessary connection with the sea or with darkness. As river-goddesses in flight are personifications of rivers, so do these Fomors personify the hills they inhabit. Scottish mountain-giants never leave their mountains. They fight continuously one against the other, tossing boulders over wide valleys or arms of the sea. To each is allowed one throw daily: A flings his boulder against B on Monday; B retaliates on Tuesday, and so on. The Holmgang duel would therefore appear to be of hallowed antiquity. These giants sleep at night and share men's terrors in darkness. Three friendly Inverness giants throw from one to the other, each morning, a stone hammer to signify that all is well. Greater than the males are their mothers, the Hags[2], who also fight with boulders, but have power to change their shapes. There are also Thunder-cloud hags who throw fireballs, tempest-hags, firebrand-hags, sea-hags, &c. They invariably wrestle with human beings like the giants of Cornwall.

Another class of Scottish giants inhabit caves, and some of them are many-headed. They hoard and guard treasure. Heroes who fight against them are invariably assisted by dogs (dogs "which have their day"), and they are instructed by indispensable wise women[3] who possess magic wands. What appears to be the oldest Thor story belongs to this class. When Thor sets out to visit Geir-

---

[1] In Scottish Gaelic, Fomhair and Famhair, pronounced "foo-ar" and "faa-har". The Fomorib (men of the sea) theory has long been abandoned by Prof. Rhys.

[2] In Gaelic, Cailleach Mor.

[3] In pre-Christian times witches were the friends of man, and helped him to combat against hags and giants.

rod he has neither hammer nor belt of strength. The Hag Grid, like the Scottish "wise-woman", warns and instructs him, and gives him her belt and magic wand. In this story Thor flings a boulder and breaks the back of a giantess. He may have wielded thunder-boulders ere his iron hammer was invented.

Scottish giants, therefore, are more like the Scandinavian than the Irish variety. If it is held that they were imported by the Vikings, it might be asked why Thor was forgotten, and why the Asa-gods and the Vans were left behind? If they are classed as Irish, it should be noted that the Danann gods, who overcame the Fomors in Erin, are not found in Scotland. Can it be maintained that the Irish brought over their "gods of Night" and left behind their "gods of Day"? In Wales and Cornwall there are also giants of the Scottish type. Geoffrey of Monmouth, in fact, tells us that giants were the sole inhabitants of ancient Britain when Brute and the first men arrived.

> Beyond the realms of Gaul, beneath the sunset
> Lieth an island, girt about by ocean,
> Guarded by ocean—*erst the haunt of giants.*[1]
>
> S. *Evans's Trans.*

It would appear that archaic giant-lore is pre-Celtic and pre-Teutonic, and therefore a common inheritance. In the wars of the Olympians and Titans, of the Irish Danann gods and the Fomors, and of the Asa-gods and the Jotuns, we may have echoes of ancient racial conflicts. The old tribal peoples attributed their successes to their gods, and remembered their battles as the battles of rival gods. For these giants are also gods of archaic conception. In Scotland certain of them are associated with the fortunes of families and tribes. On the other hand, gods

[1] In Old English the giants are "eotens".

are but exalted giants; the boisterous Olympians find their counterpart in the boisterous Scandinavian Jotuns rather than in the more refined Asa-gods and Vans.

With these giants are associated the elves. In Teutonic lore, which is not necessarily wholly of Teutonic origin, the male elves predominate. In Scotland, as in Greece, elves are mainly females, who are ruled over by a queen. There are also Scottish fairy-smiths, but they are one-eyed and Cyclopean, and not always distinguishable from giants. In fact, the Fian-giants are confused with fairies in an Inverness mound, and Thomas the Rhymer is added in the character of one of the "Seven Sleepers". Danann gods and fairies are similarly mingled in Ireland. It should be noted in this connection that Teutonic elf-smiths are allies of the giants, and they are sometimes stronger than them. When Siegfried overcame the giant doorkeeper of Nibelung, he found that the dwarf was a still more powerful opponent. Thor is friendly with the elves, but Svipdag, son of Egil, the elf, destroys the thunder-god's hammer with the "Sword of Victory".

The other class of elves—the "Light-elves"—are vaguely defined in Northern Teutonic Mythology. Frey was their ruler in his youth, which suggests that he is himself an elf exalted to a god. The wise Vans are also elfin in character, and were probably the spirit-folk of an early seafaring people. The story of the unhappy marriage of Njord and Skade may contain a germ of historic fact—the uncongenial association of a tribe of seafarers with a tribe of huntsmen.

The female elves of the commoner type become valkyries; they are also swan-maidens who have tragic liaisons with mankind. Brynhild is a swan-maiden and a valkyrie; she is also in the Nibelungenlied a boulder-throwing hag. The Balder story, regarding which much has been written, is not, therefore, the only one that underwent radical changes in the process of Mythology-making. According to Professor Frazer in the *Golden Bough*, Balder was originally a tree-god whose soul was in the mistletoe. The theory is as weighty as is the reputation of that Darwin of folklore.

But perhaps the most interesting class of elves are the sons of Ivalde—Volund and his brothers. They display the attributes now of dwarfs, now of giants, and anon of star deities. It would appear that they absorbed more than one ancient personality in an older Mythology than that in which the Odin cult predominates. Rydberg shows that Volund (Wieland) and the giant Thjasse are indistinguishable. A close study of northern folklore supports that view, and an intimate acquaintance with the mental habits of fairy-and-giant-believing people assists one to appreciate it fully. Thjasse is the only giant who is winged like Volund, as Loke and Freyja are the only members of the Asa-clan who can assume bird guise. Thjasse and Volund are also symbolized as mountain wolves; they are both star deities; they are more like one another than the two Balders, and appear to be products of the same ancient welded lore of an earlier mythological system.

In the Northern "Story of Creation" these elves, or black dwarfs, are, it is evident, intentionally belittled. They have their origin, like maggots, in Ymer's flesh. Yet they provide the gods with indispensable gifts—Odin with his spear, Thor with his hammer, and Frey with his boar and wondrous ship. In Thjasse's flight to Asgard we may have a story invented purposely to account for his fall, because, like Odin, he is a spirit-god. His other names, Byrr and Gustr, signify wind and gale.

It is not possible now to reconstruct what appears to be a pre-Odin-cult Mythology, in which Ivalde and his sons predominate. The "Milky Way" is "Irmin's Way", and Irmin, invoked by old Hildebrand in the Dietrich story, is "the ruling god". It is also Bil's way (Bil is Ivalde's daughter), and as "Bil-rost", according to Rydberg, is the original of Bif-rost. The Anglo-Saxons called the "Milky Way" "Watling Street".[1]

Volund's brother Egil, the archer, is associated with the clouds and the sea. Sleet and rain are his arrows; his arrows are also "herrings that leap from the hands of Egil", and herrings are "arrows of the sea".[2] Egil's son, the Iceland Hamlet, is the guardian of the World-Mill; his son Svipdag, with shining sword, resembles a light-hero.

In the older moon-myth Gevar, the Gewar of the Hother-Balder story, is the ward of the moon-ship, and it is attacked and burned by Ivalde. The myth is obscure but suggestive; it survives in fragments only. The swan-maids are wooed by Ivalde's three sons, and Ivalde and Gevar have quarrelled violently as rival lovers.

This group are hunters, skee-runners, and musicians. They are also connected with an early form of the Balder story. Svipdag, as Hotherus, is the wooer of Gevar's daughter Nanna, and Balder, his rival, falls a victim to his "magic sword" in the heroic story in Saxo. If Balder, as a tree-god, was associated with the tree-well, he may have wooed Nanna of the moon by reflecting her image. In this connection it may be noted that wells sprang up in the hoof marks of Balder's horse,

---

[1] In Ireland the "Milky Way" is "Lugh's chain". Lugh is the dawn-god, and grandson of the night-god.

[2] Saga Library, Morris and Magnusson, Vol. I, 339.

and in Saxo's story he provides wells for his thirsting soldiers. His rival would thus be the light-hero Svipdag, with his shining summer sword, which was concealed for a season in the Underworld cave where lie the Seasonal "Seven Sleepers". In Northern Teutonic Mythology the popular Balder becomes the Summer Sun-god instead of Svipdag, and the only husband of Nanna. If the original story was thus transformed by displacing or changing a hero, the process is a familiar one. The shadowy Hoder may be the original rival lover altered to fit into the new mythological system.

It is to this group of ancient tales of rival lovers and swan-maids and moon-maids that we owe the treasures of Middle Age popular romance. The Volsunga-saga and the Nibelungenlied and the Balder heroic story were developed from what Rydberg calls the "Ivalde myth". Svipdag, too, is the original of Siegfried and Sigurd. In his character as a wronged son he suggests Hamlet and Finn-mac-Coul. The latter has a hammer (Ord na Feinne) which links him with Thor, as Thor links with the other giant-killers—Sigurd, Siegfried, and Dietrich. A tribal hero invariably absorbs the attributes of his predecessors, and develops and changes to suit the tastes of audiences and minstrels in various ages and in various countries. In Scandinavia, when the Asa-gods were threatened by the advance of Christianity, Svipdag, as Eric, was exalted as a rival to Christ, and suffered the fate of being associated with the Devil, who was afterwards called "old Erik". Odin was similarly treated; as Nik he became "the old Nick" of Perdition. Finn-mac-Coul was also pictured by early Christian missionaries as an inhabitant of "the lower regions".

The Beowulf story is an interesting link between the

heroic lore of the northern Continental peoples and that
of the early Britons. Beowulf, like Dietrich, may have
been a historical personage, but in the poem he is a hero
of the Svipdag order, yet not necessarily a "light-hero".
He slays the warrior-devouring Grendel. Dietrich, in
one of the poems of his cycle, also rids the neighbour-
hood of Attila's court of a man-eating monster. In the
next part of *Beowulf*, which is evidently an addition,
whether by the same author or another it matters not
here, the hero slays Grendel's mother. Although the
poet suggests that she is less formidable than her son,
she proves to be a more ferocious opponent. Only by
the familiar "magic sword" can she be slain. In this
respect she resembles Hilde, the wife of Grim, in the
Dietrich story; but she bears a closer resemblance to
the British Hag, the mother of the giants. Finn-mac-
Coul, when in "The Kingdom of Big Men," had
similarly, after slaying sea-giants, to contend against the
terrible Sea-Hag-mother. There are several similar
stories in Highland giant-lore, and no doubt they were
prevalent at one time throughout Britain, especially
among members or descendants of the Matriarchal tribes
referred to by Cæsar.

Stopford Brooke, in his *History of Early English Literature*, "wonders if the Grendel tale may not be a Celtic
story which in very ancient times became Teutonic," and
quotes the close Icelandic parallel, the Glam story. "It
is a curious question," he says, "how it came to pass
that the story of Beowulf and Grendel did not, like
the other Sagas of the north, become a part of the
north German cycle of romance. . . . I have sometimes
thought that the Angles alone threw the myths and tales
of it into lays, and that when the whole body of them
emigrated to our island, they left the Continent naked

of the tale. . . . I conjecture that something broke the literary connection on the Continent, or that the story was developed only when the Angles got into Britain." The latter supposition, considered in the light of existing Scottish giant-lore, which was evidently at one time general in ancient Britain, is the more convincing of the two. The theory of a complete and wholesale Anglian migration is as improbable as the theory of a complete and wholesale extermination of the early Britons, which, although still surviving, has really no reliable basis. Dr. Clark Hall, the scholarly translator and editor of *Beowulf*, accepts the hero as "a thoroughly historical character". So was Dietrich as the Emperor Theodoric. But while, like Stopford Brooke and other rationalistic critics, he dismisses the solar-myth theory, he errs, we think, in the opposite direction. He says: "Is it not possible that besides performing many heroic deeds in war against ordinary mortals, our hero (Beowulf) had two or three mysterious encounters with wild beasts, which grew into our Grendel and dragon stories by the process of exaggeration. . . . I have myself heard, in the nineteenth century, from the lips of an ancient mariner, a passably truthful and not very imaginative man, an amazing yarn about a sea serpent which I have no doubt had some foundation in fact."[1]

To the audiences who heard the *Beowulf* poem sung, Grendel was as real as the hero; and no doubt there were, in those ancient days, many similar tales which perished because no great poet enshrined them in enduring verse.

It is believed by scholars that *Beowulf* was composed in the early part of the eighth century. Whether it was the work of one man or of several is a disputed point.

[1] *Beowulf*, Clark Hall, Introduction, lix-lx.

There appears, however, to be general agreement that it is of Pagan origin, and that the Christian references are interpolations. The only surviving manuscript, which is in the handwriting of two copyists, is preserved in the British Museum. "There are clear indications," says Dr. Clark Hall, "that the poem was originally composed in the Anglian (probably Mercian) dialect, but it has come down to us in West Saxon, with some Kentish forms, in the part copied by the second scribe."

Scattered through the poem are older stories told by the minstrels, including the myths of Scyld and Hermod and the ancient Sigmund story, which found its highest artistic development in the Volsunga-saga and Nibelungenlied. Reference has already been made to the theory that certain lays of the Elder Edda show traces of British influence. Those students who desire to have fuller knowledge of the literature, mythology, and history of our mingled ancestors may examine with profit the conjectures of the various scholars, including Schwartz, Frazer, Bugge, Stopford Brooke, York Powell, Vigfusson, and others.

The Nibelungenlied, or "Lay of the Nibelung", dates in its united form from the latter part of the twelfth century, and is supposed to be, as a poem, of Austrian or Tyrolese origin; but on this point there is no generally accepted opinion. The versification is in Middle High German. There is a large number of existing old manuscripts. The three most important were made by copyists in the thirteenth century. When the oldest of these was discovered in 1755, it was published by a Swiss scholar. Other manuscripts were subsequently brought to light, but the first complete published edition did not attract much attention. In fact, Frederick the Great, to whom it was dedicated, refused to have it in his library, and said it was hardly worth a charge of powder. To-day it is the pride of Germany.

It is evident that the Sigurd and Siegfried stories had a common origin in an ancient nature myth of which the Svipdag legend is an early form. The stories developed as popular stories; their mythological significance was forgotten, and, in course of time, historical personages were identified with certain of the characters. Other legends, like those of Helgi in the Norse version, and of Dietrich in the German, were also attached to the original plot. Both great Sagas were coloured by the civilizations in which they developed.

How floating myths and legends gathered round the memory of a popular hero is clearly shown in the lays of the Dietrich cycle. Dietrich von Bern is Theoderic the Great.[1] Although he was born two years after the death of Attila, Emperor of the Huns, he is found at his Court in the Nibelungenlied. Ermenerich (Hermanric) was Emperor of the Ostrogoths, and, when an old man, his dominions were overrun by fiery and savage Huns from Asia. He is believed to have died on the battlefield, where his power was shattered (about 374 A.D.). The Ostrogoths were subject to the Huns until Attila's death in 453 A.D. King Walamer defeated them in a great battle in 454 A.D., and once again the Ostrogoths were made independent. The king's two brothers were Theudemir, father of Theoderic (Dietrich) and Widemer, and they were subsidized from Rome for protecting the frontiers of the Eastern Empire. When payment was suddenly discontinued, Illyria was successfully invaded by Widemer, with the result that the treaty was renewed. Theoderic

---

[1] Dietrich is the High German equivalent of Theoderic. Bern is Verona.

was taken as a peace hostage to Constantinople, where he
resided for ten years and received a Roman education.
Theudemir succeeded his brother, and when he died,
Theoderic ruled the wandering Ostrogoths.

In 480 A.D. Odoacer, a German captain of mer-
cenaries, deposed Romulus Augustulus, the last of the
Western Emperors, who was but a boy of seventeen.
Eight years later Zeno, the Eastern Emperor, com-
missioned Theoderic to invade Italy. Odoacer was
overthrown, and our Dietrich of the legends became a
great and powerful king in Rome, owing nominal allegiance to the Eastern Emperor. He died in 526, and
was buried in a great marble tomb at Ravenna. A fine
statue of him, clad in full armour, may be seen in the
church of the Franciscans at Innsbruck.

In the Dietrich story Ermenerich is confused with
Odoacer, and the hero is depicted as an exile, and thus
identified with his father. A mass of floating legends
attached to the memory of Dietrich, including the Hildebrand story, which originated in the ancient and
world-wide father-and-son conflict theme, and the myths
of Thunor (Thor) the thunder-god, the slayer of giants
and dwarfs. But even Thor has his human side. He
may have been originally a tribal hero who was identified
both with an oak - deity and the central figure of a
Nature-myth.[1] He remains "the friend of man" even
when elevated to Asgard. All the heroes of the minstrels of Europe link one with another as the fictional
descendants of an ancient deified personage, or a

---

[1] The western Hittites had a storm-god, named Tarku, at the head of their pantheon. The eastern Hittites called him Teshup. This god is a warrior who holds in
one hand a hammer, and in the other three wriggling flashes of lightning. The
hammer is the symbol of fertility. Thor brings his goats back to life by waving his
hammer over them.

humanized deity, of a remoter and simpler mythology than that in which Odin is the chief ruler.

One of the most interesting problems associated with Teutonic Mythology refers to the story of the "Seven Sleepers". Mimer's seven sons lie in magic sleep in the Underworld, awaiting the blast of the horn at Ragnarok. This horn hangs in a cave. Thorkill, who visited Geirrod's domains with King Gorm and his company, saw the suspended horn which turned into a dragon when a man seized it greedily.

Rydberg argued that the various "Seven Sleepers" legends in Europe and North Africa originated in Scandinavia, and were distributed by the northern warriors who overran Italy, Greece, Asia Minor, and Egypt. His main argument rests on one very remarkable coincidence. The "Seven Sleepers" of Ephesus were Christians who were condemned to death by the Emperor Decius. They were given time to renounce their faith, but concealed themselves in a cave, where they lay wrapped in sleep "for 360 years".[1] During the reign of Theodosius, the Roman Emperor, a shepherd entered the cave, and the sleepers were awakened. Rydberg notes that Decius fell in battle with the Goths "who a few years later invaded Asia Minor and captured Ephesus among other places".

Seven men, who were attired like Romans, lay asleep in a cave in Western Germany. An eighth-century legend relates that a man who discovered them attempted to disrobe one, and his arm withered. In the vicinity dwelt a tribe of Skritobians (Skridfinns).

In Arabia a dog lies with "the sleepers". Mahomet made them foretell his coming, and the dog, named

---

[1] This calculation is according to the legends.

Kratim, is one of the ten animals which will enter Paradise.

If the legend originated in Scandinavia, it is a curious fact that this dog should be found also in the Highland stories, with which Rydberg and others who have dealt with the legend were unfortunately unacquainted. The sleepers are found in Craig-a-howe, Black Isle; Ossian's Cave, Glencoe; and Smith's Rock, in Skye. In each case they are Fians (Fingalians), and beside Finn-mac-Coul lies his dog Bran.[1] In Tomnahurich, Inverness, the chief sleeper is Thomas the Rhymer, who also reposes under the Eildon hills.

In the Scottish caves a horn hangs from the roof. When it is blown three times, the sleepers will issue forth. A shepherd found the cave (it is always a shepherd) and blew two blasts on the horn. But he was so terrified by the ferocious appearance of the warriors and by a voice which cried, "If the horn is blown once again the world will be upset altogether", that he fled, leaving the warriors resting on their elbows. The Fians cried, "Alas! you have left us worse than you found us". The shepherd locked the door and threw the key into the sea. At Inverness there is a Gaelic saying, "When the horn is blown, True Thomas shall come forth".

If this Highland story was imported by the Norsemen, why should the Arabian dog be a "sleeper" also? It is possible that in Arabia and in the Highlands the tale is found in its most archaic form, and that it is part of the floating material from which Teutonic Mythology was constructed.[2]

What appears to be a very old version of the legend

---

[1] See *Finn and His Warrior Band.*
[2] The dog also figures in a "Seven Sleepers" legend in North Afghanistan.

is found in South Uist. It was taken down from a minister thirty years ago by an Inspector of Schools, who related it to the writer as follows:—

> The Fians (Féinne) were lying in a cave, each resting on his elbow, chin upon hand, self-absorbed, not asleep.
>
> They heard the falling waters, and the storms went over them unheeded. . . . Thousands of years went past.
>
> They were still resting there, musing, when one of them moved his elbow and said :—
>
> "Och! och! 's mi tha sgith." (Och! och! it's me that's tired.)
>
> Thousands of years went past. . . . They heard the falling waters, and the storms went over them unheeded.
>
> Then a great Fian said sharply, "Mur a' sguir sibh dhe 'n chonnspoid seo, theid mi mach 's fagaidh mi an uaimh agaibh fhein." (If you do not stop this wrangling I'll go out, and leave the cave to yourselves.)
>
> Thousands of years went past. . . . They heard the falling waters, and the storms went over them unheeded.

In various legends the movements of the " sleepers" (who do not sleep in Uist) were associated with sorrow and disaster or seasonal changes. Edward the Confessor had a vision, while sitting at a banquet in his palace at Westminster, in which he saw the Ephesian sleepers turning round. A messenger was sent to Ephesus, and it was found that they had turned from their right sides to their left. This was taken as a sign of approaching disaster, and was, in fact, associated with the miseries that Christendom endured from the Saracens. The seasonal reference survives in the St. Swithin's day belief.

Various heroes lie asleep, including Charlemagne, Frederick of Barbarossa, William Tell in Switzerland, Brian Boroimhe in Ireland, and Arthur in Wales. The warning that when the sleepers leave the cave "the world will be upset" was transformed into the popular belief that certain heroes would issue forth in the hour of their country's direst need. The French peasants believed in the coming of Napoleon, as the Swiss did in the return of William Tell. During the Russo-Japanese war the peasantry of Russia were confident that General Skobeleff would hasten to Manchuria to lead the armies to victory. To this day there are many Highlanders who remain convinced that General Sir Hector Macdonald is not dead, but is waiting his hour of return. A similar belief attached to James IV, who fell at Flodden. So do "immemorial modes of thought" survive in the twentieth century from, perhaps, that remote Stone Age period when the fair-haired and blue-eyed "long-heads" spread from North Africa over the undivided lands of ancient Europe to mingle with earlier inhabitants and later "broad-heads" from Asia.

# CHAPTER I

## Story of Creation

The Beginning—Ginnunga-gap—All-father—Nifel-heim and Muspel-heim—How Life began—Ymer, the Clay Giant—Audhumla, the Cow—Vana-gods, Giants, and Asa-gods—War in Space—Ymer-deluge—The Great World-mill—How the Earth was made—Moon-god and Sun-goddess—Hyuki and Bil—The Pail of Song Mead—Wolf Giants pursue Sun and Moon—Mimer and Nat, "Mother of Gods"—The Day-god—The Eagle of Winds—First Man and Woman.

In the Ages, when naught else was, there yawned in space a vast and empty gulf called Ginnunga-gap. Length it had, and breadth immeasurable, and there was depth beyond comprehension. No shore was there, nor cooling wave; for there was yet no sea, and the earth was not made nor the heavens above.

There in the gulf was the beginning of things. There time first dawned. And in the perpetual twilight was All-father, who governs every realm and sways all things both great and small.

First of all there was formed, northward of the gulf, Nifel-heim, the immense home of misty darkness and

1

freezing cold, and to the south, Muspel-heim, the luminous home of warmth and of light.

In the midst of Nifel-heim burst forth the great fountain from whence all waters flow, and to which all waters return. It is named Hvergelmer, "the roaring cauldron", and from it surged, at the beginning, twelve tremendous rivers called Elivagar, that washed southward towards the gulf. A vast distance they traversed from their source, and then the venom that was swept with them began to harden, as does dross pouring from a surface, until they congealed and became ice. Whereupon the rivers grew silent and ceased to move, and gigantic blocks of ice stood still. Vapour arose from the ice-venom and was frozen to rime; layer upon layer heaped up in fantastic forms one above another.

That part of the gulf which lay northward was a region of horror and of strife. Heavy masses of black vapour enveloped the ice, and within were screaming whirlwinds that never ceased, and dismal banks of fleeting mist. But southward, Muspel-heim glowed with intense radiance, and sprayed forth beauteous flakes and sparks of shining fire. The intervening space between the region of tempest and gloom and the region of warmth and light was a peaceful twilight, serene and still as is windless air.

Now when the sparks from Muspel-heim fell through the frozen vapour, and the heat was sent thither by the might of the All-father, drops of moisture began to fall from the ice. It was then and there that life began to be. The drops were quickened and a formless mass took human shape. Thus came into being the great lumbering clay-giant who was named Ymer.

Rough and ungainly was Ymer, and as he stretched himself and began to move about he was tortured by the pangs of immense hunger. So he went forth ravenously to search for food; but there was yet no substance of which he could partake. The whirlwinds went past him and over, and the dark mists enveloped him like a shroud.

More drops fell through the gloomy vapours, and next there was formed a gigantic cow, which was named Audhumla, "void darkness". Ymer beheld it standing in the gloom beside blocks of ice, and groped weakly towards it. Wondering, he found that milk ran from its teats in four white streams, and greedily he drank and drank until he was filled with the seeds of life and was satisfied.

Then a great heaviness came over Ymer, and he lay down and fell into deep and dreamless slumber. Warmth and strength possessed him, and sweat gathered in the pit of his left arm, from which, by the might of All-father, were formed a son named Mimer and a daughter named Bestla. From Mimer were descended the Vana-gods. Under the feet of Ymer arose a monstrous six-headed son, who was the ancestor of the evil frost giants, the dreaded Hrimthursar. Then Ymer awoke.

For Audhumla, the great cow, there was no verdure upon which to feed. She stood on the verge of gloom, and found sustenance by licking constantly the huge boulders that were encrusted by salt and rime. For the space of a day she fed in this manner, until the hair of a great head appeared. On the second day the cow returned to the boulder, and ere she had ceased to lick, a head of human semblance was laid bare. On the third day a noble form leapt forth. He was endowed with great beauty, and was nimble and powerful. The name he received was Bure, and he was the first of the Asa-gods.

There followed in time more beings—noble giants and wicked giants, and gods. Mimer, who is Mind and Memory, had daughters, the chief of whom was Urd, Goddess of Fate and Queen of Life and Death. Bure had a son named Bor, who took for his wife Bestla, the sister of wise Mimer. Three sons were born to them, and the first was called Odin (spirit), the second Ve, whose other name is Honer, and the third Vile, whose other names are Lodur and Loke. Odin became the chief ruler of the Asa-gods, and Honer was chief of the Vans until Loke, the usurper, became their ruler.

Now Ymer and his evil sons were moved with wrath and enmity against the family of gods, and soon warfare broke out between them. To neither side was there early victory, and the fierce conflicts were waged through the long ages ere yet the earth was formed. But, at length, the sons of Bor prevailed over their enemies and drove them back. In time there followed great slaughter, which diminished the army of evil giants until one alone remained.

It was thus that the gods achieved their triumph. Ymer was stricken down, and the victors leapt upon him and then slit open the bulging veins of his neck. A great deluge of blood gushed forth, and the whole race of giants was drowned save Bergelmer, "The Mountain-old", who with his wife took refuge on the timbers of the great World-mill, and remained there. From these are descended the Jotuns, who for ever harboured enmity against the gods.

The great World-mill of the gods was under care of Mundilfore (Lodur-Loke). Nine giant maids turned it with much violence, and the grinding of the stones made such fearsome clamour that the loudest tempests could not be heard. The great mill is larger than is

*The giant Ymer.*

*The death of Ymer.*

the whole world, for out of it the mould of earth was ground.

When Ymer was dead, the gods took counsel among themselves, and set forth to frame the world. They laid the body of the clay-giant on the mill, and the maids ground it. The stones were smeared with blood, and the dark flesh came out as mould. Thus was earth produced, and the gods shaped it to their desire. From Ymer's bones were made the rocks and the mountains; his teeth and jaws were broken asunder, and as they went round at their labour the giant maids flung the fragments hither and thither, and these are the pebbles and boulders. The ice-cold blood of the giant became the waters of the vast engulfing sea.

Nor did the giant maids cease their labours when the body of Ymer was completely ground, and the earth was framed and set in order by the gods. The body of giant after giant was laid upon the mill, which stands beneath the floor of Ocean, and the flesh-grist is the sand whicn is ever washed up round the shores of the world. Where the waters are sucked through the whirling eye of the millstone is a fearsome maelstrom, and the sea ebbs and flows as it is drawn down to Hvergelmer, "the roaring cauldron", in Nifel-heim and thrown forth again. The very heavens are made to swing by the great World-mill, round Veraldar Nagli, "the world spike", which is the Polar Star.

Now when the gods had shaped the earth they set Ymer's skull over it to be the heavens. At each of the four corners they put as sentinels the strong dwarfs East and West and North and South. The skull of Ymer rests upon their broad shoulders.

As yet the sun knew not her home, nor the moon her power, and the stars had no fixed dwelling place.

Now the stars are bright fire-sparks sprayed from Muspel-heim over the great gulf, and these the gods fixed in the heavens to give light to the world and to shine over the sea. To these and to every wandering fire-flake they assigned due order and motion, so that each has its set place and time and season.

The sun and the moon were also regulated in their courses, for these are the greater fire-disks that were sprayed from Muspel-heim, and to bear them over the paths of the heavens the gods caused the elf-smiths, the sons of Ivalde and the kinsmen of Sindre, to fashion chariots of fine gold.

Mundilfore, who has care of the World-mill, aspired to rival Odin. He had two beautiful children, and one he called Mani (moon), and the other Sol (sun). The gods were filled with anger because of Mundilfore's presumption, and to punish him they took from him his two children, of whom he was exceedingly boastful, to drive the heavenly chariots and count the years for men. Fair Sol they set to drive the sun-chariot. Her steeds are Arvak, which is "Early Dawn", and Alsvid, which signifies "scorching heat". Under their withers were placed skins of ice-chilled air for coolness and refreshment. They enter the eastern heaven at Hela-gate, through which the souls of dead men pass to the world beneath.

Then the gods set Mani, the handsome youth, to drive the chariot of the moon. With him are two fair children whom he carried away from earth—a boy who was called Hyuki, and a girl whose name is Bil.[1] They had been sent out in the darkness of night by Vidfinner, their father, to draw song-mead from the mountain spring Byrger, "the hidden", which broke forth from

[1] The Jack and Jill of the nursery rhyme.

the source of Mimer's fount; and they filled their pail Saegr to the brink, so that the precious mead spilled over as they raised it on the pole Simul. When they began to descend the mountain, Mani seized them and took them away. The spots that are ever seen by night on the fair-faced moon are Hyuki and Bil; and beauteous Bil do skalds invoke, so that hearing them she may sprinkle from the moon the magic song-mead upon their lips.

In Mani's keeping is a bundle of thorns from which evildoers among men must needs suffer the punishment of piercing pains.

The sun is ever in flight, and so also is the moon. They are pursued by bloodthirsty enemies, who seek to compass their destruction ere they reach the sheltering forest of the Varns, behind the western horizon. These are two fierce and gigantic wolves. The one whose name is Skoll, "the adherer", chases the sun, whom one day it will devour; the other is Hati, "the hater", who races in front of "the bright maiden of heaven", in ceaseless pursuit of the moon.

Skoll and Hati are giants in wolf-guise. They were sent forth by the Mother of Evil, the dark and fearsome Hag, Gulveig-Hoder, whose children they are. She dwells in the Iarnvid, the black forest of iron trees, on the world's edge, which is the habitation of a witch family dreaded both by gods and by men. Of the Hag's wolf-sons the most terrible is Hati, who is also called Mana-garm, "the moon devourer". He feeds on the blood of dying men. The seers have foretold that when he comes to swallow the moon, the heavens and the earth shall turn red with blood. Then, too, must the seats of the mighty gods be reddened with gore, and the sun-shine of summer made dim, while great storms burst in fury to rage across the world.

Again and again, at dreaded eclipse, would these giant wolves have swallowed now the sun and now the moon, had not their evil designs been thwarted by spells which were wrought against them, and the clamour of affrighted men.

Now Nat, which is Night, is the swarthy daughter of the Vana-giant Narve, "the Binder", whose other name is Mimer. Dark is her hair like all her race, and her eyes are soft and benevolent. She brings rest to the toiler, and refreshment to the weary, and sleep and dreams unto all. To the warrior she gives strength so that he may win victory, and care and sorrow she loves to take away. Nat is the beneficent mother of gods. Three times was she wed. Her first husband was Nagelfare of the stars, and their son was Aud of bounteous riches. Her second husband was Annar, "Water", and their daughter, Jörd, the earth-goddess, was Odin's wife and the mother of Thor. Her third husband was Delling, the red elf of dawn, and their son was Dagr, which is Day.

To mother Nat and her son Dagr were given jewelled chariots to drive across the world, one after the other, in the space of twelve hours. Nat is first to set forth. Her steed is called Hrim Faxi, "frosted mane". Swiftly it gallops over the heavens, and every morn the sweet foam from its bit falls as dewdrops upon the earth beneath. Dagr's fair steed is called Skin Faxi, "shining mane". From its golden neck is shed radiance and beauty upon the heavens and over all the world. Of all coursers that are, he is praised most by faring men.

There are two seasons, and these are Winter and Summer. Vindsval, son of gloomy Vasud, "the ice wind", was father of grim Winter, and the mild and beneficent Svasud was the sire of fair Summer, beloved by all.

The wonder of men is whence comes the wind that shakes the ocean with fear, that fans the low spark into bright flame, and that no eye can behold. At the northern summit of heaven there sits in eagle-guise a great giant called Hraesvelgur, "the swallower of dead men's flesh". When his wide pinions are spread for flight the winds are stirred beneath them and rush down upon the earth. When coming or going, or travelling hither and thither across the heavens, the winds are driven from his wings.

As yet there were no men who had their dwelling upon the earth, although the sun and moon were set in their courses, and the days and seasons were marked out in due order. There came a time, however, when the sons of Bor were walking on the world's shores, and they beheld two logs of wood. They were grown from Ymer's hair, which sprang up as thick forests and verdure abundant from the mould of his body, which is the earth. One log was of an ash tree, and from it the gods shaped a man; and the other, which was an alder tree, they made into a fair woman. They had but life like a tree which grows until the gods gave them mind and will and desire. Then was the man named Ask and the woman Embla, and from them are descended the entire human race, whose habitation is called Midgard, "middle ward", and Mana-heim, "home of men".

Round Midgard is the embracing sea, and beyond, on the outward shores, is Jotun-heim, the home of giants. Against these the gods raised an ice bulwark shaped from the eyebrows of turbulent Ymer, whose brains they cast high in heaven, where they became heavy masses of scattered cloud, tossing hither and thither.

## Address to Odin

In the beginning, ere the gods were born,
Before the Heavens were builded, thou didst slay
The giant Ymir, whom the abyss brought forth,
Thou and thy brethren fierce, the sons of Bor,
And cast his trunk to choke the abysmal void.
But of his flesh and members thou didst build
The earth and Ocean, and above them Heaven.
And from the flaming world, where Muspel reigns,
Thou sent'st and fetched'st fire, and madest lights,
Sun, moon, and stars, which thou hast hung in Heaven,
Dividing clear the paths of night and day.
And Asgard thou didst build, and Midgard fort;
Then me thou mad'st; of us the Gods were born.
Last, walking by the sea, thou foundest spars
Of wood, and framed'st men, who till the earth,
Or on the sea, the field of pirates, sail.
And all the race of Ymir thou didst drown,
Save one, Bergelmer;—he on shipboard fled
Thy deluge, and from him the giants sprang.
But all that brood thou hast removed far off,
And set by Ocean's utmost marge to dwell;
But Hela into Nifelheim thou threw'st,
And gav'st her nine unlighted worlds to rule,
A queen, and empire over all the dead.

—*From "Balder Dead", by Matthew Arnold.*

# CHAPTER II
## The Nine Worlds

Asgard—River and Vafer-Flame—High Thingstead of the Gods—Odin's Throne—"Abode of Friends"—The Golden Age—Dwarfs—Ygdrasil, "the Tree of Existence"—Roots in the Underworld—The Three Fountains—Eagle and Hawk—"The Cock of the North"—The Biting Deer—The Dragon Nidhog—The Squirrel Gossip—Norns, Hamingjes, and Giptes—Lower Thingstead of the Gods—Bif-rost—The Sentinel Heimdal—Judgment of the Dead—The Last Journey—Bliss of the Just—Doom of the Condemned—Regions of Torture—Valhal—Divisions of the Universe—Night Path of Day and Day Path of Night.

THE Asa-gods built for themselves Asgard, the celestial city, which is set high above the heavens. It stands there in beauty and in glory upon a holy island in the midst of a dark broad river flowing from the thunder-vapours that rise through the great World-tree from Hvergelmer, "the roaring cauldron", the mother of waters. The river is ever troubled with eddies and fierce currents, and above it hover darkly thick banks of kindling mist called "Black Terror Gleam", from which leap everlastingly tongues of vafer-flame, (lightning) filling the air and darting like white froth from whirling billows.

Round Asgard is a dark and lofty wall, and the great boiling river breaks angrily at its base. There is no entry-way save by Odin's mighty gate. And if anyone who is unworthy, be he god or giant or mortal, should cross the river unscathed by the vafer-flames, and seek to open the gate of Asgard, he would be caught sud-

11

denly by a chain which springs from the lock of strange mechanism, and crushed and utterly destroyed.

In the middle of Asgard was built stately Idavoll, the Court of Judgment, the High Thingstead of the Gods, in which their own divine affairs are discussed and arranged. The beauty of the great hall is unequalled in the nine worlds, for its roof is of shining silver and it is resplendent without and within with burnished and graven gold. Therein was set the great golden throne of Odin, the chief ruler of Asgard, and around it were placed twelve golden seats for the gods who sit with him in judgment, and to whom the All-father gave power to rule and to issue decrees.

When Odin sits on his high golden throne he looks over the homes of giants and elves and mortals and sees all things. He is silent and he listens.

Another fair and stately structure did the gods cause to be made as a sanctuary for the goddesses, and by singers of skalds who echo its praises it is called Vingolf, " the abode of friends ".

In Asgard was shaped a smithy which was furnished with anvils and hammers and tongs. With these the gods had made for them, by the cunning elf-smiths, Ivalde's sons and Sindre's kinsmen, every instrument they had need of. They worked in fine metals, and so great was the treasure of gold that all movables were made of it.

On a green place in the celestial city were found the golden tablets with which was played the Game of the Gods. This was in the Golden Age, which lasted until there came from Jotun-heim three giant maids, who brought corruption.

To the gods in ages past it became known that there dwelt in Midgard a race of dwarfs. In the deep, dark

mould of Ymer's body they swarmed as do maggots in
rotted flesh, and they went hither and thither with no
purpose or knowledge. All the gods assembled in their
high Thingstead, with Odin seated on his golden throne,
and there took counsel one with another. To the dwarfs
they gave human shape, but their hue was the blackness
of earth in which they had being. Over them the gods
set Modsognir, who is Mimer, to be king. In the
mounds of the earth dwell one tribe of these earth-black
elves, within rocks another, and a third have their habitation inside high and precipitous mountains. Besides
these are the Trolls, who fly hither and thither carrying
bundles of sticks, and have power to change their shape.

Now the wonder of the Universe, which was set in
order by the will of All-father, is the great ash tree,
Ygdrasil, the Tree of Existence, which nourishes and
sustains all spiritual and physical life. Its roots are
spread through the divisions of the worlds that fill the
yawning gulf, and its boughs are above the high celestial
city of the gods. It grows out of the past, it lives in
the present, and it reaches towards the future.

The World-ash has three great roots. In the realms
below Midgard is one root, which receives warmth and
life in Hela's glittering plains from the deep fountain
of Urd, the goddess of fate and of death; another root
reaches the egg-white well of Mimer, who is Wisdom
and Memory; and the last root is in gloomy Nifel-heim,
where it finds hardening sustenance in Hvergelmer, "the
roaring cauldron", the fount of primeval waters, ice-cold
and everlasting, which springs up on Hvergelmer mountain.

In the realm of Urd, which is Hela, the souls of
good men be. Nigh to it, in the underworld, is Mimer's
well in Mimer's grove, where dwells the race which will

regenerate the world of men. Below cold and darksome Nifel-heim are the nine divisions of torture in which the souls of the wicked are punished. At Hvergelmer the watchman of the root of Ygdrasil is Ivalde, who with his sons contend against the storm-giants who threaten Hela.

The roots of the great World-tree suck up the waters of the three eternal fountains, and these mixed together give imperishable life. In the well of wise Mimer the fibres are made white with the holy mead which gives wisdom to men, and poetry also, and is the very elixir of life eternal.

On the high branches of Ygdrasil, which overshadow Asgard, sits a wise eagle, and between its eyes is perched a hawk named Vedfolner. On the topmost bough is Goldcomb, the "cock of the north", which awakens the gods from sleep and puts the demons to flight. From Hela answers the red cock, whose fire purifies what is good and destroys what is evil.

But the great World-tree bears a more painful burden than mortals can conceive. In the well of Hvergelmer, in the black realm of Nifel-heim, is the corpse-eating dragon Nidhog, "the lower one", which chews constantly at the root; above, four giant harts are ever biting its buds and its leaves; on its side, Age rots it; and many serpents gnaw its tender fibres in the dark underworld. For there never was good to which evil came not, nor growth which has known not decay and the wasting of time.

The Norns of Hela sprinkle the great ash-tree each morning with precious mead from Urd's fount of life, so that its leaves may ever be green. Thence comes the honey-dew, which drips upon the world and is stored by the bees. And in Urd's fountain are the two mystic

*Odin takes counsel with the Norns.*

*Dwarfs.*

swans which are the ancestors of the swan race in Midgard.

Up and down the World-tree runs constantly the squirrel Ratatosk, which bears gossip between the eagle on the highest branches and the dragon Nidhog at the root, and is thus ever the cause of strife. Greatly dreaded is Nidhog, who flies to the rocks and cliffs of the lower world with the bodies of dead men beneath its wings.

The three Fates, who are called Norns, are Urd and her two sisters—Urd, "present"; Verdande, "past"; and Skuld, "future". By them are spun at will the fates of men and women. There are also Dises, who are maids of Urd, unto whom various duties are assigned. The Hamingjes are those Dises who are guardians of men through their lives, and appear to them in dreams to give warnings and noble counsel, and he whom the holy elf deserts for wrongdoing is indeed lost. The decrees of Urd are executed by the Giptes, and men who are favoured are suddenly awarded good fortune and treasure; other Dises attend upon families and even upon tribes. There are also the sweet elf-maids who have care of babes unborn in the fair realms of Urd, and find them kindly mothers in the world of men; and there are maids who conduct the souls of the dead to Hela's glittering plain.

Now in Hela is the lower-world Thingstead of the gods, where the souls of the dead are judged, and rewards and punishments are meted out by Odin. There is but one road thither from Asgard for all the gods save Thor, and that is over the curved bridge Bif-rost, "the rainbow", which has its foundation beyond the edge of the world of men. The southern span reaches to the fount of Urd in the realms of green verdure that never know decay.

Bif-rost is built of air and water, and is protected by red fire flaming on its edge. Frost giants and mountain giants ever seek to capture the bridge, so that they may ascend to Asgard and overcome the gods; but its sentinel, Heimdal, is constantly on guard against them.

The gods set Heimdal, son of the waves, to protect the bridge forever against the enemy. He is clad in silvern armour, and on his head is a burnished helmet with ram's horns. Horsed on his swift steed, Gull-top, he now watches at the highest point of Bif-rost from his fortified citadel, Himinbjorg, "the ward of heaven", where his hall is supplied with precious mead. Anon he crosses over from side to side of the bridge. His sight is so keen that he can see by night as well as by day the length of a hundred leagues, and he listens so keenly that he can hear the grass growing. He sleeps as little and as lightly as a bird. When the giants and monsters come to assail the gods at Ragnarok, Heimdal shall blow a thunderblast on Gjallar-horn which is hidden in the deepest shade of the World-tree. With his great sword he shall combat with the Evil One in the Last Battle.

Heimdal is loved both by gods and by men, and he is also called Gullintani because his teeth are of gold. There was a time when he went unto Midgard as a child; he grew up to be a teacher among men, and was named Scef.

Every day the horses of the gods thunder over Bif-rost as they descend to and return from the lower-world Thingstead. Thor, the thunder god, cannot travel thus because the fire of his thunder chariot might set the bridge aflame and destroy it. He must needs wade across the four great girdling rivers in the underworld to reach Hela's glittering plains.

When the gods come unto Hela they leap from their horses and take their seats in the Thingstead. The dead are then brought before them.

A weary way and long these dead men and women have travelled. Down the valley of thorns they came, and those who were given hel-shoes in their graves, because they had shown mercy to others while they lived, suffered indeed little; but the feet of the wicked were torn and bleeding. Then they crossed a river full of weapons. The just walked over on boards, but the unjust waded, and were sorely wounded and covered with scars, so that their bodies dripped blood.

To the Thingstead come men and women in full attire, with the jewels and ornaments which those who loved them placed on their bodies ere they were laid in grave-chambers. Warriors carry their weapons, and all are clad so that they may be recommended to the gods as the well-beloved among men. But silent are the dead, save the happy ones under whose tongues were placed, ere yet they were laid in their graves, magic runes, so that they might make answer when accused, and give reasons to justify their deeds. But the Hamingjes can also speak for the dead, and those who have not Hamingjes to speak for them are known to have done evil and to be deserted by their Dises in sorrow and wrath. Those who are justified pass to the eternal realms of Hela, where joy prevails, because they have lived upright lives, and have been honourable and full of pity and have helped others; because they were brave and feared not to die; and also because they worshipped the gods and gave offerings in the temples.

But those who are condemned are sent to Nifel-hel, the region of torture. They are judged to be unworthy if they injured others by falsehoods or wicked deeds, if they were adulterers, or murderers, or despoilers of graves, or cowards, or were traitors, and profaners of the temples.

Those who are to share eternal joy are given to drink from the horn of Urd, which imparts to them enduring strength. In it are mixed the three meads from the wells which sustain Ygdrasil, the World-ash. But the doomed are given a draught of burning venom which changes them to monsters. Their tongues are then for ever bereft of speech and they can moan only.

The happy dead disport themselves on the green plains of Hela, where they meet lost friends and ancestors from the earliest years of the world. And many beauteous ways they travel, and wonderful tales they hear. The children are cared for in the realm of Mimer, "memory", where joy is theirs forever and their food is honey-dew.

The doomed are fettered and are driven towards Nifel-hel by black elves, who carry thorny rods with which they lash those who falter or seek to turn back. Their first punishment is received when they must needs pass through the regions of eternal bliss, and behold with grief unutterable the joy of the blessed. Then they cross the rivers which girdle Hela, and climb towards the dark mountains of Nifel-hel. The wolf dog barks at them in the shadowy valley where it guards the borders of Hela, and there is blood on its breast. And as they climb tortuous paths and tread the narrow path on the edge of dizzy precipices they hear the barking of the terrible watchdogs at Nifel-hel's gates. The dreaded dragon, Nidhog, hovers near them, and ferocious birds of prey sit on the rocks.

Then they enter the Na-gates and die the second death. Punishment is given in the nine realms of torture according to the sins that were committed. Some are seized by the dragon and some by the birds of prey, according to their deserts. Others are tempted for ever by illusions of sinful things they sought in life, and there are those who are torn to pieces by the great wolf.

In the Venom-dale is a river called Slid, and it is full of daggers and sharp spears. Through it must wade the perjurers and murderers and adulterers, who are continually suffering new and fierce wounds. Others sit together on benches of iron, while venom drips on them, within a hall which is full of stench unbearable. Traitors are hung on trees, and cowards are drowned in pools of foulness. Eternal night broods over all.

Naglefar, the "ship of death", lies in the Gulf of Black Grief, in the outer regions of Nifel-hel, made fast to a dark island with chains that shall not sever until Ragnarok, "the dusk of the gods". It is constructed of the parings of dead men's nails—the wicked men, hated by their kind because of their evil deeds, whose bodies were cleansed not at life's end, and whose nails were not pared ere they were laid in grave-chambers. When Naglefar breaks loose the avenging hosts shall sail in it to battle against the gods.

The warriors who are slain in battle, or drowned at sea, are borne to Valhal in Asgard by the maids of Urd, who are called Valkyries. They are horsed on swift steeds, and first they pass to Hela, where the gods give judgment and reject the unworthy. Then they are carried by the Valkyries over Bif-rost, and the hoofs of their steeds resound in Asgard. In great Valhal the heroes feast with Odin in eternal triumph and happiness.

Now these are the divisions of the Universe. In the midst is the earth, Midgard, which is encircled by the ocean. On high, and above all else, is Asgard, and below it is the realm of white elves, who flit between the branches of the great World-tree. Then Vana-heim, the home of the Vana-gods, is in the air and in the sea; and in the depths of the western sea is the hall of Æger, god of Ocean. Alf-heim, the home of elves, is to the east. In the lower world, below Nifel-heim, are the Nifel-hel regions of torture, and under Midgard are the Hela realms of Mimer and of Urd. Far below the path of the gods towards Hela's fields of bliss are Surtur's deep dales on the borders of Muspel-heim, where the great giant Surtur, the swarthy sentinel, keeps watch with his flaming sword. Jotun-heim is to the north and the east, beyond the world's edge.

Billing is the elf-guardian of the western heaven, and when the cars of Day and of Night and of the Sun and of the Moon enter the forest of the Varns, "the protectors", they pass through the lower-world realms of Mimer and of Urd towards the gates of Delling, the elf of dawn, in the east. When Nat reaches Hela, where she must rest, darkness falls around her, and the blessed are given sleep, and light comes again with Dagr, as Nat covers the earth above with shadow and deep slumber.

# The Descent of the Gods

. . . the Gods arose,
And took their horses, and set forth to ride
O'er the bridge Bifrost, where is Heimdall's watch,
To the ash Ygdrasil, and Ida's plain;
Thor came on foot, the rest on horseback rode.
And they found Mimir sitting by his fount
Of wisdom, which beneath the ash-tree springs;
And saw the Nornies watering the roots
Of that world-shadowing tree with honey-dew.
There came the Gods, and sate them down on stones.
—*From " Balder Dead ", by Matthew Arnold.*

# CHAPTER III

## The Deeds of Odin

The Brooding God—Mimer's Well—Draught of Wisdom—The Eye Sacrifice—Revolt of Ivalde—Murder of Moon-god—Combat with Hyuki—The Stolen Song-Mead—Odin seeks to Recapture it—Descent to Surtur's Deep Dales—The Giant Suttung—Odin's Bridegroom-Guise—"The Champion Drinker"—Marriage with Gunlad—Ivalde's Fate—Odin's Escape—"The Man in the Moon"—Hyuki is Slagfin and Hengest—Odin's Apparel—His Ravens and Wolf Dogs—Odin the First Poet—Saga—Secret Runes—Thor and other Gods—Odin's Wives.

ODIN was the chief ruler of the gods. He was tall and old, and his aspect was wise and reverend. White was his beard and long, and he seemed ever to brood deeply over the mysteries of life and death. He had but one eye, because the other he sacrificed so that he might be dowered with great wisdom. Indeed he had in his youth drunk deeply of the magic mead of Mimer's well.

Every morning grave Mimer drank a draught with the Gjallar-horn, and Odin when he was yet young had deep desire to receive the wisdom and strength which the egg-white mead alone can give. He entreated Mimer to give him a draught, and the price he paid was an eye, which was cast into the well. From that hour when he drained Gjallar-horn he became worthy to rule over gods and men. 'Twas thus he sang in after-time of the powers which the mead imparted to him:

Then began I to bloom,
To be wise,

21

To grow and to thrive;
Word came to me
From word,
Deed came to me
From deed.

Thus Odin taught to all men that in youth there must needs be self-sacrifice of great account so that wisdom and power may be obtained.

From the moon-car in heaven did Odin also drink of the song-mead which was in the pitcher that Hyuki and Bil had carried from the secret well on the mountain, and Mani, the moon-god, captured. But wroth was Vidfinner at his loss, and he mourned more for the mead than for his children. Vidfinner is also called Ivalde, the sworn watchman of Hvergelmer and the Rivers Elivagar, and another of his names is Svigdur, "the champion drinker". There came a day when he broke his oath of fealty to the gods and fled from his post. Then raging heavenwards he attacked the moon-god, whom he slew and burned. His son Hyuki fought against him without avail, and suffered a fierce wound— as a maker of poems has sung—"clean to the thigh bone". For this dread crime Ivalde-Svigdur was condemned, but he fled towards Surtur's deep dales and unto the dwelling of Suttung, son of Surtur, the giant sentinel of Muspelheim. For Surtur and his clan were at enmity with Mimer and the Vana-gods, and also with the gods of Asgard since the creation of Asgard and the dividing of the worlds. To Suttung Ivalde gave the previous skaldic mead, and for reward he was promised for wife Gunlad, the giant's daughter.

Odin, seeing all that happened as he sat in his high throne, resolved to recapture the mead by cunning. So he set out to visit the hall of Suttung, "the mead wolf".

Now the realm of Surtur is difficult to reach, and full of peril for the gods. It lies in the dark underworld which is lower than and beyond Hela. Suttung's hall is within a mountain to which, in a deep abyss, there is but one entry, and it is guarded by a fierce dwarf sentinel.

But Odin secured the confidence of the dwarf, who promised to aid him so that his enterprise might be crowned with success. Heimdal, the sentinel of Bif-rost, also gave his service. His other name is Rati, "the traveller", and he bored through the mountain a narrow tunnel through which Odin might escape in eagle-guise. Thus, having completed his designs, Odin went towards the door of the dwelling of the great fire-giant Suttung, who is also called Fjalar.

A great feast was held within, and the evil frost-giants were as guests there to welcome Svigdur, the wooer of the giant-maid Gunlad. Odin assumed the form of Svigdur, and like him he spoke also, lest he should by uttering words of wisdom and weight be suspected and put to death. Thus he prevailed against the sons of Surtur with their own methods, for they were given to creating illusions and travelling forth in disguise to work evil and destruction.

A high seat of gold awaited the expected wedding-guest, and when Odin entered in the form of Svigdur, "the champion drinker", he was welcomed with ardour. And well he played the part, for he was given to drink of the nectar of the giants, and partook to the full, so that he was made drunk. Yet he observed great caution, that he might not be discovered.

As he sat at the feast, Gunlad came forward and gave him a draught of the stolen mead. Then was the marriage celebrated with solemnity and in state. The holy ring was placed upon the finger of the giant-maid, and she swore to be faithful to him who wooed her.

Meantime Ivalde-Svigdur, the real lover, reached the door of Suttung's hall, and came to know that Odin was within. He was filled with wrath, and he sought to denounce the high god so that he might be slain by the giants. But the dwarf sentinel accomplished Ivalde-Svigdur's destruction. He created an illusion, and opened a door on the side of the mountain which showed a lighted hall within and the wedding guests as they sat round Suttung's board. Gunlad was at Odin's side. Ivalde-Svigdur leapt towards the vision of the high god of Asgard, and thus dashed himself against the rock. The door was shut behind, and the mountain swallowed him.

Ere the wedding feast was ended Odin had spoken words which caused the giants to suspect him. But he retired with Gunlad to the bridal chamber, and there he found the precious mead which Ivalde-Svigdur had robbed from the moon-god. Then Gunlad came to know that her lover was Odin, but she helped him to make his escape in eagle-guise. So Odin flew through the tunnel which Heimdal-Rati had made, and reached Asgard in safety with the precious mead.

In the morning the giants went towards the bridal chamber, remembering the words that their guest had spoken, and when they found he had escaped they called him Bolverkin, "the evildoer".

But although Odin conferred great good upon gods and men by capturing the mead, the consequences of the evil he wrought towards that end were doomed to bring disaster in after-time, when Surtur, issuing forth to avenge the wrong done to Gunlad, set the world aflame. For good cannot follow evil, even although it is accomplished for the sake of good.

Odin's joy was great when he returned in triumph to Asgard, but he spoke words of pity for the giant-maid whom he had betrayed, and who wept because he left her.

Ivalde - Svigdur, who perished in the mountain, was refused an abode among the blessed dead in Hela's glittering plains.   Him the gods condemned to dwell forever in the moon.   There he suffers eternal punishment for his evildoings, for he is ever drunk with the stolen mead, which is venom to him, and is ever beaten with the rod of thorns by the god he slew and to whom life was again given.   Ivalde's son, Hyuki, is revered among men.   Another name he bears is Slagfin, and by Saxon warriors he is called Hengest.   He is also Gelder, and his symbol is the gelding.   Among skee - runners he is the chief upon land and on the sea.

Many names have the gods, and for Odin there are nine-and-forty.   And the reason is, as skalds have told, that people speaking different tongues must needs call the gods by different names, while the gods have also been given names according to their various attributes and the great deeds they have done.

Thus Odin was called All - father, like the Mighty One who was at "time's first dawn", because he was father of the gods; and Val-father, the father of the brave who dwell in Valhal in high Asgard.

When Odin sat in his high golden throne, he wore a cloak which was striped with many colours of sunset splendour and summer radiance.   Its hood was blue as is the sky, and speckled with grey like clouds.   His hat was blue also, and its broad brims curved downward like the heavens.   When he left Asgard to travel over the worlds he wore a burnished helmet, and sometimes he went among men wearing a hat which was tilted to conceal the hollow of his lost eye.

As Odin sat brooding and listening in Asgard two ravens perched on his shoulder. Their names are Hugin, which is "reflection", and Munin, which means "memory". When day dawned Odin sent them forth, and they returned at eve to whisper in his ears all the doings of men. Thus was he called Rafnagud, the "raven-god". He had also two wolf dogs, and they are named Gere, "the greedy", and Freke, "the voracious". These Odin fed with the food which was placed before him at the feast of heroes, for he ate not and for nourishment drank nectar.

When Odin drank of the song-mead he composed poems which for sweetness and grandeur have never been surpassed. He was the first poet, and knew well the magic of the mead. For the source of it was secret, and was discovered only by Ivalde, the watchman of the primeval fount from which life first came and by which life is ever sustained. Then was it carried to the beauteous car of the moon, and from thence to the regions of fire. There it was won by love mixed with wrong, and when the high god who descended to the deeps drank of it, he soared as an eagle to heaven, which he filled with song. From heaven has song descended upon earth, and in song are all the sufferings which were begotten over the mead.

Odin is also the friend and companion of the goddess Saga, whose dwelling in Asgard is Sokvabek, "the deep stream". Precious thoughts well up from the fountain source and flow along as words of gold. They tell of things that were, and Odin ponders. Day after day and night after night the high god sits with the goddess listening to the flowing stream, which grows deeper and wider as it wends its way onward, and their minds are refreshed by the glories of the past.

Secret runes, which have magical influence, did Odin also invent. For nine whole nights he hung on the high branches of Ygdrasil, pondering and searching out the secrets of the mind and of the Universe. For the power of runes was before the beginning of man. They are mixed with fate, and their potency did Odin discover when he drank from Mimer's well. They have also power over death and the world beyond. Runes there are to ward off strife and care, to charm away sickness and disease, to blunt the foeman's sword, to break fetters that bind, to still the storms, to ward off the attacks of demons, to make the dead to speak, to win the love of a maid, and to turn away love that is not desired. And many more there be also.

When runes are carved in mystic symbols the powers they convey are given to the weapons, or to the men that bear them, for they govern all things and impart power to conquer and power to subdue. He who has a certain desire shall achieve it if he but knows the rune which can compel its fulfilment, for the runes come from Odin, the chief ruler of the Universe, the god most wise. His power and great knowledge are enshrined in them.

Next to Odin the mightiest of the gods was his son Thor, whose mother was Jord, "the earth". In Asgard was built for him a great mansion called Bilskirnir, with five hundred and forty halls and a roof of shining silver. He drave forth in a car which was drawn by two goats. Three precious things were his possessions : the great hammer Mjolnir, which struck fire from the mountains and has slain many frost giants ; the belt of prowess, which gave him threefold strength ; and his mighty iron gauntlets, which he put on ere he could wield his hammer.

Another of Odin's sons was Balder the Beautiful,

whose mother was Frigg, queen of goddesses, daughter of Nat and sister of Njord. Fair and comely was Balder, with silver hair that shone like sunshine. He was full of wisdom and was exceedingly mild and had great eloquence. In Asgard and Midgard there was no god more greatly loved than Balder.

Njord of the Vans was in Asgard as hostage to the Asa-gods. He was father of the god Frey and the beautiful Freyja, who was next to Frigg among the goddesses. Honer, Odin's brother, was sent to Vanaheim, where he was made ruler over the Vana-gods. He chose not his part and his judgments were weak.

Great was Tyr, the war-god, who gave valour to warriors and by whom he was invoked.

Brage, god of music and poetry, had for wife Idun, Ivalde's daughter, who was keeper of the apples of immortal youth.

*Thor and the giants, from the painting by Winge.*

*Brage and the beautiful Freyja.*

# CHAPTER IV

## How Evil entered Asgard

Odin and his Brothers—Gifts to First Man and Woman—Loke's Fall—
"The Mother of Evil"—Plot to capture Freyja—How Asgard's Wall was
built—Loke's Evil Counsel—World-disaster averted—Odin's Horse—Rape
of Sif's Locks—Loke threatened—Visits to Elf-Smiths—Wonder Works—
The Gods appeased—Rivalry of Elf-Smiths—Loke's Wager lost—Demand
for his Head—Elf-Smith outwitted—Loke's Plot causes Winter War—Children of Ivalde—Idun and the Swan Maids—Thjasse-Volund and his Brothers
—The Giantess Greip—Fenja and Menja—Freyja lured from Asgard.

If Odin sought after wisdom and loved justice his
brother Loke had the desire to do evil and work wrong,
and he became the instrument of dissension among gods
and men. In the Golden Age, when there was peace
and concord in Asgard, he was yet innocent and of good
repute. He was fair of countenance and his form was
stately, and pleasant indeed were his converse and his
ways.

With Odin and Honer, his brethren, he endowed
with their various attributes the first man and the first
woman. But the gifts of the gods were of unequal
account. Odin gave Spirit which yearns for what is good
and inspires courage and veracity, and the love of mercy
and justice. Honer imparted understanding and memory
and will, and by Loke, who is also called Loder, the man
and the woman were given the semblance of the gods,
and endowed with passions and desires and longings
which ever tend to work evil and bring weakness and

distress. Thus the gifts of Loke are continually at strife with those of Odin and Honer.

But not until the Golden Age was ended did Loke fail and man turn to evil ways. The innocence of gods and men passed from them when from Jotun-heim, as the Skalds have told, came three giant maids, who brought corruption. These three were combined in one form, which was outwardly fair and seemingly good. For the giants had plotted to accomplish the downfall of the gods, and one, whose name was Grep, desired to possess beauteous Freyja, the goddess of Fertility, who sat with her maids beneath the fruitful bough of the World-tree Ygdrasil.

The thrice-born maid whom the giants sent from Jotun-heim was Gulveig-Hoder, whose other name is Aurboda, Hag of Iarnvid and "The Mother of Evil", who assumed the guise of one both fair and young. A maid attendant was she among others to Freyja in the fairest grove of Asgard. She was loved by Loke and became his bride. She fostered his ambition to be chief ruler of the gods, and imparted to him her evil nature and her cunning, while she herself constantly sought to lure Freyja from her secure abode. There came a day when her desire was fulfilled, and war followed war because of her evil doings.

Loke was the chief instrument of her designs. She spread unrest throughout Asgard and set Asa-gods and Vana-gods at enmity, while Loke also plotted with the evil giants to bring ruin to his kindred.

The great wall of Asgard was not yet constructed, and by Loke's secret desire there came before the gods in the guise of a dwarf a Frost-giant who was a cunning artificer. He offered to build a residence so well forti-fied that it would be ever secure against the attacks of the Frost-giants and the giants of the mountains. This vast work he undertook to complete in the space of a single winter.

The gods were willing that the fortification should be made, and enquired of the artificer what reward he sought for his service. His answer was that his demand would be possession of the goddess Freyja, together with the sun and moon. But if the work were not completed in the time allowed him, he would receive no reward whatsoever.

His words were not pleasant to the gods, and they took counsel among themselves. There were those among them who desired to reject his offer, and others who were in sore doubt. Yet all of them desired that the fortification should be built.

Then Loke counselled that the offer which the artificer made should be accepted, provided that he would do the work alone and within the time allotted to him. "For," said Loke, "the dwarf can finish not the building in time, and we shall have it for ourselves without payment of any reward."

So the gods agreed as Loke counselled them, but when their will was made known to the artificer he stipulated that he should be allowed to use his horse, named Svadilfare, in performing the work. By the advice of Loke this condition was granted to the cunning artificer. The bargain was sealed and confirmed by solemn oaths.

The work was then begun without further delay. On the first day of winter the giant in dwarf-guise prepared for the laying of the foundations, and during the night his horse drew the stones towards Asgard. When day broke the gods were amazed at the prodigious size of the boulders which were gathered together, and they perceived that the greater part of the work was performed by the great steed Svadilfàre. All winter did the heavy work proceed, and rapidly did the great and vast walls rise around the habitation of the gods.

When the summer drew nigh, the work was far advanced, and the gods perceived that the artificer was certain to finish it before his allotted time was completed. The buildings were already so strong and so high as to be impregnable, and when only three days had to pass, before summer came, the gateway alone remained to be completed.

Wroth were the gods because of the disaster which threatened them, and they sat in council together and asked one of another who had given advice that the terms of the artificer should be accepted and that Freyja should be given away to Jotun-heim, and the sun and moon taken out of the heavens. They agreed that it was Loke and no other who had brought this danger with his evil designs. Him they condemned as the worker of evil, and they said they would put him to death if he did not contrive some means to prevent the artificer from finishing the work and receiving the reward which he had demanded.

The gods immediately seized Loke, who was stricken with great fear. He saw that he would be put to death if he did not cause hindrance to the giant, so he swore a solemn oath that, no matter what disaster might befall him, he would prevent the giant from accomplishing the disaster which was threatened.

In the darkness of night Loke went forth to outwit the artificer. When the great steed Svadilfare was being driven towards the last boulders which were to complete the gateway, a mare ran forth from a deep forest and neighed loudly. Svadilfare leapt with excitement and turned to follow, and the artificer sought in vain to hold him in restraint. But the steed broke free and ran after the mare, which took flight through the forest, and the great builder made search for him in vain. Thus a whole night was lost, and in the morning the artificer perceived that the work could not be completed in time. He was filled with exceeding great anger, knowing well that a plot had been laid against him. In his wrath he was moved to be revenged, and he assumed his giant form again and rose against the gods. Then it was perceived that he was a fierce and terrible Frost-giant.

Finding themselves deceived, the gods no longer observed their oaths, which had been sworn with one so treacherous. Odin called upon Thor, who seized his great stone hammer and went forth to combat. For him the giant was no match, and the great thunder-god paid him his wages, not with Freyja and the sun and moon, but with death, for the first blow he struck shattered to pieces the great giant's skull. Then the gods seized the body and flung it into the lowest depths of Nifel-hel, the place of sorrow and eternal torture.

The mare which Svadilfare followed brought forth a cloud-grey foal with eight legs. It grew up to be the swiftest steed in the nine worlds, and the name it bore was Sleipner.

To Odin was Sleipner given for his own especial use. On its teeth were graven sacred runes, and it was on the back of Sleipner that Odin ever went forth on his great hunt across the heavens and over the "Milky Way" when the winds were loud and the stars burned in splendour. The great steed he also rode daily to the lower Thingstead of the gods on the bridge which is called Bif-rost.

Thus among men was the riddle propounded: Who are these two who ride forth to the Thingstead? They have in all ten feet, three eyes, and but one tail.

The answer is Odin and Sleipner, for Odin has but one eye; the horse has eight feet and Odin two; and the horse alone has a tail.

Sleipner is not only Odin's steed of war and of the hunt, he is also the steed on which poets rise to divine heights, as Odin, who is the first and greatest of poets, was raised also.

Now Loke and his wife, although frustrated in their desire to work evil against the gods, were still filled with resolve to achieve their wicked ends. There came a season when a new disaster befel the dwellers in Asgard, and caused great dissension throughout the worlds. Sif, the harvest goddess, who was Thor's ward, was beauteous to behold, and her beauty and her power were in her rich and plenteous growth of shining golden hair.

Her harvest locks did the fierce Hag in maid's guise desire to possess, and while Sif slept Loke seized a sharp sword and cut them off and took them away.

Then was Thor filled with wrath, as were also Odin and the rest of the gods, for in Sif's locks there was abundance and prosperity.

Loke was again seized, and, fearing he would be put to death, he promised to restore Sif's harvest hair and bring gifts of appeasement to the greater gods. Oaths were laid upon him to fulfil his promise, and Loke departed from Asgard to visit the underworld, where gold and treasures were concealed in abundance. But even while he feared punishment, the desire to work evil did not leave his heart, and he sought, while he fulfilled his promise, to work great and lasting dissension.

To the elf-smiths, who are subject to wise Mimer, did Loke proceed, and their services he besought with cunning and evil intent.

Now there were two families of elves who were

accomplished artificers and workers in fine metals, and these were the sons of Ivalde and the sons of Sindre, in whose golden halls in Mimer's realm there were great treasures. They lived at peace with the gods, whom they rendered ofttimes great service by providing ornaments and embellishing the palaces of Asgard with their beauteous work.

Loke plotted to work enmity not only between the families of elf-smiths, but also to estrange them against the gods.

First he went to the sons of Ivalde and besought them to make golden locks for the goddess Sif which would grow like other hair. They set to work ,and accomplished his desire, and they also made at his request a great spear for Odin, which was named Gungner. There was made for Frey, the god of golden sunshine, a wondrous ship, named Skidbladner, which could hold all the warriors of Asgard, and was ever accompanied by soft and favourable winds. Yet, great as the vessel was, it could be folded into small space like a napkin.

The gods were reconciled to Loke when the golden hair of Sif was restored. The spear was given to Odin and the great ship to Frey.

Then Loke went with evil in his heart to the kinsmen of Sindre, and them he challenged to produce works as wondrous and finely executed as those of the sons of Ivalde. Brok, who was Sindre's brother, protested the greater skill of his fellows, and Loke wagered his own head that such treasures as were already made could not be surpassed. The wager was readily accepted. Sindre made a great smithy, and he and his kinsmen set to work. Loke assumed the guise of a great blood-drinking fly, to harass them while at work.

Sindre first put a pigskin into the smithy fire. Then

he bade Brok to blow the bellows without ceasing until the work was finished. That he did with great activity. But a great fly set itself upon his hand, stinging him sorely and drinking blood. He would have fain ceased his labours because of the fly, but if he did so the charm would be broken and the work rendered utterly without avail. So, suffering as he did, he persisted at the bellows handle, and at length Sindre drew out a wondrous boar with golden bristles, which was a thing to marvel at.

Then Sindre put much precious gold into the furnace, and Brok again blew the bellows. But the great fly attacked his neck, and drew more blood, nor could he smite it or drive it away. At times it seemed as if he must cease to labour, but he prevailed over his sufferings until Sindre drew out a magic ring, which was named Draupner, "the dropper".

A mass of iron did Sindre next place in the furnace, and when Brok began to blow the bellows the great fly became more ferocious than ever, and it stung him between the eyes, so that blood flowed down and nearly blinded him. Brok laboured heavily, and only once did he pause to drive the fly away. Then Sindre drew from the furnace a great hammer, which none save Thor could wield.

"These works," said Sindre, "no son of Ivalde can equal."

Brok carried the gifts to Asgard, and Loke went with him.

Then sat the high gods in council to decide whose treasures were of greatest account. They appointed, as judges, Odin and Thor and Frey, and the various works they considered together.

Between the sons of Ivalde and Sindre's kinsmen

there was ever keen rivalry, and Loke knew well that the clan which was given the award would win the hatred of the other, and that the gods would be despised by those who were not favoured.

Each of the gifts received the praises of the gods. But those of Sindre were to them of greatest account. The ring Daupner was a charm for fruitfulness and fertility; every ninth night eight gold rings of equal size dropped from it. It was a ring that grew to a chain without end. To Odin was it given, and the high god had it with the spear Gungner, which the sons of Ivalde had made. Oaths were sworn on the point of the great spear, which, when Odin throws it, gleams brightly as it falls through the stars. Upon great warriors is conferred the power of Odin's spear.

To Frey was given the golden boar on which to ride over the heavens or over the sea. Faster it could run than any steed save Sleipner, and in thick darkness it shone in splendour. When Frey went forth at morning or evening the rays of the golden bristles gleamed high in the heavens.

But the greatest gift of all was the mighty iron hammer, Mjolner, which was given to Thor. It had but one defect, and that was the shortness of the handle, for Brok had ceased to blow when the fly blinded him momentarily. So with the great gift came the defect which Loke had caused. The hammer had power to return to Thor each time it was thrown.

The sons of Ivalde were deeply incensed against the gods because they awarded chief praise to the kinsmen of Sindre, and they departed vowing fierce vengeance. Thus was the end of Loke achieved.

Brok, who thirsted for revenge, demanded his prize for the hammer, and that was Loke's head, which he had wagered. Loke offered to redeem it, but the elf-smith would have naught else.

Now Loke had shoes of swiftness, and could speed swiftly through the air and over the sea. Crying to Brok: "Then take me," he vanished from sight.

But the angered elf-smith appealed to Thor to seize Loke, and that great irresistible god set forth and returned with him.

"Thy head is mine," exclaimed Brok, who prepared to cut it off.

"Thine indeed is the head," answered Loke, "but not the neck."[1]

Brok appealed to the gods, and they gave judgment that favoured Loke. They told Brok that he might take the head, but the neck he must not injure.

Then was Brok possessed with great wrath, and he demanded to sew the lips from which evil counsel came. Loke's head being his by right of wager, none could gainsay him. He took his knife to pierce the evil god's lips, but it was not of sufficient sharpness. So he cried: "Would I had my brother's awl." When he said that, the awl was immediately beside him, and he took it and sewed up the mouth of Loke, and left him there confused with silence.

In great wrath did Brok leave Asgard. Thus was Loke's end doubly achieved, for Sindre's kinsmen were also incensed against the gods because of the judgment they had given when the wager was claimed.

The sons of Ivalde rose in revolt and leagued themselves with the Frost-giants to wage war against the Asagods and bring disaster to Asgard.

Let it be told that twice wedded was Ivalde, the rebel watchman of Hvergelmer and the rivers Elivagar. His

---

[1] In like manner was Shylock thwarted when he demanded his pound of flesh.

first wife was Sol, the sun-goddess, and their daughters were Idun, who became wife to Brage, and also the swan maids who sang on the borders of the western realm of Njord. Then had Ivalde for wife the giantess Greip, and they had three sons who were elf-smiths—Thjasse-Volund, Orvandel-Egil, the great archer, and Ide, whose other names are Hyuki, Hengest, and Gelder, "the Gelding".

Greip, the mother of these sons of Ivalde, had afterwards, with marriage to a giant, two sons whose daughters were Fenja and Menja.

So, as has been told, it came about that through Loke's evil workings a winter war was proclaimed against the gods by the sons of Ivalde and the Frost-giants.

At this time too was the goddess Freyja lured secretly from Asgard by Gulveig-Hoder, the Hag in maiden guise, and was caught in ambush by the great giant Beli, father of Grep, who fled with the goddess to Jotun-heim and concealed her in his strong castle. A double disaster thus fell upon the gods.

## The Dwarfs

Loke sat and thought, till his dark eyes gleam
    With joy at the deed he'd done;
When Sif looked into the crystal stream,
    Her courage was wellnigh gone.

For never again her soft amber hair
    Shall she braid with her hands of snow;
From the hateful image she turned in despair,
    And hot tears began to flow.

In a cavern's mouth, like a crafty fox,
    Loke sat 'neath the tall pine's shade,
When sudden a thundering was heard in the rocks,
    And fearfully trembled the glade.

Then he knew that the noise good boded him naught,
    He knew that 't was Thor who was coming;
He changed himself straight to a salmon trout,
    And leaped in a fright in the Glommen.

But Thor changed too, to a huge seagull,
    And the salmon trout seized in his beak;
He cried: Thou, traitor, I know thee well,
    And dear shalt thou pay thy freak!

Thy caitiff's bones to a meal I 'll pound,
    As a millstone crusheth the grain.
When Loke that naught booted his magic found,
    He took straight his own form again.

And what if thou scatter'st my limbs in air?
    He spake, will it mend thy case?
Will it gain back for Sif a single hair?
    Thou 'lt still a bald spouse embrace.

But if now thou 'lt pardon my heedless joke,—
    For malice sure meant I none,—
I swear to thee here, by root, billow and rock,
    By the moss on the Beata-stone,

By Mimer's well, and by Odin's eye,
    And by Mjolmer, greatest of all,
That straight to the secret caves I 'll hie,
    To the dwarfs, my kinsmen small;

And thence for Sif new tresses I 'll bring
    Of gold ere the daylight 's gone,
So that she will liken a field in spring,
    With its yellow-flowered garment on.

.    .    .    .    .    .

Loke promised so well with his glozing tongue
    That the Asas at length let him go,
And he sank in the earth, the dark rocks among,
    Near the cold-fountain, far below.

He crept on his belly, as supple as eel,
   The cracks in the hard granite through,
Till he came where the dwarfs stood hammering steel,
   By the light of a furnace blue.

I trow 't was a goodly sight to see
   The dwarfs, with their aprons on,
A-hammering and smelting so busily
   Pure gold from the rough brown stone.

Rock crystals from sand and hard flint they made,
   Which, tinged with the rosebud's dye,
They cast into rubies and carbuncles red,
   And hid them in cracks hard by.

They took them fresh violets all dripping with dew,
   Dwarf women had plucked them, the morn,—
And stained with their juice the clear sapphires blue,
   King Dan in his crown since hath worn.

Then for emeralds they searched out the brightest green
   Which the young spring meadow wears,
And dropped round pearls, without flaw or stain,
   From widows' and maidens' tears.

  .    .    .    .    .    .    .

When Loke to the dwarfs had his errand made known,
   In a trice for the work they were ready;
Quoth Dvalin: O Lopter, it now shall be shown
   That dwarfs in their friendship are steady.

We both trace our line from the selfsame stock;
   What you ask shall be furnished with speed,
For it ne'er shall be said that the sons of the rock
   Turned their backs on a kinsman in need.

They took them the skin of a large wild-boar,
   The largest that they could find,
And the bellows they blew till the furnace 'gan roar,
   And the fire flamed on high for the wind.

And they struck with their sledge-hammers stroke on stroke,
   That the sparks from the skin flew on high,
But never a word good or bad spoke Loke,
   Though foul malice lurked in his eye.

The thunderer far distant, with sorrow he thought
   On all he 'd engaged to obtain,
And, as summer-breeze fickle, now anxiously sought
   To render the dwarf's labour vain.

Whilst the bellows plied Brok, and Sindre the hammer,
   And Thor, that the sparks flew on high,
And the slides of the vaulted cave rang with the clamour,
   Loke changed to a huge forest-fly.

And he sat him all swelling with venom and spite,
   On Brok, the wrist just below;
But the dwarf's skin was thick, and he recked not the bite,
   Nor once ceased the bellows to blow.

And now, strange to say, from the roaring fire
   Came the golden-haired Gullinburste,
To serve as a charger the sun-god Frey,
   Sure, of all wild-boars this the first.

They took them pure gold from their secret store,
   The piece 't was but small in size,
But ere 't had been long in the furnace roar,
   'T was a jewel beyond all prize.

A broad red ring all of wroughten gold,
   As a snake with its tail in its head,
And a garland of gems did the rim enfold,
   Together with rare art laid.

'T was solid and heavy, and wrought with care,
   Thrice it passed through the white flames' glow;
A ring to produce, fit for Odin to wear,
   No labour they spared, I trow.

They worked it and turned it with wondrous skill,
    Till they gave it the virtue rare,
That each thrice third night from its rim there fell
    Eight rings, as their parent fair.

．    ．    ．    ．    ．    ．    ．

Next they laid on the anvil a steel-bar cold,
    They needed nor fire nor file;
But their sledge-hammers, following, like thunder rolled,
    And Sindre sang runes the while.

When Loke now marked how the steel gat power,
    And how warily out 't was beat
—'T was to make a new hammer for Ake-Thor,—
    He'd recourse once more to deceit.

In a trice, of a hornet the semblance he took,
    Whilst in cadence fell blow on blow,
In the leading dwarf's forehead his barbed sting he stuck,
    That the blood in a stream down did flow.

Then the dwarf raised his hand to his brow for the smart,
    Ere the iron well out was beat,
And they found that the haft by an inch was too short,
    But to alter it then 't was too late.

．    ．    ．    ．    ．    ．    ．

His object attained, Loke no longer remained
    'Neath the earth, but straight hied him to Thor,
Who owned than the hair ne'er, sure, aught more fair
    His eyes had e'er looked on before.

The boar Frey bestrode, and away proudly rode,
    And Thor took the ringlets and hammer;
To Valhal they hied, where the Asas reside,
    'Mid of tilting and wassail the clamour.

At a full solemn ting, Thor gave Odin the ring,
    And Loke his foul treachery pardoned;
But the pardon was vain, for his crimes soon again
    Must do penance the arch-sinner hardened.

                    —*Longfellow.*

# CHAPTER V

## The Winter War

The Great Earthquake—Frost-giants swarm Southward—Njord intervenes—Frey in Power of Giants—Asgard's Archer put to Shame—Peace-
makers baffled—Vengeance of Thjasse-Volund—"Sword of Victory" forged
—Mimer intervenes—Sword captured and Thjasse bound—Coming of Half-
dan—Omens at his Birth—The Swords Accursed—Marriage, and Hadding's
Birth—Conflicts with Giants—Groa taken Captive—Orvandel-Egil's Trial—
The Mythical "William Tell"—Birth of Gudhorm—Groa's Promise to Svip-
dag—Her Incantations—Ull's Boyhood—Svipdag overcome by Halfdan—
Visit to Hela—"Sword of Victory" recaptured—Svipdag's Great Victory—
Thor put to Flight—Halfdan's Death.

A GREAT earthquake shook the nine worlds when the
winter war was proclaimed. Midgar trembled and the
heavens were disturbed. In Asgard the gods heard the
dread clamour and the strong walls shivered as with fear.
And it was thus that the earthquake was caused. When
the sons of Ivalde withdrew their services from the gods,
and made compact with their enemies, the terrible Frost-
giants, the two giant-maids, Fenja and Menja, seized the
handle of the great World-mill and turned it so violently
that it went out of order, and disaster was threatened to
the Universe. Then southward swarmed the Frost-
giants to make war with the gods and their allies.

Now the Vana-god Njord sought to make peace
between the gods and the sons of Ivalde, because at that
time his son, the sunshine-god, Frey, was with them in
northern Alf-heim, where he reigned as a king. He
was still but a youth, and the sons of Ivalde had power
to do him harm.

With Njord went Bjorno-Hoder, the fair god Balder's brother, the famous archer, who had not yet grown blind. Forsete, Balder's son, was also an envoy, for, like his father, he was a just judge and settler of disputes. Gifted he was with persuasive speech and manners which could subdue the most stubborn disputants. But they discovered that Frey had been given to Beli, " the howler", the great giant with enormous body who held him in thrall.

Bjorno-Hoder waxed wroth, and he drew his bow to slay Volund-Thjasse and Egil-Orvandel, Ivalde's sons. But Egil-Orvandel was also a great archer, for which he was named Avo. Ere Hoder could shoot, Orvandel's arrow severed his bowstring. Then the god tied the string, and Orvandel's second arrow passed through his fingers without hurting them. Ignoring this dread warning, Balder's brother still persisted, and his third arrow was struck from the bowstring by Orvandel just as he was pulling the string. Thus was Hoder put to shame.

Then the peacemakers turned to take their departure, and Ivalde's sons continued their journey to the north.

Thjasse-Volund, son of Ivalde, was filled with boundless vengeance against the gods, and went to his smithy, where he forged the great Sword of Victory. Never was there such a weapon since the beginning of time. It shone like the sun in heaven, and there was no substance that it would not cleave. More terrible was it than Thor's hammer, which the sons of Sindre had made, for he who wielded the sword could prevail over the Thunder-god. Thjasse-Volund was resolved to subdue the gods and conquer Asgard. He also made a ring which multiplied till it became a chain to bind the wind.

But grave Mimer-Nidhad, who is also called Narve, " the binder", came to know of the dread sword which his rebellious subject had constructed, and he still remained the faithful friend of the gods. He knew well the power possessed by the sword, and feared the disaster which it would cause. So he went to Wolfdales, in Nifel-heim, where Thjasse-Volund had built his great smithy, and seized the elf-smith, whom he bound with chains. Then The Binder took with him the sword, and also the magic ring from among seven hundred other rings, which it had produced. These he bore unto river-girdled Hela, where he concealed them in his deep cave, heaped with treasure, over which his son was guard. There the sword and the ring were kept until they were recaptured by The Shining One, who prevailed over Thor and became a god in Asgard— Svipdag the Brave, the hero of heroes. But ere that day came many great battles were fought, and mighty warriors perished in their pride.

The great hero who fought against the giants and Ivalde's sons in the winter war was Halfdan, son of Thor, who by tellers of old tales has also been called Mannus.

At his birth there were dread omens which foretold his glory and his doom. Eagles screeched, the clamour of thunder was heard, and the shadow of Thor fell over the house. Norns came and twisted the threads of fate. Of gold they made the warp of the web and fastened it under the moon; the ends were hid in the east and the west. One fateful thread was drawn northward towards Jotun-heim, the giants' home, and Urd decreed that it should hold there forever.

Hungry ravens cawed one to another, and welcomed the wolf-eyed child who would cause them to thrive with blood and the flesh of slaughtered men. They rejoiced that the battle-feast would soon be spread for them.

Halfdan's mother heard the ravens' song and dreaded

his fate. Two swords there were in her home and they were accursed. She buried them deep in the earth, so that the child, when he grew strong, would not find them. But Halfdan soon displayed his warrior strength. When yet a youth he wrestled with a giant-bear and slew it.

Then came a day when Halfdan found a hidden sword, and in a conflict he slew with it his half-brother, nor did he know it was he. Thus was the sword accursed indeed.

Halfdan had knowledge from his father of sacred runes, and he knew the speech of birds, which gave him advantage over his enemies, for he was warned when danger was at hand.

When he grew into years of knowledge and strength, he went forth to seek his fortunes. One day he met Signe-Alveig, which means "nourishing drink", and her he loved and married. She was the fair swan-maiden whose sister Groa was wed to Egil-Orvandel, son of Ivalde, and their son was Hadding. But although Halfdan lived for long at peace with Ivalde's clan, he fought against them when they leagued themselves with the Frost-giants to combat with the gods and their allies.

A strenuous campaign did Thor's son wage against the Frost-giants on the borders of Midgard, which they sought to possess and put under thrall. The giant Froste was their leader, and with him was Fjalar-Suttung, the fire-giant from Surtur's deep dales. Their march southward Halfdan stayed, and to the bleak north he drave them in confusion. A great battle he fought at Svarin's mound, where he slew Sigbrygg, the sire of his wife and Groa, her sister. Groa he took captive, and he put shame upon her, and with her he took her son Svipdag.

With Halfdan on his triumphant march northward

went Odin's victorious Valkyries, and nightly the heavens
flamed with their splendour, by men called "The Northern
Lights".

On the borders of Jotun-heim Halfdan overcame
Orvandel-Egil, the great archer, whose house he surrounded in the night.

Then it came about that Halfdan caused Orvandel to
make trial of his skill, for hearing he had boasted that he
could with the first arrow from his bow hit a small apple
placed upon a stick at a great distance, he ordered Svipdag to stand with an apple upon his head.[1]  Then he
commanded Orvandel to perform the deed of which he
had boasted on penalty of his life, but promised him his
freedom if he achieved success.

Svipdag was led forth.  To him his sire spoke words
of encouragement and good counsel, so that he might
bear the trial with courage and .unflinchingly, and also
lest he should move and thus cause the arrow to miss its
mark.  Svipdag he made to stand with his back turned
so that he might not behold the drawing of the bow.

Three arrows did Orvandel take from his quiver.
Then one he aimed at the apple upon his son's head.
Careful aim he took and shot it from the bow, and he
clove the apple in twain nor harmed his son.

Then did Halfdan ask him why he had taken three
arrows from his quiver, and Orvandel-Egil bade him
know that it was his purpose, had his son fallen, to slay
the man who had compelled the sore trial of skill.

But the risk was not avenged upon Halfdan until the
day of Svipdag's triumph.

In sorrow did Groa pass weary days with Halfdan, to
whom she bore a son who was named Gudhorm.  Then
was Groa rejected with deeper shame.  When she, with

[1] Saga version of William Tell myth.

*A Valkyrie, from the sculpture by Sinding.*

*Two Valkyries.*

her son, Svipdag, returned to Orvandel, she was heart-broken and had come nigh to life's end. Svipdag she called to her side and told him she must soon die with the sorrow she bore for the death of her sire and the shame that Halfdan had put upon her. Then she told him that he must needs endure great troubles and much strife, and be ofttimes in death-shadowing peril. "If mine aid you need at any time," she said, "come to my grave chamber and invoke my spirit, and I shall rise to help you." Soon after she spake thus Groa died, and Svipdag wept for her.

Then Orvandel took for wife the beauteous Sith. Their son was Ull, and he grew up to be a strong young warrior like his half-brother.

Svipdag was overcome with desire to be avenged upon Halfdan, and sought to wage war against him. But Sith prevailed upon him to promise that he would go towards the mountains of Jotun-heim, and rescue the goddess Freyja and the god Frey from the giant who kept them imprisoned in his strong castle.

But Svipdag deemed Sith to be moved with cunning intentions, and he feared that if he went forth upon such an enterprise he would never return. He had need of counsel and of help, and in the darkness of night he went to the stone grave-chamber of his mother and called upon her.

"Awake," he cried, "as thou didst promise me, and come to me, O mother, in my sore straits!"

The spirit of Groa rose out of Hela, where she heard her son's voice calling upon her, and from the grave-chamber she spoke. She told him that he must indeed go on a long journey and meet many perils ere yet he would find Freyja, but she bade him remember that his Norn of fate would be his guide.

Then sang she incantations over Svipdag to protect him from danger and to heal his wounds, to give him courage and set him free from prisons. She also sang incantations to protect him against raging rivers he must needs cross, and against ocean's perils and the perils of vast and high mountains over which he must climb.

Nine incantations did Groa utter, and the last gave him security to traverse Nifel-hel and enter Mimer's grove.

Whereupon Groa's voice was silent, and her spirit returned to the Underworld.

Satisfied he would be indeed safe from all danger, Svipdag went northward towards the battleground of the giants. It was his desire to first avenge his grandsire's death and his mother's shame ere yet he would search to find Freyja. So he set himself to lead a giant host against the army of Halfdan, and a dread conflict was fought.

Svipdag was in the midst of the battle, and with Halfdan he waged a duel, but he was overcome and taken prisoner. Then made the giants hurried flight towards the north.

Deep was Halfdan's admiration for the prowess of the young hero, and he offered him his friendship if he would become his ally and help him to continue the campaign against the giants with whom Ivalde's sons were in league. But Svipdag scorned his friendship with defiance, and Halfdan in his wrath caused him to be bound to a tree in the midst of a thick forest, so that he might become the prey of wild beasts.

Groa's son, when he was alone, bethought him of the incantations which his mother had uttered, and one he repeated till the chains that bound him flew away and he was set free. Hither and thither he wandered disconsolately, nor giant nor foeman could he see, nor could he discover which way he should go.

Then came he to the moon-god ere he rose on his path through the heavens, and by him was Svipdag told where he would find the Sword of Victory which Thjasse-Volund had forged.

"In Mimer's cave," the moon-god said, "it is concealed, and thou must needs overcome the Keeper of Hela's gate to obtain it."

Towards the trackless regions that lead by Hvergelmer's mountain did Svipdag then journey, and over the caves in which giants guard their accursed hoards of treasure. Intense and bitter cold prevailed as he traversed over frostbound ways and wreaths of blocking snow. Now he had need to climb great precipices, and ofttimes he found himself on dizzy mountain ridges, while dread chasms yawned below him. Through many places of horror and peril did Svipdag traverse until he reached the borders of Hela. There he beheld a fair land that gleamed before him, full of flowers of rich fragrance.

He crossed a dark valley, and a hel-hound pursued him, barking loudly. Then came he to the River of Blades, which was spanned by a bridge of gold, and beyond there was a stone door in Hela's wall, guarded by a strong watchman. With him Svipdag fought and was victorious, and he entered the land of spirits where dwells Mimer and the regenerating race unborn.

Protected by the enchantment of Groa, Svipdag went towards the cave in which the treasures of Mimer are concealed, nor did he let his shadow fall upon it lest Mimer's son Mimingus, who kept watch, should take fear and shrink back into the mountain.

Mimingus lay asleep, and Svipdag overcame him and

bound him where he lay. He took from the wall the glittering Sword of Victory and the great Arm-ring which Thjasse-Volund had forged, and then hastened to return by the way he had come. So traversing again the mountains of snow and misty blackness, and escaping the dread perils about him, Svipdag returned with his treasures from the Underworld.

Then without delay did the vengeance-seeking son of Groa open a new campaign against Halfdan. In Asgard it was known that he had secured the dreaded sword which Thjasse-Volund had made so that he might overcome the gods. Mighty Thor seized his iron hammer and went forth to help his son.

Great was the battle which was waged. Svipdag mowed down his enemies before him, and Halfdan was sorely wounded by an arrow shot from the bow of Orvandel-Egil. Then did Thor press into the midst of the fray, fighting fiercely against the giants, who fell before him until he came against Svipdag. But the hammer which Sindre had made was of no avail against the young hero, for with the Sword of Victory it was struck by The Shining One and severed from the handle.

When Thor was repulsed he fled from the field, and Halfdan went with him.

Thus did victory come to Svipdag, and thus was the judgment of the gods defied, for they had placed the workmanship of Sindre's kinsman above that of the sons of Ivalde.

Halfdan died of his wounds, and Thor made haste to Asgard, where the gods awaited the coming of Svipdag with the Sword of Victory, which had been forged so that they might be utterly overcome and Asgard laid waste.

# CHAPTER VI

## Triumph of Love

Freyja and Frey in Captivity—Svipdag's Promise—Food of Wisdom—
Voyage to Jotun-heim—Beli, "The Howler"—The Brothers Grep—God and
Goddess under Enchantments—Svipdag and Ull in Giant's Castle—Freyja
Rescued—The Shame of Frey—Freyja deserted—Her Wanderings—How the
Spell was broken—Return to Asgard—Idun is lost—Loke and the Eagle—
His Promise—The Angered Gods—Idun rescued—Thjasse - Volund slain—
Svipdag climbs Bif-rost — The Wolf Dogs on Watch — Odin's Warnings—
Glimpse of Asgard's Beauties—Lovers meet—The Sword of Victory—Gods
and Elves reconciled.

WHEN Svipdag had triumphed over Halfdan he returned to Sith, remembering the promise he had made
to rescue Freyja and Frey from the castle of the giant
who held them in captivity. Then he prepared to set
out with Ull, his stepbrother, towards the giants' country
—cold and darksome Jotun-heim. But ere he went, Sith
made for the twain the food of wisdom with the fat of
three serpents, so that they might be rendered able to
perform their long and perilous journey. Of the magic
food did Svipdag secure the better portion for himself.

They had need to cross a great magic sea on which
dread tempests roared and whirlpools and treacherous
currents were an ever-present danger. When far from
shore the storm-giant came against him, but Svipdag
overcame him in combat. Protected by the incantations
of Groa did Svipdag with Ull make the voyage in safety,
until they reached a harbour nigh to the bleak castle of

Beli, "the howler", in which Freyja and Frey were imprisoned.

Three sons of the giant met them on the strand. Each of them had Grep for name, and one, who was a skald, desired to have Freyja for his bride. With Svipdag and Ull he entered into angry dispute, and sought to prevail upon them to return from whence they came. But this they scorned to do, and in the end the giants retreated from the strand.

Then went Svipdag and Ull towards the castle to seek for Freyja and Frey. The giants were filled with anger, and sought to affright the young heroes by howling like beasts and bellowing like the storm-god. The clamour they made was indeed fearsome, and none but brave hearts could have ventured to make entry to that place of horror.

Within the court Frey and Freyja came to meet them, and they were surrounded by giant attendants. Svipdag greeted Freyja with a kiss, and she knew that she would become his bride.

But enchantments had been put upon her and upon Frey by the giants. They had been given to drink the potion of forgetfulness, so that they had but vague memory of the past, while deep discontent and haunting misery were their dower. Frey had deep shame upon him, and he sought nor flight nor expected happiness any more. In dark despair he lived within the strong castle of Beli.

Freyja was pale and sorrow-stricken. In her heart was keen loathing, which tortured her, against the Grep who would fain be her favoured suitor. Her golden locks were twisted hard above her forehead, for Beli had thus punished her when he took her captive. In vain she had endeavoured to comb them and win back her extreme beauty, but the spell that was put upon her she could not break. Her eyes were vacant and sad. She rejoiced not that Svipdag and Ull had come to rescue her, for her heart was cold and passionless.

Svipdag and Ull entered the wide hall of the castle amidst the bestial howlings of the dread giants. A great fire burned there because of the bitter cold that prevailed.

With the giants they sat at feast, and Frey was on a high seat with pale, unhappy face, while the giants sang loudly and drank deeply about him.

Now deeply were these fierce furies incensed against Svipdag and Ull, whom they sought to overcome and put to death. In sharp dispute they engaged. At length, the Grep who wooed Freyja flung himself upon Svipdag, but Ull cut him down with his sword and slew him. Then many fought against Egil's sons, but they were driven back.

In the end the heroes prevailed upon Freyja to flee with them, but on Frey they could not prevail, for so deeply did he feel his shame that he could not again appear, he said, before the gods in Asgard.

To Svipdag was Freyja cold and indifferent, nor did she ever raise her eyes to look at him or open her lips to speak. When they had crossed the magic sea, they set out to climb the great mountains towards Orvandel's home, where Sith awaited them; but Freyja showed neither joy nor gratitude at her escape from the giants.

Then was the heart of Svipdag filled with anger, and he left Freyja to wander alone. She went towards a desolate land which was the abode of giantesses, and was found by one, who took her for a slave to tend her goats. But Svipdag repented, and when his anger passed away he went again in search of Freyja, for his heart was moved with deep tenderness towards her.

From the giantess he rescued her, and they went together on their way. But that great Hag followed quickly, and swift was the flight of the lovers, running on skees. Nearer and more near came the monster, but suddenly the sun rose over the mountains, and she was turned into a great boulder at the sea's edge.

In Freyja's heart there was yet no gratitude, because of the spells that were upon her. Nor answer would she make when Svipdag spoke, nor would she gaze in his eyes to reward him. One brief look was all he desired, and yet she stared upon the ground disconsolate and silent.

Again did Svipdag wax wroth and leave her to wander alone; and she went down among the rocks. Then took she the guise of a bird and flew over the mountains and over the river that separates that wild country from the land in which Svipdag had his dwelling. She reached the house of Orvandel. To Sith, who recognized her not, she said that she was a poor woman who had no home, and she was received with welcome.

But Svipdag knew her and claimed her for his bride, and a wedding feast was set, and the marriage oath sworn in solemnity and state. Yet was Freyja cold and passionless. To the bridal chamber they went, and in her hand Freyja held a candle. She stood motionless before Svipdag until the candle burned low; and when the flame stung her hand, Svipdag spoke words of warning. But Freyja felt not the pain because of the greater pain within her heart.

Then was the spell broken by fire, and she raised her face and looked with eyes of love upon him who had rescued her. Thus had Svipdag his exceeding great reward.

But Freyja vanished from before him, and in falcon-guise she soared to Asgard, undefiled and pure, and was received with rejoicing by the gods. Then did Svipdag take his Sword of Victory and set forth towards Asgard to win Freyja.

But a sorrow no greater than when Freyja was lured away had fallen upon Asgard because the goddess Idun was lost. For it was she who had in her keeping the golden apples of eternal youth. In her fast-shut casket she kept them, and for each one she drew forth another took its place. From the apples did the gods receive immortality, and when Idun was taken away they began to grow old. Well they knew that both giants and trolls had much desire to rob the golden apples from Asgard. So they were sore troubled, fearing that disaster would fall speedily upon them. On evil Loke did suspicion fall, and when Odin challenged him, for Idun had last been seen in company with him, he confessed that he had delivered her to Thjasse-Volund, her brother, who had forged the Sword of Victory so that the gods might be overcome.

'Twas thus it fell that Idun was taken from Asgard. One day there went forth together on a journey Odin and Honer and Loke. It was their desire to visit the country of Ivalde and his sons, beside Hvergelmer and the rivers Evilagar, so as to cause the conflict to have end. Thjasse-Volund, who had escaped from the bonds of Mimer in the guise of an eagle, had knowledge of their coming and waited for them. In a valley of oaks the gods rested. There they saw grazing a herd of bears, and one they caught on which to feast, for they hungered and were weary. The bear they slew, and when a fire was kindled they roasted it for their feast. Near by lay a magic rod which Thjasse-Volund had forged with intent to wreak his vengeance upon the gods, and especially Loke.

Then a great eagle came towards them, and the gods knew it was Thjasse-Volund who had dominion there.

Hard was the bear to carve, for Ivalde's son had put enchantments upon it, and of this had Odin full knowledge. So he addressed Thjasse and said: " Why hast thou done this, thou maker of ornaments in eagle guise?"

Thjasse said that he desired his share. Odin had not, however, any knowledge of the evil intent of the eagle, and consented that he should divide the meal with them. Whereupon Thjasse flew down and sought to take so large a share that Loke, in his wrath, seized the magic rod to strike at him. When he did that he was in the eagle's power. He could not unclasp his hands from the rod, and the other end was fixed in the claws of the eagle, which flew high, carrying Loke with him. In vain did he seek to be released, and over the oak trees was he dragged and sorely beaten until he was near to being torn to pieces. Loke was heavy and the eagle sank to the ground. Then Loke offered Thjasse any ransom he would demand if he would but let him escape, for he was compelled to plead for his life.

Thjasse demanded his sister Idun, who had been taken away by Loke when the sons of Ivalde were the willing servants of the gods. Loke promised to deliver her to him secretly, and was then released by his dread captor. The gods returned to Asgard together, and evil Loke fulfilled his promise, nor gave Odin knowledge of his doings.

Thus it came that when he made confession of his deed the gods were moved to anger against him, and threatened to put him to death. But Loke made vows to restore Idun to Asgard, and flew forth towards the dominion of Thjasse-Volund in the bird-guise of Freyja.

The loss of Idun had dread effect in Midgard as in Asgard. Cold winds blew from the north. The power of the Frost-giants increased, and they swarmed southward in great hosts. Halfdan, they knew, was slain, and that the gods had loss of power because that Idun had been taken away. Icy arrows were shot over the earth, killing man and beast and each thing that grew. The heavens were disturbed. Nearer sun and moon crept the giant wolves. From Urd's fountain was slowly departing the power to give warmth to the World-tree Ygdrasil. Out of Jotun-heim rose songs of rejoicing and vengeance that were heard in Asgard, and the gods, growing old, feared that the end of all things was drawing very nigh. To Mimer's grove were sent swift messengers, so that from the Norns might be received knowledge of the world's fate and that of the gods.

So did gods and men suffer because Idun, the goddess of regeneration, was taken away. The death-cold storm-spears were turned against gods and men. The murder-frost held Midgard with iron grasp.

Idun was found by Loke in Thjasse's dwelling, and he put enchantments upon her and she became a nut. Then he flew with her in his claws towards Asgard. But ere he set off, Loke, the tempter, made known to Thjasse what he had done, and challenged him to follow. In eagle-guise angry Thjasse pursued the god. So swiftly did he fly that he came very nigh to Loke ere yet he had reached the safety of Asgard. Then he flew midst the vafer-flames in the kindling vapour cloud, and fell scorched within the walls. Thor seized his hammer, which Sindre had again forged, and slew him. Thus did Thjasse-Volund, who had shaped the Sword of Victory, fall in his shame and perish because of Loke's evil doings.

Meanwhile in Asgard did Freyja await the coming of Svipdag, whom she loved; and him the gods awaited also, because he carried the Sword of Victory.

Svipdag's heart was filled with longing for Freyja, nor could he sleep or rest until he found her. The protection of Groa's incantations was still upon him, and it was Urd's will that he should reach Asgard. So he went again on a perilous journey. Unto Hela he went, over bleak tremendous mountains and through storms and blinding mist, until he reached the foundations of Bif-rost. Heimdal, the shining sentinel, beheld him as he stepped upon the Bridge of the Gods with the gleaming Sword of Victory girdled by his side. But no warning did he sound, for it was the will of Odin that Freyja's lover should stand before the gate of Asgard. So Svipdag ascended until he beheld the ramparts of the celestial city. There he perceived Odin nor knew who he was.

Roughly did the god receive his greetings. "This", he said, "is no place for beggars; return by the moist ways whence you came."

But Svipdag remonstrated, and claimed hospitality, being a weary traveller, and Odin made answer again that he could not enter, although less harshly, for the noble bearing of the youth gave pleasure to his eyes.

"From here," cried Svipdag, "I cannot turn my eyes away because of its exceeding great beauty. Here would I find happiness and peace."

"Who art thou?" Odin asked.

"My name," said Svipdag, "is Windcold, and I am the son of Springcold, whose sire was Very-cold."

Now Svipdag had caught a radiant glimpse of Asgard's beauties. He saw its halls of glittering gold, and especially the Hall of Gladness, which is the dwelling of Freyja, and is nigh to the gate. He also beheld Freyja, whom he loved, sitting on the flower-decked Rock of Joy, which gives health to those who seek it with prayer. She was surrounded by her maids—Eil, the healer; Hlif, the protectress; Bjort, the shining; Blid, the blithe; and Frid, the fair—they had power to give healing to men and women who called upon them from Midgard and offered up sacrifices. Freyja was silent and in deep thought. Like a graven statue she sat in virgin beauty, blue-eyed with golden hair—she who has care of love-lorn maidens and mothers and their babes. She wore her gleaming necklace which the elf-smiths had made with sparkling jewels of the sky and bright spring-flowers, for the fair goddess was " The Lover of Ornaments ".

Freyja sat beneath the branches of Ygdrasil, and these Svipdag beheld with wonder. He saw its magical fruit, and in the branches sat the cock Goldcomb, with feathers of gleaming gold.

Svipdag turned his eyes upon Asgard's wondrous gate, and saw before it the two great wolf-dogs which kept watch by night and by day, for when one slept the other was awake. They had power to kill giants and put to flight through the air the flying trolls that came against Asgard in the darkness.

" Can a stranger enter ? " the young hero asked of Odin.

" No stranger can come within," the god made answer, " unless he brings with him the Sword of Victory."

" How can the dogs be passed ? " asked Svipdag.

Odin made reply that no one could pass the dogs unless he could give them to eat of the flesh upon the legs of Goldcomb.

When Svipdag asked how the cock which sat on the

World-tree could be killed, Odin said that there was but one sword with which it could be slain, and it had been kept in Hela's cave, nor could it be obtained from the watchman unless he were given the ankle bones of Goldcomb.

"Can no man enter the city and go unto Freyja?" the hero asked.

"No man can enter," was Odin's answer, "save Svipdag."

"Then open the gates," the hero cried, "for I am he. Svipdag has come to seek for Freyja."

Then he crossed the river unscathed by vafer-flame, for the gates of Asgard flew open. The dogs fawned to him and bayed joyous welcome.

From the rock on which she sat hastened Freyja, and when she knew that it was indeed Svipdag who had come, she cried: "Welcome, my lover! Now is my great desire fulfilled. Long have I waited, sitting on the rock, looking for you by day and by night. All my desires are indeed fulfilled because you are once again by my side."

'Twas thus that Svipdag entered Asgard, bearing with him the Sword of Victory which had been forged to bring ruin to the gods. Love had triumphed over hate, and the designs of Loke were thwarted, for Svipdag had Freyja for his wife and the sons of Ivalde were reconciled to the gods.

Then was Ull brought to Asgard, and Sith also. The eyes of Thjasse-Volund were placed in heaven to shine as stars, and Orvandel, who was dead, was also raised among the star-heroes.

Meanwhile Njord had journeyed to Jotun-heim, where he rescued from the giant's castle his son Frey. In his wrath did Frey kill Beli, "the howler", with a stag's horn which he plucked from the wall when the spells that bound him were taken off.

To Frey was given by Svipdag the Sword of Victory, and the joy of peace fell upon Asgard when he returned.

But still the Hag abode among the gods in the guise of a maid who sat at Freyja's feet. It was fated that she would cause yet another and greater war in Asgard and in Midgard ere her power would be overcome.

# CHAPTER VII

## The Lost Sword of Victory

The Wrath of Skade—The Demand for Vengeance—Challenge to the Gods—Loke's Cunning Device—Thjasse-Volund a Star-Hero—Skade chooses a Husband—Marriage with Njord—The Vision of Gerd—Frey's Love-Madness—Skirner's Mission—Visit to Gymer's Castle—Gerd's Disdain—Bridal Gifts scorned—Threats of Torture—Horrors of Nifel-hel—Frey accepted—The Price of Gerd—Gymer receives the Sword of Victory—How Surtur will be avenged.

WHEN Skade, the proud and powerful daughter of Thjasse-Volund, came to know that her father had been slain by the gods, she put on her armour of chain mail and her shining helmet, and she seized her great spear and poisoned arrows to avenge his death. Then, hastening to Asgard, she stood without, challenging a god to combat. Bold was she and beautiful, and serenely fearless in her wrath.

The gods took counsel together, and deemed that her cause was just. Thus it came that they spoke words of peace unto her, and, indeed, they desired not to slay one so fair. But she scorned their entreaties, and, raising her spear, demanded the life of him who had slain her father.

Then went cunning Loke without and set to dancing before her, while a goat danced with him, whereat she was amused. He danced long, and, when he had ceased, he bowed before her and besought her for his bride, the while the goat did bleat mournfully. Skade was moved to laughter, and her wrath passed away.

Nat rode forth, and shadows fell upon the heavens and the stars came forth. Then was Skade besought to enter Asgard. To her came Odin, and, pointing to the sky, he said:

"Behold! thy father's eyes are made bright stars,[1] which shall ever look down upon thee. . . . Amidst the gods thou mayest now dwell, and one thou canst choose to be thy husband. But, when this thou shalt do, thine eyes must be blindfolded, so that his feet only may be beheld by thee."

On the assembled gods she gazed with wonder and delight. Her eyes fell on Balder the Beautiful, and him she loved. In her heart she vowed he would be her choice.

When her eyes were veiled, she beheld a foot that was beautiful, and she deemed it was Balder's. Her arms went out, and, crying: "Thee I wed," she snatched aside the veil, and lo! it was Njord who stood before her.

Stately and fair was Njord, the summer sea-god, who stilled the tempests of Æger and the blast of Gymer, the storm-giant of the bitter east. But the heart of Skade took no delight in Njord.

Yet was the Vana-god her choice, and with him was she wed in pomp and state in Asgard. Together they departed to Noatun, where Skade wearied of the sea and the cries of birds on the cliffs, which bereft her of sleep. Deep was her sorrow that she dwelt no longer in the forest of Thrym-heim, and she yearned for the thundering waterfall, the high mountains, and the wide plains where

---

[1] The Ivalde family is associated with star worship. Ivalde is Vate, or Wate, of "Watling Street", the old English name of the Milky Way. Thjasse is connected with Sirius, and Orvandel with Orion. "Watling Street" was also applied to one of the Roman military roads extending from near Dover by London to North Wales.

she was wont to follow the chase. And the love she bore to Balder was ever gnawing her heart.

Then sought Frey a bride, and with love of her he was possessed to madness.

One day he ascended the golden throne of Odin and looked over the worlds, seeing all things, and that was the day of his sorrow. Wondering, he gazed east and west, and to the south he gazed. Then northward towards the land of giants he turned his eyes, and there shone before him a light of great radiance that filled with beauty the heavens and the air and the sea. A maiden, fairer than ever he beheld before, had opened the door of her dwelling. Divinely tall was she, and her arms gleamed like silver. For a moment he saw her, his heart leaping with love, and then she vanished, whereat his soul was stricken with deep sadness. So was he punished for sitting in Odin's throne.

Homeward went Frey, nor speak would he, nor would he eat, or drink, so great was his love for the giant-maid, whose name was Gerd, the daughter of Gymer. Much did the gods marvel because of his silence and his deep sighs. But none could find reason for the madness of Frey. To him came his father Njord, and Skade also, and as they found him so they left him, in melancholy and possessed with secret sorrow. Then spake Njord to Svipdag, who, in Asgard, was named Skirner, "the shining one", and entreated him to discover what caused his son to suffer, and to find a remedy whereby he would be restored to gladness.

As reluctant was Skirner to go unto Frey as he was when Sith besought him to rescue Freyja from the giant Beli. Yet when he found Frey sitting alone in silence, and stricken with keen longing for her whom he loved, he spoke to him boldly and with confidence.

*Frey, from the design by Burne-Jones.*

*Frey, as portrayed by Doré.*

"Together", he said, "we have had adventures in other days, and faithful should we now be one to another. Nor should there be any secret between us. Speak, O Frey, and tell me why you grieve alone and refuse to eat and to drink."

Frey answered him: "How can I disclose, fond friend, the secret of my sorrow. Bright shines the sun-goddess over heaven, but cheerless to me are her rays."

But Skirner pressed him to confide his sorrow, and Frey told of his love for beautiful Gerd, the giant-maid. But his love, he said, was foredoomed to sorrow, for neither god nor elf would permit that they should dwell together.

Then went Skirner to the gods and revealed the secret of Frey's silence and despair. Well they knew that if Gerd were not taken to him the god of sunshine would pine and die, so to Skirner they made known their will that he should haste to Gymer's abode and win his fair daughter for Frey.

Then was Frey less sad, and he gave Skirner the Sword of Victory to be his defence, and from Odin he received Sleipner to ride through fire and over the heavens. The bridal gifts he bore when he set forth were the magic ring Draupner and eleven apples of immortal youth from Idun's precious casket. A magic rod which subdues took he also with him.

Over raging sea and bleak mountains rode Skirner, over chasms and the mountain caves of fierce giants, until he came to Gymer's Castle, which was protected by a moat of fire. Fierce bloodhounds guarded the entrance gate.

On a mound sat a shepherd alone, and him Skirner addressed, beseeching how he could lull the fearsome hounds that kept constant watch, so that he might reach the giant-maid.

"Whence come ye?" asked the shepherd; "for surely you are doomed to die. You may ride by night or by day, but never can you win nigh to Gerd."

Skirner had no fear. "Our fates," he said, "are spun when we are born. Our doom we can never escape."

Now was the voice of Skirner heard by Gerd, who was within, and she besought her maid-servant to discover who it was that spoke so boldly before the castle.

Then Skirner spurred his horse, which rode over the hounds and the fiery moat, and the castle was shaken to the foundations when the door was reached.

The maid-servant told Gerd that a warrior stood without and demanded to be admitted to her.

"Then haste," cried Gerd, "and take him within, and mix for him the sweet and ancient mead, for I fear that he who murdered Beli, my brother, is come at length."

Skirner entered and stood before the giant-maid whom Frey loved so well, and she spake to him and said: "Who art thou—an elf, or the son of an Asa-god, or one of the wise Vans? Daring, indeed, art thou, to come alone unto this our strong abode."

"Neither elf, nor god, nor Van am I," Skirner made answer. "I am a messenger from the god Frey, who loves thee. From him I bring the ring Draupner as a gift, for he seeks thee for his bride."

Then was Gerd's heart filled with disdain, and the bridal gift she refused to take. "While life remains in me," she said, "Frey I shall not wed."

Skirner next made offer of the golden ring Draupner, but that she disdained also.

"Of thy ring I have no need," she told him, "because my sire hath great treasure of jewels and of gold."

When she spake thus the heart of Skirner was filled with anger, and he drew forth the shining Sword of Victory.

"Behold this blade!" he cried; "with it I can slay thee if Frey is rejected."

Proudly did Gerd arise. "By force nor threat," said she, "will I ever be led. My strong sire Gymer is armed and ready to punish thee for thy boldness."

Then Skirner said wrathfully: "With this blade I shall slay thy sire, the old giant Gymer, if he should dare to oppose me. And thee I can conquer with this magic wand, which shall subdue thy heart. If I must needs do so, no happiness will ever again come nigh thee. For thee it will remove to the regions of Nifel-hel, where nor god nor man can ever behold thee in beauty again."

Silent and pale sat Gerd as Skirner told her of the fate which would be hers if she continued to refuse to become the bride of Frey.

The place in Nifel-hel to which she must go, he said, was a region of torture where dwell the spirits of the giants who were ground in the World-mill. Power to love she would not have, nor tenderness or sympathy. Alone she must live, or else as the fruitless bride of a monstrous three-headed giant. Gladness and enjoyment would be banished from her heart. Staring eyes would ever watch her coldly and with more hatred than do the Frost-giants regard Heimdal, the sentinel of Bif-rost, or do the Trolls the wolf-dogs of Odin. Nor would the demons ever leave her at peace. Evil witches would bow her to the rocks. Morn, who gives "agony of soul", would fill her being. There in the place of torment prepared for her dwell the demons of sickness, who would increase her sorrow. Never would she be free from the torture of Tope (madness) and Ope (hysteria), and no rest would she know by night or by day. For food she would have loathsome meat, and venom for drink. Each morning would she crawl painfully to the mountain top and behold Hela in glory and in beauty, and ever would she seek in vain to reach its glittering plains of bliss and delight.

" Such, O Gerd, must be thy fate," cried Skirner, " if Frey by thee is disdained."

Then prepared he to strike her with the magic rod which subdues; but Gerd besought him to hear her.

" Fulfil not thy threat," she pleaded, " and drink of this sweet and ancient mead. Never dreamed I that I should love a god of the Vans."

But Skirner would not be appeased until she gave to him a message to Frey. Whereat she promised that after the space of nine nights she would consent to become the bride of the Vana-god if the Sword of Victory were given to her sire.

Pleasant were her words to Skirner, and hastening without he leapt upon his horse and returned with all speed to Asgard. There did Frey await him with impatience, but the lovelorn Vana-god was filled with sadness when he came to know that he must needs wait the space of nine nights ere he would be by Gerd received.

" Long is one night without her," he cried; " longer are two nights—how can I endure to wait for nine? Longer has this half night of waiting seemed to me than a month of greatest bliss."

Slowly for Frey passed the days and nights that followed. Then at the appointed time he went to Gerd, who became his bride.

Unto Gymer he gave for his daughter the Sword of

Victory, which had been forged to bring disaster upon the gods. And in this manner was Asgard deprived of the fruit of the triumph which Freyja had brought thither when Svipdag's wrath was turned aside and his love for her caused peace to be made between gods and elves.

Long had the giants sought to possess the Sword of Victory, and especially the wife of Gymer, Gulveig-Hoder, the dreaded Hag of Iarnvid, who had still her dwelling in Asgard, where she ever strove to work evil.

For with the Sword of Victory will Surtur be armed when he issues forth to avenge the wrong done to Gunlad by Odin.

Thus did Loke taunt Frey. " Treasure gave you to Gymer with which to buy his daughter, and the Sword of Victory also. Lo! when the sons of Surtur come over Ironwood, in sore distress you shall indeed be, for then you shall know not, O unhappy one, with what weapon to fight."

# CHAPTER VIII

## Fall of Asgard

Vengeance of the Gods—Burning of the Hag—War of the Gods—Skade leaves Njord—Mimer is slain—The Vans before Asgard—The Strategy of Njord—How Sleipner was captured—A Spy in Asgard—Odin's Gate burst Open—Invaders Victorious—Flight of Asa-Gods—The War in Midgard— The Sons of Halfdan—Odin rescues Hadding—Loke's Evil Designs—Giants in Conflict—Defeat of Hadding—How the Dead spoke—A Dread Curse— Forest Peril—The Great Hand—Death of Giant Maid—Heimdal protects Hadding.

THE gods marvelled greatly at the disasters which had befallen them, and they sat in council together to discover how Freyja had been lured from Asgard, and who had plotted to work this evil.

Suspicion fell upon Loke's wife, Aurboda-Gulveig-Hoder, the Hag of Ironwood, who dwelt among the gods in the guise of a maid-attendant to Freyja. Wife she was also to Gymer, who had become possessed of the Sword of Victory, and her son was Beli, "the howler", whom Frey had slain. So well did she act her part, while she schemed to work evil, that among the maids none seemed fairer or more faithful. Many missions did she perform for Freyja. Once, indeed, she was sent to confer divine favour upon mortals. A king and queen had long been married, and they had no children. Prayers they offered up to Freyja, and sacrifices made they that an heir to the kingdom might be theirs. In compassion were they heard, and Aurboda was sent earthwards by Freyja in the guise of a crow, bearing with her the fruit of fertility from the branches of Ygdrasil. When the queen partook of it, her desire was fulfilled, and in due season an heir was born, whereat there was great rejoicing in the kingdom.

Thus Aurboda[1] had fair repute in Asgard despite her evil character—she who was mother of the wolves that pursue son and moon; she who was Hag of Eastern Winds which bear the burden of her fearsome song and drive fair vessels into the very jaws of Ægir, the storm-god of western ocean.

When the gods came to know she was indeed the Mother of Evil, and had lured Freyja from her secure abode, they were moved with great wrath and with horror against her. They found, too, that it was dread Aurboda who had filled the air with witchcraft and wrought evil spells that enchanted both gods and men. Black sorcery did she practise to stir up the evil passions with which Loke had endowed human kind.

Thor sprang up in the High Thingstead of the gods and went forth hastily to find her. By him was she seized and struck down. Then the gods burned her as punishment for her witchcraft. A great pyre they reared in Valhal, and they spitted her body with their spears, holding it over the flames until it was consumed. But she came to life again. Thrice they burned her and thrice was she restored, for evil is hard to destroy. The third time they flung her ashes away, but her heart, which is the seat of life, was but half-burned, and Loke found it and swallowed it. Thereafter he partook in still greater measure of the evil character of the Hag, who, however, came to life the third time in Ironwood, where she must ever dwell despite the vengeance of the gods and their

[1] Also Angerboda.

wrathful desire to destroy her.  But Asgard she could never again enter.

Now the Hag was the mother of Gerd, the giant maid whom Frey the Vana-god had married.  As kinswoman of one of their clan she was under the protection of the Vana-gods, although, like the Asa-gods, they had fear and hatred of her witchcraft.  They therefore began to dispute with the Asa-clan because the Hag had been burned.  Long and loud the quarrel waged, but suddenly it was brought to an end by Odin, who flung his spear into their midst to signify that the war of words must end and the war of arms ensue.

Thus was the breach between the gods accomplished by the fearsome Hag.

On earth, too, was a conflict begun between the tribes of men.  Thus came to be waged, as skalds have sung, "the first great war in the world".  Whereat the primeval cold heart of "the old one in the Ironwood" was made glad.  With her rejoiced Egther, "the sword-guardian", who is also named Gymer, and is shepherd of her foul herds.  On the Day of Vengeance, when Surtur prepares to issue forth, Egther shall be visited by Fjalar-Suttung, in the guise of the red cock of Hela, to obtain from him the Sword of Victory with which to slay the gods.

Now when the Vans became hostile to the Asa-gods, they issued forth from Asgard.  With them went Njord. Skade, his wife, refused to dwell any more with him when she found she had no longer need to fear the Asa-gods.  She wearied of the western seashore, for she loved Thrym-heim, the domain of Thjasse-Volund, her father, with its serene mountains and wide plains and forests of oak.  For nine days and nine nights would Njord go with her to the mountains, and then for a time would she

dwell with him beside the loud-voiced sea. Njord hated
Thrym-heim as she did Noatun, and with heavy heart he
sang:

> I am weary of the mountains,
>     The barren plains and lone,
> And dismal chasms of the winds
>     Where fettered demons groan;
> I am weary of the forests
>     And the wolves that howl by night,
> For I love the singing of the swans
>     Upon the ocean bright,
> The flash of oars on boundless seas
>     And billows plunging white.

In the kingdom of Njord did Skade sing:

> O never mine eyes are closed in sleep
>     On my lonesome couch by the sea,
> For the clamour the restless seagulls keep
>     Is weary and strange to me.
> I pine for my mountains free, and the woods,
>     For the snow-clad plains and the chase;
> And I hate the cold-lipped shore that broods
>     In the shifting sea's embrace.

So Skade parted with Njord and went towards her
ancient home, from which she never returned. When the
star-eyes of Thjasse-Volund are gleaming bright in heaven,
and winds are abroad, she runs on her skees adown steep
mountain slopes; and with her arrows and her spear she
hunts the bear and the wolf in dim forests and over
snow-white plains.

Mighty Njord was leader of the Vans in their war
against the Asa-gods. And to the Vans was it given to
triumph. In sore plight were Odin and his strong warriors, for the Sword of Victory was no longer theirs,
and the hammer of Thor had been broken. Yet with

indomitable courage did Thor and brave Tyr and all the gods of Odin's clan defend Asgard. Loke usurped Honer, for he desired to rule over the Vana-gods.

Mimer, in the Underworld, was ever faithful unto Odin. So the Vana-gods slew him, and to Odin they sent his head, and the great Asa-god embalmed it. Then sang he sacred runes, so that in after time Odin spake with Mimer's head, and heard words of wisdom from it, and received guidance as of old. Honer was sent unto Mimer's realm, where he spoke without confidence or clear knowledge, but he had not chosen his part.

Asgard fell, and by cunning strategy was it taken. Unscathed by the vafer-flames did the Vans cross its fearsome river, for Njord burst open the mighty gate with his great battleaxe and caused it to fall. So did the Vans achieve gigantic triumph.

It was thus that the gods were overcome. Before Asgard their foes assembled, and skirmishings there were when Odin's warriors issued forth. On a silent evening the gate was lowered, so that it bridged the river, and a god rode forth upon Sleipner. But in ambush was he taken by Njord, and he leapt from his horse and hastened back to Asgard, crossing the bridge, which was hastily raised again. But Sleipner was captured, whereat there was sorrow and deep foreboding in Asgard.

Next morning the gods found Odin's horse outside the gate, and they rejoiced and took it within. The robes of Njord they saw also in the river, and what they thought to be his dead body, so they deemed themselves secure.

But Njord was already in Asgard. He had gone to the river, horsed on Sleipner, in the darkness of night. There he slew his attendant and wrapped his own kingly robes about him, throwing the body into the dread waters.

Whereupon he crossed over on Sleipner, unscathed by the vafer-flames, scaled the great wall, and concealed himself within the High Thingstead of the gods.

When he came to know of the gods' plans, and perceived that he had naught to fear, he crept forth and struck the gate with his battleaxe. Across the river it fell like a bridge, and over it surged the conquering Vana-gods. Thus did they become possessed of Asgard, the celestial city.

Njord was chief of heroes, and with him fought Frey and Ull, the warlike son of Sith, and Svipdag, Freyja's husband. Frigg espoused the cause of the Vana-gods, her kinsmen, and remained in Asgard.[1]

Odin made swift escape on the back of Sleipner, and Thor yoked his goats, and in his thundering car departed with those who remained faithful to his sire. Thus were the Asa-gods bereft of their power, and thus became the Vana-gods the world-rulers in Asgard. Ull was chosen as the chief, and to him did mortals offer up prayers and sacrifices.

Then did wicked men, by reason of great offerings which they made, seek to win Hela's secure abode.

While the war was waged about Asgard there were mighty conflicts in Midgard, for Halfdan's tribe sought to be avenged on the tribe of Svipdag. But ere the tale of the battles be told it must needs be known how the war upon earth came to be.

When Halfdan was wounded unto death, in the great fight in which Svipdag overcame Thor with the Sword of Victory, his forces were driven hither and thither. He had two sons—Hadding, whose mother was Signe-Alveig, and Gudhorm, whose mother was Groa. They were in

---

[1] Hence the Heimskringla story of Odin going a long journey, and the wooing of Frigg by his brothers, who thought he would never return.

great peril when Halfdan died, and Thor carried them
unto Jotun-heim.  Gudhorm he gave to the giant Halfe,
and Hadding to the giant Vagnhofde, so that they might
be cared for until they became great warriors.

When the Vans conquered Asgard, Loke sought to
win their favour.  He perceived that they were scorned
by Hadding's tribe, whom Saxons called "the Heardings", and he laid snares against Hadding.  But there
came to Hadding one day a tall old man with one eye,
who rode a great horse.  He lifted Halfdan's son into his
saddle, and round the lad he wrapped his cloak.  Then
he set off with him.  So swiftly did the horse travel, and
yet so smoothly, that the lad was curious to know whither
they were going.  There was a small hole in the horseman's mantle, and when Hadding peered through he saw
the wide ocean far beneath and the clouds about him.
Fear filled his heart and he trembled, and the rider bade
him to look not forth again.  For it was Odin who had
rescued Hadding, and he bore him to the place of refuge
which the gods had selected when they were driven out
of Asgard.

Odin trained Halfdan's son to become a great leader
of men.  Over him he sang magical incantations which
had power to free him from fetters and chains.  He also
gave him to drink of the Splendid Draught, which was
called "Leifner's Flames".  Its virtue was such that it
imparted to Hadding strength beyond that of all men,
and bravery that was unequalled.  Then did Odin warn
him that he would soon have need to use his powers
against his enemies.

Hadding returned on Odin's horse, as he had come,
to the home of the giant Vagnhofde.  But soon he fell
into Loke's snare.  The evil god seized him and chained
him in a forest, as Svipdag had been chained by Halfdan,

so that he might become the prey of wild beasts. Guards were set over him to prevent his escape. But when these allies of Loke kept watch, Halfdan sang an incantation which Odin had taught him, and they fell into a magic sleep. A great wolf came towards him to tear his body to pieces, and he sang the incantation which makes free, and his chains and fetters fell from him. Then he attacked the wolf and killed it, and its heart he did eat. With the might and ferocity of the wolf was Hadding then endowed, and the guards he slew, and went upon his way.

He returned to the giants' home, and prepared to depart so that he might raise his tribe to battle against the tribe of Svipdag. Now Hardgrep, the giant's daughter, loved him and besought him not to leave her. She had power to change her shape. Now she had stature which reached to the stars, and anon she was of human size. In vain did she remonstrate with Hadding because he scorned her love and sought to follow arms, thirsting for throats.

But although at length she gained his love as a comely maid, he had still resolve to be gone. So she attired herself as a male warrior and went with him.

Then did Svipdag come from Asgard, and he sought to make peace with the sons of Halfdan. To both he offered kingdoms, and his half-brother Gudhorm, son of Groa, he made ruler over the Danes. But Hadding refused his favours, and with anger and fierce scorn he vowed that he would avenge his father's death and take no favour from the hands of his enemy. Until his life's purpose was fulfilled he vowed to cut neither hair nor beard, and long were both and very fair. It was thus that he was called Hadding, "the hairy"

His eastern tribe of Swedes did the young warrior

raise to battle against Svipdag's tribe and their allies, and war he declared against his brother Gudhorm, King of the Danes. Between the two brothers did Loke work much evil. As a blind man he went to Hadding with words his brother uttered, and with Gudhorm he was Bikke, a leader of his army.

So the brothers fought one against another. To Gudhorm's aid went Halfe, the giant who had nourished him, and to Hadding's went Vagnhofde. Svipdag's Scandian tribe fought with the Danes.

On the night before the battle the opposing armies beheld the great hairless giants contending in mid-air, the starlight gleaming on their bald, horrible heads. Monstrous were the efforts of these foul gigantic warriors. When the dread conflict was ended, victory was with Halfe.

On the morrow did Loke set in cunning battle array the forces of Gudhorm, which triumphed on the field as Halfe had in mid-air.

The eastern Swedes were scattered, and Hadding became a fugitive in the woods. With him was Hardgrep, the giant's daughter, who was a constant protection to him. Great hardships did they endure together, and they were ofttimes in peril.

But her aid he was doomed to lose. One night they entered a lonely dwelling to seek hospitality, and there they found that the master of the house was lying dead. His funeral rites were being performed. Now, it was Hardgrep's desire to peer into the future, and she took a piece of wood and on it engraved magic runes, which she caused Hadding to place under the dead man's tongue, so that he might speak.

Angry, indeed, was the spirit thus compelled to make utterance. Nor did it reveal what was sought, but cursed the worker of the spell. Terrible was the voice that spoke and said: "Cursed be the one who dragged me back from the Underworld! Let her perish by the demon who called a spirit out of bale!"

Then fled from the house Hadding and Hardgrep and sought refuge in the deep forest. Over the narrow path of a grove they made a shelter with branches of trees and concealed themselves there. In the middle of the night a rustling was heard in their secret dwelling, and a Great Black Hand was perceived to move about, groping with iron fingers for its prey.

Hadding was stricken with terror, and he awakened Hardgrep and besought her to rescue him. Swiftly rose the giant-maid, and she assumed great stature to defend her lover. With strength of her kind she clutched the Great Hand round the wrist, and bade Hadding strike it with his sword. Many blows did he give, seeking to hew it off, and his blade rang noisily against the hard flesh.

Blood flowed from the wounds he made, but more venom than blood came forth.

Then suddenly was Hardgrep caught by the Hand, which clutched her in terrible embrace. Into her flesh sank the sharp claws, and her bones were crushed, and she sank in death in the sheltered dwelling. Whereat the Great Hand vanished.

Hadding was now alone and in great peril, for demons compassed him about in the dark forest.

But Odin, in his compassion, sent forth Lyfir, "the shining one", who was Heimdal in human guise, to protect the warrior in his loneliness. Him did Hadding meet as a rover, and a bond of friendship they made together by sprinkling one another's feet with their blood.

Soon again did Hadding appear in the east, leading his hosts to battle.

# CHAPTER IX
## The Gods Reconciled

Svipdag leaves Asgard—Hadding's Strategy—Fleet sunk by Odin—Fate of Svipdag—Freyja's Sorrowful Quest—The Sea-Dragon—Slain by Hadding—The Curse of Freyja—Loke and Heimdal's Ocean Fight—Hadding's Peril—The Gods and the Last Battle—Death of Svipdag's Son—His Faithful Queen—Giants threaten Asgard—Odin's Warning—Thor wins Ull's Favour—Asa-Gods return to Asgard—The Decrees of Odin—The Seven Sleepers—St. Swithin's-Day Myth.

Svipdag descended out of Asgard and urged his tribe to help the Danes in their campaign against Hadding. Ing was he called by his people. They were ruled over by his son, Asmund, who had chosen to live among men.

The fame of Hadding had already gone forth because of mighty deeds he had done. He had conquered King Hadvanus, although the city in which he was besieged was protected by strong battlements. The cunning warrior desired the speedy surrender of his foemen. He caused birds that nested within to be caught, and to their feathers slow-burning lights were attached, so that when they flew over the battlements they set the roofs aflame. The people hastened to quench the great fires that raged about them ; soldiers left the fortresses, and the guards ran from the gates. Then did Hadding make sudden and fierce assault and capture the town. Not until he gave payment of much gold was the stricken king ransomed and saved from death.

A great fleet sailed eastward with Svipdag's warriors.

In one ship, the name of which was Gnod, went three thousand men. But Odin sank it, and all on board perished in the waves.

There are some who tell that Svipdag was drowned with his warriors, and there are others who hold that he was punished by enchantments, for by reason of Groa's incantations the sea could not harm him, and none there were who had power over him save the Asa-gods. Indeed he had reason to fear them greatly, for they were stirred with wrath against him because he would not permit the war to have end. He was Odur, the one " endowed with spirit ".

It is told that enchantments were put upon Svipdag by the Asa-gods, and that he was transformed into a great sea-dragon which dwelt beneath a grey rock guarding much treasure.

The heart of Freyja was sad because that Svipdag came not nigh to her with loving words and shining face. Deeply she yearned for him in Asgard, wondering what evil had befallen The Shining One.

Then came she to know that he had suffered because of Odin's wrath, and forth she went to search for him. Tears fell from her eyes, and they became drops of pure gold, and those that showered into the sea were changed to amber.

Through Midgard she went searching for Svipdag, and she roamed over hills and plains and over rivers and lakes enquiring of whom she met if her lost one had gone this way or that. And without ceasing she wept, so that her tears of gold may be found in all lands, and her tears of amber on the shores of wide seas. Faithful was she to Svipdag, and ever did she sorrow as she went because she found him not.

At length she came to the shore of the sea where her

husband sorrowed also in dragon-guise. Horrible was he to behold and of haggard seeming.

She was neither repulsed nor was her love turned cold, for the eyes of the dragon were still the eyes of Svipdag, without change or lack of beauty.

Then endeavoured she to comfort him, and wept more tears of gold. Great indeed did the dragon's treasure become, for great was the sorrow of Freyja. But break the spell she could not, for who can remove the curse of Odin?

Long she stayed nigh to Svipdag, nor sought to return unto Asgard. And when she entered the sea to comfort him her great necklace glittered through the waves, and in darkness fire flashed from it. Beneath the grey stone she left the necklace on the day when lasting sorrow was her dower.

There came on that day to bathe in the sea Hadding, the vengeful son of Halfdan. But he wondered because his body was scorched with great heat and the waves boiled all around. Then suddenly he beheld the dragon coming against him. With haste he seized his sword and made fierce attack. Great was the might of Hadding, and by Odin was he given power to prevail. With many strong blows he slew the monster, and he bade his men to carry it to his camp.

Now, as he went thither, a lady came towards him. She was of such great beauty that he was made silent before her. Golden was her hair, and gleaming and blue were her eyes as the radiant, sun-kissed sea. But Hadding knew not that it was the goddess Freyja who stood before him.

When she beheld the dragon she was stirred to divine wrath. Hadding she cursed upon sea and upon land. "Suffer shalt thou," she cried, "the vengeance of

the gods in Asgard.   On battlefield and empty plain shall
their wrath attend thee.   On seas eternal tempests shall
thee follow.   Wherever thou dost wander thou shalt be
accursed.   Bitter cold shall follow thee to thy dwelling;
at its fire thou shalt be oppressed.   Thy flocks shall die.
All men shall shun thee, for through the world thou shalt
go as foul and as hated as is the plague.   Such is the
wrath of the gods against thee, for with sacrilegious hands
thou hast slain a dweller in Asgard who was enchanted
in a form that was not his own.   O slayer of the god
I loved! when thou art cast into the deep the wrath of
demons shall fall upon thee.   Ever will you be under
our curse until with prayers and sacrifice to the Vana-
gods our wrath is appeased."

All things that Freyja said came to pass.   Stricken
was Hadding by a tempest and cast into the raging sea.
Despised was he by strangers when he was washed ashore,
and shunned was he as if he were plague-smitten and
foul.   Many disasters, indeed, fell upon him, until he
offered up dusky men in sacrifice to the god Frey.
Then was the wrath of the Vana-gods melted and the
curse removed.

Each year did Hadding ever afterwards give Frey
great offerings, as did also his sons and their sons for
generations.

Now Loke had watched the conflict between Hadding
and the dragon while yet afar off.   When he perceived
that Svipdag was slain, he hastened to secure the treasure,
and especially the necklace of Freyja, from below the
grey rock.   In seal guise did he enter the sea, and he
saw gleaming through the dark waters the jewels of the
divine Lover of Ornaments.   But Heimdal, the keen-
eyed, followed him, and in seal guise was he also.   Thus
did Loke and he meet in the sea's dim depths.   By their

eyes did each know the other, and fiercely they fought on the grey rock to be possessed of the jewels.

Heimdal, son of the waves, was victorious. He drave off Loke, and possessed himself of Freyja's necklace, which he kept secure until he returned to Asgard with the Asa-gods.

Then came the day of great battle between Hadding and the tribes that were combined against him. Ere it began, he slew Henry, son of Asmund, son of Svipdag. Then was Asmund filled with great wrath, and he vowed to slay the warrior who had killed his sire and his son also.

But Odin was with Hadding, and the great god caused his favoured warrior to marshal his army in wedge shape, so as to pierce and scatter the foe. For long years after did the descendants of Hadding enter battle in this manner.

Now when the conflict was at its height, Hadding was sore pressed because of the strength of Asmund's arm, which was made greater by his exceeding great wrath and desire for vengeance. Odin perceived his peril, and hastened from the battle to bring him aid.

The Vana-gods gave help to Asmund, and over Hadding's army there passed a fierce rainstorm and wreaths of mist that caused confusion. Then came Thor on a black thundercloud which drave back the rain-clouds over the hills, and the sun broke forth in clear splendour.

Hadding's wedge-shaped army pressed forward, until Asmund was nigh to his enemy, whose death he sought above all else. Then did Hadding call upon the Asa-gods in his sore need. Asmund had flung his shield over his back, and with both hands grasping the hilt, he wielded his great sword so fiercely that he mowed down his enemies before him. Nigh to Hadding came he indeed, when Odin returned on his horse Sleipner, bearing with him the giant Vagnhofde. By Hadding's side was the giant placed in the guise of a warrior bearing a crooked sword.

When Asmund saw the weapon which the giant wielded he cried: "Thou mayest fight with a crooked sword, but my short sword and my javelin shall be thy doom this day. And thou, Hadding, holding thy shield against me, art foul with crimes. Thy bold lance shall I bear down, and thee shall I cover with shame."

But the giant engaged Asmund, and Hadding flung his lance, which pierced Asmund's body so that he fell dying of his fierce wound. Yet was he not without strength to strike a last blow, for he grasped his javelin and flung it at Hadding, whose foot he pierced. Then died Asmund unrevenged, but ever afterwards did the slayer of his sire and his son limp with the wound he gave him in his last hour.

When Asmund fell, Hadding became victorious, and his foemen he drave in confusion from the field.

The body of Asmund was buried with pomp and state. Bitter was the grief of his queen Gunnhild, who desired not to live after him. With Asmund's sword she slew herself, and with him was she laid in the tomb. She loved him more than life, and with her arms around his body was she laid to rest in his tomb. The whole tribe mourned them, sorrowing greatly for many days.

Now the Frost-giants and the giants of the mountains plotted together to conquer Asgard, and in Surtur's deep dales and in Iarnvid there was promise and offer of help. Weak were the Vana-gods to resist the disaster which impended, nor did they know aught of the evil plans of their dread foes. But to Odin came full knowledge in his exile.   Well he knew that disaster irretrievable would befall both gods and mortals if the high celestial city fell before the giants.

Sleipner he mounted, and towards Asgard sped he, bearing the tidings of dread import.   Then it was that the Vana-gods knew they had exceeding great need of his wise and constant counsel.   Deeply moved were they towards the leader they had dethroned and driven into exile, because he had forewarned them of the giants' plans.

To Thor went Ull, who sat in Odin's throne, and together they conferred.   With eloquent words did the Thunder-god fill the heart of Ull with friendship towards the Asa-gods, so that he returned to Asgard to plead their cause.   Nor long did he speak when the Vana-gods sent speedily unto Odin to beseech him to become once again their great chief ruler.

So were the Asas and Vans reconciled, but on the day of Ragnarok, when Suttung comes forth to wreak vengeance, the wise Vans shall depart from Asgard.

Soon after Odin had returned to sit supreme again upon his throne, the giants made vain attempt to overcome the gods, but great punishment was meted out to them for their presumption.   Many were slain, and those that survived were driven back to Jotun-heim.   Then peace unbroken reigned in Asgard.   In Midgard, too, was peace restored, and men laid down their arms, weary with fighting.

Odin then, remembering the evil wrought by the Hag of Iarnvid, issued decrees which condemned magic and the practice of black sorcery.   The great sacrifices made by evil men did he also condemn, and he made known that not only by the quantity of offerings would the gods be appeased or the wicked recommended before the

Thingstead of the Lower World. Those of his chosen warriors who were borne by the Valkyries to his place of exile were brought unto Asgard to share the joys of Valhal.

So ended the first great war in the world. But the dread effects of Loke's evil had not yet their end.

When Mimer was slain, the fount of wisdom was without a watchman, and Ygdrasil, the World-tree, ceased to draw sustenance therefrom, so that it began to wither. Many leaves faded, and its branches knew swift decay.

The seven sons of Mimer, who were guardians of the seven months of change,[1] fell into deep stupor in their golden hall, which was heaped with great treasure. Clad in splendid robes, they lay upon the floor wrapped in magic sleep. Sindre-Dvalin was there in the midst; his brothers were about him. Mortals who have penetrated Hela and reached Mimer's realm have beheld them lying asleep beside their treasure, but they feared to enter; for if anyone touched the robes, or sought to be possessed of the gold, his hand and his arm would wither.

The Seven Sleepers shall awake not, as mortals have been told, until Ragnarok, "the Dusk of the Gods". When Heimdal blows a thunder blast from Gjallarhorn on the day of the Last Battle, the sons of Mimer shall start from sleep. They shall then arm themselves and issue forth. On the wall have mortals beheld suspended and bright, seven long swords which none save the sons of Mimer can wield.

---

[1] These are St. Swithin's mythical predecessors. The ancient belief was that if it rained on "the day of the Seven Sleepers" there would be rain for seven weeks thereafter.

# CHAPTER X

## Loke's Evil Progeny

Ironwood Brood—The Midgard-Serpent, Hel, and the Wolf—Odin's Acts of Vengeance—The Binding of Fenrer—Its Silk-like Chain—The Gulf of Black Grief—Its Island—How Tyr lost his Hand—Wolf-River Von—The Great Watchdog—Loke's Taunts—His Doom foretold—Human Sacrifices—The Runes of Tyr—Warriors' Sword Charm—Commander of the Valkyries.

Now by divination did Odin come to know that in Ironwood the Hag, Angerboda (Gulveig-Hoder) was rearing the dread progeny of Loke with purpose to bring disaster to the gods. Three monster children there were—Fenrer, the wolf; Jormungand, the Midgard serpent; and Hel. From these the Trolls are sprung.

Together the gods took counsel, and a Vala revealed dimly the fate that would be theirs if these monsters were not overcome, for the wolf, it was foretold, would slay Odin, Thor would fall in combat with the serpent, and Hel would come with the hosts of destruction against the gods and men.

So it was deemed of great import that the foul children of Loke and Angerboda should be brought to Asgard, and by Odin was Hermod sent to Ironwood to take them captive. That he did right speedily, bringing them one by one.

When Odin beheld the foul serpent, which was yet young, but of great length and very fierce, he seized it in his wrath and flung it far over the walls of Asgard.

Yet by reason of its terrible weight it did not pass beyond the world's edge, but fell into the depths of Ocean, where in after-days it grew and grew until it encircled the world of men. There on the sea bottom it lies, holding its tail in its mouth. When it shakes itself the waves rise in great fury and surge high upon the world's shores.

Next came Hel, and foul was she of aspect, for one-half of her body was of hue like to raw flesh, while the other was livid and horrible. In wrath did Odin seize her also, and he flung her afar. Beyond the edge of Ocean she went, falling through space, until she reached the black depths of Nifel-hel. There in the realms of torture became she a queen.

High are the walls and strongly barred the gates of her habitation, which is named Hel-heim and also Elvidner, the Place of Storm. The doomed have terror of her fearsome countenance, and of the place where she sits. About her are her servants, who do her will. Delay is her man servant and Slowness her maid servant; Hunger waits at her table, and her knife is Starvation. The threshold of Hel's home is Precipice, her bed is Care, while Burning Anguish forms the hangings of her apartment.

Unto Elvidner, as it hath been told, went the doomed ere they were committed to the realms of torture. By Hel were their punishments ordered according to the judgments passed upon them. And especially to her came trembling, warmen who died without valour and were unworthy, as did also those who were traitors in the hour of trial.

Now when the wolf Fenrer was brought to Odin, he sought not to destroy it. Indeed it was reared by the gods in Asgard; but when it grew large, it became so fierce that none save brave Tyr had courage to feed it. The day fell when Odin perceived that the wolf must needs be overcome, or else it would devour him. So prodigiously did it increase that there was terror in Asgard.

Then the gods caused to be made an iron chain which was named Leding. Tyr bore it to Fenrer, who knew well its purpose. Without resistance was it bound, and when that was done the gods were well pleased. Then rose Fenrer to struggle with the chain, which it snapped right speedily. So the wolf again went free, and grew more ferocious than ever.

Another chain, which was named Dromi, was there-afterwards made by the artisans of the gods. It had double the strength of Leding. Then went Tyr to the fierce wolf, and constrained it to be bound.

"If this chain by thee is burst," Tyr said, "then will thy mighty strength be proved indeed."

Well did the wolf know that the second chain was more powerful than the first, and that it could not easily be snapped. But much had Fenrer grown in bulk and in strength after Leding was broken. So the monster lay down, and, although somewhat afraid, allowed Tyr to fetter its legs. . . . The gods stood nigh and deemed the wolf secure forever. . . . They saw it rise and struggle fiercely without avail. Then it rolled upon the ground in monstrous strife, until at length the chain burst asunder and Fenrer was again free. More fierce than ever, and more terrible did the wolf become.

Thus had origin the proverb that men use in dire straits when they know that wondrous efforts must needs be made: "I must now get loose from Leding, and burst free out of Dromi".

In despair were the gods when they saw Fenrer

again at liberty, and they feared he would never be bound.

Then did Odin give to Hermod his horse Sleipner, and him did the wise god send unto the Underworld, so that he might prevail upon the dark artisans of the gods to fashion the cord Gleipner, "the devourer".

Readily indeed did the cunning workers give Odin their service. Soft as silk was the cord they made, and light as air. When it was cast down it made no noise. Of six things was it made:

> A mountain's root,
> A bear's sinews,
> The breath of fish,
> A cat's footfall,
> A woman's beard,
> The spittle of birds.

"Of all these things thou mayest not have heard before," a skald has said, "yet a mountain hath no roots, fish breathe not, and cats make no noise when they run. Women have no beards, as thou hast seen.

Soft and smooth was the cord indeed, but yet of exceeding great strength. Hermod bore it to Asgard with great speed, and by Odin was he thanked for his service.

Then did the gods challenge Fenrer to a supreme trial of strength. To the depths of Nifel-hel they went, and to the Gulf Amsvartner, which means "black grief". In the gulf is an island, and on the island a misty grove, with trees shaped from jets of water sent forth by boiling springs.

To the island did the gods take Fenrer, and they showed him there the cord Gleipner. Each of them in turn tried its strength but could not snap it.

"None but thee, O Fenrer, can break cord," Odin said.

The wolf answered: "Methinks no great fame can come to me from breaking such a cord, so light and slender does it seem."

Then with fierce eyes it spake thus: "If the cord is made with magic cunning, although it seems slender, never shall I permit it to bind my feet."

The gods answered, and said: "Surely Fenrer can burst asunder a cord both silken and light, when it hath already severed chains of iron."

The wolf made no answer, watching them sullenly with fiery eyes.

"If thou canst break this cord," Odin said, "then shall the gods know that they have no cause to fear thee, and then may well set thee at liberty."

The wolf answered sullenly, and said: "Much I fear that if I am fettered, and cannot free myself, thou shalt not haste to unloose me. Loath indeed am I to be bound with this cord. But I am not without courage. Know now that I shall give consent to be bound if a god but place his hand in my mouth, as a sure undertaking that ye practise no deceit towards me."

At one another the gods looked in silence. No choice had they between two evils, and they knew that the wolf must needs be bound.

Then stepped forth brave Tyr, the valiant god without fear, and between the fierce jaws of the monster wolf he placed his strong right hand. Thereupon the gods bound Fenrer with the soft silk-like cord of magic power. Securely they tied him; his legs they fettered so that he could not rise.

Holding Tyr's right hand in its jaws, the wolf then began to struggle with purpose to break free from the

magic bonds. Great wrath possessed its heart because
its efforts were vain. No loop could be displaced, nor
knot unloosed. On its back and on its side it struggled
in vain, for the more it sought to be free, the tighter became the cords. Blood streamed from Tyr's hand, and
in the end Fenrer gnawed it off at the wrist.

When the gods perceived that the wolf was bound
indeed, all of them save Tyr shook with great laughter.

A gallow-chain, named Gelgja, was then fixed to the
cord, and the gods drew it through a black rock named
Gjoll, which was sunk deep in the earth. The other end
of the cord they tied to Thviti, a great boulder, which was
buried still deeper. The wolf was then so well secured
that it could not move. Yet it snapped its jaws, endea-
vouring to sever chains and cord; and, perceiving this,
the gods thrust in its evil mouth a great sword. It
pierced the under jaw up to the very hilt, and the point
touched the monster's palate.

Then did the wolf's struggles come to an end, and
horribly did it howl. Foam streamed from its mouth,
and a roaring cascade began to fall, which ever after fed
the great and turbulent River Von.

To guard the island of the Gulf of Black Grief the
gods bound there, nigh to Loke's monster son, the great
watchdog Garm, which is greater than Hate-Managarm,
the moon devourer, so that it might bark with loud alarm
if Fenrer broke free. There, too, beside the fettered
wolf, was Loke bound in after days.

Now when Loke fell to dispute with Tyr he said:
"Thy two hands thou canst not use, since thy right one
was taken from thee by the wolf."

To him did Tyr make answer: "A hand I lack, but
thou, O Loke, dost lack a good reputation. That is
indeed a great defect. But the wolf fares not well.

On the island of the Gulf of Black Grief it shall pine in fetters until the world's end."

Loke was angered and spoke bitterly. "Thy wife", he said, "loves me."

Frey cried: "Silence, thou mischief maker! I see Fenrer, thy offspring, lying fettered at the source of Von, where it shall remain until the gods perish and all things have end. If thy tongue is not silent, then shalt thou be bound also."

It was then that Loke taunted Frey for giving unto the giant Gymer the Sword of Victory as a gift for Gerd.

Wroth was Bygver, who served Frey, when he heard the words that Loke uttered. He it was who ground the barley for those who give honour to his master, the god of harvests.

"Were I the honoured Frey," he said unto Loke, "I would grind thee finer than sand, thou evil crow! I would crush thee limb by limb."

But Loke turned, with wrinkling lips and cold disdain, and said: "What child is this? What parasite starts up before me? Ever in Frey's hearing he clatters from under the millstone."

"My name is Bygver," the servant answered, "and by gods and men am I called nimble."

Loke answered: "Be silent, Bygver! never couldst thou divide fairly food between men. Ugly indeed is thy slave wife Beyla, who is ever filthy with dust and dirt."

Valiant was Tyr, whose sire was Odin and whose mother was a beauteous giantess of the deep. Brave men honoured him, and by Saxons was he called Saxnot. With Odin did heroes name him ere they entered battle, and when they were victorious they offered up to Tyr burnt sacrifices of war prisoners. On earth his temple symbol was the sun-flashing sword which he wielded, and on the swords of warriors were his runes graven. Thus hath a skald sung:

> The runes of Tyr give victory—
> And these we needs must lilt
> When on the guard a sword we rist,
> Or on the blazing hilt.
> When we the magic words engrave,
> Twice name we Tyr, the wise, the brave.

Tyr was commander of Odin's wish maidens, the Valkyries, who bore to Valhal the sword-slain battle warriors.

With great Thor did Tyr go forth when he contended against the giant Hymer and the Midgard serpent. Of that great enterprise the story must now be told.

# CHAPTER XI

## Thor's Great Fishing

The Ocean Storm-god—His Hall—The Brewing Kettle—Ran and her
Net—Her Nine Daughters—Thor and Tyr seek Hymer's Kettle—The
Friendly Giantess—The Fisher of Whales—A Great Feast—Giant marvels
at Thor—The Midgard Serpent—A Dread Conflict—Hymer's Terror—How
Thor was baffled—The Broken Goblet—Hymer's Kettle captured—Flight of
Thor and Tyr—A Running Battle—Mead for the Feast.

ÆGIR, the Ocean Storm-god, had long heard of the fame
and wisdom of Odin and his Asa clan, and there fell a
day when he went to visit them. Thus it came that
vows of lasting friendship were sworn between them.
The gods were in due season invited to a harvest-end
feast in the dwelling of the storm-god in the midst of
the Western Sea, and thither they journeyed together.
It was from Ægir's hall that Thor and Tyr set forth to
do valiant deeds in the realm of the giant Hymer.

The kingdom of Ægir is beyond Noatun, the safe
ship haven of the god Njord, which ever had peace save
when it was visited by Skade, "the stormy one". A
fierce and aged giant is Ægir, with long and foam-white
beard, and black is his helmet. When he rises in the
midst of Ocean, cold-hearted and turbulent, he shatters
fair vessels in his wrath. Many ships has Angerboda,
Hag of Ironwood, driven by her wild easterly winds into
the very jaws of Ægir.

In Ægir's hall gold is used for fire, and his brewing
kettles seethe and boil like stormy seas. His wife is

Ran, the fair traitress. She is possessed of a great net, in which she catches seafarers when their ships are broken. So are men " drowned to Ran ". At the sea bottom is her home, which gleams phosphorescent and golden ; its roof is of silver and sun-gemmed azure. Nigh is it unto the House of Death. Eager is Ran to make captives, and those who would win her favour must needs, when they are drawn down to her, take with them offerings of gold, for she loves treasure, and her hoard is great. To those whom she receives without anger she offers a seat and a bed.

Nine giant maids are the chief daughters of Ran, and these are the mothers of Heimdal, the shining sentinel of beauteous Bif-rost. In gowns of blue they go forth. They have foam-white veils, and their locks are pale as sea froth. The sea maidens are ever at Ægir's command, and by him are they sent abroad to be ship-tossing billows. Great rocks they love to scatter and throw down, and the shoreland they devour.

These giant maids at the beginning ground Ymer's body on the World-mill. And ever do they turn the great mill at the sea bottom. Angeyja and Eyrgjafa grind mould ; Jarnsaxa is the crusher of the iron which comes from clay and the sea ; Imder, Gjalp, and Greip are fire maids, for from the World-mill is fire sparked forth, and there is fire in the sea ; Eistla, Eyrgjafa, and Ulfrun are also at work like the others. The sire of Gjalp and Greip was Geirrod, the fire-giant.

Now when Ægir went to Asgard he was received by Odin and the other gods with pomp and in state. Together they drank mead, ancient and sweet, in spacious Valhal, which was adorned with burnished shields and made bright by shining swords. High sat the gods in their doom seats, and in full grandeur. By Bragi's side

was Ægir, and the sweet-voiced divine poet sang of Idun
and her apples of immortal youth, and of Thjasse's death,
and of how Odin took from Suttung's dwelling the
skaldic-mead which Ivalde had stolen.    Pleasant were the
tales to Ægir, and the gods, as we have told, he besought
to visit him in his Ocean kingdom.

Thither at autumn equinox went Odin and his Asa
clan to drink mead and hear ancient tales and the singing
of skalds.    But of mead there was not sufficient, because
Ægir was in need of a brewing kettle large enough to
give due hospitality to the gods.    He besought Thor to
fetch the greatest kettle in the nine worlds ; but nor Asa
nor Vana-gods knew where it could be found until Tyr
spake and said :

"Hymer, the dog-headed, my foster-father, hath the
great kettle, which is exceedingly strong and a mile in
depth.    His dwelling is beyond the Rivers Elivagar, nigh
to the borders of Nifel-heim."

"Thinkest thou that the kettle can be captured?"
asked Thor.

"Yes," Tyr answered, "by stratagem it may be procured."

Then took Thor and Tyr the guise of young men,
and they set forth in the thunder-god's chariot drawn by
the two goats Tanngnjoster and Tanngrisner over ocean
and through air.    Nearly all day did they travel thus until
they came unto the dwelling of Orvandel-Egil.    There
did Thor leave the horn-strong goats and his sublime car.

Across Elivagar they went, and past the vast fishing
ground of Hymer, where he is wont to catch whales on
great hooks.    Then a great distance journeyed the gods
on foot towards Hymer's dwelling through dense mountain woods and past dismal rocky caverns where dwell
the fierce giants and monsters of Hymer's clan.

When they came to their journey's end, they entered the king giant's great stronghold, and there Tyr saw his grandmother—a giantess with numerous heads, who was fierce and awesome to behold. But his mother, who had great beauty, brought them mead to drink. When they were refreshed and strong again, she bade them hide behind a great post at the gable end, and beneath the Kettles of Hymer; because, as she warned them, the giant was wont to give ill treatment to strangers who came nigh to his dwelling.

At nightfall Thor and Tyr heard a mighty shout which was raised by the giant's servants. Whereat Hymer entered, carrying the whales he had caught. His long beard was white with hoar frost.

"Welcome art thou, indeed, O Hymer," his wife said. "My son, for whom I have long waited, has come to thy hall, and with him is one who is an enemy of the giants and a friend of men. Behind yonder gable post have they with cunning concealed themselves."

Hymer was ill-pleased, and he turned fiercely towards the post, which suddenly went to pieces before his piercing gaze. Thereat the beam above it broke, and the Kettles fell down. Seven of them were thus broken, but one was so large and so strong that it was left whole, although it sank deep in the floor.

Forth then came Tyr and Thor. The giant had no pleasure in receiving them, but he bade them be seated at his table.

A great feast did he cause to be prepared. Three oxen were slain and roasted, and placed before the giant and the gods. Two of these did Thor eat, for he sought great strength. If the giant was angry before, he was still more angry when the meal was ended, for it was his purpose to slay his guests, as was his wont, if they failed to eat an equal share with him; but in this he was indeed thwarted.

"Extravagant is our fare," Hymer growled in his displeasure; "on the morrow we must eat of fish."

Then to bed went they all, and sound was their sleep throughout the night.

At dawn Thor rose, and from the window he perceived that the giant was making ready his boat to go fishing. Hastily did the Asa-god dress himself. He placed his great hammer in his belt. He went towards the shore, and then he besought the giant to allow him to row with him in the great boat.

Hymer looked down upon him with contempt, and said: "Too small and frail art thou to be of help to me; besides, I row so far and stay at sea so long, that thou wouldst be chilled to death."

Thor answered: "I shall row as far as thou hast need of me, as far from land as is thy desire. Nor am I certain which of us twain would wish to return first."

The thunder-god was filled with wrath against the ice-giant because of his presumption, and was minded to strike him down with his hammer; but he remembered that he had need of all his strength elsewhere, and must not do aught to lessen it.

"What bait hast thou for me?" asked Thor.

Hymer answered with surly voice: "If thou wouldst fish, find thine own bait."

That Thor did with impatience. He hastened towards the giant's herd of great cattle, and seizing the largest bull, named Himinbrjoter, which signified "sky-cleaver", he snatched off its head and carried it towards the shore. Hymer watched him and received him in silence, and together they entered the boat and put to sea.

Both then seized the great billow-raising oars. At the bow rowed Hymer, and Thor was aft. So strongly did the Asa-god pull that the boat went through the water with great swiftness, whereat the giant was amazed. Endeavour as he might, putting forth his utmost strength, Hymer could not pull with half the strength of the Asa-god, who was still in youthful guise.

The giant at length grew weary, and when they reached the grounds where he was wont to catch flat fish, he bade his companion cease rowing. But that Thor refused to do.

"We have not yet," he said, "gone far enough to sea."

Soon they came to the grounds where whales are caught, and again the giant bade Thor to take rest, but he would not consent to do so.

"We must needs," Thor said, "go much farther yet."

Farther and farther out to sea they rowed with exceeding great speed. Then was the cold heart of Hymer filled with sharp alarm.

"If we stop not now," he cried, "we shall be in danger of the dread Midgard serpent."

But Thor refused to pause, and rowed stronger and faster than before. Not once nor twice did Hymer, resting wearily on his oars, remonstrate with him, but in vain. Far out to sea the boat still sped, and rapid and strong were the oarsweeps of Thor. Nor did he pause until they were a great distance from land.

Then began the fishing. Hymer baited his hooks, and cast his line in the deep waters. Ere long he caught two great whales, and hauled them aboard. His eyes were bright with pleasure, and he turned towards Thor and challenged him to do as well.

Then did the great thunder-god get ready his fishing tackle, which was of great strength. An immense hook he baited with the head of Hymer's bull. Into the deep waters he flung his line, which, as it splashed, raised big billows, and he ran it out until the bait was dragged along the floor of the ocean.

Now right below the giant's boat lay the Midgard serpent, all slimy and horrible, on the sea bottom, with its mouth clutching the tail of its world-encircling body. When that great monster beheld the bait it was deceived, not perceiving that Thor's hook was within. Greedily it seized the bull's head and sought to devour it. Then did the great hook sink deep into its throat and stick there. Tortured was the serpent with terrible agony, and it began to writhe violently to be free; but its struggle was without avail. So the line it tugged fiercely to draw angler and boat beneath the waves.

But greater than the serpent's was the strength of Thor. With both hands the god grasped the line, and against the side of the boat he placed his feet and began to pull, twisting the line round the oar pins as he did so, and now and again making it fast. Violently rocked the boat, and the waves rose high, as the great Midgard serpent struggled with the thunder-god.

But Thor put forth his entire divine strength and he grew in stature as he pulled the line. At length his feet went through the boat's side, as it tilted over, and they reached to the ocean floor. Harder and harder he pulled, and unwillingly the serpent, stung with fierce pain, was hauled through the deep, until its monstrous head came in sight.

Awesome was the spectacle to Hymer, nor can words picture it. With fierce wrath did the thunder-god dart fiery looks at the serpent, while the great monster tossed on high its terrible head and spouted floods of venom upon him.

Hymer trembled with fear; his face was white as mountain snow. Scarce could he look upon the ferocious serpent, for ghastly it was, and bearded and venom-spotted. Great waves washed over the gunwale, and the giant feared that the boat would be swamped.

Still Thor struggled with the fierce monster until he dragged its head close to the edge of the boat. Then, twisting the line round the oar pin, he seized his great hammer and struck a mighty blow on the serpent's head.

The mountains shook with thunder, the caves howled loud, the ocean trembled with violence, and the whole world shrank together, but the Midgard serpent was not yet killed.

Thor prepared to strike another great blow, but Hymer in his fear cut the line, whereat the writhing monster sank back into the deep. The waves tossed high and the boat plunged with them.

Angrily Thor turned upon Hymer, and with his great right fist struck him a resounding blow. Headlong plunged the giant into the sea, but speedily and in great fear he scrambled back again into the boat. Yet if his fear of the serpent was great, no less was his fear of Thor.

Then set they to row back, and the boat went speedily. Thor spake not; he sat in sullen silence. Deep indeed was his wrath because he had slain not the serpent which ever threatened the gods in Asgard.

When the shore was reached the giant leapt out. Proudly he flung the two whales over his shoulder. But Thor carried the great boat, and went with it to the giant's stronghold.

They entered the castle. They sat down with Tyr

beside them. Ill at ease was the giant because of Thor's great deeds, and him did he challenge to perform another feat of strength. He brought forth a goblet, and asked him to break it. Without rising from his seat, Thor flung it violently against a post, which was shattered in pieces; but the goblet remained whole, and it was brought back to the giant, who smiled well content.

Then Tyr's mother, whispering to Thor, bade him fling the goblet at Hymer's forehead, which was harder than aught else there. Thor did that right speedily. He seized the goblet, and struck the giant with it midway between his eyes. Nor broken was the giant's head, although the goblet fell shivered into small pieces on the table before him.

"A great treasure have I lost," Hymer cried. "Hot was the drink that came from my strong goblet."

The giant's heart was filled with anger against Thor, and him he would fain put to shame. So he challenged the Asa-god once again.

"One feat of strength remains for thee yet to do, thou boastful one," cried Hymer. "Seize yonder great kettle and carry it forth from my dwelling."

Tyr rose eagerly and ran to lift the kettle, which the gods waited for in Ægir's hall; but in vain did he try to lift it. Twice he made endeavour without avail.

Then did Thor seize the kettle. He grasped it at the edge and shook it violently. Then he began to lift it. So heavy was it, and so great was the strength of Thor, that his feet went through the floor.

Hymer watched him with angry eyes, fearing he would take with him the great treasure. That was what Thor did, for he lifted the kettle first upon his shoulder and then upon his head, while the rings fell round his feet.

Then he darted outside, and Tyr went with him.

Nor did they stay to await the giant, but right speedily they hastened on their way. Thor took also with him Hymer's great boat.

A great distance did the gods journey through the wooded mountain recesses, and then behind them there rose a great clamour. Hymer was hastening in pursuit. From the rocky caverns his foul and strange-headed clan were issuing forth, and following fast as well. They bellowed like winter tempests, and from hill to hill cliff their voices rang. Trees groaned and were bowed down, and the earth shook.

Thor looked back, and when he beheld the host pursuing him he put down the boat and the kettle, and seized his hammer, Mjolner. That murderous weapon did he fling against the giants, and they were mowed down by it as oat straw is by a scythe. Not until he had slain all those who fled not did Thor swing high the boat and the kettle upon his shoulders, and with Tyr again pursue his way.

Elivagar they could not have crossed in safety had they not had Hymer's boat, for the waves ran high because of the violent writhings of the Midgard serpent as it lay wounded by hook and hammer on the rumbling floor of Ocean.

In due time did Thor reach the hall of Ægir with the great kettle of Hymer. Then was brewed sufficient ale for the feast of harvest-end, and host and guests were made merry.

But Thor rejoiced most because of the blow he had struck the great Midgard serpent. For thus was he avenged upon it for causing his shame in the dwelling of the giant Utgard-Loke, who had so cunningly deceived him. Of that, his most strange adventure, the tale must next be told.

# Thor's Fishing

On the dark bottom of the great salt lake
Imprisoned lay the giant snake,
With naught his sullen sleep to break.

Huge whales disported amorous o'er his neck;
Little their sports the worm did reck,
Nor his dark, vengeful thoughts would check.

To move his iron fins he has no power,
Nor yet to harm the trembling shore,
With scaly rings he is covered o'er.

His head he seeks 'mid coral rocks to hide,
Nor e'er hath man his eye espied,
Nor could its deadly glare abide.

His eyelids half in drowsy stupor close,
But short and troubled his repose,
As his quick heavy breathing shows.

Muscles and crabs, and all the shelly race,
In spacious banks still crowd for place,
A grisly beard, around his face.

When Midgard's worm his fetters strives to break,
Riseth the sea, the mountains quake;
The fiends in Naastrand merry make.

Rejoicing flames from Hecla's caldron flasn,
Huge molten stones with deafening crash
Fly out,—its scathed sides fire-streams wash.

The affrighted sons of Ask do feel the shock,
As the worm doth lie and rock,
And sullen waiteth Ragnarok.

To his foul craving maw naught e'er came ill;
It never he doth cease to fill;
Nath' more his hungry pain can still.

Upward by chance he turns his sleepy eye,
And, over him suspended nigh,
The gory head he doth espy.

The serpent taken with his own deceit,
Suspecting naught the daring cheat,
Ravenous gulps down the bait.

His leathern jaws the barbed steel compress,
His ponderous head must leave the abyss;
Dire was Jormungander's hiss.

In giant coils he writhes his length about,
Poisonous streams he speweth out,
But his struggles help him naught.

The mighty Thor knoweth no peer in fight,
The loathsome worm, his strength despite,
Now o'ermatched must yield the fight.

His grisly head Thor heaveth o'er the tide,
No mortal eye the sight may bide,
The scared waves haste i' th' sands to hide.

As when accursed Naastrand yawns and burns,
His impious throat 'gainst heaven he turns
And with his tail the ocean spurns.

The parched sky droops, darkness enwraps the sun;
Now the matchless strength is shown
Of the god whom warriors own.

Around his loins he draws his girdle tight,
His eye with triumph flashes bright,
The frail boat splits aneath his weight;

The frail boat splits,—but on the ocean's ground
Thor again hath footing found;
Within his arms the worm is bound.

Hymer, who in the strife no part had took,
But like a trembling aspen shook,
Rouseth him to avert the stroke.

In the last night, the vala hath decreed
Thor, in Odin's utmost need,
To the worm shall bow the head.

Thus, in sunk voice, the craven giant spoke,
Whilst from his belt a knife he took,
Forged by dwarfs aneath the rock.

Upon the magic belt straight 'gan to file;
Thor in bitter scorn to smile;
Mjolner swang in air the while.

In the worm's front full two-score leagues it fell;
From Gimle to the realms of hell
Echoed Jormungander's yell.

The ocean yawned; Thor's lightnings rent the sky;
Through the storm, the great sun's eye
Looked out on the fight from high.

Bif-rost i' th' east shone forth in brightest green;
On its top, in snow-white sheen,
Heimdal at his post was seen.

On the charmed belt the dagger hath no power;
The star of Jotun-heim 'gan to lour;
But now, in Asgard's evil hour,

When all his efforts foiled tall Hymer saw,
Wading to the serpent's maw,
On the kedge he 'gan to saw.

The sun dismayed, hastened in clouds to hide,
Heimdal turned his head aside;
Thor was humbled in his pride.

The knife prevails, far down beneath the main,
The serpent, spent with toil and pain,
To the bottom sank again.

The giant fled, his head 'mid rocks to save,
Fearfully the god did rave,
With his lightnings tore the wave.

To madness stung, to think his conquest vain,
His ire no longer could contain,
Dared the worm to rise again.

His radiant form to its full height he drew,
And Mjolner through the billows blue
Swifter than the fire-bolt flew.

Hoped, yet, the worm had fallen beneath the stroke,
But the wily child of Loke
Waits her turn of Ragnarok.

# CHAPTER XII

## The City of Enchantments

Loke flatters the Thunder-god—The Feast of Goats—Loke's Evil Design—Journey in Jotun-heim—Terror of the Night—The Great Giant Skrymer—How Thor was thwarted—The Three Blows with Mjolner—Utgard-Loke's Castle—The Giant's Challenge—Loke and Thjalfe are beaten —Thor and the Drinking Horn—The Great Cat—Thor wrestles with the Hag—He is put to Shame—Utgard-Loke's Revelation—The Ocean, the Midgard Serpent, and Old Age—Wrath of the Thunder-god.

THE Frost-giants were sending forth from Jotun-heim ice-cold blasts which blighted Midgard's fields and arrested all growth. Thor, the friend of man, was made wroth thereat, and he caused his swift goats to be yoked to his sublime chariot, for he was resolved to punish the Jotuns for their presumption and evil workings. To him came Loke and made flattering address, praising the thunder-god for his valour and good intentions. Thor took Loke with him because he had knowledge of the northern wastes they must needs traverse.

All day they journeyed from Asgard, and at nightfall they came to the dwelling of Orvandel-Egil on the banks of Elivagar, and fronting the mountains that fortalice icebound Jotun-heim. The fare which Orvandel set before them was meagre because of the plunder accomplished by the giants, so Thor slew his two goats, and when they were skinned he placed their flesh in a kettle.

The feast that was thus prepared was abundant, and

Thor invited Orvandel and his family to eat with Loke and himself, requesting them to throw each flesh-stripped bone into the skins of the goats.

It was Loke's desire to stir up enmity between Thor and Orvandel, who were fast friends, because at the house of the skilful archer did the thunder-god ever rest on his journeyings to and from Jotun-heim. The Evil One made Orvandel's son, Thjalfe, the instrument of his designs. To him Loke whispered at the feast that the marrow of the bones was of exceeding sweetness, and he constrained upon the lad to break open the thigh bone of a goat's hind leg.

Next morning Thor arose and took his hammer, Mjolner, which he waved over the skins filled with loose bones. Then did the great animals spring to life again, but one limped because a hind leg was broken. Thor was moved to immense wrath, and with black brows, and with knuckles that grew white as he clutched the handle of his hammer, he turned upon Orvandel, who was stricken with much fear. The house shook because of Thor's anger. But the evil designs of Loke were put to naught, for Thor consented to take for ransom-servants, Orvandel's son, Thjalfe, the swift runner, and his beauteous daughter, Roskva, the vivacious, and his love for them made stronger the bond of friendship between the thunder-god and Orvandel.

Leaving his chariot and goats behind, Thor went on his journey with Loke and Thjalfe and Roskva. Soon they came to a great mountain forest, and through its immense depths they wandered until night came on. Fleet-footed Thjalfe carried Thor's meat sack, but it was wellnigh empty because it was difficult to hunt the deer in that confusing forest.

In the darkness they all sought a dwelling in which

to rest, and ere long they found one. The door was exceedingly large, for it opened up the whole side of the house. Within there was a vast hall. Beyond were five long rooms like to mountain caves; but they entered them not. In the outer hall they prepared their couches and lay down to sleep.

In the middle of the night a great earthquake made the forest tremble, so that the house shook with much violence.

Then Thor arose and sought for his affrighted servants a place of greater safety. So they entered together the widest of the cave chambers in the vast house. Thor stood at the door on guard, with his great hammer in his hand, ready to strike down any fierce giant who would dare to enter. The others crept to the farthest end of the chamber, and, trembling greatly, again sought their couches.

Then was heard a rumbling and a roaring that continued long and then ceased awhile, but began again. It was a night of blackness and great terror.

At early dawn Thor went forth, for the clamour had not yet ended. He walked through the forest and found that a great giant lay sleeping on the ground. He snored as loudly as roars the outer sea, and his breath burst forth like wild gusts of tempest. Then did the Asa-gods realize from whence came the clamour which had filled the night with terror.

Around his waist Thor tightened his magic belt so that his great strength was increased, but as he grasped his hammer to strike, the mighty giant awoke, and rose hastily to his feet. High above Thor he towered, so that the thunder-god was filled with amaze at his great bulk and forgot to wield his hammer.

"What is thy name, O giant?" Thor asked.

"My name is Skrymer," was his answer, and he said: "Thine I need not ask, for I perceive thou art Asa-Thor."

Then the giant looked about him, and sneered: "But what hast thou done with my glove?"

Skrymer stretched forth his hand, and in the midst of the trees he found his glove and picked it up. Then with amazement did Thor perceive that it was the great dwelling in which, with his companions, he had found shelter for the night. The broad cave chamber into which they had crept was the thumb of the giant's glove.

Skrymer besought Thor to take him for his travelling companion through that vast country, and when the Asa-god gave his consent, the giant opened his meat sack and began to munch his morning feast. Thor and his companions did likewise in a place apart.

Now when they had finished their meals and were satisfied, Skrymer said they should put their food together. Thor was willing that such should be done, and the giant thrust all the provisions into his own meat sack, which he threw over his back.

All day long they travelled eastward with great speed, because of the rapid pace of the giant, and when darkness began to fall they rested under the branches of a vast and lofty oak tree. Skrymer said he was weary and must needs sleep, so he flung his meat sack to Thor, and bade him feast with his companions. But Thor found that the sack was bound so securely that he could not untie it. Each knot defied him; not one could he unloose; and struggle as he might, he was unable to slacken any portion of the cord.

Great wrath possessed the Asa-god because of the deceit which had been practised upon him; so, casting the sack from him, he sprang up and seized his hammer. He went swiftly towards the giant as he lay snoring heavily, and on his skull struck a mighty blow.

Skrymer awoke, and, rubbing his eyes, asked if a leaf had fallen down from the great oak. On Thor he gazed, and asked him if he had eaten his supper, and was ready for sleep.

Thor made answer gruffly that he was about to lie down, and went towards another tree. But there he found that it was not possible to get sleep, for Skrymer snored so loudly that the woods were shaken with tempest clamour.

Angrily rose the Asa-god, and hastening towards the giant he swung his great hammer and struck him flat on the forehead. So great was the blow that Mjolner sank down to the heft.

Skrymer awoke suddenly and growled: "What hath happened now to disturb my slumber? Did an acorn fall down from the branches? Is that thee, Thor, standing nigh me? How fares it with thee?"

"I have just awakened," was Thor's answer, as he turned, wondering greatly, and again lay down beneath his oak. But he sought not to sleep. He was resolved to be avenged on the giant for his deceit, and because his own rest was broken. As Thor lay there he was convinced that if he dealt but one more blow on the giant's skull he would kill him. So he remained watching and waiting until Skrymer would again fall to sleep. Ere dawn broke his opportunity came, for the giant's loud snoring once more made fearsome clamour in the forest.

Thor arose and tightened his strength-giving belt. His iron gloves he put upon his hands, and seized his mighty hammer. Then he went towards the giant and struck so great a blow that Mjolner was buried in one of his temples.

Skrymer sat up, rubbing his eyes. Then he stroked his chin in vacant wonder, and, seeing Thor beside him, said: "Do birds sit above me in the oak branches? Methinks that some moss from a bird's nest fell upon my forehead as I awoke. . . . So thou art also awake, O Thor. . . . The dawn has broken, and it is time to set forth upon your way, for a long journey lies before thee ere thou shalt reach the castle which is called Utgard (outer-ward). Whispers I have heard between thee and thy companions that ye regard me as one of no mean stature, but larger men shalt thou find when thou dost reach Utgard. . . . Wilt thou take from me good advice? When thou comest to Utgard, do not boast overmuch. The courtiers of Utgard-Loke, will not permit of boasting from such insignificant beings as are thou and thy companions. . . . If my advice is not pleasant to thee, O Thor, thou hadst better turn back; and, indeed, that is what thou shouldst do. . . . But if thou wouldst go farther, thy way lies eastward; mine is to the north, towards yonder high mountains. Fare thee well!"

When he had spoken thus, Skrymer flung his meat sack over his shoulder and vanished amidst the trees. Nor was it ever known whether or not Thor desired to meet with him again.

Thor and Loke went eastward upon their way, and with them went Thjalfe and Roskva. They journeyed until midday, when they came to a city in the midst of which was a great ice castle. So lofty were its towers that Thor and those with him had need to bend back their heads to survey it aright. They saw no one nigh to the castle, and its ponderous gate was shut and securely locked. In vain did Thor attempt to open it; but being anxious to gain admittance he crept between the bars. The others followed him. They then perceived that the palace door was wide open, and they entered together.

Round the hall many giants of immense stature were seated upon benches. No word was spoken nor greeting given, but Thor and his companions went past, and entering a wide room they stood before King Utgard-Loke in his high throne, and to him they made obeisance. A cold look gave the monarch, nor did he return their salutations. After a long pause he spake with a voice of keen scorn, saying:

"It would be wearisome to have tidings of your long journey. If I be not mistaken the greatest of the striplings who stand before me is the Asa-god Thor."

Upon Thor he gazed intently, and then addressing him, said: "It may be that thou art stronger than thou dost seem. What feats art thou able to perform? Thou must know that no one can remain here who cannot perform deeds which excel those of all other living beings."

Wroth was Thor and made no answer. But Loke spoke and said: "I know a great feat, and am ready to perform it. I can eat quicker than anyone else, and I am now an-hungered and ready to give proof of that against him who may be chosen to contend with me."

"If thou shalt do as thou sayest," Utgard-Loke said, "thou shalt perform a great feat indeed. Let us have trial of it without delay."

The king ordered Loge, one of his men, to come forward to compete with Asa-Loke.

A great trough of meat was prepared, and the two were seated—Loke at one end and Loge at the other.

Then they began to eat with great speed, nor did they falter until they met at the middle. To neither seemed the victory, until it was found that Loge had consumed the bones as well as the flesh, and the trough also, while Loke had eaten but the flesh. So the Asa-god was accounted beaten.

Utgard-Loke then addressed Thjalfe, and asked him what feat he was able to perform, and the young man answered that he was a swift runner. He offered to run a race with anyone whom the monarch would select.

"If thou dost win," Utgard-Loke said, "thou shalt indeed perform a wondrous feat. But come without, for thine opponent awaiteth thee."

The king left his throne, and together they all went to a fine racecourse that lay nigh to the castle walls.

A dwarf named Huge was called forth by Utgard-Loke. Thrice did he run with Thjalfe. At the first contest the dwarf ran so fast that he met the other as he turned back.

"Thou canst run well," the king said to Thjalfe, "but thou must needs be more nimble-legged if thou art to win this contest, for there is no swifter runner than Huge."

At the second trial Thjalfe went speedier, but he was a bowshot space behind the dwarf when that swift runner made pause.

"Indeed thou must needs have greater speed if thou wouldst win the race," said the king to Orvandel's son; "but another chance awaiteth thee. The third trial shall decide the contest."

Again the race was started; but if Thjalfe went swiftly there was more speed in the dwarf, for he reached the goal ere yet his opponent was halfway.

So was Thjalfe vanquished and put to shame.

Together they all returned to the hall, and the king, turning to Thor, asked him if he could perform any wonderful feats that day. The Asa-god made prompt answer and said: "I shall hold a drinking contest with anyone thou mayest select."

"First," said the king, "thy power must be tested."

To this condition Thor gave his ready consent.

Then came a cupbearer carrying an immense drinking horn, which he gave unto the Asa-god.

"He who trespasseth the laws of this place when at feast," the king said, "must needs drink from that horn. He who is a good drinker can empty it at a single draught. Some men, however, must make two attempts, but it is only the weakest who cannot exhaust it at the third trial."

Now Thor was tortured with exceeding great thirst after his long journey, and at first he deemed the horn not to be too large, although it had great length indeed. To his mouth he raised it, and drank deep, until his thirst was quenched; and he continued drinking until he was forced to cease and lower the horn. With great wonder he then perceived that the liquor seemed not to have diminished at all.

"Thou hast drunken well," the king said, "yet there is naught of which boast can be made. Had I been told that Thor would drink no more when in thirst I would not have believed it. But perhaps it is thy resolve to surpass thyself when thou shalt take the second draught."

Again did the Asa-god raise the horn with firm resolve to empty it. Ill-pleased was he with himself because he deemed he had drunk less than before. But that was not so, for when he had done his utmost the horn could be carried without spilling.

"Thou dost spare thyself indeed," the king exclaimed;

"but if thou art resolved to empty the horn thou must pull with greater strength at thy third trial. If more skill at this feat is not shown by thee, methinks," the king added with scorn, "thou shalt be accounted a lesser man here than thou seemest to be among the gods in Asgard."

Angry was Thor because of the words which Utgard-Loke spake, and a third time he seized the horn and put forth all his power to empty it; but long and deep as he drank, be seemed not to exhaust it any.

He laid it down, and then he perceived that the liquor was slightly lower than before.

"No further trial shall I make," he said, as he thrust the horn back to the cupbearer.

"Ha! thou'rt of less strength than we deemed thee to be," exclaimed Utgard-Loke, smiling grimly at the thwarted Asa-god. "Yet, mayhap, thou wouldst try another feat to prove thy power, although I am assured that thou shalt have no better success."

But Thor was ready for any other trial. "I shall contend with whom thou wilt," he said. "Although I have failed with the horn, yet can I assure thee that the draughts which I have taken would not be counted meagre in Asgard."

"There is a trivial game which we play betimes," the king said, "but I would not have asked thee to perform it, because among us here it is only an exercise for children. Yet as thou art, it seems, not of so great power as we deemed heretofore, thou hadst better try it. The game is merely to lift my cat from the floor."

As he spake, a big grey cat leapt forward and sat before the throne. Thor at once went towards it, and grasped it firmly, placing his hands under its body. Then he attempted to lift the cat, but it bent its great back, and although he put forth all his strength Thor could lift but one paw from the floor.

Knowing well that he could not do better, he made no further attempt.

"Thou hast failed, as I foresaw thou wouldst," the king said. "The cat is too large for Thor, who is weakly and small compared with the men of my race."

"Say what thou wilt," cried Thor, whose wrath was great because of the shame put upon him, "but I now challenge anyone here to wrestle with me whom ye call weakly and small."

Utgard-Loke looked calmly about him, and answered with chilling voice: "I see no one nigh me who would not deem it an unworthy thing to wrestle with Thor. . . . But let the old woman, my nurse, whose name is Elle, be called, and if Thor would perforce wrestle, let him try his strength against hers. Many a stronger man than he hath Elle thrown down."

Then came into the hall an aged woman, who was toothless and heavily wrinkled. Her back was bent, and she walked slowly. Utgard-Loke bade her wrestle with Thor.

There is little to tell. The firmer Thor clutched her the mightier she became; the stronger his grip, the more securely did she stand. The struggle was long and violent, and although Thor realized ere long that he could not overcome the Hag, his endeavour was to prevent her from casting him down. Yet was he at length unable to keep his footing, and he was brought to his knee.

Then did Utgard-Loke bid the wrestlers to cease, and walking forward he placed himself between them. To Thor he said: "Thou canst not ask now to wrestle with anyone else in the hall, for the hour is late and darkness is falling."

Nor did he seem to be eager that Thor should have further trial of skill.

At dawn of next day Thor and his companions arose and prepared to take their departure from the castle. Food and drink in plenty were placed before them, and they made hearty feast. Then went they to take leave of the king, and Utgard-Loke walked with them until they were without the gate of the city. Ere they bade one another farewell, the king asked Thor if he was satisfied with his journey and the results thereof, and whether there were any others among the Asa-gods who were stronger than he.

"I cannot deny," Thor said, "that great shame has been put upon me. But what pains me most is that thou shouldst call me a man of little account."

"Be not mistaken," the king said, "for we hold thee in greater account than thou dost deem. Now must the truth be told, seeing thou art no longer in the city which, if my will shall prevail, thou must never enter again. This I swear: if I had known that thy strength was so mighty thou shouldst never have been allowed to come through the castle gate. Nigh, indeed, didst thou bring me unto a great disaster.

"Thou mayest now know," the king continued, "that I have all along deceived thee greatly with my illusions."

Thor stared with much amaze at Utgard-Loke, who spake thus:

"First, it was I whom thou didst meet with in the forest. My meat sack thou couldst not unloose because I had bound it securely with a rope of iron, and thou couldst not discover how the cunning knots were devised.

"Thrice thou didst strike me with thy great hammer.

From any of these blows of thine I would have received speedy death, but thee I deceived by creating an illusion and placing betwixt thee and me a great rocky mountain, which thou didst cleave with thy blows. On thy way back thou shalt see it, and the three broad valleys thou didst make, for thrice thou didst cut it asunder.

"In my palace I did also deceive thee with illusions. Asa-Loke, like hunger, devoured speedily all that was placed before him; but his opponent Loge, who is Fire, consumed not only the food, but the bones also, and the trough.

"Huge the dwarf, with whom Thjalfe ran, is Thought. Swift indeed must the runner be who is more speedy than Thought.

"Then came thine own feats, O mighty Thor. When thou didst attempt to drain the horn, thou didst perform a feat so wonderful, that if I had not beheld it with mine own eyes I should ne'er have believed it to be possible. For the horn was long, and one end reached out to the sea, which thou didst not perceive, and the sea filled it. When thou dost come to the shore thou shalt realize how much thou hast made the sea to shrink, for thy great draughts have caused what men shall henceforward call the ebb.

"No less marvellous was thy struggle with the great cat. Much fear possessed us when we saw thee lift but a single paw from the floor, because the cat was no other than the Midgard serpent, which encircles the earth. So high didst thou lift him that his head reached unto heaven.

"Great indeed was thy feat also when thou didst contend against the old woman, my nurse. No man ever before prevailed so wrestling, nor shall any man ever again do as thou hast done, for Elle is Old Age,

and sooner or later she lays low all who await her
coming."

Still was Thor silent, for he was filled with great
wonder by reason of the things of which Utgard-Loke
spake to him.

"Now, O Thor," the king said, "we are about to
part. This must I say unto you. It were better that
we two should never again meet; but if thou shouldst
come against me any more I must needs defend myself
with illusions as I have already done, so that thou shalt
never seem to thyself to prevail."

When the king spake thus he vanished from before
the eyes of Thor and his companions.

Then was the thunder-god moved to great wrath,
because he had been deceived, and seizing his mighty
hammer he turned towards the city again to wreak his
vengeance upon Utgard-Loke and his people. But he
found that city and castle had vanished, and he beheld
nothing save a broad level plain.

So with his companions Thor then went gloomily on
his way, and pondering over what had happened he
resolved to combat with the Midgard serpent from
Hymer's boat. And of this adventure the tale has been
told, but of how Thor lost his great hammer and the
strange adventure that ensued, the story follows.

# CHAPTER XIII
## Thor in Peril

The Theft of Mjolner—Loke's Mission—Thrym demands Freyja—The Wrath of the Goddess—Thor disguised—Giant Bridegroom's Amaze—A Hungry Bride—The Hammer recovered—Vengeance of Thor—Loke in Geirrod's Castle—Plot to capture Thor—Grid intervenes—Vidar the Silent—Crossing Elivagar—The High Flood—Giant Maid is punished—Geirrod's Flaming Javelin—Thunder-god's Victory

Now there was a king of giants whose name was Thrym, and he desired to have Freyja, the beauteous Asa-goddess, for his bride. A deep plot he laid, nor did the gods become aware of it until a grievous misfortune befell Thor. He was returning with Loke from Jotun-heim, and together they lay down to sleep. In great wrath was the thunder-god when he awoke because he could find not his hammer, Mjolner. He grasped his red beard and shook it, and fear crept over him as he searched around and about, because without his hammer he was powerless to contend against the giants.

When the other awoke, Thor spoke to him, saying: "Listen to me, and I shall tell thee what is known not in heaven nor upon earth—Mjolner is stolen!"

Speedily they took flight towards high Asgard, and to the dwelling of Freyja went they. Thor spake abruptly, and said: "Wilt thou lend thy falcon-guise to me, for my hammer hath been stolen, and I would fain find it."

"Gladly shall I give it thee, O Thor," Freyja

answered, "even although it were made of silver; yea, if it were of fine gold thou wouldst have it without delay."

To Loke gave Thor the falcon-guise, and he flew speedily from Asgard to the northern coasts of distant Jotun-heim. Nor did he pause or stay until he reached a high mountain on which sat Thrym, king of giants, twisting bands of gold for his dogs, and anon smoothing the gold mane of his horse.

When he beheld Loke in falcon-guise he said: "How fare the gods, and how fare the elves? Why dost thou come alone unto these shores?"

Loke answered: "Ill fares it with gods and ill fares it with the elves. Hast thou hidden the hammer of Thor?"

Thrym answered boldly and with gladness: "I have indeed done so. Nine miles below the ground have I buried Mjolner. Nor shall it ever be recovered or returned unto Thor until I am given the goddess Freyja for my bride."

Having spoken thus he smoothed leisurely the golden mane of his fleet-footed steed, and Loke flew back towards Asgard.

Thor awaited him on the battlements, and when the falcon drew nigh he cried: "Hast thou indeed performed thy mission, O Loke? Tell me what thou knowest ere thou dost descend. What is spoken by one who sits is often of small worth. He who reclines is prone to utter what is untrue."

Loke answered and said: "I have discovered all that needs be known. Thy hammer hath been stolen by Thrym, King of Jotuns, and he hath buried it nine miles down below the mountains. Nor will he deliver it to thee again until Freyja is given him to be his bride."

Then Thor and Loke went unto Freyja and told her what the giant had said. Impatient, indeed, was the thunder-god, for he feared that if it became known to the Frost-giants that his hammer was lost they would fall upon Asgard and overcome the gods.

"Right speedily thou must don thy bridal attire, O Freyja," Thor exclaimed, "and together shall we hasten unto Jotun-heim."

Freyja was filled with anger, and as she raged she broke her flashing necklace that gave her great beauty. "A love-sick maid, indeed, I would be," she exclaimed, "ere I would hasten to King Thrym."

To the high Thingstead of Asgard went Thor, and the gods assembled there to hold counsel one with another and decide how the hammer should be recovered. To the hall Vingolf went the goddesses, to consult regarding the fate of Freyja.

In the Thingstead, Heimdal, the wise Van, the shining god, spake with foreknowledge and cunning, and thus he advised: "Let Thor be dressed in the bridal robes of Freyja, and let him also don her sparkling necklace, which gives its wearer great beauty. In a woman's dress let Thor go forth, with keys jingling at his waist. His hair must be pleated, and on his breast must be fixed great brooches."

But Thor made protest, and declared that the gods would mock him if he were attired in woman's dress. Ill-pleased was he with Heimdal's words. "Be silent, Thor," Loke exclaimed; "thou knowest well that if thy hammer is found not the Frost-giants will come speedily hither and build over Asgard a dome of ice."

The other gods spake likewise, and Thor consented to be attired as a bride. When this was done, Loke was dressed, at his own desire, as a maid attendant, and together they went forth from Asgard in Thor's sublime car. The mountains thundered and fire swept from the heavens over Midgard as Thor journeyed to Jotun-heim.

Thrym was sitting on the mountain top, and to the Jotuns about him he spoke, when he beheld Thor in female-guise coming nigh, saying: "Arise, O giants! let the feast be spread, for Freyja comes hither to be my bride."

Then were driven before him into his yard his red cows with golden horns, and his great black oxen.

"I have great wealth indeed," the king exclaimed; "all that I desire is mine. I lack naught save Freyja."

The feast was made ready, and at the board sat Thor, whom Thrym deemed to be Freyja, and Loke, who was "maid attendant".

Thor had great hunger, and he ate an ox, eight salmon, and all the sweets which had been made ready for the giantesses. Then he drank three great barrels of ancient mead.

Wondering, Thrym sat and watched him. Then he cried: "Hath anyone ever beheld a bride so hungry? Never have I known a maid who ate as Freyja hath eaten, or a woman who ever drank so great a quantity of mead."

Loke, the cunning one, fearing that Thor would be discovered, said: "For eight days hath Freyja fasted, so greatly did she long to come unto Jotun-heim."

Thrym was well pleased to hear what Loke said, and he rose and went towards Thor. He lifted the veil he wore and sought to kiss, but he shrank back suddenly. Indeed he retreated to the hall end, where he cried: "Why are the eyes of Freyja so bright and so fierce? They seem to glow like hot embers."

Then spake cunning Loke again, and said: "Alas!

O Thrym, for eight nights Freyja hath slept not, for she longed to be here with thee in Jotun-heim. Thus are her eyes a-fire."

Thrym's sister then entered, and she went towards Thor humbly and with due respect, and asked to be given golden bridal rings from his fingers.

"Thou shalt gift them to me," she said, "if thou desirest to have my friendship and my love."

But naught did she receive from the angry and impatient god of thunder.

Thrym then desired that the wedding ceremony should be held, but Loke asked that as proof of his friendship, and to complete the bargain the giant had made, Thor's hammer should be laid upon the maiden's lap.

Then did Thrym order that Mjolner be lifted from its hiding place deep in the bowels of the earth.

In Thor's heart there was great laughter when Thrym spoke thus, yet was his mind solemn, and he waited anxiously until Mjolner was laid upon his knees.

A servant came forward with it, and Thor clutched the handle right eagerly. Then he tore off the bridal veil from his face and the woman's dress from about his knees, and sprang upon King Thrym, whom he killed with a single blow. Around the feasting board he went, slaying the guests, nor one would he permit to escape from the hall, so fierce was he with long-restrained wrath.

Thrym's sister, who had begged from Thor the bridal rings, he slew with the others. A blow she received from the hammer instead of golden treasure.

Cunning Loke watched with pleasure the devastation accomplished by the fierce thunder-god as he raged round the hall and through the castle, wreaking his fierce vengeance on the whole clan of Thrym.

Then together hastened they to where the goats were bound at the home of Orvandel, nor did they pause to rest. Across the heavens was speedily driven the black sublime car. Swiftly o'er mountain and sea it went, blotting out the sparkling stars. Mountains thundered and the wide ocean trembled with fear as the car rolled on. The earth was filled with fire.

Thus did Thor return in triumph unto Asgard, because Mjolner was recovered and the King of Mountain Giants was slain.

But although Loke had served Thor well when his hammer was stolen by Thrym, there came a time when he brought the god of thunder nigh to great misfortune. It was in the days ere the winter war was waged between the Asa-gods and the sons of Ivalde, and the cunning artisans were yet friendly with the dwellers in Asgard.

Loke had gone forth in the falcon-guise of Freyja to pry round Jotun-heim, and especially the castle of King Geirrod, whose daughter he desired for a bride. He flew towards a window, and sat in it while he listened to the words that were being spoken, and surveyed the guests who were there. A servant beheld him with curious eyes, and perceived that he was not a real falcon. So, making cautious approach, he seized Loke and brought him before the king. The eyes of the falcon were still the cunning eyes of Loke, and he was recognized by Geirrod, who demanded ransom ere he would release him. In vain did Loke endeavour to escape. He flapped his wings, he pecked with his beak, but the servant held his claws securely.

Silent was he before Geirrod, and no answer would he make when he was addressed. So to punish him the giant locked him in a chest, in which he was kept for three months. Then was Loke taken forth, and ready indeed was he to speak. To Geirrod he confessed who he was, and the giant constrained him to promise, by swearing a binding oath, that he would bring Thor to Jotun-heim and unto that strong castle without his hammer or his belt or his iron gloves. For greatly sought the giant to have the thunder-god in his power.

Loke then flew back to Asgard, and with great cunning he addressed Thor, so that he secured his consent to visit the castle of Geirrod without taking with him his hammer and gloves and his strong belt. For Loke assured Thor that the castle stood on a green and level plain, and that they were invited to attend together a feast of friends.

Thor set forth, and Loke went with him. All day they travelled on their way until they came to the borders of Elivagar in Alf-heim, where dwelt the sons of Ivalde.

There dwelt also in that realm and in the midst of a deep wood a giantess who was friendly towards the gods. Her name was Grid. She was the mother of Odin's son Vidar, the Silent One, whose strength was so mighty that none save Thor was his equal. A great shoe he had; its sole was hard as iron, for it was formed of the cast-off leather scraps of every shoe that was ever made. This son of Grid was born to avenge his father's death. When Odin is slain at Ragnarok, then shall Vidar combat with the wolf Fenrer and tear its jaws asunder. Nor shall Surtur destroy him with his firebrands, for the wood-god perishes never in Nature's deep solitudes.

Now Grid, mother of Vidar, had power to work magic spells, and she possessed a magic rowan wand which was named Gridarvold. When she beheld Thor going unarmed towards Geirrod's castle, she warned him that the giant was as cunning and treacherous as a wolf-dog, and dangerous to meet without weapons. So to Thor she gave her magic staff, her belt of strength, and her iron gloves, and when he set out he took with him the sons of Ivalde. Together they travelled in safety until they came to Vimur, which is the greatest of the rivers Elivagar. The clouds drove heavily above them, and hailstones fell around. Wild and mountainous was the country which Loke had said was green and level. There were swift and treacherous eddies in the swollen waters.

But Thor put on the belt of strength which Grid had given him, and in his hand he took her magic staff. Rapidly did the river rise as he entered it with his men. From the mountains icy torrents poured down with increasing strength, and the sons of Ivalde were soon in great peril. They thrust their spears into the shingle as they tried to ford the river, and the clinking of the steel mingled with the sharp screams of the waters. When they were but halfway across a high wave burst out from a great mountain torrent, and the waters rose to Thor's shoulder. The others were swept down towards him ; for, perceiving their peril and desiring to be a protection to them, he had chosen the deepest part through which to wade. Orvandel leapt upon Thor's shoulder, and there stood, bending his bow. Loke and the others clung to the belt of Grid, which was about Thor's body. Towards the bank the thunder-god laboured, and when he came nigh to it he beheld at the torrent's source a daughter of Geirrod, whose name was Gjalp. It was she who, standing high on the hillside, caused the river to increase so that Thor and his followers might be drowned. The angry god seized a boulder and flung it towards her. Sure was his aim, for it struck her heavily, so that her back was broken.    Thus was the Hag overcome and the torrent stayed.

Then did Thor seize a rowan-tree branch which overhung the river, and with its aid he pulled himself up the bank.    Thus had its origin the ancient proverb: " Thor's salvation, the rowan ".

Up the steep mountain did the thunder-god climb with all his men.    Against them came the giants who sought to destroy Ygdrasil, " the World-tree ".    Bravely fought Thor, and the arrows of Orvandel sped fast until the horde of giants were put to flight.    Speedily did the heroes follow them.    They pressed onward and reached Geirrod's castle amidst the clamour and the howling of the storm-giants and the giants that dwell within the caves of the mountains.

When Thor entered Geirrod's hall the giant king cast at him a red-hot flaming javelin from behind a great pillar of wood.    But with Grid's iron gloves Thor caught it, and past Orvandel's head he flung it back, so that it went through the pillar and through Geirrod, who was slain ; and it passed through the wall of his castle ere it sank deep into the earth.

Then loudly thundered the din of battle in Geirrod's hall, which was shaken to its foundations.    With slings and boulders did the giants contend, but from Thor and his men they received their deathblows.

Thus was Geirrod and his clan overcome in dread conflict ; but no less terrible was the battle which Thor waged against Hrungner, the stone-giant, the tale of which now follows.

## Thor

I am the god Thor,
I am the war god,
I am the Thunderer!
Here in my Northland,
My fastness and fortress,
Reign I forever!

Here amid icebergs
Rule I the nations;
This is my hammer,
Mjolner, the mighty
Giants and sorcerers
Cannot withstand it!

These are the gauntlets
Wherewith I wield it
And hurl it afar off;
This is my girdle,
Whenever I brace it
Strength is redoubled!

The light thou beholdest
Stream through the heavens,
In flashes of crimson,
Is but my red beard
Blown by the night-wind,
Affrighting the nations.

Jove is my brother;
Mine eyes are the lightning;
The wheels of my chariot
Roll in the thunder,
The blows of my hammer
Ring in the earthquake!

Force rules the world still,
Has ruled it, shall rule it;
Meekness is weakness,
Strength is triumphant;
Over the whole earth
Still is Thor's-day!

—*Longfellow*

# CHAPTER XIV

## The Great Stone Giant

Odin in Jotunheim—Two Swift Steeds—Race to Asgard—The Boastful Giant—His Challenge to Thor—An Island Duel—The Clay Giant—A Lightning Conflict—Thor is wounded—His Son Magni rescues Him—Groa's Incantation—Story of Orvandel's Rescue—The Spell is broken—Odin as the Ferryman—How he taunted Thor—A Divine Comedy.

THOR was in the east battling against the Trolls when Odin went forth from Asgard towards the dwelling of Hrungner, the great stone giant of Jotun-heim.

Hrungner watched him coming through the air in splendour and beauty, and he cried: "Who cometh towards me? On his head is a helmet of gleaming gold. He rides over ocean and high upon the air. Swift indeed is his mighty steed."

Ere the giant was silent the ruler of Asgard was nigh to him, and he spake proudly. "In all Jotun-heim," Odin said, "there is not a horse that is Sleipner's equal."

Then twitching the reins, he turned Sleipner back towards Asgard, and he rode swifter than the wind.

"Thy steed is fast indeed," the giant bellowed, "but my nimble-footed Goldfax (gold mane) hath greater stride."

As he spake, Hrungner leapt upon his horse's back and set out in swift pursuit of the Asa-god. But although he urged Goldfax to hasten, he could not win nigh unto Odin. Yet would the giant pause not in his speedy flight, for his heart was afire with ambition to prevail over the rider of Sleipner. Swiftly indeed he rode, and ere he was aware he found himself entering the gates of Asgard over the gate-bridge which had been set down for Odin.

By the gods was he received with hospitality as he demanded. They took him to the great feasting hall, and there he drank ancient mead and sweet. The bowls from which Thor was wont to refresh himself were placed before him, and Freyja filled them. Each of the bowls the giant emptied in turn at a single draught. Indeed, so much did he drink that the mead surged in his veins and his eyes rolled with redness, for he was made drunk. Then was his tongue unloosened, and he gave forth loud boastings.

"Valhal," he cried, "shall be mine. . . . The warrior's hall must I carry away with me to Jotun-heim."

More mead did Freyja pour out to him, filling the bowls of Thor.

Then Hrungner boasted that he would bring utter ruin to Asgard, and cast down its wall and palaces. . . .

"The gods," he cried, "and all that are within the city shall I slay save Freyja and Sif."

As Freyja filled the bowls he said: "Ha! all the mead in Asgard I must consume this day. None shall I leave for the gods."

Weary grew the gods of the braggart giant and his vain boastings, and Thor they named. . . . Immediately Thor was in their midst. Black were the brows of the thunder-god when he beheld Hrungner; white were his knuckles as he clutched his great hammer.

"Who hath permitted this Jotun," Thor roared, " to drink the mead of Asgard? Why doth Freyja pour it forth to him as if she were honouring a feast of gods?"

Evil was in Hrungner's eyes as he scowled at Thor.
"By Odin's wish am I here," he sneered, "and under his
protection I remain."

"When thou dost seek to go forth," Thor growled
sullenly, "thou mayest regret the invitation."

"Unarmed have I come," Hrungner protested with
sudden alarm, "and of little honour would it be to thee,
O Asa-Thor, if thou didst slay me now. If thou
wouldst fain put thy valour to proof, thee I dare to
contend against me on the borders of my kingdom."

Thor cast at him defiant eyes, and the giant was
troubled. "Alas!" he cried; "I have done foolishly
to come hither, leaving my stone shield and my flint
weapon in Jotun-heim. Were I armed, we might well
fight. This shall I say unto thee, O Asa-Thor: I would
brand thee as a coward if thou didst seek to slay me
undefended. . . . I challenge thee to contend with me
in an island duel."

Now never before had Thor been challenged thus.
For the island duel (Holmgang) which Hrungner desired
was fought by dealing blow for blow, and the Asa-god
would have the right to strike first because he was challenged by the other. In the contest each would have
a shieldbearer. His consent did Thor give to the giant's
terms, and in silence they parted.

Through Jotun-heim the duel challenge was gravely
debated by the giants, and keen was their desire that
Thor should be worsted, because Hrungner was their
strongest and greatest warrior, and they feared that if he
fell the thunder-god would do them more injury than
heretofore.

On an island on the borders of rocky Grjottungard.
where Hrungner had his dwelling, the Jotuns made a
giant of clay who was in height nine miles, and three

in breadth between the shoulders. Him they called Mokker-kalfi (Mist-wader), and they gave him a mare's heart. He was shieldbearer to Thor's enemy.

Now Hrungner had a heart of stone; his head was of stone also. Broad and thick was his stone shield, and in his right hand he grasped his great flint weapon, which he swung over his shoulder. A terrible combatant was Hrungner.

To the island duel did Thor set forth. His shield-bearer was his faithful Thjalfe, son of Orvandel, who ran swiftly to the place of combat. To Hrungner he cried:

"Although thy shield is held in front, thou dost stand unprotected, for Thor cometh to attack thee from the earth beneath."

Then did Hrungner cause his shield to be cast down. Defiantly he stood upon it, while with both hands he grasped his great flint weapon.

In fear and trembling was Mokker-kalfi. His mare's heart quaked within him because Thor was coming, and sweat ran from his body in torrents.

Thunder broke forth and lightning flashed before Hrungner. Then he beheld rushing swiftly towards him the black-browed thunder-god, who swung his hammer to strike. Nor did Hrungner wait till he was nigh. He raised his great flint weapon and flung it with might against Mjolner, which Thor, divining his purpose, hurtled simultaneously. In mid-air the weapons met and flashed forking fire that rent the heavens and covered the ocean with flame. The flint was utterly shattered. On the ground fell a portion, and there to this day are the flint hills, and a great splinter pierced the forehead of the Asa-god, so that he was thrown down.

Meanwhile the sublime hammer smote Hrungner and crushed his skull, and he fell also. The giant's foot struck Thor and lay heavily upon his neck, so that he could not rise to his feet.

On the affrighted Mokker-kalfi had Thjalfe flung himself, and him he overcame right speedily. Then ran he to help Thor, but in vain he strove to lift Hrungner's foot from his neck. . . . He named the Asa-gods, and they hastened from Asgard to the place of combat. When they found that Thor was cast down, they put forth their strength to free him, but unable were they to lift the giant's foot.

Then came Thor's son, Magni, whose mother was Jarnsaxa, the iron-crusher of the World-mill. He was but three nights old, but had already exceeding great strength. The giant's foot he seized and flung it from his sire's neck, saying:

"Alas! I should have come sooner. Hrungner's head would I have broken with my fist!"

Thor leapt up, and his arms he threw about his son, embracing him with great love.

"To thee, O Magni," he said, "I shall give Goldfax, Hrungner's great steed."

But Odin was ill-pleased with Thor, and to him he said: "Thou hast done wrong to give unto a Hag's son the speedy horse of the giant. 'Twere better if thou hadst gifted it to thy sire."

In wrath he turned away with the gods of his clan, and went towards Asgard.

Now the day of the great island duel was long ere the time when the sons of Ivalde waged the winter war against the Asa-gods. As Thor returned towards Orvandel's dwelling, his resting place on the borders of Jotun-heim, where he was wont to leave his swift, strong goats and his sublime car, he met with Orvandel, who was in great peril. The elfin archer had gone forth to fight against the Frost-giants, but with ill success as it proved, for they pressed nigh to him and sought to take him captive.

Thor rescued his friend speedily, and placed him in the meat basket, which he carried on his shoulders, as he waded through deep Elivagar. Orvandel thrust a toe through a hole, and a spell was put upon it by the giants, so that it was frozen. Then did Thor snap it off and fling it high in the heavens, where it became a bright star, which unto this day is called " Orvandel's Toe ". Thus it was that the elfin archer (Avo) became a star hero.

When he parted with Orvandel, Thor yoked his goats, and in his sublime car he hastened towards his dwelling in Thrud - Varg. In grievous pain was he because of the wound which Hrungner had given him. Deep in his forehead was the flint flake embedded. In vain did Sith seek to alleviate his sufferings.

Now gentle Groa, Orvandel's wife, was dwelling in Thor's stronghold, as was her wont when her husband went forth against the Frost-giants. She had the power to work magic spells. She who was the " elf of growth " could make rocks to move, and she had power to arrest the turbulent floods. It was Groa who restored to strength those whom the Frost-giants had wounded, and it was she who gave beauty again to the places which they laid waste.

Unto Thor she came to heal his wound, and take from his forehead the splintered flint which stuck fast there. Incantations she sang over him. First she charmed away the pain which afflicted the god. Then the stone quivered and grew loose.

The heart of Thor leapt within him when he perceived that Groa would give him healing, and he was consumed with desire to reward her, and to gladden her heart without delay. So ere she sang further, he spake and she was silenced.

Of Orvandel's peril Thor gave Groa tidings, and of how he had rescued the elf from the power of the Frost-giants who encompassed him about. With joy was Groa's heart filled, but the spell she wrought was broken, and the memory of the magic song passed away. Thus was she unable to take from Thor's forehead the splintered flint, and there it ever remained because of his impatience to give premature reward.

So there was ever after weakness in Thor. Nor must mortal fling across his dwelling a flint weapon, lest the stone in the Asa-god's forehead be shaken, for then he would have suffering, and be moved to wrath against an offender.

Great were the deeds of Thor, which brought security to gods and men, for by him were the giants driven back and their power suppressed. Unto him, therefore, was willing service at all times rendered.

But there fell a day when Odin went forth from Asgard and towards the east. He saw Thor coming out of Jotun-heim, and sought to mock him so that he might have mirth.

Elivagar ran deep, and Odin waited on the opposite shore in the guise of Greybeard, the ferryman. Thor called upon him, but Odin refused to cross, whereat there rose a dispute between them. The valour of Thor did Odin question, and his feats belittle. With scornful laughter, too, did he receive the angry threatenings of the thunder-god.

"Nimble is thy tongue," cried Thor, "but it would help thee little if I waded across to thee. Louder than the wolf thou wouldst howl if I struck at thee with Mjolner."

"Better wouldst thou be engaged," Odin answered, "if thou didst hasten home; because there is one there whom Sif loves better than thee."

Thor was wroth. "Well dost thou know," he cried, "that thy cruel words sting me. A coward art thou who speakest what is untrue."

Odin answered: "Truly I speak indeed. . . . Thou art tardy in returning. Why art thou lingering on thy way? 'Twere better if thou hadst set forth on thy journey at early morn."

"'Tis thou who delayest me, villain," Thor answered wrothfully.

Odin smiled. "Can one of so little account as I am," he said, "delay the journey of the great Asa-god Thor?"

"Cease thy bantering," cried Thor; "hasten hither with thy boat, and thou shalt have the friendship of the sire of Magni."

"Begone!" cried Odin. "I shall not cross thee."

Then said Thor, with pleading voice: "Show me the ford then, since thou wilt not come over."

Odin wagged his head. "That is easy to refuse," he said. "The way is long. Thou canst go a little way this direction, and a little way in that; then thou canst turn to thy left till thou dost reach No-man's-land. There wilt thou meet thy mother, who shall guide thee unto Odin's land."

"Can I go thither to-day?" Thor asked.

Odin answered: "By sunrise, if thou dost travel quickly, thou mayest get there."

"Mocker," exclaimed Thor, "our talk is ended! Thou hast denied me crossing this day, but by the holy waters of Leipter, I swear that I shall reward thee indeed when next we meet."

Odin smiled : "Begone !" he cried ; "and may demons seize thee."

Then took Thor his departure in great wrath, nor did he ever discover again the ferryman Greybeard who had mocked him and put him to shame.

# CHAPTER XV
## Balder the Beautiful

The Summer Sun-god—Blind Hodur—Nanna the Brave—The Light Battles—A Dread Omen—Balder's Dreams—Frigg's Alarm—World Vows taken—Odin descends to Hela—The Vala invoked—Her Prophecies—Loke's Evil Design—The Mistletoe Arrow of Pain—Balder is killed—Hermod's Mission—The Funeral of the God—Odin whispers—Hermod in Hela—Urd's Decree—World Tears—Hag seals Balder's Fate.

BALDER THE BEAUTIFUL was the most noble and pious of the gods in Asgard. The whitest flower upon earth is called Balder's brow, because the countenance of the god was snow-white and shining. Like fine gold was his hair, and his eyes were radiant and blue. He was well loved by all the gods, save evil Loke, who cunningly devised his death.

Balder, the summer sun-god, was Odin's fairest son; his mother was Frigg, goddess of fruitful earth and sister of Njord. His brother was blind Hodur. On Balder's tongue were runes graven, so that he had great eloquence. He rode a brightly shining horse, and his ships, which men called "billow falcons", were the sunbeams that sailed through the drifting cloudways. For wife he was given Nanna, the moon maid, the brave one who fought with him the light battles. On a bright horse she rode also, and tender was she and very fair.

There came a time when Odin and Balder went forth to journey through a wood. A dread omen forewarned them of disaster, because the leg was sprained of Balder's

146

horse — the horse from whose hoofmarks bubbled forth clear wells. Charms were sung over the sun-god by Nanna and by her fair sister Sunna, the sun maid. Frigg also sang, and then Fulla her sister. Odin uttered magic runes to protect him from evil.

But soon after Balder began to languish. The light went from his eyes, care sat on his forehead, and melancholy were his lips. To him came the gods beseeching to know what ailed him, and he told that nightly he dreamed fearsome dreams which boded ill, and revealed to him, alas! that his life was in dire peril.

Now Frigg, who had fore-knowledge of all things save Balder's fate, sent forth her maid-servants to take oaths from all creatures living, from plants and metals, and from stones, not to do any hurt unto the god Balder. To her, in due time, the maidens returned, and she received from them the compacts and vows that were given. All things promised to spare him, save the mistletoe, slender and harmless, from which no vow was asked, for it clung, as was its need, to a strong tree for protection. Then was Frigg's heart filled with comfort, and no longer did she fear the fate of her noble son.

But the heart of Odin was filled with foreboding. He mounted his horse Sleipner, and went over Bif-rost towards the north, and descended unto darksome Nifel-hel, where dwelt the spirits of the great giants who were crushed in the World-mill. On the borders of Hela, as he rode speedily, a great and fierce hel-dog came after him. There was blood on its breast, and in the darkness it barked loudly. When it could go no farther, it howled long with gaping jaws.

Over a long green plain went Odin, while the hoofs of Sleipner rang fast and clear, until he came to a high dwelling, the name of which is Heljar-ran, of which the keeper is Delling, the Red Elf of Dawn. Therein have their Hela-home the fair Asmegir—Lif and Lifthraser and their descendants who shall come at Time's new dawn that shall follow Ragnarok to regenerate the world of men.

To the eastern gate went Odin, where he knew there was the grave of a Vala (prophetess). Dismounting from Sleipner, he chanted over her death chamber strange magic songs. He looked towards the north; he uttered runes; he pronounced a spell, and demanded sure response. Then rose the Vala, and from the grave chamber her ghostly voice spake forth and said:

"What unknown man cometh to disturb my rest? Snow has covered me in its deeps; by cold rains have I been beaten and by many dews made wet. . . . Long indeed have I lain dead."

Odin answered: "My name is Vegtam and my sire was Valtam. Tell me, O Vala," he cried, "for whom are the benches of Delling's hall strewn with rings, and for whom are the rooms decked with fine gold?"

The Vala answered and said: "Here stands for Balder mead prepared, pure drink indeed. Over the cup shields are laid. Impatiently do the Asmegir await him and to make merry. . . . Alas! by compulsion hast thou made me to speak. . . . Now must I be silent."

Odin said: "Silent thou must not be until I know who shall slay Balder—who shall bereave Odin's son of life."

The Vala answered: "Hodur shall send his brother hither, for Balder shall he slay, and Odin's son bereave of life. . . . Alas! by compulsion hast thou made me speak. . . . Now must I be silent."

Odin said: "Silent thou must not be until I know

who shall avenge the deed on Hodur, who shall raise Balder's slayer on the funeral pyre."

The Vala answered: "A son, Vale, shall Rhind bear in the halls of Winter. He shall not wash his hands nor comb his hair until to the funeral pyre he beareth Balder's foe. . . . Alas! by compulsion hast thou made me to speak. . . . Now must I be silent."

Odin said: "Silent thou shalt not be until I know who are the maidens that sorrow and throw high their veils with grief. Sleep not until thou dost answer."

The Vala spake and said: "Thou art not Vegtam, as I deemed, but Odin, ruler of all."

Odin said: "No Vala art thou, but the mother of three giants."

Then cried the Vala: "Return, O Odin, unto Asgard. Never again shall I be called upon until Loke escapes from bonds and the world-devastating Dusk of the Gods is at hand."

To Asgard did Odin return; but there was no sorrow there nor foreboding, because of the vows which Frigg had taken from all creatures and all things that are, so that no harm might be done unto her fair son. And of this had the gods full proof. Balder they made to stand amidst a rain of javelins that harmed him not. Some flung at him stones, others smote him with their swords; yet was he not injured. Of Balder were they all proud because he was charmed against wounds. To honour him did they make fruitless attack on his fair body.

Evil there was in the heart of Loke, and in woman's guise he went unto Frigg, who spake and said: "Why do the gods thus assail my fair son Balder?"

Loke answered: "It is in sport they fling at him javelins and stones and strike him with swords, because they know full well that they can do him no hurt."

Frigg said: "By neither metal, nor wood, nor stone, can he be injured because of the world-vows which I have received."

"Have all things indeed sworn to protect Balder?" Loke asked with downcast eyes.

"All things save the mistletoe," answered Frigg; "and so slender and weak is the mistletoe that from it no vow was demanded."

Then Loke went from Frigg and plucked a mistletoe sprig, which he carried to a cunning elf-smith named Hlebard, whom he robbed of his understanding. With the mistletoe twig the smith shaped a magic arrow—a deadly arrow of pain. . . . Loke made haste with it to Asgard, and he went to the green place where the gods assailed Balder and made merry. He saw blind Hodur standing apart, and to him he went and spake thus:

"Why, O Hodur, dost thou not join the game and cast a missile at Balder also?"

"Alas!" cried Hodur; "am I not blind? I can see not my fair brother, nor have I aught which I can throw."

"Come and do honour unto Balder like the others," Loke urged him. "I shall give thee an arrow for thy bow, and hold thine arm so that thou mayest know where he stands."

Hodur then took from Loke the magic arrow which the elf-smith had made and placed it in his bow. Then raised he his left arm, while evil Loke took certain aim.

"Thou canst now share in the sport," said the Evil One unto the blind god, and went to a place apart.

The gods beheld Hodur standing with bent bow, and paused in their game. . . . Then did the arrow dart forth. . . . It struck Balder; it pierced his fair body, and he fell dead upon the sward.

*Loke and Hodur, from the sculpture by Qvarnström.*

*Fenrer, the wolf, with Tyr's hand.*

In horror, and frozen with silence, the gods stood around. . . . Where there had been joy and merrymaking, dumb grief prevailed. . . . Alone stood Hodur wondering and in mute amaze.

But ere long angry cries broke forth, and the gods sought to slay Death's blind archer; but the sward on which they stood was consecrated to peace, and unwillingly were their hands withheld.

Then a loud voice cried through Asgard: "Balder is dead! . . . . Balder the Beautiful is dead! . . . ."

Every voice was hushed and every face turned pale because of the disaster which had befallen the gods in that black hour.

Thereafter arose the sound of loud lamentations, and a tempest of grief swept over the Celestial City. Frigg wept in silence and alone. Odin grieved inwardly, and more than the rest he realized the great disaster which Balder's death would bring unto the Asa-gods.

The spirit of Balder descended to the Lower World and crossed the golden bridge over the River Gjoll.

The Asmegir in their gold-decked hall awaited him, for they desired that he should be their ruler until the dawn of the world's new age.

But Frigg would not suffer that Balder should remain in Hela. She went forth when the gods ceased to cry aloud in their sorrow and said:

"Who among thee hath longing to win my gratitude and my love? For such shall be given unto him who rideth to Hela to find Balder. It is my heart's desire, in this my hour of grief, that a great ransom be offered unto Urd, Queen of Death, so that she may permit my fair son to return unto me again."

Forth stepped Heimdal the Young. He was a messenger of the gods and a son of Odin. He spake forth and said: "Unto Hela shall I go, O Queen of Asgard, as thou desirest, to find Balder and to offer great ransom unto Urd, so that she may permit him to return unto thee once again."

Then was Sleipner taken forth for Hermod, who leapt nimbly into the saddle. Swift as the wind he went over the gate bridge, and through the air and across the seas he sped and descended unto Nifel-hel towards the north to search for Balder.

The gods bore Balder's body unto the bleak shore of Ocean, where lay his great ship, Hringhorn. On its deck they built a pyre covered with much treasure, and then they sought to launch it.

But that they were unable to do, because the keel stuck fast in the sand and would not be moved seaward. So they sent unto Jotun-heim for the storm-giantess, Hyrrokin, who was Angerboda, that ancient-cold Vala of the east, who sweeps wind-tossed ships into the very jaws of Æger. On a great wolf she came and the bridle was a writhing snake. She leapt on the beach and with disdain regarded the gods. To four giants were given the keeping of the wolf. Then went she to the ship and thrust it speedily into the sea. Fire blazed from the rollers and the earth shook.

Angry was Thor when he beheld the Hag, and he swung his hammer to strike her down; but him did the gods restrain, for they sought not bloodshed in that hour.

Then was Balder's body carried to the ship and laid upon the pyre, and his steed beside him. Beautiful was he in death. In white robes was Balder clad, and round his head lay a wreath of radiant flowers.

On the shore were gathered the gods and goddesses of Asgard. Odin was there, and he went first. His ravens hovered over the ship, and his wolf-dogs wailed. Beside him was wise Frigg, who was wont to spin golden cloud-threads from her jewelled wheel. Queen of Asgard was she and goddess of Maternal Love. She was robed in black who was erstwhile attired in cloudy whiteness; on her golden head were the heron plumes of silence; a golden girdle clasped her waist and on her feet were golden shoes. Tall was she and stately and surpassing fair.

Dark-browed Thor was nigh to Odin, and Brage and Tyr also. Njord, black-bearded, and clad in green, strode his stately way. With his golden-bristled boar came Frey, and Heimdal, horsed on Gulltop, shone fair as sunshine. Beauteous Freyja, veiled in tears, rode her chariot drawn by great cats, and fair Idun was there also, and Sith with harvest hair. Loke stood apart with tearless eyes.

The valkyries leaned on their spears. Frigg's maids were nigh the Queen of Asgard, and these were Fulla, her sister, Hlin, who carries to Frigg the prayers of mortals; Gna, the speedy messenger who passes to and fro over the earth, beholding and remembering: Lofn, guardian of lovers, in whose name vows are made; Vjofr, the peacemaker, who unites lovers, and husbands and wives who have quarrelled; Syn, the wise doorkeeper; and Gefjon, guardian of maids who shall never wed.

White elves were assembled on that sad shore to sorrow, and even black elves were there. Many Frost-giants and Mountain-giants gathered around, for there was sadness everywhere because Balder was dead.

But none mourned more than Nanna, Balder's wife. Silent was she; her heart wept, and fire burned in her eyes.

Then Odin mounted the pyre. On Balder's breast

he laid the gold ring Draupner, and bending low he whispered in Balder's ear. . . .

From that hour have gods and men wondered what said Odin in his son's ear.

When Odin whispered
In Balder's ear,
Nor god nor man
Was nigh to hear.

What Odin whispered,
Bending low,
No man knoweth
Or e'er shall know.

In silence Odin returned to the shore, and then Thor consecrated the pyre with his hammer. A dwarf named Littur, who ran past him, he kicked into the boat, where he was burned with Balder.

So ended the ceremony of grief, and the torch was placed to the pyre. High as heaven leapt the flames, and the faces of the gods were made ruddy in the glow. . . . Nanna cried aloud in grief, and her heart burst within her, and she fell dead upon the cold sea strand.

Seaward swept the burning ship. . . . The whole world sorrowed for Balder. . . .

Meanwhile Hermod made his darksome way through Nifel-hel towards Hela's glittering plains. Nine days and nine nights he rode on Sleipner through misty blackness and in bitter cold over high mountains and along ridges where chasms yawn vast and bottomless. On Hela's borders the terrible wolf dog of the giant Offotes followed him, barking in the black mist. . . . Then Hermod reached the rivers. Over Slid, full of daggers, he went, and over Kormet and Ormet, and the two rivers Kerlogar, through which Thor wades when he goes to the Lower Thingstead of the gods. He crossed shining Leipter, by whose holy waters men swear oaths that bind. At length he came to the River Gjoll and its golden bridge.

Modgud, the elf maid who watches the bridge, cried aloud: "Whence cometh thou who hath not yet died?"

Of her did Hermod ask who had crossed before him. Impatient was he to brook delay.

"But five days since," she said, "there passed five troops of warriors who rode over with valkyries, yet made they less noise than thee alone. . . . Whom seekest thou?"

Hermod answered and said: "Balder, my brother, son of Odin and Frigg, do I seek. If thou hast seen him, speak forth and tell me whither he hath gone."

In silence did Modgud point towards the north, whereat Hermod spurred Sleipner and went on. . . . Soon he came to Hela's great stone gate. Strongly barred it was and very high, and guarded by a great armed sentinel. To none was given entry save the dead who are brought to judgment.

Hermod leapt to the ground. He tightened the girths of Sleipner. He remounted again. Then he spurred Odin's horse towards the gate, and with a great bound it leapt over, nor ceased to go onward when it came down. . . . Swiftly rode Hermod until he came to the palace in which Balder dwelt with the Asmegir.

From the saddle he leapt and went within. . . . There in a golden hall he saw Balder seated on a throne of gold. Wan was his face and careworn, for the gloom of death had not yet passed from him. On his brow was a wreath of faded flowers, and on his breast the ring Draupner. He sat listening, as if he still heard the

voice of Odin whispering in his ear. Before him stood
a goblet of mead, which he had touched not. Nanna
sat by his side, and her cheeks were pale.

Hermod beheld nigh unto them Urd, the queen of
Hela. In cold grandeur she stood, silent and alone.
Deathly white was her face, and hard and stern, and she
looked downward. On her dark robe gleamed great
diamonds and ornaments of fine gold. . . .

To Balder spoke Hermod, and said: "For thee
have I been sent hither, O my brother. In Asgard
there is deep mourning for thee, and thy queen mother
beseecheth thy speedy return."

Sadly did Balder shake his head, and to Nanna he
pointed. But she leaned towards him and whispered:
"Love is stronger than death, nor can the grave destroy
it. . . . With thee, O Balder, shall I ever remain. . . ."

They would have wept, but in Hela there are no
tears.

Throughout the night did Hermod hold converse
with the twain, and when morning came he besought
Urd to release Balder from death's bonds.

With eyes still looking downwards she heard him
speak.

"In Asgard," Hermod said, "the gods sorrow for
Balder, and on earth is he also mourned. All who have
being and all things with life weep for Balder, and beseech thee that he may return again."

Urd made answer coldly: "If all who have being
and all things with life weep for Balder and beseech his
return, then must he be restored again. . . . But if one
eye is without tears, then must he remain in Hela
forever."

Hermod bowed himself before Urd in silence, and
turned again to Balder and to Nanna, who went with

*Balder, the bright god.*

The gods attempt to destroy Balder.

him to the door. . . . Ere their sad farewells were spoken, Balder gave Hermod the ring Draupner to carry back unto Odin, for in Hela the ring was without fertility. Her veil Nanna did send unto Frigg, and a bride's gold ring she gave for Fulla.

To Asgard did Hermod make speedy return, bearing the gifts of Balder and of Nanna, and unto gods and goddesses assembled together he made known the stern decree of Hela's queen.

Over all the world did Frigg then send messengers to beseech all who have being and all things with life to weep for Balder, so that he might be restored again. Then did sorrow indeed prevail. The frost of grief was broken, and the sound of weeping was heard like to falling streams. Men wept, as did also every animal, peaceful and wild. Stones had tears, and metals were made wet. On trees and plants and on every grass blade were dewdrops of mourning for Balder.

But as the messengers of Frigg were returning to Asgard, they came to a deep dark cavern in which sat Gulveig-Hoder, the Hag of Ironwood, in the guise of Thok (darkness). Her they besought to weep, so that Balder might return. She spake coldly and said:

"Thok shall weep tears of fire only because Balder is dead. No joy hath he ever given unto me living or dead. . . . Let Hela's queen hold what is her own."

Great was the sorrow in Asgard because that the Hag would weep not and free Balder from death's bonds. Upon Loke was laid the blame, because he never ceased to work evil among the gods. But not afar off was the day of his doom.

## The Passing of Balder

I heard a voice, that cried,
"Balder the Beautiful
Is dead, is dead!"
And through the misty air
Passed like the mournful cry
Of sunward-sailing cranes.

I saw the pallid corpse
Of the dead sun
Borne through the Northern sky.
Blasts from Nifel-heim
Lifted the sheeted mists
Around him as he passed.

And the voice for ever cried,
"Balder the Beautiful
Is dead, is dead!"
And died away
Through the dreary night,
In accents of despair.

Balder the Beautiful,
God of the summer sun,
Fairest of all the Gods!
Light from his forehead beamed,
Runes were upon his tongue,
As on the warrior's sword.

All things in earth and air
Bound were by magic spell
Never to do him harm,
Even the plants and stones:
All save the mistletoe,
The sacred mistletoe!

Hoder, the blind old god,
Whose feet are shod with silence,
Pierced through that gentle breast
With his sharp spear, by fraud
Made of the mistletoe,
The accursed mistletoe!

They laid him in his ship,
With horse and harness,
As on a funeral pyre.
Odin placed
A ring upon his finger,
And whispered in his ear.

They launched the burning ship!
It floated far away
Over the misty sea,
Till like the sun it seemed,
Sinking beneath the waves.
Balder returned no more!

*—Longfellow.*

# The Descent of Odin

Uprose the King of men with speed,
And saddled strait his coal-black steed;
Down the yawning steep he rode,
That leads to Hela's drear abode.
Him the Dog of Darkness spied,
His shaggy throat he opened wide,
While from his jaws, with carnage filled,
Foam and human gore distilled;

Hoarse he bays with hideous din,
Eyes that glow, and fangs that grin;
And long pursues, with fruitless yell,
The father of the powerful spell.

Onward still his way he takes,
(The groaning earth beneath him shakes,)
Till full before his fearless eyes
The portals nine of hell arise.

Right against the eastern gate,
By the moss-grown pile he sate;
Where long of yore to sleep was laid
The dust of the prophetic Maid.
Facing to the northern clime,
Thrice he traced the runic rhyme;
Thrice pronounced, in accents dread,
The thrilling verse that wakes the dead;
Till from out the hollow ground
Slowly breathed a sullen sound.

### Prophetess

What call unknown, what charms presume,
To break the quiet of the tomb?
Who thus afflicts my troubled sprite
And drags me from the realms of night?
Long on these mould'ring bones have beat
The winter's snow, the summer's heat,
The drenching dews, and driving rain!
Let me, let me sleep again.
Who is he, with voice unblest,
That calls me from the bed of rest?

### Odin

A Traveller, to the unknown,
Is he that calls, a Warrior's son.
Thou the deeds of light shalt know;
Tell me what is done below,
For whom yon glitt'ring board is spread,
Drest for whom yon golden bed.

*Prophetess*

Mantling in the goblet see
The pure beverage of the bee,
O'er it hangs the shield of gold;
'T is the drink of Balder bold;
Balder's head to death is given.
Pain can reach the sons of Heaven!
Unwilling I my lips unclose;
Leave me, leave me to repose.

*Odin*

Once again my call obey.
Prophetess, arise and say,
What dangers Odin's child await,
Who the Author of his fate.

*Prophetess*

In Hoder's hand the Hero's doom;
His brother sends him to the tomb.
Now my weary lips I close;
Leave me, leave me to repose.

*Odin*

Prophetess, my spell obey,
Once again arise, and say,
Who th' Avenger of his guilt.
By whom shall Hoder's blood be spilt.

*Prophetess*

In the caverns of the west,
By Odin's fierce embrace comprest,
A wondrous Boy shall Rinda bear,
Who ne'er shall comb his raven hair,
Nor wash his visage in the stream,
Nor see the sun's departing beam,

Till he on Hoder's corse shall smile
Flaming on the fun'ral pile.
Now my weary lips I close;
Leave me, leave me to repose.

### Odin

Yet a while my call obey.
Prophetess, awake, and say,
What Virgins these in speechless woe,
That bend to earth their solemn brow,
That their flaxen tresses tear,
And snowy veils, that float in air.
Tell me whence their sorrows rose;
Then I leave thee to repose.

### Prophetess

Ha ! no Traveller art thou,
King of Men, I know thee now
Mightiest of a mighty line—

### Odin

No boding Maid of skill divine
Art thou, nor Prophetess of good;
But mother of the giant brood !

### Prophetess

Hie thee hence, and boast at home,
That never shall enquirer come
To break my iron sleep again;
Till Lok has burst his tenfold chain.
Never, till substantial Night
Has reassumed her ancient right;
Till wrapped in flames, in ruin hurled,
Sinks the fabric of the world.

*Gray*

## The World's Tears

Odin . . . thus addressed the Gods:
" Go quickly forth through all the world, and pray
All living and unliving things to weep
Balder, if haply he may thus be won."
When the Gods heard, they straight arose, and took
Their horses, and rode forth through all the world;
North, south, east, west, they struck, and roam'd the world,
Entreating all things to weep Balder's death.
And all that lived, and all without life, wept.
And as in winter, when the frost breaks up,
At winter's end, before the spring begins,
And a warm west-wind blows, and thaw sets in—
After an hour a dripping sound is heard
In all the forests, and the soft-strewn snow
Under the trees is dibbled thick with holes,
And from the boughs the snowloads shuffle down;
And, in fields sloping to the south, dark plots
Of grass peep out amid surrounding snow,
And widen, and the peasant's heart is glad—
So through the world was heard a dripping noise
Of all things weeping to bring Balder back;
And there fell joy upon the Gods to hear.
        But Hermod rode with Niord, whom he took
To show him spits and beaches of the sea
Far off, where some unwarn'd might fail to weep—
Niord, the God of storms, whom fishers know;
Not born in Heaven; he was in Vanheim rear'd,
With men, but lives a hostage with the Gods;
He knows each frith, and every rocky creek
Fringed with dark pines, and sands where seafowl scream—
They two scour'd every coast, and all things wept.
And they rode home together, through the wood
Of Jarnvid, which to east of Midgard lies
Bordering the giants, where the trees are iron;
There in the wood before a cave they came,

Where sate, in the cave's mouth, a skinny hag,
Toothless and old; she gibes the passers by.
Thok is she called, but now Loke wore her shape;
She greeted them the first, and laugh'd, and said :—
   " Ye Gods, good lack, is it so dull in Heaven,
That ye come pleasuring to Thok's iron wood?
Lovers of change ye are, fastidious sprites.
Look, as in some boor's yard a sweet-breath'd cow,
Whose manger is stuffed full of good fresh hay,
Snuffs at it daintily, and stoops her head
To chew the straw, her litter, at her feet—
So ye grow squeamish, Gods, and sniff at Heaven!"
   She spake; but Hermod answer'd her and said :—
" Thok, not for gibes we come, we come for tears.
Balder is dead, and Hela holds her prey,
But will restore, if all things give him tears.
Begrudge not thine! to all was Balder dear."
   Then, with a louder laugh, the hag replied :—
" Is Balder dead? and do ye come for tears?
Thok with dry eyes will weep o'er Balder's pyre.
Weep him all other things, if weep they will—
I weep him not! let Hela keep her prey."
               *From " Balder Dead ", by Matthew Arnold.*

# CHAPTER XVI
## The Binding of Loke

Balder's Avenger—Odin woos Rhind—Winter's Cold-hearted Queen—
The Coming of Vale—At Valhal's Feast—The Sword-slain Warriors—Hodur
is killed—Odin and the Riddle-Giant—The Unanswered Question—Æger's
Feast—Loke reviles the Gods—His Confession and Flight—His Salmon
Guise—Caught in his Net—The Evil One is bound—Skade's Revenge—
Faithful Sigyn.

As the Vala had foretold, a son was born to Odin, who
took vengeance upon Hodur because that he slew Balder.
His mother was Rhind, Earth's Winter Queen, whom
Odin wooed in the time of ice. Cold-hearted was she,
although of great beauty, and long she withheld her
love. Her sire was Billing, the Elf of Twilight, whose
dwelling was in the west. Guardian was he of the forest
of the Varns, whither fled the deities of sun and moon
to find safety from the pursuing wolves of Ironwood.
Strong-armed were the Varns, and when Sol sank into
her golden bed, their chosen warriors, who guarded her,
kept watch with burning brands. By day they slept, but
when Sol again drave her chariot towards Billing's gate[1]
they lit their torches, which flamed with red fire and
gold.

When Odin went unto Billing he revealed his love
for Rhind, but the stern maid spurned with scorn the
Ruler of Asgard. Displeased with himself was Odin.

[1] According to Geoffrey of Monmouth, the mythical Belinus, King of Britain,
made in London a gate of marvellous workmanship " which the citizens do still in
these days call Billingsgate ".

Nor, as the skald hath sung, is there "a worse disease to afflict a wise man". Among the reeds sat Odin all alone, awaiting Rhind, yet she would favour him not. Her heart was frozen and cold.

A second time Odin went towards Billing's dwelling. He bore with him a bracelet and rings of fine gold and radiant flower-gems, and these gifts of golden summer he offered to Rhind. But she refused them with bitterness, for her heart was indeed cold. Her lover she despised.

A third time did Odin seek to woo the stern daughter of Billing. He went unto her attired as a young warrior, his helmet on his head and his sword by his side. Stately was he as is a viking who plunders on summer seas. But the warriors of Varn stood nigh unto Rhind. Their torches were in their hands, and she slept. Sun-bright she lay upon her golden couch. . . . At morn when all the household slumbered a hungry wolf-dog guarded her. Odin she again rejected. Contumely she heaped upon him, nor could he hope to gain her love.

At length Odin went unto Rhind in Hag guise. Earth's Winter Queen languished in sickness, and he promised to cure her. Over her then Odin muttered spells, so that she was moved to tempest madness. Then was she bound with ice chains. Thereafter did Odin reveal himself to her. He took off the spell. He released her from ice bonds. Whereupon her heart melted towards him and she became his bride.

Meanwhile in Asgard the gods sought to be avenged on silent-footed Hodur for slaying Balder. But him they could not discover. All day he hid in a deep forest, and in nighttime only was he abroad. A magic shield he bore, and a magic sword, and none would dare go nigh to him when darkness fell. Ever did he move restlessly and without sound through the forest, fearing that the avenger would come; ever did he seek to make escape, for of his fate he had full foreknowledge.

There came a day of brightness, and it was the May day of Vale's coming. In the night was he born in full strength, and towards Asgard he went speedily and entered therein. He had the face of a child and a warrior's body. Straight to Valhal strode Vale, and the watchman sought to hold him back, because his hands were unwashed and his hair uncombed. A strong bow he carried and three arrows.

Vale spurned the watchman and entered the warrior's hall. At feast sat Odin and the rest of the gods, and about them were the fearless heroes, the sword-slain warmen whom the valkyries had chosen.

Odin received Vale with pride, and to gods and heroes he announced: "Behold it is Vale, son of Rhind, who shall avenge the death of Balder."

The gods spake one to another and said: "How can this tender youth overcome night-haunting Hodur and escape his magic sword?"

Vale answered them saying: "But one night old am I, yet shall I avenge Balder, my brother."

Then sat Odin's new-born son at the feast. With the sword-slain warriors he shared the joys of Valhal, and ate of the boar Saehrimnir which was devoured daily and became whole again each night.

Odin sate in his high chair. But he partook not of the food, for he had no need of it. His portion he flung to his dogs Gere and Freke, and drank only of the mead which nourished him forever.

For drink the heroes had the mead milk of the goat Heidrun, which ate the leaves of Laerath, the tree which overshadows Valhal.

When the warriors had feasted with Vale in their midst, they issued forth in vast numbers from Valhal's doors, which numbered five hundred and forty. From each door eight hundred warriors came out, as they shall do at Ragnarok, to combat against the hordes of Surtur.

Thus daily do the warriors go forth as on the morn of Vale's coming. On a great field they fight battles, and one another they cut to pieces. On steeds they ride and the steeds fall. On foot they rush into battle to be slain.[1] Yet are they ever restored again.

Vale beheld the heroes in conflict. He saw them slay one another. He saw them rising to return unto Valhal.

When night fell, and Sol was laid on her golden couch in Billing's hall, Vale went forth to seek silent-footed Hodur. Through the wood of blackness he went, for he had knowledge of where the blind god was hidden. Then heard he a voice which cried:

"The avenger cometh, O slayer of Balder."

Hodur held high his magic shield. His sword he drew, and went in silence towards the sound of Vale's footsteps.

The bow of Vale was bent. He shot an arrow towards Hodur and it went past him. A second he cast and it struck the magic shield. The third arrow pierced the heart of Hodur and he fell dead.

Thus was the death of Balder avenged by Vale, son of Odin and Rhind, the young May-god with a child's face and the body of a strong warrior.

A pyre was built and the body of Hodur was burned

---

[1] "They went forth to the war, but they always fell."—Macpherson's *Ossian*. The reference is to Scandinavian invaders. Matthew Arnold applied the quotation to the Celts.

thereon.  The gods rejoiced that he was dead, but Balder awaited him in Hela.  Loke was yet unpunished; his day of doom was drawing nigh.

Ere that time came, Odin went forth from Asgard and journeyed unto Jotun-heim.  There he sought the dwelling of the ancient giant, Vafthrudner, to hear from him the secrets of the past.  He was the strongest of the giants and the most cunning.  He was also a maker of riddles, and those who could answer them not he put to death.  His head he wagered that none equalled him in wisdom.

Odin went towards the giant's dwelling in the guise of a mortal named Gangraad.

"Why comest thou hither?" Vafthrudner asked.  His sword was in his hand.

Odin answered: "I come hither to know whether thou art so wise and all-remembering as men say."

The giant was wroth, and to Odin he said: "If thou art not wiser than I am, and if thy knowledge is less than mine, thy head shall speedily be struck from thy shoulders.  If thou art proved the wiser, mine own head is forfeit."

First the giant asked Odin if he had knowledge of who drave the chariots of night and of day, and if he could name the world-dividing rivers.  Odin answered him.

Then the giant asked where the last battle would be fought, and Odin gave ready response.  "On Virgrid Plain," he said.

Much did the giant marvel.  He besought Odin to sit by his side.  When Odin was seated, he in turn put questions to Vafthrudner.  He asked of the old giant how far back he remembered, and Vafthrudner said that he had beheld Ymer's son, Bergelmer, who escaped the blood deluge, when he was laid on the World-mill to be ground.

Of the beginning of things Odin did ask him, and of the end. The giant made answer with great wisdom. There was naught of which he could not speak with full knowledge.

Then did Odin rise from his seat and say: "One last question shall I put thee, O Vafthrudner, and if thou canst not answer it, thy head is forfeit."

The giant was without fear. He listened, fully assured that he could make ready response.

But Odin spake and said: "Tell me if thou canst, O maker of riddles, what did Odin whisper into Balder's ear?"

Then was the giant stricken with great fear, because he perceived that the stranger was none other than Odin himself. With trembling voice he confessed that he was vanquished. So he who sought to slay the stranger was himself slain. By Odin was his head struck off.

By the gods was Odin called Jalk[1] when he slew the great giant.

But although Odin brought judgment upon the tyrant Vafthrudner, as he was wont to do unto all evil-doers, it was long ere he meted out just punishment to him who had in secret devised the death of Balder. But his hour was very nigh. His place beside Fenrer awaited him.

Shunned was Loke in Asgard, and rarely he went thither; for Balder he mourned not nor shared the grief of the gods, by whom he was suspect.

The time came when Æger sent messengers to the high Celestial city to invite the dwellers there to the harvest-end feast of the autumnal equinox. Thither

---

[1] Jack the Giant-killer.

they journeyed, robed in state, to drink of Æger's mead.

Now, while they sat round the board, Loke, who was not bidden to the feast, entered with stealthy steps. Funafeng, the guardian of the door, sought to hold him back.

"No seat awaits thee here," he said. "Thou hadst better haste to Ironwood and feast with Angerboda, mother of the Fenrer wolf."

Wroth was Loke with Æger's servant, and more wroth was he when he heard the gods praising Funafeng because of the words he had spoken. So he turned on the bold guardian of the door and slew him.

The gods rose in anger, and seized their weapons to be avenged, but Loke fled forth in the darkness and concealed himself in a deep forest at the sea bottom.

Then was the feast resumed. Mead flowed plenteously from Æger's vessels, for, like the horn of Utgard-Loki, they could never be emptied, and they were ever full.

Again Loke returned. Eldir guarded the door. The Evil One spake freely to him and said: "Of what do the gods speak as they drink their mead?"

"They speak of thee," Eldir answered, "and the evil deeds thou hast done."

"Then shall I enter," said Loke. "I shall revile them one after another until they are covered with shame."

Silent in their anger were the gods when they beheld Loke in their midst once again. But he demanded a seat at the board.

"Am I not an Asa-god?" he cried. "The golden mead I claim as my due."

Brage, god of music and song, spake fiercely and said:

"Thou shalt never again be an equal of the gods.  For thy villainy art thou become an outcast.  For thee is now prepared a drink of revenge."

To Odin did Loke make stern appeal, saying : "Promised we not each to the other in olden days, when our blood we mixed together, never to drink mead that was offered not unto both ?"

When Loke spake thus, Odin consented that he should sit at the board, for indeed he had spoken truly.  His claim was just according to ancient vows.

A goblet of mead did Loke receive, and he cried : "Hail to all who are here save Brage, who refused me hospitality."

When he drank from the goblet he taunted Brage with scorn, and the Song-god challenged him to combat ; but Loke heeded him not.  He heard him with silent scorn.

To Njord then turned Loke and flouted him because that he was but a hostage of the Vans.

Njord answered and said that he was father of Frey, who was hated by none, whereat the Evil One heaped abuse upon the harvest-god.  But Tyr said that Njord's fair son was the best of all chiefs among the gods, and that his doings were ever benevolent, so that by mortals was he well loved.

Loke cried : "Silence, O Tyr.  Thou hast but one hand since the Fenrer wolf seized thee."

Tyr answered : "Better to lose a hand than a good reputation, for that thou hast not, Loke."

Frey in wrath then said : "If thou art not silent, with thy wolf son shalt thou be bound."

Then did Loke taunt Frey because he had given to Gymer the Sword of Victory with which to buy Gerd.

Shame fell upon Frey and on all the gods whom

Loke reviled in that hour. Then Frigg spoke angrily
to the Evil One and said:

"If I had here in Æger's hall a son like to Balder,
who is dead, thou wouldst never go from hither, for in
wrath thou wouldst be slain."

"Ha!" cried Loke, leaping to his feet; "is it thy
will, O Frigg, that I should speak further? Now hear
and know that I am the cause of Balder's death. To
Hela was he sent by me, for to Hodur did I give the
mistletoe arrow that struck thy son down."

The gods seized their weapons to attack their evil
reviler, when suddenly thunder pealed in the hall, and
Thor stood there in their midst.

Now Loke knew well that the gods sought not to
defile the dwelling of Æger by shedding blood. So he
went and stood before Thor, whom he addressed, saying:
"Dost thou remember, O Asa-Thor, when thou didst
hide with fear in the thumb space of Skrymer's glove?"

"Silence, thou evil one," roared Thor, "or else with
my hammer shall I strike thy head off and end thy life!"

Then did Loke answer humbly: "Silent indeed I
shall be now, O Thor, for I know well thou shalt
strike."

So saying he left the hall. But the gods rose to
pursue him, so greatly angered were they because that he
had caused Balder's death. But Loke assumed the guise
of a salmon and escaped through the sea, and in vain
they sought him. Never again could he enter Asgard.

The gods took counsel together and decreed that
Loke should be bound because of the many evils he had
done, and especially because he devised the death of
Balder. They searched for him in Midgard and in
Jotun-heim, but found him not, for a cunning retreat
had Loke discovered. In a cliff he dwelt behind a great

waterfall.   Four doors there were in his cavern, and they were ever kept open, so that he might make quick and sure escape.   There he devised plots to overcome the Asa-gods.

But wearily passed the days of his solitude.   One morning he took flax and yarn and fashioned a net with which to capture fish, and in the manner which he made it have fishermen ever since fashioned theirs.   He took pride in his cunning work, but for what end he devised it no man knoweth.

Meanwhile the gods sought greatly after him.   Then Odin mounted his golden throne and looked over the nine worlds, searching for the place in which Loke was hidden.   He saw the cavern behind the waterfall.   He perceived Loke sitting within.   Then he called the gods and told them where the Evil One could be found.

Then set they forth and made cunning approach to the cavern.   They divided tó enter all the four doors. Loke perceived them, but not until they were very nigh to him.   Then he flung his net upon the fire, and in salmon guise leapt into the pool which was below the waterfall.   There he concealed himself betwixt two stones.

When the gods entered the cavern they knew that the Evil-worker whom they sought was not far distant, for the fire still smouldered.   Kvasir, son of Njord, who was keen-eyed as Heimdal, at once beheld on the white embers the ashes of the net which Loke had made.   So the gods sat down and speedily they wove another of like kind.   When it was finished they threw it into the stream, knowing that he whom they sought was there. But the net went over Loke.

Then did the gods take the net a second time, and weighted it with stones so that it could be dragged along the stream's bed. Loke divined their purpose, and leapt over the net into the waterfall.

But the gods espied him, and Thor went into midstream so that he might not escape. On either bank did the avengers drag the net towards the pool.

Loke perceived that there were but two means of escape left to him. One was to again leap over the net; the other was to swim out to the sea and brave the perils that are there. He chose to leap. But he escaped not, for Thor grasped him in his hand. In vain Loke sought to wriggle free, but Thor closed his strong fingers over his tail. That is why the salmon's tail has been narrow since that day.

When Loke found he could not escape, he assumed his wonted shape. Then did the gods do as Frey had threatened at Æger's feast. Him they bore unto the place where his son the wolf Fenrer was already bound on the geyser-sprayed island in the gulf of Black Grief.

Loke's two sons, Vali and Narvi, followed him, as did also gentle Sigyn, his wife, whom he had despised and wronged. Incantations were sung over Vali, and he became a fierce wolf. Upon his brother Narvi he sprang and tore him to pieces.

Then did the gods lay Loke on three sharp-edged rocks next to the Fenrer wolf. With the sinews of Narvi (the binder) they made chains which were like iron, and with these they bound the Evil One securely.

Skade came from her mountain home rejoicing because that he who had caused the death of her father, Thjasse, was at length overcome. She bore with her a poisonous snake, and bound it on the rock above Loke's head. From its jaws dropped burning venom, which tortured the Evil One with great agony.

Then took the avengers their departure, leaving Loke

in torment. . . . His faithful wife Sigyn remained behind. Over Loke's head she is ever holding a goblet to receive the dripping venom. So does she constantly guard her evil husband. But when the vessel is filled to the brim she must needs bring it down, so that it may be emptied. Then do venom drops fall upon Loke's face, burning him fiercely. . . . When that happens he struggles madly with his bonds, and the rocks shake and Midgard trembles to its foundations. . . . It is thus that earthquakes are caused.

On the island of the Gulf of Black Grief must Loke and the Fenrer wolf remain until Ragnarok. The wolf dog Garm shall bark aloud when they escape from their bonds.

# CHAPTER XVII

# The Dusk of the Gods

The Vala's Song—Signs of Ragnarok—Evil among Men—Fimbul Winter—Goldcomb's Warning—Giants assail Bif-rost—Heimdal's Horn is blown—The Quaking of Ygdrasil—Loke and the Monsters freed—Ship of Death—Fear in Hela—Harper of Ironwood—The Midgard Serpent rises—Coming of Monsters—The Last Scene—Gods in Battle: their Doom—Odin avenged—Sun and Moon devoured—The End of All—World's New Age—Balder's Return—The Regenerating Race—All-father's Decrees.

THERE was a Vala who sang of the end of all things, of the doom of gods and men, of the last dread battle and Odin's death, and of the coming of Surtur, whose flames shall consume the world. In mid-air she sang, and at high noon. Odin, sitting in his throne of gold, was silent, and listening he understood, for from the beginning he had foreknowledge of the end. Yet was he not afraid. He awaited Ragnarok, "the Dusk of the Gods", as in youth he had waited, and now he was grown old.

$$\cdot \qquad \cdot \qquad \cdot \qquad \cdot \qquad \cdot \qquad \cdot$$

It was thus the Vala sang:

"The Age of Evil hath come upon earth—the Knife Age, the Axe Age, and the Age of Cloven Shields. The violent fall upon the peaceful; brothers slay brothers, and the children of sisters are shedding one another's blood. Great luxuries do men seek, and sensual sin prevails. The world is doomed, yet is it hard and cruel and full of sin. Thick-pressed in Hela's heavy streams doth Urd behold wading confusedly perjurers and murderers and evildoers without number. . . .

"Follows the Age of Northern Winds. Sword blasts
are cleaving the darkened skies. Fierce beasts from
forests and mountains and barren wilds seek their prey
among men. None spares his neighbour, nor lifts a
hand to save. . . .

"Fimbul Winter is now come. Heavy snows are
driven and fall from the world's four corners; the
murder frost prevails. The sun is darkened at noon;
it sheds no gladness; devouring tempests bellow and
never end. In vain do men await the coming of summer.
Thrice winter follows winter over a world which is snow-
smitten, frost-fettered, and chained in ice. . . . Yet wars
are waged, blood is shed, and evil grows greater. . . .

"Suddenly Goldcomb crows loud in Asgard; from
Hela's depths the Red Fire-Cock makes answer. On
a hilltop in Ironwood the Storm-Eagle flaps heavily its
wings, and tempests bellow over ocean and land. . . .

"The giants have gathered to assail Asgard. To
Bif-rost they hasten: at the north end are Frost-giants
and Mountain-giants; at the south end are the dread
sons of Suttung. Heimdal beholds them. In his hand
is the Gjallar-horn, which has long been hidden in the
deepest shade of Ygdrasil, and from it he blows a
thunder blast which awakens the nine worlds. . . .
Mimer's seven sons start from sleep in Hela's golden
hall, and arm themselves for conflict. . . . Odin talks
with Mimer's head; he divines the end of all things,
and unafraid he plans his battle array in the last conflict.

"With clamour and speed the giants ascend Bif-rost,
and the sublime bridge breaks with the weight of riders,
whereat Ygdrasil quakes—the old ash, deep-rooted and
strong-rooted, trembles standing, so that the worlds are
shaken and the bonds of fettered giants are broken.
Loud barks Garm on the rocky isle of the Gulf of Black

Grief, for the wolf Fenrer escapes and Loke is set free. Snapped are the cords that bind Naglefar, the great Ship of Death; it breaks loose. . . .

"The gods are unafraid; they sit in counsel in their High Thingstead. But Njord leaves Asgard and returns to the wise Vans, for the war is waged against the Asagods, and Suttung seeks to be avenged upon Odin. . . .

"The elves tremble, and the dwarfs shudder in dim-discovered caverns; they hide behind their rocky walls. In Jotun-heim there is loud bellowing and defiance, and terror spreads among men in Midgard. White fear passes over Hela, for the uncertain conflict is at hand. The sons of Mimer guard the gate: their long swords are in their hands. . . .

"In gloomy Ironwood the ice-cold heart of Anger-boda is made glad. Gymer sits upon a mound alone, playing a harp; he is merry because of what is at hand. Long hath he awaited the hour of doom. To him comes Fjalar-Suttung, creator of illusions, in the guise of Hela's red cock, and he seeks the Sword of Victory which Gymer hath guarded—the sword which Thjasse-Volund forged with spells to wreak vengeance upon the gods, which Mimer captured and Svipdag found, the sword which Frey should wield in the last battle, and he yet gave to Angerboda for love of Gerd. To Fjalar-Suttung is the Sword of Victory given up, and he hastens to Surtur. . . .

"Now from the east drives Hrym; a buckler covers him, and his hordes follow. The Midgard serpent is shaken with giant rage, for its hour hath come; it writhes and wallows on Ocean's slimy floor, so that billows are raised and driven over Midgard high as the mountains; it rears its shaggy head out of the sea; venom-spotted is its body, and fire fumes it sends forth.

In Ironwood the storm eagle rises with beating wings.
It snaps its sharp beak; it hungers for dead men's
flesh. . . .

"The Ship of Death is sailing over the sea. On
board are the sons of Muspel, who were bound; the
stricken Jotuns, freed from bonds; Garm, the watch-dog;
and the unfettered wolf Fenrer. Monsters gaunt and
grim are in the ship, and Hel is there also. Loke is
the pilot and holds the rudder. To Ironwood he steers;
over it his host he shall lead to the plain of Vigrid. . . .

"From the south comes black Surtur. In his hand
flames the Sword of Victory, which he hath received from
Suttung. Seething fire gleams from the sunbright blade,
and his bleak avengers follow him. . . .

"Mountains are shaken and the rocks tremble. The
giant maids are stricken with fear. Mortals in Midgard
are strewn in death, and their shades crowd the path to
Hela. Heaven yawns; it is rent in twain because that
Surtur issues forth. . . .

"On the plains of Vigrid is the last battle fought. A
hundred miles it stretches in length, and a hundred miles
in width, enclosing the wood of Vidar the Silent, where
Odin is doomed to die. . . . The hosts of evil come
against the hosts of Asgard. Frey leads the heroes of
Valhal in the fray. He goes against black Surtur, unarmed and without fear, and by the Sword of Victory he
is slain.

"Against strong Tyr leaps Garm, the fierce wolf-dog,
and in dread conflict they engage; and one by the other
is wounded, so that both fall dead.

"Loke battles with Heimdal, but against the shining
hero the Evil One cannot prevail. Terrible is Loke's
aspect after long torture, for his beard and hair have
grown like horns. With his bright sword the watchman

of Bif-rost takes his head. But even after death is the
Evil One avenged, for his head strikes the body of
Heimdal, who is grievously wounded thereby and
brought to life's end.

"There is no longer fear in Hela; the sons of Mimer
rejoice because that Loke is dead.

"Thor is engaged in fierce combat with the Midgard
serpent. Long is the strife and uncertain. The serpent
is coiled and uncoiled; it writhes before Thor; it avoids
his hammer blows, and over him it pours floods of
venom. Terrible is the wrath of the thunder-god, and
fain would he smite his enemy, dreading that he will be
overcome. But at length he prevails. Thunder bellows
loud and Mjolner flashes fire as Thor smites the death-
blow, and the monster is stretched dying upon the plain.
Great renown, indeed, hath the God of Thunder gained,
yet pays he life's cost for the victory. With its last fierce
breath the serpent sends forth suffocating venom fumes,
and Thor staggers back nine paces. Then with a thunder
groan the victor falls dead. . . .

"How fares Odin in this dread hour? He combats
with the ravenous wolf Fenrer, the avenging monster
which broke free from its bonds. From earth to heaven
its jaws gape. Fiery flames dart from its nostrils and
from its eyes. Odin fights with his spear Gungner, and
violent are his blows. He rides on Sleipner; on his
head gleams his helmet of gold; his blue robe streams
behind. Fearless is Odin and proud, and his form is
stately in this his hour of doom. Naught can avail him
in the great combat. He is stricken down in his splendour, and by the wolf is he devoured.

"Yet shortlived is the triumph of Fenrer. Strong
Vidar the Silent advances speedily to avenge his sire's
death. His iron-shod foot is stamped on the monster's

under jaw. He struggles fiercely with the terrible wolf, for he is stronger and must prevail. In the end he tears asunder the great jaws, and plunges his spear in Fenrer's heart through that throat of fire. Thus Odin is avenged. . . .

"How fares the Asa-hosts when Odin and Thor fall, and Tyr and Frey lie dead? The heroes of Valhal are scattered, hordes of giants are killed, and the field is wet with blood. The black dragon Nidhog is soaring through the air with rustling wings. It flies towards the plain of battle and swallows the bodies of the dead. . . . Surtur alone prevails.

"In Heaven there is disaster. Closer and closer hath the giant wolf Skoll crept towards the sun, and now he swallows it. By Hati-Managarm is the moon devoured.

"So is the sun darkened at high noon, the heavens and the earth are turned red with blood, the seats of the mighty gods drip gore. So is the moon lost in blackness, while the stars vanish from the skies.

"Now Surtur completes creation's doom. He casts his firebrands against the scattered Asa-hosts, and those who remain are burned up, save Vale and Vidar, sons of Odin, and Modi and Magni, sons of Thor. Midgard is swept by flame; the smoke curls round mountain tops; all things are burned up; nothing with life remains. Asgard is scorched, and fire envelops the withering trunk of Ygdrasil. Even Nidhog is destroyed in its flight. . . . Earth, smouldering and black, sinks into Ocean; the billows cover it. . . .

"Now there is naught but thick blackness and silence unbroken. The end hath come—Ragnarok, 'the Dusk of the Gods'!"

.    .    .    .    .    .

Silent was then the voice of the Vala in mid-air and

at high noon.   Odin sat in his throne of gold listening through the stillness, unafraid, waiting for Ragnarok and his own doom.   Waited he also for the song's end and the promise of Time's new morning, when evil would cease to be and Balder would come back.

The skylark soars till its song falls weakly; at morn is its singing fresh and sweet.   Sweet, too, and fresh was the song of the Vala when Odin heard, sitting in his throne, her voice falling through the stillness, afar off but clear.

.     .     .     .     .     .

"In Hela's realms there is sure defence.   None goeth thither to conquer, and the long swords are unstained with blood.   The fire hath reached not the Underworld.   Mimer's seven sons, who have awakened, sleep not again.   The roots of Ygdrasil are watered once more from Mimer's well; fire has destroyed not the tree save those branches which had withered; it grows green again.

"The World's New Age hath dawned.   The sun is bright in heaven, for Balder hath returned.   Earth rises a second time, from the deep sea; it rises clad with green verdure.   The sound of falling waters fills the morning air.   High soars the eagle; from the mountain ridge he espies the fish. . . .

"Asgard is again made fair.   The young gods arrive. Balder is there, and Hodur, his brother; Vale and Vidar are there also, and Mode and Magne, who bear with them Mjolner, the hammer of Thor.   Honer, who reads the future, is in their midst; he is able to choose his part.

"Of the evils and perils of past time do the gods converse.   Midgard's serpent they call to mind and the wolf Fenrer.   They forget not the judgments of the gods and the antique mysteries. They remember the sacred runes of mighty Odin. On the grass they find the tablets of gold with which in the Golden Age was played the game of the gods. So did the Asa clan find them on Time's fair morning ere yet by the Hag was Asgard corrupted.

"The world is decked in beauty. Fields yield produce without being sown. Evil is ended and every ill hath ceased. Balder hath indeed returned, and with Hodur he dwells in the holy halls of Odin.

"The sons of the two brothers are in the vast abode of the winds, the wide free hall of the cloud drift. In the sun chariot is Sol's daughter, who is more beautiful than was Sol, and she drives in brightness over a heaven of blue.

"Lifthraser and Lif and their descendants, who are the regenerating race, have come from Mimer's realm to inhabit Midgard. Pure are they and without stain. Honey-dew is their food in Time's new morning: their children shall overspread the earth.

"The new race shall dwell, when life ends, in their hall which is named Gimle. Brighter it shines than the sun, and its roof is of gold, and it stands in high heaven. There indeed shall the holy ones dwell in peace and eternal joy for evermore.

"Northward on Nida mountains is a golden hall. The sons of Mimer and Sindre's race have dwelling within it. In heaven there is also the hall Brimer, where mead drinkers sit round the board amidst plenty and in peace.

"The evil ones who have fallen from their high state dwell in Naastrand. A vast hall it is, and of great height. Its doors are open to the north. With serpents was it built; they are entwined so that their backs are outward and their heads are within. Venom drops from

their jaws; it burns the sinners on the benches beneath;
they wade through venom floods in the hall. . . .

"Odin returns not again, nor Heimdal. Another
comes who is more mighty. Him I dare not name, for
he is All-father. He comes to the great judgment; he
utters decrees. He governeth all realms, by him are all
things swayed. He settles strife; he makes war to cease.
He ordains sacred laws which are inviolable and shall
flourish for ever."

  .  .  .  .  .  .

The Vala's song was ended, and Odin sat in his
golden throne, pondering in silence.

## Regeneration

Far to the south, beyond the blue, there spreads
Another Heaven, the boundless—no one yet
Hath reach'd it; there hereafter shall arise
The second Asgard, with another name.
Thither, when o'er this present earth and Heavens
The tempest of the latter days hath swept,
And they from sight have disappear'd, and sunk,
Shall a small remnant of the Gods repair;
Hoder and I shall join them from the grave.
There re-assembling we shall see emerge
From the bright Ocean at our feet an earth
More fresh, more verdant than the last, with fruits
Self-springing, and a seed of man preserved,
Who then shall live in peace, as now in war.
But we in Heaven shall find again with joy
The ruin'd palaces of Odin, seats
Familiar, halls where we have supp'd of old;
Re-enter them with wonder, never fill
Our eyes with gazing, and rebuild with tears.
And we shall tread once more the well-known plain

Of Ida, and among the grass shall find
The golden dice wherewith we play'd of yore;
And that will bring to mind the former life
And pastime of the Gods, the wise discourse
Of Odin, the delights of other days.

*—From "Balder Dead", by Matthew Arnold.*

# CHAPTER XVIII

## The Coming of Beowulf

The First Parents—Heimdal's Mission—A Wise Ruler—Passing of Scyld
—Hrothgar builds Heorot—The Demon Grendel—Warriors devoured by
Night—Reign of Terror—Beowulf of the Geats—He sets forth to fight the
Demon—The Voyage—Challenged by the Shore Guardian—The King's Wel-
come—Beowulf asks a Boon—Waiting for Grendel—Beowulf keeps Watch.

To Ask and Embla, the first man and the first woman,
did the gods impart divine attributes when they had
but tree life, and were of little might and without destiny.    Naked they stood before Odin at the seaway
end.    Perceiving their conscious shame, he gave unto
them divine garments, and in these they took pride.    In
Midgard they dwelt, on the shore edge of Western
waters, and their children multiplied, and their children's
children.    The lives of mortals were long in those days;
they were yet innocent, and dwelt together in peace.    The
Golden Age prevailed in Asgard, nor had the Evil One
of Ironwood corrupted the gods.

In after days Heimdal, son of Odin and of the nine
Vana-mothers who were daughters of sea-dwelling Ran,
was given from out of Gjallarhorn a wisdom draught of
Mimer's mead.    Then became he a child in human guise.
In a fair ring-stemmed ship was he laid, wrapped in soft
slumber, and his pillow was a golden grain sheaf, the gift
of Frey, god of harvest.    Around him were heaped great
treasures, war glaives and full armour, weapons and tools,

which the gods had made in Asgard. The sacred fire-borer took Heimdal also with him—he who was called Stigande, the journey-maker.

There came a sunbright morn when men, looking westward from Scedeland's high shore, saw drifting towards them over the blue sea a fair ship, and on the stem shone golden rings. Nigh it came, and it found a safe harbour and lay therein. With wonder the people beheld on the deck a man-child wrapped in soft slumber; his pillow was a golden grain sheaf, and they named him Scyld[1] of the Sheaf. Him they took unto their chief's home, and there he was nourished and fostered tenderly. The treasures that were in the ship gave great riches and power unto the tribe, and they received knowledge to grow grain and to use the sacred fire. When the child reached to wise manhood, he became a ruler among men, and long were his years.

Of Heimdal have skalds sung that thrice were sons born to him of earth mothers. The first was Thrall, from whom thralls are descended; the second was Churl, sire of freemen; and the third Jarl, from whom all nobles have sprung.

So when warriors assembled to feast together and drink mead, and ere the song was raised, have skalds spoken thus:—

"Give ear all ye divine races, great and small, sons of Heimdal".

Scyld of the Sheaf achieved great renown. He who was received as a helpless child became a great and good king. He drove invaders from the shores, he scattered ravaging bands, and among the tribes he was regarded with awe. Indeed he waxed so powerful that tribute

[1] As in Beowulf. Elsewhere Scyld is called son of Sheaf.

was paid to him by the people who dwell beyond the seaway of whales.

A man-child was born unto Scyld. He was named Beowulf[1], and when he came to years of strength and knowledge he won fair repute. Among the followers of his sire he distributed many money gifts, so that he won their favour; ready were they indeed to serve him in wartime.

When Scyld was of great age, he departed at his fateful hour to go into the keeping of the Lord. According to his dying request his faithful subjects carried him down to the seabeach. There in the small harbour lay the ship in which as a child he had come over the waves. Ready to go seaward, the vessel waited him in wondrous wintry beauty, glistening with hoar frost and ice. By the mast, on the broad bosom of the ship, the mourners laid down their well-beloved lord, the generous giver of golden money rings. Great treasures they heaped around him—graven ornaments from distant lands, armour and weapons of war and bright swords— and on his breast they put many gems. As rich and numerous were the gifts they gave as were those they had received with the child in other years.

Over the dead king they hoisted a banner of gold. . . . Then was the boat let loose. . . . The tide bore it away to the heaving ocean. . . . Thus in deep sadness was the king given unto the sea, while his people sorrowed for him, watching from the shore. . . . No man can tell who received that fair ship's burden

Beowulf then reigned over the Scyldings, and was honoured and well loved. His son Healfdene[2], who followed him, was famed afar as a warrior, and when he waxed old he was yet fierce in battle. Four children

---

[1] The elder Beowulf; not the hero of the poem.     [2] Halfdan.

he had—Herogar, a captain of war men; Hrothgar, who
became king; Halga the Good; and Elan, the queen of
a Swedish chieftain.

Hrothgar was a strong leader, and won many great
battles. He received willing service, and under him the
young war-men increased in numbers, until he commanded a mighty army. Then bethought he to have
a great Hall built, with a larger feasting room than was
ever heard of among men. For that purpose were
workers from many tribes put in service, and in due
season was erected the high, horn-gabled building which
was called Heorot, and it awaited the devouring flames.

There was much feasting and merriment in the great
Hall. A fierce man-eating monster, which dwelt in darkness, was made angry by the revelry, the music of harps,
and the cheerful songs of skalds. One[1] was in the hall,
too, who told how the Almighty did create man and the
earth in the midst of the encircling sea, and did set the
sun and moon in the heavens to give light and cover
the land with branches and leaves.

Thus did war-men live happily indeed in the Hall,
until the Hell-fiend began to work evil. Grendel was
his name, and he hovered by night on the marches and
held moorland and fen. By the Creator were he and his
kind banished to their dark lairs, because they were the
kindred of Cain, the slayer of Abel, whose evil progeny
were monsters and elves and sea-demons, as well as the
giants who fought with God, for which he paid them
their reward.

Now it happened that in the midst of the night the
demon Grendel entered the silenced hall to discover who
were lodged there after beer-drinking. He beheld a

---

[1] Evidently an interpolation by a Christian copyist. Further on offerings are
made to idols.

band of high war-men who had feasted, and were wrapped in deep slumber; they had forgotten sorrow, that woeful heritage of men.

With fury was the demon possessed, and thirty of the war-men he carried off while they slept, hastening with exulting heart to his lair with that fill of slaughter.

At daybreak there was grief and loud wailing in the Hall. The great and honoured prince sat moodily, stricken with great sorrow, and gazed at the blood track of the fierce demon. His distress was long-lasting, and deep.

On the next night the demon Grendel returned, and did more murderous deeds. Nor had he any regret thereat, so much was he steeped in crime. Then was it easy indeed to find men who sought inner chambers by night. He alone who found farthest retreat escaped the fierce fiend.[1]

Then became Grendel the master indeed. For the space of twelve long winters Hrothgar endured because of the demon great sorrow and deep loss. Minstrels went abroad making known in song the ceaseless outrages and fierce strife. No offering would Grendel take, nor could the greatest war-man who was seized expect to escape his doom. He entrapped young and old; on the mist-dark moorlands he seized his victims night after night. In vain did Hrothgar lament and make offerings unto idols, and pray that the soul destroyer would give them release from the demon. So did the heathen, as was their custom, remember hell, for they knew not the Creator, the Judge of Deeds, the Lord God, nor could they praise the Lord of Glory.

Then did Beowulf, a thane among the Geats, come to hear in his fatherland of the deeds of Grendel. In his

---

[1] Grendel could enter the hall only: other dwellings were "taboo".

time he was the strongest among living, men, and he was noble as he was indeed mighty.

"Get ready my good wave-traverser," he said. "I shall go unto Hrothgar over the swan-way; he hath need of men."

The prudent, who depended on his aid, sought not to hold Beowulf back; they urged on the stout-hearted hero, and looked eagerly for favourable omens.

Beowulf selected fourteen of the finest war men to go with him, and took also a sea-skilled mariner, who knew the landmarks along the path of Ocean. Then to the ship they all went together: it lay beached below a sheltering headland. The warriors, bearing their arms, walked on to the stem, while the sea waves were washed against the sand. The armour and ornaments were placed on board, and then the willing heroes pushed into deep water the strong timber-braced ship. Like to a bird was that swift floater, necked with white foam, driven by favourable winds over the sea waves. All night they sailed on, and next day they beheld high and shining cliffs, steep mountains, and bold sea-nesses. So came they to the seaway end; the voyage was over and past.

The heroes leapt speedily from the ship and made it fast to the shore. Their armour clinked as they turned inland, while they thanked God that the seaway had been made easy to them.

Then there came towards them the Coast Guardian of the Scyldings, riding upon his horse along the shore. He shook his strong spear shaft as he drew nigh, and he spake, saying:

"Who are ye who in a high ship have come over the seaway, well-armed and bearing weapons? Know ye that I keep watch over the shore so that sea plunderers may not do harm to Denmark. Never have I beheld armed men landing more openly; nor know ye the password of friends. Nor ever have I beheld a greater earl than this one among you. Unless his looks belie him, he is no home-stayer. Noble is his air. . . . Ere you advance farther to spy out the land, I must know who ye are. Now, listen to me, sea travellers from afar, my frank advice is that ye reveal at once from whence ye come."

That shore guardian did Beowulf answer thus : " We are Geats, the hearth friends of Hygelac. My sire Ecgtheow, the noble leader, was renowned among the people ; he is remembered by every wise man. Now know that we come seeking thy king, the son of Healf-dene, protector of the people. Be thou our guide. A great mission is ours, nor need its purpose be concealed. To us hath it been told, and thou knowest if it is true, that a malignant foeman works evil by night among the Scyldings. I can council Hrothgar how the fiend may be overcome and his misery have end."

On his horse sitting, the fearless shore guardian spake in answer, saying : " A shield war man shall judge well between your words and deeds. Friendly are you, I hear, to the ruler of the Scyldings. Then pass onward in armour carrying your weapons. I shall guide ye. My comrades shall guard thy ship, so that the well-loved man, thy leader, may return over the sea tides to the borders of the Weders. To him it is assured that he shall come unscathed through the battle crush."

Together they went on their way until they came to the high and gold-decked Hall of Hrothgar. The shore-guardian pointed towards it and said: " Now must I take my departure. May the Almighty protect you all in your adventure. To the seashore I must hasten to keep watch against hostile bands."

Beowulf and his heroes reached the Hall. Sea-weary

they all were, and they placed their shields and armour against the wall; they put their spears together and rested on benches.

A warrior, who was Hrothgar's messenger, asked them whence they came. "Never," said he, "have I seen bolder strangers. It would seem that ye have come to seek Hrothgar, not because of exile, but because of your bravery and noblemindedness."

Then did Beowulf reveal who he was and seek audience with the king, and his message did Wulfgar bear unto Hrothgar, who sat, grey-headed and old, among his peers.

"As a youth I knew Beowulf," the aged ruler said. "He comes to a sure friend. Of him have I heard that his hand hath the strength of thirty men. The holy God hath sent him hither as a help against the dreaded Grendel."

So he bade the messenger welcome Beowulf and his men and usher them to his presence.

When Beowulf entered he hailed Hrothgar, the kinsman of Hygelac, standing before him in shining armour.

"In my youth," he said, "I have undertaken great exploits. In my fatherland heard I of the evil deeds of Grendel, and my people counselled me, knowing my great strength, that I should come hither. For they know well that I avenged the sorrow of the Weders, bound five of their foes, slew a brood of giants, and killed sea monsters by night. . . . Alone shall I go now against this demon, this giant Grendel!"

Then asked Beowulf as a boon that he alone with his warriors should be left to cleanse the hall of the monster. Having heard that Grendel had no fear of weapons, he also made known his desire to contend with him unarmed. "With the fiend," he said, "I shall wrestle for life, foe against foe."

Hrothgar accepted Beowulf's offer with gladness, and granted him the boon he sought. Then was a bench cleared for the noble heroes. They sat there in pride and drank of bright liquor. Songs were sung by a clear-voiced minstrel. There was much joy in the hall among the Danes and the Weders, who were no small company.

When they had feasted, and the queen bore the cup round the heroes, young and old, she greeted Beowulf, who, when he had drunk, said he had vowed to slay Grendel or perish in his clutches.

The old queen was much pleased to hear the words which the great hero spake.

Loud revelry was heard in the hall once more until Hrothgar desired to go to his couch. Well he knew that the night-haunting monster would attack the hall when the sun's radiance was dimmed and shadows fell, and dusky shapes were stalking under the clouds.

Then the whole company arose and greeted the heroes. Hrothgar greeted Beowulf and wished him success and power in the hall.

"Be mindful of thy renown," the king said, "make known thy great might, be watchful against the foe. . . . Thou shalt lack naught that thou dost desire if thou shalt survive this conflict."

Whereupon Hrothgar went forth with all his warriors, leaving the hall to Beowulf and his men.

When he was thus left alone with his heroes, the chief of Geats took off his armour, and gave his decorated sword to his thane. Ere he lay down in bed he said :

"No less in fighting strength than Grendel do I

account myself. I shall not slay him with my sword as I well might. He knows not the noble art to strike back, splitting my shield, although he hath courage and strength in evildoing. No weapons shall we use if he dares combat without them. . . . May the wise God, the holy Lord, give victory to the side which may seem meet to Him.

On his pillow Beowulf then laid his head. Around him on beds lay his warriors, nor did one of them expect ever again to return to his home; for each of them had heard how, in times past, the Danish warriors were taken from the Hall in bloody death.

In the blackness of night Grendel, the shadow-goer, came striding towards the Hall. . . . The warriors, sea-weary and spent, lay wrapt in deep slumber, nor kept watch — all save one. He alone was defiantly awake, awaiting the issue of the conflict with increasing wrath.

# CHAPTER XIX

## Conflict with Demons

Grendel enters the Hall—A Warrior devoured—Struggle with Beowulf
—Terror-stricken Danes—The Hero Triumphant—Flight of the Demon—
The Great Feast—Beowulf honoured—Grendel's Mother takes her Revenge
—The Hero follows her—His Great Dive—Fight in the Cave—The Ancient
Giant-sword—The She Demon slain—How Beowulf became a Prince.

OVER the moor in the black mist Grendel came
stalking. The wrath of God was upon him. He saw
the high hall and hungered for human flesh. . . .
Stealthily he strode below the dark clouds, so that he
might peer into the feasting chamber, which was decorated with gold and shining with ornaments. . . . It
was not the first time he had entered it, but never before
did he meet therein with a mightier warrior and braver
watchmen.

So came that accursed fiend towards the Hall. The
door was shut and strongly barred with iron bands; but
he smote it with his great hands and it flew open. The
demon was bent upon evil and swollen with fury as
he tore through the entrance. With swift footsteps he
strode his silent way over the finely paved floor. . . .
He raged inwardly, and in the darkness awesome lights,
like to fire, burned in his eyes. . . . He surveyed the
hall; he saw warriors asleep on the benches and his heart
exulted as he resolved to devour each one separately ere
the night was spent. . . . But he had come to his last
feast of human flesh.

Beowulf lay watching Grendel. Soon the hero beheld how suddenly the fiend snatched up his prey. Without delay that grim monster clutched a sleeping warrior, tore him asunder, chewed his flesh, and drank his blood, swallowing great mouthfuls quickly, until he completely devoured the man, and even his hands and feet.

Then Grendel came nearer; his claws darted out to wards Beowulf as he lay in bed. But the hero divined the demon's purpose, and he clutched the monstrous arm and threw his weight upon it. . . . Never before did Grendel feel a stronger hand-grip, and he was suddenly stricken with terror and sought to escape. . . . In vain he struggled to break free, so that he might take flight into the blackness of night—back again to the demons of his gang.

But Beowulf was mindful of his evening boast; he leapt from bed; he stood erect; tightly he grasped the monster; his fingers burst. . . . Grendel twisted and swayed; backward he sprawled towards the door, but the hero went with him, nor relaxed his grip. The wily fiend sought to slip without, if it were possible, and then flee to the darksome fen. He realized what strength there was in Beowulf's hands. . . . A luckless visit indeed had the monster made to Heorot.

Loud rang the clamour in the hall. Terror seized upon the Danes in their safe dwellings without; there was panic among them. . . . Beowulf and Grendel raged with fury; the building resounded as they struggled and crashed round and about. . . . It was a wonder that the feasting-hall was not shattered, and that it ever survived the savage conflict; it might well have fallen to the ground, but the timbers were bound together by well-forged iron bands. . . . Never could it be destroyed by hands, although the flames might devour it.

Then arose a loud and awesome scream. . . . The Danes were stricken with terrible dread, because they heard the demon's cries of despair—his screeching song lamenting for his wound.

Beowulf held fast; he would not suffer the man-eating fiend to escape alive. . . . Of little account was Grendel's life to the world of men. . . .

The battle heroes in the hall sought to help their lord. They fell upon the monster without fear, and smote him with their war swords, but without avail, for Grendel's body was charmed against weapon wounds, and they could do him no hurt.

But miserable was to be the life ending of the fiend; his alien spirit was fated to travel afar to be bound by devils. The crime worker, the devourer of men, the enemy of God, realized that his body would endure not or give him help and sure defence. Brave Beowulf had him in his power; each loathed the other with fierce hate.

In agony was Grendel. . . . A wound gaped on his shoulder; it was torn wider and wider; the sinews snapped; the flesh burst. . . . The glory of battle was given to great Beowulf. . . . Sick unto death Grendel must indeed escape to his joyless lair below the darksome fen: he knew that his life days were spun to an end. . . . So tearing away, he left his arm and shoulder in Beowulf's hands.

Thus was the desire of the Danes achieved, and the boast of the great hero fulfilled. The high hall was cleansed of Grendel. That indeed did the people who were stricken and put to shame realize when they entered Heorot, for from the great roof had Beowulf suspended the arm of the night demon with its iron-strong hand and clutching claws.

In the safety of morning the warriors hastened to the

Hall; from far and near the people gathered to gaze with wonder on the traces of the conflict. The blood tracks of the monster were on the ground. The warriors followed his trail on horseback until they came to the water of sea demons, which they beheld weltering with blood; the waves surged red and hot with gore. The death-doomed Grendel had laid his life down in his lair —his heathen soul. There Hela[1] snatched him away.

Then the mounted warriors rode back and proclaimed the tidings and the glory of Beowulf, of whom they said that no other warrior between the seas and the world ever was his equal or worthier of a kingdom.

Then was great rejoicing. Warriors held races on horses, one with another, and a minstrel thane sang of Beowulf's deed, and of Sigemund, the Volsung, who slew the dragon. To the Hall went many retainers to behold the arm of Grendel. The king went to view it with his nobles, and the queen went with her maidens.

Hrothgar gave thanksgiving to God because that the dread of Grendel was ended, and, addressing Beowulf, whom he called "the valiant hero", he vowed that henceforth he would love him as a son. . . . "Thy fame," he said, "shall endure for ever."

Beowulf spake in answer, and said he had done the deed with great goodwill. "Would", he said, "that thou hadst witnessed the conflict. I thought to hold down the fiend on his deathbed until he died, but I could not prevent his going away."

The warriors were silent about him: they looked on the arm suspended from the roof; they saw the finger-claws which were like steel. Then they said that no weapon could have cut off that bloody battlehand of the demon.

[1] Urd, Queen of Hela.

A great feast was given in Heorot in Beowulf's honour. Hrothgar gave unto the hero as gifts a golden banner, a helm and war armour and richly jewelled sword. Eight battle steeds gave he also, and on one was the king's war saddle, adorned with embroidery and gems. To each of the hero's followers was given a sword, and blood money was paid for the warrior whom Grendel had devoured.

At the feast a minstrel sang of the deeds of King Finn[1] and of Hengest, Hnaef, and Hildeburgh—how Finn married Hildeburgh, the sister of Hnaef, who was afterwards slain and burned at the king's hall, and how Hengest went against Finn and slew him, returning to the fatherland with Hildeburgh.

When the song was ended, Hrothgar's queen, Wealtitheow, gave the golden cup to the king, and then bore it to Beowulf, to whom she also gave two golden armlets, a mantle, and a jewelled collar which was as precious as the collar of the Brisings,[2] which Hama took from Eormanric. The wondrous collar did Beowulf afterwards gift to his king, Hygelac, who wore it when, in after days, he fell fighting against the Frisians, when to them it passed.

The feast was then spread; men drank wine. They knew not stern Wyrd[3]—Destiny—as had many of the nobles before them there. And when evening came, Hrothgar rose and left the hall, and Beowulf went also to sleep in an outer dwelling. The benches were cleared and laid out as sleeping couches. . . . One among the revellers was doomed that night to die. . . . Each of

[1] One of several heroic poems founded on the Ivalde moon-myth.
[2] Probably a legend founded on the fight between Heimdal and Loke, when the latter tries to steal Brisingamen, Freyja's necklace. Hama is Heimdal.
[3] Urd, Queen of Fate (as chief Norn) and of Death.

the warriors hung his armour and weapons on the wall at his head, ready for sudden alarm and night attack. Brave men were they!

Now demon vengeance was brooding against the warriors because that Grendel was slain. His mother, a female demon, was filled with woe in her dwelling amidst awesome waters and cold streams. Ravenous and wrathful she resolved to go forth to avenge her son's death.

In the darkness she made her sorrowful way, and came to Heorot while the warriors slept on the benches. When she broke in there was again terror in the hall, which was just as much less than before as is a woman's strength unto a man's on the battlefield.

Swords were drawn hastily: there was no time to don armour. The she demon, perceiving that she was discovered, made haste to depart, but she had seized in her grim claws a sleeping noble, and she carried him off towards the fen. He was Hrothgar's comrade warrior and shield bearer, Æschere, who was famed between the two seas and well beloved. . . . A wailing arose in Heorot; the demon had taken life for life.

The old king was sorrow-stricken when he knew that his chief warrior was slain. He summoned Beowulf to a council, and the hero went with his followers. Along the floor strode the war-famed hero, while the timbers resounded his steps. He asked of the king if he had passed, according to his desire, an easeful night.

"Ask not of my welfare!" the king cried. "Sorrow has again fallen upon the Danes. Æschere is dead — my right-hand man, my councillor, my teacher. The death demon is his murderer. By her is her son's death avenged. My comrade she hath slain because thou didst kill Grendel, who for long slaughtered my people. So is the feud continued against us." . . .

Then did the king tell Beowulf that ofttimes he heard that two dread stalkers held the moors by night. One of them had a woman's seeming; the other was Grendel. None knew if there was a sire in times past. Their lair was under the cliffs where a stream fell downward—in an underworld flood below a tree-girt mere. Nightly was a wonder beheld there—fire in the flood! No man knew how deep was the mere. The hart when close pursued will die rather than enter the water. An awesome place it is!

Thence do the waves surge to the clouds when the wind stirs up fearsome storms, the air is filled with mist, and the heavens weep.[1]

Then said the king unto Beowulf: "Once more do we look to thee for aid. Thou knowest not yet the demon lair, the perilous retreat, where the monster may be found. Seek it if thou art unafraid! Then shall I reward as heretofore with gifts of gold if thou shalt survive."

Beowulf was, indeed, without fear. He besought the king to sorrow not. "Better it is," he said, "to avenge a comrade than to grieve without end." So he counselled that they should go forth quickly and follow the demon's blood trail to her den. Bravely he spoke thus:—

"Not in earth's bosom, in mountain wood, or in the sea depths, go where she may, shall the kin of Grendel escape me! . . . Be patient in thy grief this day, O king, as I expect of thee."

With joy the king leapt up, hearing the words that Beowulf spake. He called for his horse, and, followed by his men, went forth with Beowulf and his warriors.

[1] Ironwood and the Hag are suggested. Hati-managarm, Angerboda's son, is also a maneater like Grendel.

They followed the track of the demon over the moor, and came to the stony places and the cliffs and the homes of sea-monsters. They reached the grey rock[1] overhung by trees, and below they beheld the mere surging and red with blood. On a cliff top they found Æschere's head.

In the water they beheld serpents and awesome sea dragons. On a ledge were sea monsters that go down the ocean paths. When the horn gave out a battle-lay they rushed seaward, and one did Beowulf wound unto death with an arrow so that he swam slowly in the water. The war-men thrust barbed boar spears at it and dragged it ashore. With wonder they gazed on their awesome guest.

Beowulf then girded on his armour, and on his head put his battle helmet. Then gave Hrothgar's spokes-man, Unferth, unto him the strong blade which was named Hrunting. Of iron was it made, and tempered with blood of battle; it had been forged with twig venom and never had it failed in battle.

Then Beowulf addressed Hrothgar and besought him to be guardian of his comrades should he himself sur-vive not, and to send unto Hygelac the treasures he had received.

"I shall achieve fame with Hrunting," Beowulf cried, "or death shall take me."

He awaited no answer and plunged; the surging waters received him. Downward he sank a day's space ere he found the bottom. . . . Soon the demon dis-covered that an alien being came against her, and she clutched Beowulf in his finger claws, but by reason of his strong armour she could do him no hurt. Sea

---

[1] The Svipdag-dragon is also under a grey rock. The treasures he guards, and especially Freyja's necklace, also shine like fire in the water.

monsters attacked him with sharp tusks,[1] so that he could not use his sword, and they followed as the demon drew him into her lair. Then did Beowulf perceive that he was dragged into a hall beyond the sea's reach. The glow of fire-like light was shining bright, and Beowulf perceived that the mere wife had taken him. He smote her with his sword—a great free blow he gave, and the blade rang on her head. But no wound could he inflict. Never before had the sword failed in conflict! Then did the hero fling down the blade. He would have his strength of arm for sure defence. So, desperate-minded, does a battle man fight when he hopes for fame and recks not of life. . . . The shoulder of Grendel's mother he seized and in great fury wrestled and flung the demon down. . . .

But fiercely she clutched at him. In her claws she held him securely. They struggled together thus until the battle hero, heart-weary, at length was overthrown. On the ground he fell and the she demon sat upon him. . . . She drew swiftly her broad and bloodstained dagger to avenge her only son. . . . Then would the hero have died there, but over his shoulder lay his chain armour and that saved him. . . . To his feet he leapt again.

Beowulf suddenly beheld among the armour in the demon's lair an ancient giant-sword. It was a blade without an equal. No other living man could wield it, for it was the choice of splendid weapons, and giants had made it. The hero seized it and wielded it.

Strong was Beowulf, and in battle fury he swung the giant-sword and smote the demon a fierce blow, cleaving her at the neck and shattering her bone-rings. Right through her body went the blade, and she sank

[1] Walruses?

in death. . . . Blood-wet indeed was the sword, and Beowulf gloried in his deed.

Then light flashed through the hall, as when heaven's candle gleams from on high. . . . The hero gazed about him. . . . He saw Grendel lying maimed and dead on his resting place, and in vengeance for the evil that monster had done, Beowulf smote his body so that it was split open. Then the head he struck off.

On the cliff top the warriors waited, watching the angry waters. . . . In time, Hrothgar beheld the waves rising red with blood. Old and grey-haired war men spoke one to another about the brave one; nor did they expect to see him return again in triumph, for they deemed that the wolf demon had torn him asunder. . . . So they spoke and waited, until in the ninth hour the Scylding heroes turned away. Hrothgar went with them to his home. . . . Nor did the Geats expect ever to behold Beowulf again; yet they waited, gazing at the blood-red waters.

Meanwhile, in the demon's wave-protected hall, the giant sword which the hero had wielded began to waste away in the bloodstream. A strange thing was that! Like ice it melted, as when the Father unties the frost chains and the flood flows free.

Beowulf took not any of the other arms that were on the wall, but he kept the gold and graven swordhilt of which the blade was burnt up by reason of the fiend's hot and poisonous blood. Then, seizing the monstrous head of Grendel, he entered the waters and soon again he was swimming—he who survived fearsome strife, for by this time were the waters purged of blood and he rose quickly. He came to shore, and his war men rejoiced, as did also the brave hero, for he was proud of his mighty load of sea spoil.

Quickly did his men unloose his armour, and with glad hearts they went inland with him. Heavy was the burden of Grendel's head, which was carried to the hall on a spear shaft, the warriors marching in triumph.

Into the feasting-chamber they strode, where people sat drinking, and dragged Grendel's head along the floor. . . . An awesome sight was that to the nobles and the queen who sat with them. In silence the warriors gazed upon the monstrous head, wondering greatly.

Then did Beowulf address the king, telling him of the dread peril he endured ere yet he slew the demon. " But now," the hero said, " thou canst sleep in Heorot among thy warriors as heretofore, nor fear murderous attacks in the darkness."

To Hrothgar gave Beowulf the sword-hilt rich in victory, the work of a wonder-smith. It was a heritage of the past, and upon it was engraved that primeval war when the surging sea engulfed the race of giants[1]. Terribly were they punished — that people who were alien to the Eternal Lord; the Supreme Ruler gave them their final deserts in the flood. A gold plate upon the hilt had engraved in runes the name of him for whom that choicest of weapons was first made with decorated hilt and serpent ornament.[2]

There was silence in the hall when Hrothgar, son of Halfdane, spoke of Beowulf's deed. Well may he say, an aged guardian who promotes truth and right among the people and remembers all from the far past, " that this nobleman is of high birth. Beowulf, my friend, thy renown is raised above all people, far and

[1] The sons of Ymer.

[2] The traditional Sword of Victory, made by Thjasse-Volund, which was in the keeping of the Hag of Ironwood and her shepherd, Gymer. The runes, the smith's name, and the serpent charm suggest its magical qualities. It was evidently intended to achieve as great a disaster as did the Ymer deluge.

wide. With modesty and prudence thou dost bear thyself. My friendship thou shalt have, as I promised thee. Thou shalt ever be a strength to thy people and an aid to war men.

Not so was Heremod[1] to the children of Ecgwela, the renowned Scyldings. Not for their happiness did he flourish, but to bring cruelty and slaughter to the Danes. God had given him power and strength greater than any other man, but he had a fierce heart; he gave not money rings; he was without joy, and he endured grief because of his savagery and never-ending enmity with his people. Follow not that example. Have manly virtue. Many winters have made me wise, and for thee I have told this tale."

Further did the king give wise counsel to Beowulf, advising him to distribute gifts to his people, so that he might ever have their support, and to avoid vaunting pride, because the day would come when his strength would depart, and in the end death would take him.

A great feast was held in the Hall, and there was much rejoicing, and Beowulf slept there until the raven, with blithe heart, proclaimed the joy of dawn.

Then did the hero bid Hrothgar farewell. An alliance of peace was formed between the Scyldings and the Geats. The old king kissed the hero and shed tears.

To the coast guardian Beowulf gifted a gold-hilted sword. Then with his followers he went aboard the ship in which were the treasures and armour and horses which Hrothgar had given.

---

[1] A reference to an older heroic tale. Hermod, the son of Odin, who visited Balder in Hades, has some connection with the Svipdag myth. Indeed, Rydberg identifies him with Svipdag. Beowulf is a hero of similar cast. Each has the attributes of the age in which their deeds were sung, and reflect the ideals of the people who celebrated them. Older savage conceptions, preserved by tradition, were condemned when compared with the new and nobler.

*Viking ship from Gokstad.*

*Viking ornaments.*

The good ship clove the sea waters; the sail swallowed the wind; the timbers creaked; necked with white foam the ocean traverser, with curved stem, sailed away. Favourable were the winds until they saw the Geatish headlands and the keel grated on the shore.

To King Hygelac did Beowulf relate his adventures, and then he distributed the gifts he had received, giving that monarch a coat of mail and four horses, and to the queen, Hygd, the beauteous collar and three horses. Hygelac awarded the hero a gold-headed sword, much money, a country seat, and the rank of a prince.

# CHAPTER XX
## Beowulf and the Dragon

Beowulf in Battle—He becomes King of the Geats—A Slave's Discovery —Theft of Treasure—The Dragon devastates the Kingdom—Beowulf is angered—He sets forth to slay the Monster—Address to his Followers—The Dragon comes forth—The Great Conflict—Flight of Followers—The single Faithful Knight—He helps the King—Dragon slain—The Treasure—Beowulf's Death—Wiglaf reproaches the Battle Laggards—How the People sorrowed.

BEOWULF gave faithful service to Hygelac. In peace he was his wise counsellor, and in war his right-hand battle man. Then did the king fall fighting against the Frisians and Hugs. His death was avenged by Beowulf on the field, for he seized Dœghrefn, the hero of the Hugs, and slew him, not with his sword. "I grasped him," the hero could boast; "his beating heart I stilled. I crushed his bones." Then swam Beowulf away towards home, escaping unscathed, and bearing with him the armour of thirty warriors.

Queen Hygd mourned the king's death, and to Beowulf made offer of the kingdom, but he chose to be faithful to Hygelac, and protected his young son, Heardred, until he grew to years of wisdom and strength. But the young king was slain by Eanmund, and Beowulf was given the throne. He avenged the death of Heardred by slaying his murderer's brother, Eadgils.

For fifty winters did Beowulf reign wisely and well. Then a great dragon began to ravage his country with fire. Alone did the monarch combat againt it, and in the end was the victor. But he paid life's cost for his triumph.

Now the dragon had its dwelling in a secret cavern beneath a grey rock, on the shoreland of a lonely, upland moor. No man knew the path thither. It chanced then that a slave who had been sorely beaten by his master fled towards the untrodden solitudes, and he came to the dragon's lair while yet the monster slept. Quaking with fear, he beheld it there guarding rich treasure which had been hidden in ancient days by a prince, the last of his race. All his people had fallen in a great war, and he wandered about alone mourning for his friends. Then he hid the treasures of the tribe where the slave found them. Armour and great swords were there, a banner of gold that lit up the cavern, golden cups, and many gems and ornaments, collars and brooches, the work of giants in ancient times.

The ancient dragon which went forth by night wrapped in fiery flame found the treasure unprotected, and from that hour became the guardian of it.

Now the slave who discovered the monster's lair had more greed than fear in his heart as he gazed upon the hoard. So he went lightly past the dragon's head and seized a rich golden cup, and fled away over the rocks. To his master he carried the treasure, and thus secured his pardon and goodwill.

The dragon soon afterwards awoke. He smelt along the rocks; he saw the footprints of the man on the ground, and searched for him angrily. Round about the monster went, but saw no one in that dismal solitude. Hot was the dragon's heart with desire for conflict. Then he returned to the cavern and found that the treasure had been rifled. Great was his wrath thereat, and he panted to be avenged. So waited he for night-fall, when he could go forth against mankind.

In the thick darkness the great dragon flew over the land. He vomited coals of fire over many a fair home. The flames made lurid blaze against the sky, and men were terror-stricken. It seemed that the night flyer was resolved not to leave aught alive, for far and near the countryside blazed before him. Great harm, indeed, did he accomplish in his fierce hate for the people of Geatland.

All night long the raging flames swept the land, and far and near they wrought disaster. Not until it was very nigh unto dawn did the dragon cease his vengeful work and take swift departure to its lair. Great faith had he in the security of his hiding place, but his faith proved to be futile.

To Beowulf the grievous tidings of the night horrors were sent quickly. His own country dwelling, the gift of the Geats, was smouldering in fire. Sorrow-stricken, indeed was the brave old king; no greater grief could have befallen him. In deep gloom he sat alone, who was wont to be cheerful, wondering by what offence he had made angry the Almighty, the Everlasting Lord.

The fire drake had burned up the people's strong-hold; the sea-skirting land was devastated. Waves washed inland. . . . Beowulf was filled with anger against the monster, and resolved to be avenged. So he began to make ready for the combat. He bade that a shield of iron be made for him, for a wooden shield would be of no avail against raging fire. . . . Alas! the valiant hero was doomed to come ere long to life's sad end, as was also the serpent fiend who had for so long kept guard over the secret hoard. . . .

Beowulf scorned to attack the flying monster with a

host of war men ; he had no fear of going forth alone, no dread of single combat, nor did he hold the battle powers of the dragon as of high account. Many conflicts and many war-fights he had survived unscathed since he, the hero of many frays, had cleansed Heorot and wrestled in combat with Grendel, the hated fiend.

Twelve valiant and true war men he selected to go with him against the fire drake. And as he had come to know how its dread vengeance had been stirred up against his people, he took with him also the slave who had rifled the treasure, so that he might be a guide to lead them unto the monster's den. A sorrowful heart was in that poor man; abject and trembling he showed the way, much against his will, to the mound in which was the treasure, while underneath the dragon kept guard. It was on a rocky shoreland where the waves bellowed in unceasing strife.

Beowulf sat on the grey cliff looking over the sea. His hearth comrades were about him, and he spoke to them words of farewell, for he knew that Wyrd had tied fast the life thread of his web. His soul was sad and restless, and he was ready to go hence. Not long after that his spirit departed the flesh.

Of his whole life the king spake, recounting the long service he had accomplished since that he was but seven years old, when King Hrethel took him from his father and gave him food and pay, mindful of his kinship. Of his deeds of valour he spoke, and life's afflictions, and touchingly he told of a father's sorrow when his son was taken from him. Such an one in his old age remembered every morn the lost lad. For another he had no desire. With sorrow he beheld his son's empty home, with deserted wine hall that heard but the moaning winds, for the horseman and hero slept in the grave, and no longer was heard the harp's music and the voices of men making merry.

'Twas thus he spake of Hrethel, the king who sorrowed when his son was slain and avenged not; abandoning the world the stricken monarch sought a solitary place in which to end his days.

Then spake Beowulf of Hygelac, whom he served and did avenge, and his son whom he avenged also.

"When yet young," the hero said, "I fought many battles, and now when I am old I seek fame in combat with the dragon, if he but come from his underground dwelling."

He must needs, Beowulf told his followers, wear his armour in that last fray. Naked he fought with Grendel, but now he must stand against consuming flame.

"I shall draw not back a foot's space," he said boldly and with calm demeanour, "nor shall I flee before the watcher of treasure; before the rock it shall be as Wyrd[1] decrees—Wyrd who measures out a man's life. . . . Ready am I, and I boast not before the dragon. . . . Ye warriors in armour, watch ye from the mound, so that ye may perceive which of us is best able to survive the strife after deadly attack. . . It is not for one of you to fight as I must fight; the adventure is for me only. . . . Gold shall I win for triumph, and death is my due if I fail. . . ."

Then fully armoured under his strong helmet, his shield on his left arm, his sword by his side, the valorous hero of the Geats went down the cliff path towards the dragon's cavern. . . . He saw the stream which flowed from the stone ramparts steaming hot with deadly fire; nigh to the hoard he could not endure long the flame of the dragon.

[1] Urd.

But filled was his great heart with battle fury.    A storm-like shout he gave—a strong battlecry that went under the grey stone. . . . In wrath the monster heard him ; he knew the voice of man. . . . Nor was there time then to seek peace.    Fiery flame issued forth first : it was the dragon's battle breath. . . . The earth shook. . . . Beowulf stood waiting, his iron shield upraised. . . . The monster curled itself to spring ; Beowulf waited in his armour. . . .

Then forth came the wriggling monster—swiftly to his fate he came.    The shield gave that strong hero good defence against the flame.    His sword was drawn, and it was an ancient heritage, keen-edged and sure. . . . Both the king and the dragon were bent on slaughter ; each feared the other.

Beowulf swung his great sword, and smote the dragon's head, but the blade glanced from the bone, for Wyrd did not decree otherwise.    Then the hero was enveloped in fire, for in wrath at the blow the monster spouted flame far and wide.    Greatly did the brave one suffer. . . . His followers standing on the mound were terror-stricken ; to the wood they fled, fearing for their lives.

But one remained ; he alone sorrowed and sought to help the king.    He was named Wiglaf, a shield warrior, a well-loved lord of Scyldings.    He remembered the honours and the gifts which Beowulf had bestowed upon him. . . . He could not hold back ; he grasped his wooden shield and drew his ancient sword — a giant's sword which Onela gave him.    To his comrades he cried : " Promised we not to help our lord in time of need when with him we drank in the mead-hall ?    Rather would I perish in fire with our gold-giver than that we should return again with shields unscathed. . . . Advance then.

Give help to our lord. . . . Together shall we stand side by side behind the same defence."

So speaking, that young hero plunged through the death smoke, hastening to Beowulf's aid. Never before had Wiglaf fought at his chief's side.

"Beloved hero," Wiglaf spake, "do thy utmost as of yore. Let not thy honour fail. Put forth thy full strength and I shall help thee."

Then came the dragon to attack a second time. Brightly flamed the fire against his hated human foes. The young hero's wooden shield was burnt up, and behind Beowulf's he shielded himself.

Again Beowulf smote the dragon, but his grey sword, Naegling, snapped in twain, whereat the monster leapt on the lord of the Geats, and took that hero's neck in his horrible jaws, so that the king's life blood streamed over his armour. But Wiglaf smote low, and his sword pierced the dragon, so that the fire abated.

Beowulf drew his death dagger, and striking fiercely he cut the monster in twain. So was the dragon slain; so did the heroes achieve great victory and renown.

But the king was wounded unto death. The dragon's venom boiled in his blood, and he knew well that his end was nigh. Faint and heart-weary he went and sat down, gazing on the rocky arches of the dragon's lair, which giants had made. . . . Wiglaf came and washed the bloodstained king, who was weary after the conflict, and unloosed his helmet and took it off. Tenderly he ministered unto Beowulf in his last hour. Well knew the king that he was nigh unto death.

"It is now my desire," Beowulf said faintly, "to give unto my son, if it had been granted to me to have one, this my war armour. . . . For fifty winters I have ruled over my people, nor was there a king who dared come against me in battle.  At home I waited my fateful hour, never seeking to make strife, nor ever breaking a pledged oath ; so now when I am sick unto death I have comfort because the Ruler of all mankind can charge me not with murderous doings when I die."

Then he bade Wiglaf to bring forth the treasure from the dragon's lair, so that he might behold the riches he had won ere life was spent.  The young hero did as was asked of him.  He brought forth ancient armour, and vases of gold, rich ornaments and gems and many an armlet of rare design.  A banner of gold which lit up the cavern he also bore to the king, in haste lest the last breath should be drawn ere he returned. . . . He found Beowulf gasping faintly, so once again he laved the king's face with cold water until he spake, gazing on the treasure, with thankfulness.

"To the Lord of glory I give thanks," he said, "because that he hath permitted me, ere I died, to win such great treasure for my own folk. . . . Give thou the gifts unto my people according to their needs. . . . I have paid life's cost for them. . . . No longer can I remain."

Then the king made request that on the cliff top overlooking the sea there should be raised his burial mound, and that it should be made bright with fire.  He desired also that it should be built on Hronesness, as a memorial, so that seafarers, whose ships are driven through spray mist, might call it "Beowulf's Grave".

To Wiglaf the dying hero then gave his golden neck ring, his helmet adorned with gold, and his strong armour, which Weland had fashioned, bidding him to make ever good use of the gifts.

"The last of our race, the Wægmundings, art thou, O Wiglaf," Beowulf said faintly, as life ebbed low. "Wyrd took one by one away, each at his appointed hour; the nobles in their strength went to their doom. . . . Now must I follow them. . . ."

These were Beowulf's last words. His soul went forth from his body, to the doom of good men. . . . Wiglaf sat alone, mourning him.

Then came the battle laggards from the wood and approached Wiglaf, who spoke angrily to them, because that they had fled their lord in his hour of need. Nevermore, he vowed, would they receive gifts or lands; each one would, when the lords were told of their cowardice, be deprived of their possessions.

" For a noble warrior," Wiglaf cried, "death is better than a life of shame."

When the people heard that Beowulf was dead, they feared that their enemies would renew the blood feuds and come against them. The messenger whom Wiglaf sent to bear the sad tidings spake of wars to be, when many a maiden would be taken away to exile and many a warrior slain. Then would their ghosts lift up their spears; the harp would be heard not as it awakened warriors, but instead the blood-fed raven would ask how fared it with the eagle as it fought with the wolf to devour the slain.

In sadness and sharp grief the people went towards the dragon's lair, and they saw the dread monster that had been slain. In length it measured fifty feet; horrible it was and blackened with its own fire. Round the dead king they gathered, weeping sorrowfully, and Wiglaf spake, telling them of Beowulf's last words, and his desire that he should be buried in a high barrow at the place of the bale fire.

Then, while the bier was being made ready, Wiglaf led seven men into the cave, and what treasure remained they brought forth. The dragon was thrown into the sea, and the body of grey old Beowulf was borne to the headland which is called Hronesness.

A great pyre was built, and it was hung with armour and battle shields and bright helms.   Reverently they laid the great king thereon — the well-loved lord for whom they mourned. . . . Never before was so large a pyre seen by men.   Torches set it aflame, and soon the smoke rose thick and black above it ;  the roaring of flames mingled with the wailing of the mourners while the body of Beowulf was consumed. . . .

A doleful dirge sang the old queen, and again and again she said that oft had she dreaded the coming of conflict and much slaughter.   She feared for her own shame and captivity.

Heaven swallowed the smoke. . . . The people then raised a grave mound of great height.   For ten days they laboured constructing a wall which encircled the ashes. Much treasure did they lay in the mound—all that was in the hoard—and there the riches lie now of as little use to men as ever they were.

Twelve horsemen rode round the great mound on Hronesness[1] lamenting for their lord.   All the people sorrowed together, and they said that Beowulf was of all the world's kings and of men the mildest and most gracious, the kindest unto his people and the keenest for their praise.

## The Curse of Gold

The antique world, in his first flow'ring youth,
Found no defect in his Creator's grace ;

[1] Hronesness is translated " Whales' Ness " by some : others incline to the mythological rendering, Ran's Ness.   Rydberg in this connection shows that Rhind's son, Vale, the wolf slayer, is called, by Saxo, Bous, the Latinized form for Beowulf. Stopford Brooke shows that Hronesness is next to Earnaness, Eagle's Ness, and considers that "the unmythological explanation is plainly right".

But with glad thanks, and unreproved truth,
The gifts of sovran bounty did embrace:
Like angel's life was then men's happy case;
But later ages Pride, like corn-fed steed,
Abused her plenty and fat-swoll'n increase
To all licentious lust, and gan exceed
The measure of her mean and natural first need.
Then gan a cursed hand the quiet womb
Of his great grandmother with steel to wound,
And the hid treasures in her sacred tomb
With sacrilege to dig; therein he found
Fountains of gold and silver to abound,
Of which the matter of his huge desire
And pompous pride eftsoons he did compound;
Then Avarice gan through his veins inspire
His greedy flames, and kindled life-devouring fire.
"Son," said he[1] then, "let be thy bitter scorn,
And leave the rudeness of that antique age
To them, that lived therein in state forlorn.
Thou, that doest live in later times must wage
Thy works for wealth, and life for gold engage."

—*From Spenser's " Faerie Queene "*.

[1] Mammon (Mimer) to the knight Guyon.

# CHAPTER XXI

## Hother and Balder

Hother's Accomplishments—His Love for Nanna—Balder becomes his Rival—The Valkyries' Warning—The Sword of Victory—Where it was concealed—Hother's Journey to the Other-world—Miming is overcome—Helgi and Thora—War between Gods and Mortals—Hother overcomes Thor—Love-sick Balder—Hother in Solitude—The Great Battle—How Balder was slain—Odin woos Rinda—Balder's Death is avenged.

HOTHER was but a lad when his father Hodbrodd was slain, and him did King Gewar take to his castle to be reared as his own son. Strong and nimble he became, and very comely to behold. He could perform mightier feats than any of his foster-brothers: he could swim deftly and far like to a sea bird, he was a skilled archer, and he could box well with the gloves. Great gifts of mind had Hother also. He was a singer of songs, and a sweet musician. With rare skill he fingered the harp, and played the lute, and such power had he with stringed instruments that he could at will make his hearers merry or sad; he could fill their hearts with pleasure, or stir them with strange terror.

Pleasing indeed was this fair youth, unto beauteous Nanna, his foster-sister, the daughter of King Gewar. Her heart was moved with love towards him, and no less passionately did he love her also. Dear unto Nanna were the fond embraces of Hother.

Now there came a fateful day when Balder, son of Odin, saw Nanna while she bathed. The vision held him spellbound, and he was consumed with burning love by reason of the splendour and beauty of her comely body. When she vanished, the day was made dim, and Balder sighed full oft as he thought with tenderness of the beautiful maid; but when he remembered his rival he was moved to anger, for full well he knew that Hother would be the chief obstacle between him and his heart's desire. In the end he resolved to slay the young hero.

Hother soon came to know of Balder's burning love, and his fierce and bloody purpose. One day he went hunting alone in a deep wood. A deep mist drave over the land and enveloped the trees, so that he knew not whither he was wandering. In time he came to the dwelling of wood maidens. They called him "Hother", and he marvelled greatly thereat. When he asked them who they were, they told him that it was their lot to decide the issue of battle conflicts[1]; invisible they fought in the fray, assisting those whom they favoured so that victory might be achieved. Hother wondered to hear. Then they told him that Balder had gazed with eyes of love upon Nanna while she bathed, and was possessed with burning desire to have her for his bride. Hother did they warn not to combat with his rival, because that he was a demigod whose body was charmed against wounds. But to Hother they gave a sword-proof coat of mail, so that he might have protection like unto Balder. They made promise to aid him in battle.

Then the maidens vanished, and their dwelling also vanished from before the eyes of the young hero, and he found himself standing alone upon a barren plain, where there was not tree nor any shelter whatsoever. The mist was driven before the wind.

The youth thereafter returned quickly unto King

[1] Valkyries.

Gewar, to whom he related what he had seen, and what
had been told unto him concerning Balder. He also
made request that Nanna should be his bride.

Gewar was willing indeed that his daughter should
wed Hother, but he said that he feared greatly the wrath
of Balder, if he came seeking for Nanna and were
refused.

"No weapon," Gewar said, "can do hurt to Balder
save a certain sword[1] which is guarded in a cave by
Miming, the wood satyr. A wondrous ring doth he also
possess, which hath power to increase the wealth of him
who owns it. . . . But long and dangerous is the road
which leads unto the satyr's lair," the king added; "it is
wintry cold, indeed, and hardly to be endured."

Hother, however, was resolved to win the sword with
which to combat against Balder, and Gewar counselled
him to yoke reindeer to his car so that he might be able
to traverse the region of extreme and bitter cold with
great swiftness.

"When thou dost reach the cave of Miming," Gewar
said, "thou must set up thy tent so that its shadow may
not fall upon the satyr, for if that should happen he
would remain within. Thou must needs wait until the
satyr goes out, when the sword and the ring will await
for thee."

As Gewar advised, so did Hother do. He went
swiftly with his reindeer over the bleak wintry way until
he came unto Miming's cave, where he pitched his tent.
But long he waited ere the wood satyr came forth. Sad
and dreary were the days, and restless and anxious the
nights. Then, after waiting through a night of long
darkness, Miming came forth, and his shadow fell upon

[1] The Sword of Victory concealed in Mimer's realm. Hother resembles Svipdag
very closely. Gewar is the moon-god of the Ivalde myth.

Hother's tent. The youth sprang to his feet, and struck down the satyr with his spear, and then bound him securely. Terrible were the threats of Hother, who vowed that he would slay Miming if he gave not unto him the sword and the bracelet. The satyr held life more dearly than wealth, and gave Hother the ransom which he demanded. In triumph did the young hero return unto the kingdom of Gewar, and his fame was mooted abroad.

Then Gelder, King of Saxony, came to know that Miming had been robbed, and he urged his war-men to go against Hother, so great was his desire to become possessed of the treasure. But Gewar, who had magical powers, divined Gelder's purpose, and he counselled Hother to meet him with his band, and receive the shower of his javelins until there was none left, and then to fall upon the bold invaders.

So Hother went to meet the men from Saxony; he awaited them on the seashore. Eager were Gelder's heroes to make onslaught, and fast and furious did they cast their spears and javelins. But Hother had bidden his trained war-men to resist the missiles with shields interlocked, and not to cast a weapon. When the men of Saxony saw that, they were all the more eager to attack, and soon they flung away all their spears and javelins. Then Hother's men began to hurtle the weapons against the enemy, driving them back in confusion, whereat Gelder, in great alarm, hoisted up, on the mast of his ship, a crimson shield to make known that he desired to surrender, so that his life might be spared. But Hother showed nor anger nor vengeance against him; he approached the king with smiling face and offered his friendship. Thus became he victor by reason of his kindliness as well as his might.

A strong friend to Hother was Helgi, King of Halo-galand, who loved Thora, daughter of Cuse, the ruler of the Finns and the Bjarmians. The monarch had a blemish of tongue, so that he stuttered greatly, and was unable to utter with eloquence the sweet speeches of love. Indeed, he not only shrank from addressing strangers, but rarely spoke in his own household. He sent messengers unto Cuse, pleading for his daughter's hand, but they were rejected with disdain, for the king said that the man who could not urge his own suit was unworthy of love's prize.

Then did Helgi seek the aid of Hother, who could speak with fluency and charm, and promised him his life-long service if he would win for him the heart of Thora. A great fleet did Hother fit out, and he voyaged to Norway, fully resolved to take, by reason of his strength, the maid whom words would conquer not. To Cuse he spake first with eloquent tongue, and the king said that his daughter must first be heard, for he deemed it not right that he should prevail against her wishes, or decide before her will was made known. So Thora was ushered in, and when she heard what Hother said, she gave consent to be Helgi's queen.

But while Hother was thus engaged, Balder invaded the kingdom of Gewar with an armed band, and demanded that he should have Nanna for his bride. The king said that he must needs make request of the maiden, and before her did Balder plead his cause with choice speech and flattering address. But she said that a humble maiden could not be wooed by one of divine birth, and that the pledges of the gods were often broken. Thus did the maiden reject the love of him who sought her.

When Hother returned, Gewar told him of what had happened, and the young hero was filled with wrath because of Balder's presumption. With Helgi he took counsel and together they debated how they could inflict punishment upon the god. They had no recourse save to battle-blows, and Hother fitted out his fleet and went against his rival. Helgi gave him strong aid, as did also Gelder.

Then broke out a war in which the gods fought against mortals. With Balder fought Odin and Thor, clad in full armour, and when the opposing fleets met at sea a great conflict was waged. Hother in sword-proof mail attacked the gods with fury. Now Thor was swinging his great club, and while he urged those about him to press forward, he called upon his foemen to attack. The black-browed god dealt furious blows; he struck down his enemies' shields; he broke through their ranks; for long none could withstand him. Terrible, indeed, was the slaughter, and to the gods it seemed that victory was being given. But Hother went against Thor with Miming's sword. He feared him not, and struck at the great club, which he severed in twain with his keen-edged sword. . . . Then the gods took flight before Hother, and the ships that remained were destroyed by the victors.

Hother rejoiced in his triumph, but he sorrowed greatly because that Gelder had been slain. A great pyre he caused to be built with the wreckage of Balder's war-ships, and the corpses of the oarsmen were placed there in a heap. Then above these was laid with reverence the body of the dead king. Torches were applied and the flames rose high and bright. The ashes of King Gelder were afterwards laid in a great mound which was erected to his memory, and there was much mourning for him.

Then did Hother return to Gewar, and Nanna and

he were wed with great ceremony, while the people rejoiced. To Helgi and Thora, who were also united in their joy, did the young hero give gifts of treasure. Then Hother ruled over Zeeland and Sweden.

As greatly as was Hother praised by men, Balder was mocked because that he had fled.

But the strife came not to an end. In a land battle did Balder contend against his rival, and drove him from the field. For fickle indeed are the fortunes of war. Hother took refuge with Gewar; he who had achieved victory as a subject, was defeated when a king.

Balder's army was afflicted by a water famine, but the divine one dug wells and water streamed forth, so that his parched soldiers were able to slake their thirst. To this day is a spring called Balder's-brynd.

Even by night was Balder made unhappy in his sleep, because he was tormented by dreams of Nanna. His love consumed him like fire, and he grew melancholy and thin and careworn. At length he could no longer walk, and he was taken about in his chariot. He took no pleasure in his victory, because that he had not won Nanna. There was a magical food prepared for Balder, so that he might not be brought unto death.

At this time Frey, who ruled for the gods, took up his abode nigh to Upsala, and revived the abhorrent rites of human sacrifice.

To Sweden did Hother take flight, and Balder possessed himself of Zeeland, where he received the willing service of the Danes, who before had reverenced his rival. In due season Hother, having fitted out a fleet, again engaged in war with Balder, but was defeated and put to flight. He took refuge in Jutland, in a town which to this day bears the name of Horsens; then he returned to Sweden.

Sad at heart was Hother[1]; he was weary of life and refused to be comforted, and he took farewell of all, and wandered alone through solitary places and trackless forests, for solitude is dear to the sick at heart. The people were angry with him because that he had concealed himself in a place apart.

One day Hother, as he wandered through the deep forest, came to a cave in a lonely place in which dwelt the maidens who had given to him the sword-proof coat of mail. They received him with eyes of wonder, and they asked why he paid visit to them. Whereupon Hother bewailed his fate and with sorrow spake of the afflictions he endured. The maidens did he also reproach because that they had not helped him as they had promised. But they told him that he had inflicted greater disasters than he deemed of, and promised him ultimate triumph.

"Victory will assuredly be thine," they said, "if thou shalt but find the magical food with which Balder is nourished so that his strength may have increase. Possess thyself of it and he shall certainly die."

Then once again did Hother, encouraged by what the maidens had said, raise a great army to wage war against Balder. A fierce and long conflict was fought, and when night fell the issue was undecided, because that the forces were of equal strength.

Hother could not sleep, for he was afflicted with anxiety, and he went forth to reconnoitre the opposing camp. . . . He beheld three maidens who prepared the magical food for Balder, and followed their footprints through the dewy grass when they fled from him, so that he reached their dwelling and entered therein.

The maidens asked him who he was, for they per-

[1] Like King Hrethel in Beowulf.

ceived that he was an enemy, and he said that he was a musician. Then gave they to him a lyre, and he played sweetly thereon, so that their ears were charmed.

He saw them prepare the food for Balder. They had three serpents and their venom dropped into the mixture. One of the maidens offered Hother a portion, but the elder one said that to do so would be treason, because it would increase the strength of one of their foes. But in the end Hother was given to eat, and the maidens also conferred upon him a shining girdle which had power to assure him of victory in conflict.

Then did Hother leave the dwelling to return to his camp. But he had not gone far when he met Balder. Drawing his sword he thrust it in his foe's side so that he fell wounded nigh unto death.

There was great rejoicing in Hother's camp when he returned and told how he had stricken his rival; in Balder's camp there were loud lamentations.

Next day, when the battle was renewed, Balder bade his men to carry him into the midst of the fray upon a stretcher, so that he might not meet with death in his tent.

When night again fell Balder saw standing beside him the vision of Proserpine[1], and she told him that on the morrow she would have him for her guest. At the time appointed Balder died, and he was buried in a great grave mound with pomp and deep mourning.

In after days Harold[2] and other men sought to rob Balder's mound of its treasure, but when they pierced it a great flood of water burst forth[3] and they fled in confusion. So was terror implanted in the minds of

---

[1] Urd.

[2] Believed to be a historical personage who lived in the twelfth century.

[3] Balder is associated with well worship. Wells sprang from his horse's hoofmarks, and he found water for his soldiers. Water defends his mound.

youths there, so that they feared to disturb the mound again.

Hother again ruled over his kingdom, but he had great sorrow when Gewar was attacked and burned in his castle by Gunno, a jarl who served him. He took speedy vengeance, and burned Gunno alive upon a pyre.

When Odin came to know of Balder's death, he went unto prophets to divine how he could be avenged, and he came to know that a son would be born to him of Rinda; his name would be Boe, and he would slay Hother.

Now Rinda was a daughter of the king of the Ruthenians, and Odin went forth disguised and entered the service of that monarch. He became the captain of a band and won a distinguished victory; then he fought singlehanded against a host and achieved renown above all other men. There was great wonder thereat. Great gifts were given unto him, and he was honoured in the royal household. Then he secretly told the king of his love for Rinda, and his suit was favoured, but he must needs woo the fair princess and win her heart ere he would have her for his bride.

Not easily was Rinda wooed, because when Odin sought to kiss her, she smote him with anger. A year passed by, and then he went to the Court in foreign guise and said he was a wonder-smith. With bronze did he fashion many fair ornaments, for which he received much gold. To Rinda he made offer of a rare bracelet and rings, but again she smote him when he sought to woo her. Although her sire remonstrated with her, she scorned to wed a man of many years, especially as she was herself of tender age. A third time went Odin to woo the maid. He was disguised as a young warrior, but again he was repulsed. Then had he recourse to magic arts. He had with him a piece of bark on which runes were graven, and with that he touched her, so that she was seized with madness.

Odin returned next in the guise of a woman who was a skilled physician, and offered to cure Rinda, who was prostrate with sickness. In the end he prevailed and won the maiden for himself, and she became the mother of Boe.

At this time the gods ruled at Byzantium, and they were moved to wrath against Odin because that he had practised magic arts; so they deprived him of his high honours and drove him into exile. Oller ruled in his stead. Not until ten years had passed was Odin recalled to the throne, and then Oller fled to Sweden, where he was slain by certain Danes. It is said of Oller that he possessed a bone, graven with fearsome spells, with which he could cross the ocean as if it were a ship.

Odin reigned with greater dignity and power than before, and his renown was spread far among men. Then found he Boe, his son by Rinda, and him he constrained to go forth to avenge the death of Balder.

Thus it came that Hother was slain by Rinda's son in a fierce battle, but Boe[1] was wounded unto death, so that he was borne from the field upon his shield. Next day he died, and the Ruthenian soldiers buried him in a stately mound, so that his memory might not perish in after days, but ever have renown among men.

After Hother's death his son Rorik became king.

---

[1] Vale, who in mythology is the slayer of the wolf, is thus Boe (Beowulf) in Saxo's Danish legend. He receives his deathwound when he slays Hother, who, as Svipdag, was a dragon guarding beneath a grey rock great treasure, which shone like fire in the flood. At the same time Hother is confused with Hoder, Balder's blind brother. One of Svipdag's names was Odur. So do the divine and heroic elements of a passing mythology intermix in tradition. Each age, each race, and each bard leaves in turn impresses upon a persistent legend. The memory of the mythical hero may survive, or his deeds may become associated with the traditions of a national hero. Mythological incidents which appeal to the popular imagination not infrequently develop into independent narratives.

# CHAPTER XXII
# The Traditional Hamlet

Horwendil slays King Koll—Birth of Amleth—Horwendil slain by Feng
—The Prince feigns Madness—His Witty Sayings—Polonius is slain—Amleth
scolds his Mother—His Uncle's Treachery—Visit to Britain—His Return—
How he won the Crown—Second Visit to Britain—Mission to Scotland—The
Lovesick Queen—Amleth's Victory—Over-king claims his Kingdom—His
Death—An Unfaithful Queen.

KING RORIK, son of Hother, made joint governors of
Jutland two brothers whose names were Horwendil[1] and
Feng. Their father, Gerwendil, was governor before
them. Horwendil was chief ruler, but he sought for
glory as a sea rover. King Koll, of Norway, was also
ambitious for ocean renown, and he longed to battle with
the ships of Horwendil. The rivals met together at an
island in the midst of the sea, which they each desired to
possess, and young Horwendil challenged Koll to fight a
duel. Thus it came that the two men contended one
against the other on a portion of spring-green sward.

Horwendil was the bolder and more daring of the
two. He flung aside his shield and grasped his sword
with both hands. Furious attack did he make upon the
King of Norway, whose shield he split in twain. Then
he inflicted wounds, and smote off Koll's foot so that he
sank in death before the valorous young hero. But
Horwendil honoured the sea king with stately burial, and

---

[1] Rydberg identifies Horwendil with Orvandil, Svipdag's father, and holds that there
are memories of the Svipdag myth in the Hamlet story as related by Saxo, Halfdan
being the original of Feng, and Groa of Gerutha (Gertrude).

*King Rorik, from the painting by Koekkoek.*

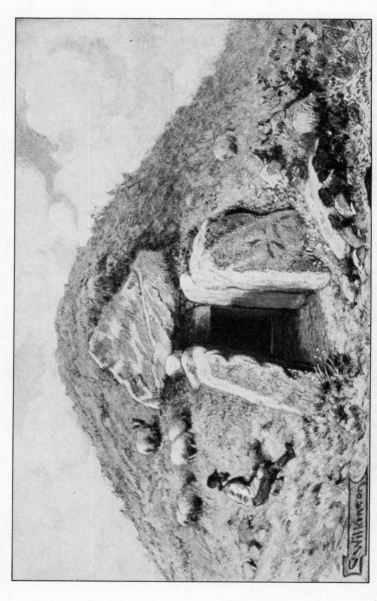

*Entrance to passage-grave at Uby, Denmark. The hiding place of Grendel —the dragon's den—was almost certainly a forgotten passage-grave.*

caused to be erected a great grave mound so that his memory might endure forever.

Many triumphs did Horwendil afterwards achieve, and to his king he gave gifts of the spoils of battle. So became he a hero in the kingdom. Rorik, who exalted Horwendil with honours, and made him King of Jutland, gave his daughter, the princess Gerutha[1], to that renowned sea rover to be his wife. To them was a son born whose name was Amleth.

Now, Feng was stricken with jealousy because of his brother's fortune and renown, and he resolved to accomplish his death. His fell purpose he achieved with treachery, and to the crime of slaying his kin he added another, for he took Horwendil's widow to be his bride. Unto men did Feng declare that he had slain his brother because that he had shown cruelty unto Gerutha, whom he had rescued when in danger. In this he was believed.

But Amleth[2] was not deluded. He perceived the evil purpose of Feng's heart, and, fearing his own safety, he feigned madness with great cunning so that he might live to slay the usurper. He went about with mire on his face. Often would he sit brooding over the fire, cutting twigs and pointing them with barbs; and when asked why he did so, he said he was preparing to avenge his father's death.

There were those who suspected that his madness was a pretence, and he was cunningly put to test, but his foster-brother[3] went about with him and gave him timely warning.

A horse was brought to Amleth, and he mounted it with his back to its neck, seeking to drive it by the tail. As he rode in this grotesque manner a wolf passed him,

[1] Gertrude.     [2] Amleth means "insane".
[3] Shakespeare's Horatio.

and those who were with him called it "a colt", where-upon Amleth said that there were too few colts of that kind in his uncle's stable.

On the shore lay a ship's rudder, and the men called it "a knife", whereupon Amleth said, pointing to the sea, that it was of appropriate size to cut such a huge ham.

To the sand dunes they then pointed, and said: "Behold the meal", and Amleth, speaking of the sand, declared that it was well-ground meal from the Mill of Storms.[1]

A maiden was sent forth to waylay Amleth, but with her he had a secret understanding. Thus were those who sought to expose the prince as one who shammed thwarted in their purposes.

A courtier[2], one of Feng's friends, who had more self-assurance than good tact, contrived a plot with purpose to make certain of knowing whether Amleth were weak-minded or a cunning pretender. He counselled Feng to leave Amleth alone with the queen, so that he might speak freely, for a son was never slow to trust his mother. Then the courtier, having convinced Feng that his proposal was a shrewd one, concealed himself under a heap of straw in the room where the queen and her son would hold converse together.

---

[1] The World-mill. In an old saga, reference is made to the Island-mill beyond the world's edge, which is worked by nine maidens. It is called "Amlode's mealbin". Thus, in the tenth century, we have an Icelandic reference to a mythical "Hamlet" who is connected with the mill. When Orvandil and the other sons of Ivalde declare war against the gods (see chapter "The Winter War") two giant maids who are relatives of Orvandil jerk the mill handle violently, and put it out of order. Here then is another link between Svipdag, the avenger, son of Orvandil, and Amleth, the avenger, son of Horvendil. Before Svipdag journeys to Hela, he is protected by Groa's incantations against the storms caused by the World-mill. In vague traditions we do not expect exact references, but rather suggestive associations. The chief actor in a popular tale absorbs all else as he develops independently through the ages.

[2] Shakespeare's Polonius.

But Amleth was too cunning to be waylaid thus. When he found, on entering the room, that the king had left on the excuse that he had business to attend to elsewhere, the prince, ere he addressed his mother, behaved with seeming madness; he crowed like a cock, and imitated the bird's wing-clapping with his hands. On the heap of straw he leapt, and then stamped about upon it. Feeling something hard below his feet, he drew his sword and drove it through the man who sought to be an eavesdropper. Then the prince hauled the body forth, cut it to pieces, and scalded it with hot water. He flung the hacked flesh to the swine.

Amleth afterwards returned to the queen, who wept and lamented her son's madness. The prince heard what his mother said, and her he addressed with great seriousness, saying:

" O, shameless woman! seek not by dissembling sorrow to conceal thy terrible guilt—thou wanton embracer of thy husband's murderer, thou harlot who took in vile wedlock the slayer of thy son's father! Thou hast mated like the brute, and with brute nature forgotten thy first husband. . . . Ask not of me why I feign madness and speak foolishly; fear I not that he who slew his brother may also do further evil unto his kindred? Although I seem to be bereft of sense, and guard myself with pretended craziness, yet am I resolute in my consuming desire to avenge my father's death, waiting patiently fit opportunity and the favourable moment. Against so foul a schemer I must needs exercise great cunning. . . . Now, canst thou—oh! thou who shouldst be wailing over thy dark shame—realize that it is needless for thee to lament my seeming madness. Better were it for thy soul if thou didst shed tears for the frailty of thine own heart, and not for the weakness of another's. . . . Thou hast heard me. . . . I counsel thee to speak not of this."

So did Amleth upbraid his mother, and reawaken in her heart, with bitterness, the memory of her murdered husband.

Soon after was the courtier, whom Amleth had slain, sought for by Feng, but of his whereabouts no man had knowledge, and the prince was laughed at when he said that he beheld him falling through a sewer to be devoured by swine. But it was ere long discovered that the courtier had indeed perished as the prince had said.

Feng would fain have put Amleth to death, but he feared the wrath of King Rorik and of his wife, so he sent the prince forth to pay visit to the King of Britain that he might be put to death by him. Ere the prince took his departure, he counselled his mother in secret to sorrow for him in a year's time as if he were dead, and to drape the walls with knitted curtains of mourning.

Two courtiers did Feng send with Amleth on his pretended mission, and he gave them a missive inscribed upon wood, beseeching the King of Britain to slay the prince. One night, while the men slept, Amleth read the missive and shaved it off the wood, inscribing in its stead a request that the courtiers should be hanged, and that he who accompanied them should be given a princess for his bride.

When they reached Britain the king read the letter, nor revealed its contents, but entertained the two messengers and the prince at a feast. Amleth made all who sat round the board wonder greatly because that he ate not of the food nor drank the wine. So, being curious to know what his guests thought of his fare, the king sent a servant to listen to their conversation after they had gone to their sleeping chamber.

Amleth's companions reproached him because of his conduct at the feast, but the prince said that the flesh smelt like human carcass, and that there was blood in the bread, and iron rust in the liquor. The king he also reviled, saying that he had the eyes of a slave, while the queen had acted like one who was low born.

It seemed to his companions that he spoke crazily, but when the king was told what Amleth had said, he sent for his chief servant and asked where the corn of which the bread was made had been grown. The servant answered him that a plenteous crop had been grown upon an old battlefield.

The monarch then asked regarding the swine, and was told that they had strayed and fed upon the body of a robber who had been slain. The liquor, he learned, was made from meal and from water taken from a certain well. The king had this well dug out, and rusted swords were found which contaminated the water.

So the king did thus prove that Amleth had spoken with knowledge. But he was not yet satisfied, and he spoke in secret to his mother, who confessed that she had been a slave.

Next day the king spoke to Amleth, whom he admired greatly because of his wisdom, and he besought of him why he had said that the queen had acted like one who was low born.

The prince gave three reasons for what he had said— she had drawn her mantle over her head like a bond servant; she had lifted her gown to walk; and she had with a small splint picked her teeth, and then chewed the shreds of food from between them.

The monarch was so enamoured of Amleth that he gave him his daughter for wife. He also had Feng's two messengers hanged, and the prince pretended to be angry thereat, so the king gave him their price in gold. Amleth had the gold melted and poured into two sticks, hollowed out for that purpose.

A year passed ere Amleth returned home, leaving his wife, the princess, in her sire's castle. When he came to Jutland he smudged his face and dressed grotesquely and went towards Feng's hall, carrying nothing save the two sticks filled with gold. There he found that the people sorrowed for him as one who was dead, and when he entered the feasting chamber he saw it was hung with mourning drapery. At first the guests were stricken with terror, because they believed him to be a ghost; but soon they made merry and cast gibes one at another because that they had been fooled.

When Amleth was asked where the king's messengers were, he lifted up the sticks saying: "This is one and that is another;" nor did they realize that he spoke truly.

The prince was in gay mood, and he poured forth plenitude of wine to the guests. They all drank freely. Once or twice Amleth drew his sword, and cut his fingers with it, so they took the weapon from him and nailed it across the scabbard upon the wall.

More wine did Amleth pour forth to the guests, because he had laid a deep plot, and soon they were all made so drunken that they could not walk. They lay down to sleep on the benches and on the floor. Then the prince tore down the mourning drapery which his mother had knitted and threw it over the slumbering lords. Each of these, by aid of the sticks, he entangled in the network, so that none of them could rise up. Thereafterwards he set fire to the building, which was consumed. All who slumbered there perished in the flames.

Amleth, meantime, made haste to Feng's sleeping

chamber, and first he snatched the sword that was hanging from the king's bed and put his own in its place. He shook his uncle from sleep and said that his courtiers were being burned alive.

"Withal I am here now, carrying my sticks," the prince cried, "with purpose to avenge my father's death."

Feng leapt from his bed and seized the mutilated sword; but while he tried vainly to draw it, Amleth slew him.

Thus did the prince put to death the man who had murdered and supplanted his sire, and all the nobles who had supported him.

Amleth then fled and concealed himself, so that he might know how the people regarded his deed. Soon he came to know that they were not greatly grieved, while a portion rejoiced that the tyrant had been overthrown. Whereupon he left his place of concealment, and gathered together his father's friends, whom he addressed.

"Ye who sorrowed for Horvendil," he said, "need sorrow not now any longer. Behold the corpse of a murderer of his kin! The hand that slew my sire made you all bondsmen.

Then Amleth revealed to the people that he had feigned madness, so that he might accomplish the ruin of Feng and his supporters. He told them how he had suffered in secret, hounded to death by his wicked uncle, disdained by his own mother, and spat upon by the nobles. "Who among ye", he cried, "is so hard of heart, that he is not moved towards me with sympathy and compassion?"

Thus he pleaded with them, and beseeched that they should honour him as their prince, and reward him with smiles of kindness.

"I have blotted out my country's shame," he said; "I have ended my mother's shame; I have stamped out tyranny. I have avenged myself on the murderer of my sire, and overcome the evil designs of my wicked uncle. . . . I have restored what you lost; your glory have I revived. The tyrant is thrown down and the butcher is slain. . . . What I have done is done, and for your sakes was it accomplished. My reward I now beg from you."

Thus did Amleth win the hearts of the people, and they declared him their king. His reward was his father's crown.

When the country was settled and well organized King Amleth crossed the seas to Britain, taking with him his choicest warriors. He had had a great shield made on which all his exploits were depicted, and it was of rare craftsmanship. The shields of his followers were covered over with gold.

When the King of Britain received him, he asked regarding Feng's welfare, and Amleth related unto him all that had happened. The king heard him with sorrow, because he had sworn a secret compact with Feng that one of them should avenge the death of the other. Nor could he consider the blood ties of his house above the sacredness of his oath. He cared not to accomplish the death of his daughter's husband with his own hands, so he contrived a plot whereby Amleth would fall by the hands of another. His queen had died, and he made request of his son-in-law to become his envoy to a queen in Scotland whom he desired to wed.

Now the King of Britain knew full well that this Scottish ruler was a lady of great chastity, who scorned to be loved, and put to death those who sought to woo her. But Amleth, although he knew the mission was begirt with peril, disdained to refuse the king's request, and, taking with him his armed followers and a few of the British war men, he went north to execute his mission.

When he drew nigh to the dwelling of the Scottish queen he went into a green dell to rest his horses, and by the side of a stream he fell asleep. Over his head he put his shield to shade him from the sun's rays.

The queen heard of his coming. She sent forth spies, who found Amleth lying fast asleep. They took away his shield and the missive which he bore from the King of Britain. Thus did the Scottish queen come to know of Amleth's great deed, because on the shield which he had made she saw depicted how he had slain his father's murderer. She read the missive and rubbed out the writing, and substituted a message from the King of Britain, expressing his desire that she should wed the bearer of it.

Amleth woke up ere the spies returned, but pretended still to sleep. When one of them was about to place the king's missive from where he had taken it, Amleth sprang up, seized him, and had him bound. Then went he to the queen's dwelling. Her name was Hermutrude. She read the altered missive, and she praised the bearer, because that he had avenged his father's death and possessed himself of the crown. She also expressed her surprise that he should have wed a slave's daughter. So noble a prince, she said, should wed one of high birth, for rank was of more account than beauty. But there was one nobly born, who was worthy of him. She herself was worthy of him, because that his kingdom and his ancestors were not greater than hers. She offered him her love and her possessions with it, and pleaded with him to set aside his marriage and have her for wife.[1]

Then the queen rose and embraced Amleth, kissing him, and he with joy embraced and kissed her in turn. A great feast was held, and they were married with ceremony and in great pomp.

Accompanied by a band of Scottish war men, Amleth then set out to return to the King of Britain; but his first wife met him and warned him against her sire. She made bitter complaint that he had slighted her, but said that her love for him was stronger than her hate of his adultery. A son was born to her, she told Amleth, who might grow up to hate the Scottish queen, but she herself would love her rival.

Then came nigh the King of Britain, and he embraced Amleth, but afterwards sought to slay him. Amleth would have fallen by the sword, which was thrust treacherously at him from behind, had he not been protected by a shirt of mail.

So it came that war broke out between them. The British king and his war men fell upon Amleth's forces and put them to flight, killing many. On the next day the young warrior found himself closely pressed, but he had resort to a cunning stratagem. He collected together all the slain war men, and set them up tied to stakes as if they were alive; on horseback even were many made fast. Thus he seemed to command an imposing array of battle warriors.

When the King of Britain's army came against Amleth, and beheld the apparent strength of his force, the soldiers were terrified, and they broke and fled in confusion. The Danes charged, and they slew the king ere

[1] Evidently a memory of Pictish marriage customs. The Irish Cuchullin has a similar experience in Scotland.

he could escape. Then Amleth ravaged the land and possessed himself of much treasure. Soon afterwards he returned to Denmark with his two wives.

It chanced that King Rorik died. His son, Wiglek, regarded Amleth as a usurper, and claimed the throne of Jutland. A war was thereupon declared, and Amleth was slain. Ere he entered the fateful battle he had fore-knowledge of his fate, and he sought to choose a second husband for Hermutrude ; but she vowed that she would share his fate on the field, saying that a woman who feared to die with her husband was an abomination. But when Amleth fell, the queen kept not her promise ; she made offer of herself to Wiglek and became his bride.

Amleth was buried on a plain in Jutland which still bears his name.[1]

## Hamlet and his Mother

*Queen.* What have I done, that thou dar'st wag thy tongue
In noise so rude against me ?
*Ham.*                 Such an act
That blurs the grace and blush of modesty;
Calls virtue hypocrite; takes off the rose
From the fair forehead of an innocent love,
And sets a blister there; makes marriage vows
As false as dicers' oaths: O, such a deed
As from the body of contraction plucks
The very soul, and sweet religion makes
A rhapsody of words!—heaven's face doth glow;
Yea, this solidity and compound mass,
With tristful visage, as against the doom,
Is thought-sick at the act.
*Queen.*              Ah me, what act,
That roars so loud, and thunders in the index?

---

[1] Muller says there are two localities named " Amelhede ".

*Ham.* Look here, upon this picture, and on this—
The counterfeit presentment of two brothers.
See what a grace was seated on this brow;
Hyperion's curls; the front of Jove himself;
An eye like Mars, to threaten and command;
A station like the herald Mercury
New-lighted on a heaven-kissing hill;
A combination and a form, indeed,
Where every god did seem to set his seal,
To give the world assurance of a man:
This was your husband.—Look you now, what follows:
Here is your husband; like a mildew'd ear,
Blasting his wholesome brother.   Have you eyes?
Could you on this fair mountain leave to feed,
And batten on this moor?   Ha! have you eyes?
You cannot call it love; for at your age
The heydey in the blood is tame, it's humble,
And waits upon the judgment: and what judgment
Would step from this to this?   Sense, sure, you have,
Else could you not have motion: but, sure, that sense
Is apoplex'd: for madness would not err;
Nor sense to ecstasy was ne'er so thrall'd
But it reserv'd some quantity of choice,
To serve in such a difference.   What devil was 't,
That thus hath cozen'd you at hoodman-blind?
Eyes without feeling, feeling without sight,
Ears without hands or eyes, smelling sans all,
Or but a sickly part of one true sense
Could not so mope.
O shame! where is thy blush?   Rebellious hell,
If thou canst mutine in a matron's bones,
To flaming youth let virtue be as wax,
And melt in her own fire: proclaim no shame,
When the compulsive ardour gives the charge,
Since frost itself as actively doth burn,
And reason panders will.
   *Queen.*                    O Hamlet, speak no more:
Thou turn'st mine eyes into my very soul;

And there I see such black and grained spots,
As will not leave their tinct.
  *Ham.*      Nay, but to live
Stew'd in corruption—
  *Queen.* O, speak to me no more;
These words, like daggers, enter in mine ears;
No more, sweet Hamlet!
  *Ham.*     A murderer and a villain;
A slave, that is not twentieth part the tithe
Of your precedent lord;—a vice of kings:
A cutpurse of the empire and the rule,
That from a shelf the precious diadem stole,
And put it in his pocket!
  *Queen.*    No more!
  *Ham.* A king of shreds and patches:—

.  .  .  .  .

My pulse, as yours, doth temperately keep time,
And makes as healthful music: it is not madness
That I have utter'd: bring me to the test,
And I the matter will re-word; which madness
Would gambol from. Mother, for love of grace,
Lay not that flattering unction to your soul,
That not your trespass, but my madness, speaks:
It will but skin and film the ulcerous place,
Whilst rank corruption, mining all within,
Infects unseen. Confess yourself to heaven;
Repent what's past; avoid what is to come;
And do not spread the compost on the weeds,
To make them ranker. Forgive me this, my virtue;
For in the fatness of these pursy times,
Virtue itself of vice must pardon beg;
Yea, curb and woo, for leave to do him good.
  *Queen.* O Hamlet, thou hast cleft my heart in twain.
  *Ham.* O, throw away the worser part of it,
And live the purer with the other half.
             *Shakespeare.*

# CHAPTER XXIII
# Hamlet's Storm-mill

When Frode was King—What the Mill ground forth—The Giant Maids
—Their Ceaseless Labour—Desire for Vengeance—Sea Rovers plunder the
Kingdom—The Maelstrom—Tale of Two Brothers—A Deal with the Devil
—Wonderful Quern Stones—The Covetous Brother—Flood of Broth—The
House by the Sea—A Skipper's Bargain—Why the Sea is salt.

"AMLODE's mealbin",[1] which the Prince of Denmark
called the "Mill of Storms", was also named by skalds
"Frode's Mill".[2]

King Frode was a wise and just king, and there was
peace when he reigned in Denmark. Harvests were
abundant, so that there was no lack of food, and treasure
was never concealed, because there were no robbers.
Strangers who visited the kingdom were received with
hospitality and allowed to depart in peace.

The king had two wonderful quern stones, which
ground at Frode's will whatever he desired of them.
When he wanted gold he named it. Then the stones
were turned round and the shining grist was poured
forth. Silver and gleaming gems were produced in like
manner. The wondrous mill could also grind peace

[1] The following is an extract from a tenth-century Icelandic saga which makes
reference to Hamlet: "'Tis said that far out, off yonder headland, the nine maids of
the Island-mill stir amain the host-cruel skerry-quern—they who in ages past ground
Amlode's (Hamlet's) meal ".

[2] Frode is the god Frey humanized. His crops were ground on the World-mill.
According to an Eddic poem his servant Bygver divided food among men. This elf
is of the mill-brownie type so familiar in folktales.

and goodwill, and thus it was that there was great prosperity when Frode reigned over the land.

Once upon a time the millstones gave forth naught, because there were no servants in the kingdom who had sufficient strength to turn the handle. In vain did Frode make search for strong workers, and at length he came to know that the King of Sweden had two slave women of great stature and strength. With a gift of gold Frode purchased them. Their names were Menja and Fenja; eight feet in height were they, and broader than the doughtiest war man; their muscles were as hard as iron.

They were set to grind the mill, and they cried: "What shall we grind?"

The king said: "Grind gold, so that I may have great wealth."

So they ground gold in plenty, and King Frode was soon the possessor of much treasure. Then they ground for him peace and plenty, and the harvests were rich, the streams flowed ever, and ships made prosperous voyages. By day and by night the giant maids ground, and they were weary, so they beseeched the king that they should have rest.

"Thou shalt pause no longer than the cuckoo is silent in the springtime," the king said.

"Rarely is the cuckoo silent in spring," they made answer; "permit that we may have longer rest."

"Thou mayest rest," the king said, "as long as the verse of a song is sung."

Frode obtained more and more wealth from the mill, but he was never satisfied. Then the maidens grew angry, and vowed vengeance upon him. One to another they said: "Are we not the daughters of mountain giants; are our kindred not greater than Frode's. We have beheld the quern in other days. In the home of giants we whirled it round, so that the earth trembled and thunder bellowed in the caves.[1] . . . Frode hath not done wisely."

Thus did they complain, weary of grinding, and Fenja at length counselled that they should no longer grind good for him who gave them no rest and was never satisfied.

Then Menja sang a weird incantation, which brought a band of warriors over the sea to work disaster with fire and sword.

Fenja called upon Frode, warning him of approaching peril, but he slept and heard her not. The warriors came to the shore; they laid waste the land, they burned the town, and scattered before them the warriors of Frode. The king was wounded grievously, so that he died.

Thus came Mysinger, the sea rover, and plundered the land, which he robbed of its vast treasures. The ships were heavily loaded thereafter, and Mysinger took with him the wondrous mill and the giant maids who turned it.

Then the sea rover set the slaves to grind salt, because there was none in the ships. As he bade them, so did they do. When night fell they asked him if they had ground sufficient for his needs; but he was no wiser than Frode, and commanded them to cease not their labours. So Fenja and Menja ground on until the ship was so full of salt that it sank into the deep.

From that day the giant maids have continued to grind the mill, for there is no one to bid them to take rest. On the sea bottom are they ever turning the stones. At the spot where they work is the great Maelstrom, a name which signifies " the grinding stream ".

[1] See chapter " The Winter War ".

It is said that Fenja and Menja still work as My-singer commanded them, and that is why the sea is salt. But there is another tale that minstrels were wont to tell regarding a wondrous mill which sank below the waves.

There were once two brothers, and one was rich while the other was poor. On a Christmas Eve the brother who was in need went unto the other and asked him in God's name for food, because that he had naught to eat.

The rich brother said: "A flitch of bacon shall I give thee if thou wilt do as I desire."

Readily did the starving man agree to his brother's terms. He took the flitch of bacon, and then he was told: "Hasten thou straight to hell with what I have given thee."

The poor brother must needs carry out the compact, so he set forth by a long and weary road. He travelled until darkness fell, and then he saw a light and went towards it. Soon he reached a dwelling. Standing outside it was an old man with a long grey beard, who hewed wood for his Christmas fire.

"Whither art thou going at this late hour?" asked the old man.

"I am journeying to hell," the other made answer, "but I know not the way."

"Thou hast no need to go any farther," the old man said, "because this dwelling is hell. When thou goest within thou shalt find not a few who will readily purchase the flitch of bacon from thee. But sell it not to any man unless thou art given the quern which is behind the door. When thou dost receive it, carry it without, and I shall show thee how to turn the handle. The quern can grind forth anything thou desirest."

The poor man knocked at the door, and it was opened.
. . . All the demons swarmed towards him, begging for
the flitch, and one did outbid the other with desire to
purchase it.

"I shall sell it," the man said, "for the old quern
which is behind the door."

The devil at first refused to barter the quern, but
soon he relented, and it was given to the man for the
flitch of bacon.

When the grey-bearded woodcutter taught the poor
brother how to use the quern, he set out with it towards
his home.

He found his wife waiting for him, and she com-
plained bitterly because that there was no food in the
house, nor fuel to light a fire. When she ceased scold-
ing him, the husband said:

"I had to travel a long way, first for one thing and
then for another, but now we shall see what we shall see."

He put the quern on the table, and he bade it grind
forth fuel and food and ale, and soon they had a warm
fire and Christmas fare in plenty. The old dame was
made happy indeed, and she said: "Where didst thou
get this wonderful quern?"

"Ask me not," answered her husband; "here is the
quern, and indeed it is an excellent one. The mill-
stream never freezes. That is enough."

Then the man made the quern to grind much food
and ale, and he gave a feast to all his friends. His rich
brother came, and when he saw that the larder was full
he grew angry because that he wished not his brother to
have anything.

"On Christmas Eve," he said, "thou didst come to
me to beg for a little food in God's name. From whence
have you received all this wealth?"

The brother who had been poor answered: "I obtained it from behind the door."

Nor would he say aught else at that time.

But ere the evening was spent the rich brother saw that the other had drunk deep, and he asked him again regarding the quern. So the man who had sold a flitch of bacon to the devil told him all. His brother pleaded for the quern, which he coveted greatly, and offered for purchase three hundred pieces of gold. The other said he would get it for that sum at the hay harvest.

Next day the man who had been poor set the quern to work, and he kept it grinding until he had enough food and drink to last him for the rest of his days. Then gave he the quern to his brother, but he told him not how to work it.

It was the beginning of the hay harvest, and the rich brother, who was a farmer, told his wife, when he carried the quern home, to go out to the field with the workers while he prepared the midday meal. Then he set the quern upon the kitchen table, and he bade it to grind forth herrings and broth in plenty.

The quern set to work, and the herrings and the broth were poured from it in abundance. First all the dishes in the house were filled, and then all the tubs, and still the food poured forth until the kitchen floor was covered over. In vain did the farmer seek to stop the supply. He seized the handle of the quern roughly, and twisted it this way and that, but without avail. The herrings were heaped high and the broth flooded the kitchen. In terror the man fled to the parlour, but the broth followed him, and he had to struggle towards the door, half-smothered in the food stream, to escape being drowned.

When the door was opened he ran down the road,

and the flood of broth and herrings went after him, roaring like a mountain waterfall and spreading all over the farm.

The farmer's wife wondered greatly that she and the workers were not called home for dinner, and she said: "Although we have not yet been bidden, we may as well return. Perhaps the master finds it harder than he expected to cook our meal, and has much need of my help."

So the dame and the workers left the hayfield and went towards the farmhouse. Ere long they beheld a strange spectacle. Pell-mell the farmer came running towards them, escaping from a torrent of herrings and broth. As he came nigh he shouted: "I would that each of ye had a hundred throats. . . . Beware, lest you are drowned in the broth!"

He ran on and hastened to his brother, and besought of him to take back the quern. But this the man who got it from the devil refused to do, unless he were paid another three hundred pieces of gold.

"If it goes on grinding for another hour," the farmer declared, "the whole parish will be covered with herrings and broth."

So he gladly paid the money demanded by his brother, who thus got back the quern again, and a goodly sum of money as well.

Then did the man who gave the flitch to the devil set the stones grinding without delay. He got all he desired from them. Before long he had a fine farmhouse, which was larger and more commodious than his brother's, and he had so much gold produced by the mill that he covered his new dwelling with plates of gold. It stood upon the shore, and far out at sea it was beheld shining in beauty. Sailors cast anchor when they came nigh to

that shore, so that they might land to see the golden
house and the rich man who inhabited it. They were
one after another shown the wonderful quern, and its
fame was spread far and near.

One day a sea captain called at the golden house, and
when he saw the quern he asked if it could grind salt.
The man who purchased it from the devil said that it
gave forth anything that was desired.

Now the captain was accustomed to go long voyages
for salt, and he offered to buy the quern. At first the
owner would not consent to sell it, but at length he
agreed to do so if he received a thousand pieces of gold.
The skipper paid that sum, and went off with the
quern, but he was not instructed how to work it. He
hastened on board his ship and sailed away. When he
was far out at sea he thought he would set the quern
a-working, so he commanded it to grind salt in plenty,
and as speedily as could be.

The quern set to work. It ground salt in plenty,
and ground very fast. Soon the hold was full, and the
skipper, feeling satisfied, sought to stop the quern. But
that he was unable to do. It ground and ground until
the decks were covered over, and at length the immense
load of salt weighed down the ship, so that it sank below
the waves.

On the floor of ocean lies the quern, and by day
and by night it grinds on as the skipper bade it to
do. . . . That is why the sea is salt.

# CHAPTER XXIV

## Land of the Not-dead and many Marvels

King Gorm and Thorkill—Voyage of Exploration—Isle of Giants—Adventures in Geirrod's Land—City of Dreadful Night—Giants in Torture—The Treasures—Battle with Demons—Thorkill's Second Voyage—Loke bound—Erik in Odainsaker—The Magic Tower—Helge Thoreson—His Demon Bride—Spells, Blessings, and Prayers—Why Helge was made blind—Hadding in the Underworld—The Flowers of Hela.

THERE was a King in Denmark whose name was Gorm, and he had more desire to obtain knowledge than to win great glory in battle.  He had royal courage, which he sought to prove in searching out the profound mysteries of the dread Unknown rather than by engaging in bloody conflict with his fellow men.

Now, Gorm came to hear of a lone, undiscovered land in the distant north, where vast treasure was concealed in caves.  The giant Geirrod dwelt there, and although the way to his abode was full of peril for mortals, Gorm was consumed with desire to explore it.  Many travellers who had ventured forth to discover the giant's country never again returned; they had to pay the dues of death.

To reach the abode of Geirrod ships must needs cross the vast tempestuous ocean that encircles the earth, and voyage on through horrors undreamt of, until the sunway is passed and the stars vanish from sight.  For in that dread land there is no light, nor warmth of summer; winter endures without end, and there is ever eternal darkness unbroken and deep.

But Gorm was without fear. No peril daunted him, nor could fear of suffering hold him back. He sought not wealth, although treasure abounded in the land of night; he desired rather the glory of achievement in searching out marvels unbeholden by living men.

So it came that the king made known his purpose to the people, and three hundred of his choicest war-men clamoured to share his renown. There was among them one braver than the rest, and it was he who had brought intelligence to Gorm of the dark undiscovered land. His name was Thorkill; he had coasted the perilous shores and knew well the path of ocean thither, so he was chosen to be leader of the exploring band.

Thorkill counselled that there should be built three strong and commodious ships, covered with thick ox hides to afford shelter from tempest spray, for vast food stores must needs be taken in them. As Thorkill advised, so did Gorm of Denmark do. He had the vessels built, they were covered with skins, and well laden with provisions and arms. In due season the voyage was begun. Northward sailed the billow-cleaving galleys, wind-driven through seething foam, and in each there were a hundred chosen men.

Ere long they came to Halogaland, and they had favoured progress on pleasant waters; but then the waves grew fierce, and the winds opposed them so that the galleys were tossed and stayed on perilous seas, driven hither and thither, and turned divers ways from their proper course. So they suffered delay, and their voyage was prolonged until their food stores were all but consumed, and hunger menaced them with death. In dire straits they made meagre pottage and fed sparingly thus on scanty fare for many days.

But at length their sufferings had end. One night in

thick darkness they heard, booming hard on the wind, the breaking surf of shoreland billows. To the masthead at dawn a youth climbed nimbly, and in the distance he saw, hazed by spray, the high beetling cliffs of a rocky isle. Towards it were the galleys steered, and with glad eyes the wasted men gazed upon the welcoming land, rough and desolate as it was. Against wind and tide they made their way, until at length they reached a haven of refuge. Then they went ashore, scrambling over broken rocks, and climbed by slippery paths the stern precipitous heights of the island until they reached the level ground.

On a green place nigh to a deep forest they beheld great herds of browsing cattle. They were easy prey, for they feared not men, whom they had never before beheld; indeed the beasts assembled together to gaze with wonder on the sea-roving band.

Thorkill had knowledge of the island perils, and he counselled the men to slay not more of the cattle than were needful for a single repast, lest the giants who kept watch there might be angered, and should seek to prevent their departure. But the men heeded him not So great was their greed that they slew many cattle and filled the galleys with their flesh. Heavily they feasted and were made glad, but there were those of them who paid dearly for their rashness.

When night fell black, there were threats of dire vengeance. The forest resounded with loud bellowing, and from the rocky beach dread monsters dashed through the surf and beset the galleys. One, greater and fiercer than the others, strode knee-deep in the sea, swinging angrily a tree-like club. He rated the seafarers because they had slaughtered the cattle, and demanded to be given a man from each galley because of the loss which the island had suffered. There was no choice but to

accept of the monster's terms; the few must oft be
sacrificed so that the many may escape. So Thorkill cast
lots, and three men were thus chosen and delivered unto
the monsters who guarded the island herds.

Thereafter a favourable wind sprang up; the sails
were set, and the ships drave onwards. Swiftly they
voyaged and far. The days grew shorter and dimmer,
until at length the sun was left behind and the stars
vanished. . . . So traversing seas unknown they came
nigh to Outer Bjarmaland. It was a dreary land, ice-cold
and dark; the snows never melt there, and eternal night
prevails.

Blacker than all else, the men saw dimly deep pathless
forests through which ever roam strange ferocious beasts,
unseen elsewhere. Many rivers were foaming seaward
over sharp and treacherous reefs.

Thorkill at length found the haven he sought, and
the ships were drawn high on the beach. Then were the
tents pitched.

"From here," said Thorkill, "the journey to Geirrod's
dwelling is short. . . . Now unto all give I timely warning. Let no man open his mouth unto any monster that
comes nigh, lest words should be spoken which would
give them power to injure you. None save one who
knows the customs of this land can converse safely with
its strange people."

Soon there came towards the seafarers a giant who
called each seafarer by his name and spoke freely. The
men were stricken with terror, and answered him not.
Thorkill told them that the giant was Geirrod's brother,
and was named Gudmund[1]; he was guardian of that
weird land, and protected from peril all men who
sojourned there.

[1] Mimer.

Gudmund spoke unto Thorkill and asked him why the men answered him not, and the wily seafarer answered that they had little knowledge of his language, and were ashamed to speak it.

Then the giant bade them all to a feast, and led the way along the banks of a river. Soon the travellers came to a golden bridge, and they desired to cross it, so fair did it seem, but Gudmund warned them that the river which they gazed upon divided the land of mortals from the land of horrid sights, and that the opposite bank was by sacred decree declared unlawful for mortals to tread.[1] So they went onward by the road they had taken, until they came to the dwelling place of Gudmund.

Privily did Thorkill then speak unto his companions, and warned them to eat not of the food placed before them, or drink of the liquor, or touch any man who was there.

As he commanded them so did they do, and at the feast they partook of their own viands only.

The feasting hall was ablaze with splendour. With Gudmund were his twelve stately sons and twelve beauteous daughters, and they made merry. But when the host perceived that King Gorm partook not of the food or the wine placed before him, and that the others likewise refused the fare, he spake to Thorkill, protesting that his hospitality was despised. But that wily seafarer said that his companions had long been unaccustomed to such rich fare, and feared to eat of the dainties lest they should be sickened.

Gudmund was ill-pleased, because the food was prepared with spells so that the guests might be made forgetful of the past and compelled to remain for ever in

[1] Saxo's words are: "Cujus transeundi cupidos revocavit, docens, eo alveo humana a monstrosis rerum secrevisse naturam, nec mortalibus ultra fas esse vestigiis."

the dismal shade among creatures non - human and weird.

So the giant sought to tempt them further. To the king he offered his daughter for wife, and unto the others he would fain give brides also. But Thorkill prevailed upon them to make refusal. All save four of the men obeyed him, and these were made insane.[1]

Then Gudmund invited the king to visit his garden, so that he might partake of its wondrous fruits; but Gorm was warned by Thorkill and refused to be lured thither. So the host perceived that he was baffled; and consented to guide them to the dwelling of Geirrod. He then conducted the travellers over the river, and promised to await their return.

They entered a dismal land which was fraught with peril and full of terrors. Not long did Thorkill and his companions travel when they beheld a strange city which seemed to be composed of vapour. Dismal and gloomy it was, and covered with dust and slime as if it were neglected and deserted. Yet was it thickly peopled by sorrowing folk. The not-dead inhabited it amidst horrors and illusions.

Lofty were the battlements that surrounded the city, and surmounting them on stakes were the heads of fallen war-men. The gates were situated so high that they could not be reached save by ladders, and fierce hel-hounds kept watch before them. Thorkill went first, and climbed towards the entrance, which is ever open. To the hounds he flung a horn smeared with fat, and they licked it greedily and were appeased. Then his companions followed him, and together they entered the gloomy city of the not-dead.

[1] In Highland lore these unions are followed by speedy death. The demon brides crush their lovers.

Horrible were the shades that hastened past them with faces fixed aghast, and ever screaming woefully. They came and went beholding naught—

> A great stream
> Of people there was hurrying to and fro,
> Numerous as gnats upon the evening gleam,
>
> All hastening onward, yet none seemed to know
> Whither he went, or whence he came, or why
> He made one of the multitude, and so
>
> Was borne amid the crowd, as through the sky
> One of the million leaves of summer's bier;
> Old age and youth, manhood and infancy
>
> Mixed in one mighty torrent did appear,
> Some flying from the thing they feared, and some
> Seeking the object of another's fear.
>
> *Shelley*

The streets were misty and loathsome; putrid scum and miry filth—

> Stifled the air till the dead wind stank.

Every sense was offended; every man was repulsed. The reeking foulness and nameless horrors froze Gorm and his followers with agonized loathing.

Then they came to Geïrrod's mountain lair. The door opened on the ledge of a black precipice, but they faltered with icy dread before it; they shrank back lest they might be overcome. But Thorkill spake words of encouragement and bade them fear not, but he warned them not to touch aught which might tempt them— gems, or gold, or any treasure—nor to be terrified by what was horrible and weird. If a hand were laid upon anything within, he told them, it could never be withdrawn; it would be bound; it would be knotted up. Then he bade them all to enter in companies of four. Broder and Buchi, the skilful archers, with Thorkill and the king went first; the others followed in order.

The doorposts were black with soot, which was centuries old and very deep; filth lay everywhere. Gaunt monster sentinels were on guard; they were numerous, noisy, restless, and menacing. Some leapt about with maniac-like frenzy, playing a strange repulsive game.

No man spoke. Half-stunned by belching filth reek from within they entered falteringly. The dwelling was wellnigh a ruin; the walls were dark and loathsome in the faint twilight; horrors loomed through the shadows. A roof of arrowy stings was above them, and the floors were made of venomous snakes steeped in foulness. Thorkill's companions were quaking with terror, and they could scarcely endure the violent and suffocating fumes. Yet they could not forbear gazing about them, confused with horror and mute with alarm. Vast giants were stretched as if dead upon benches of iron; in silent agony they lay as if carved from stone. Others wallowed in torture.

Thorkill led the strangers through a rocky fissure, and they beheld, sitting on a high ledge, the old giant Geirrod. His body was transfixed to the cliff by a javelin. Three giant maids with broken spines lay squirming beside him. These were the monsters whom Thor had thus punished because that they sought to overcome him with treachery.[1]

From the halls of torture the bold seafarers passed to a chamber of treasures, where the air was sweet. Fair indeed was the spectacle they beheld. Tankards of mead stood around them; these were encircled with fine gold

[1] See chapter "Thor in Peril".

and decorated with rings of silver. Among the treasures were a gleaming ivory tusk, circled with gold, a golden armlet, and a great drinking-horn, graven with pictures and set with sparkling gems.

Three men with covetous hearts could resist not their desire to be possessed of these rare treasures, and seized them greedily. Then did they pay life's cost for their boldness. The tusk became a sword which pierced the heart of him who laid hands upon it, the armlet became a venomous snake which stung to death the man who held it, and the great horn was transformed into a fiery dragon which devoured the robbers.[1]

The other men were stricken anew with terror in that dread land, and they all feared they would share the fate of their companions. But they passed in safety to another chamber, which had greater splendour than that which they left. It was filled with shining armour and bright weapons, and rich apparel radiant with silver and gold and ablaze with jewels. Fairest of all were a great king's robe, with his splendid headgear and his graven gem-decked waistbelt.

Thorkill, who had warned others, could not resist his desire to possess some of the rare treasure, so, impulsively he seized the royal mantle. . . . Then did dire disaster threaten them. The chamber tottered as if shaken by earthquake; women's screams were heard, and wailing voices asked if these despoilers were to be endured any longer. . . . The whole dwelling was stirred with noisy alarm. Monstrous beings who seemed to lie dead sprang suddenly to their feet, menacing and horrible, and with hordes of wan and shadowy furies made fierce

---

[1] Thjasse-Volund's Sword of Victory and multiplying ring. Here we have the treasure which was cursed, and the dragon guardian of Beowulf, Volsunga saga, &c. The horn is Gjallar-horn which Heimdal is to blow at Ragnarok.

attack upon the strangers, who were begirt with awesome peril. It was well for Thorkill and the others that the skilled archers, Broder and Buchi, were with them, for they bent their bows and shot magic arrows against the assailing horde. Spears were also cast and deadly missiles were flung from ready slings. So were the Furies beaten back, although many men fell, to be torn asunder by monsters. Those who survived made speedy escape from Geirrod's dwelling, and from the city of the not-dead, and returned to Gudmund, who waited for them, as he had promised. Then did the giant ferry them over the river and take them unto his own dwelling.

Again they were feasted and again did they resist the temptation to partake of the food and wine, and have for brides the demon maids that were offered to them. But Buchi, the archer, was stricken with love for a daughter of Gudmund, and he was driven insane in her embrace. He who contended against the monsters in Geirrod's dwelling was overcome by a maiden of gentle seeming, and he never again returned to his native land, for when Thorkill and the king took their departure he followed them towards the shore, but he was caught in a river and dashed to death.

The king and Thorkill, mourning for those who had fallen, and especially Buchi, made haste to leave the land of terror. But their voyage homeward was beset with perils; the seas wallowed in tempest, and the galleys were driven hither and thither by contrary winds, so that they suffered great delay. The food stores were at length exhausted and many died of hunger. Prayers were made to divers gods without avail, but at length the king made vows and offerings to Utgard-Loke, whereat the seas were calmed, and a favourable wind drove the vessels towards the haven of home. Of the three hundred men who had set forth to visit the land of the not-dead, but twenty returned to Denmark.

The king sought not further adventures over perilous seas towards distant lands. He lived at peace after sore travail, and he engaged in meditation regarding the mysteries of life and death. Certain teachers convinced him that to men's souls immortal life is given, and Gorm wondered whether the gods would cause him to suffer torture or reward him with bliss, because that he had spent his days in adoration and had given peace offerings.

Now the god whom the king favoured most was Utgard-Loke, and his friends counselled him that he should send Thorkill to appease that deity in the land of night. They also made grave accusations of treachery against the brave seafarer, who waxed wroth and demanded that these evil advisers of the king should accompany him on his fearsome voyage. Gorm forced the men to sail with Thorkill, and unwillingly they went forth to face the perils of the Unknown.

Great were the sufferings of the men who went towards the dwelling of Utgard-Loke. Many died from starvation ere they came to the land of eternal darkness. At length they reached a rocky shore on which there was a black tremendous precipice. Thorkill and his companions went ashore, and they came to the narrow entrance of a vast cavern. Iron benches were seen within by the light of the torches carried, and they perceived that the floor swarmed with venomous snakes. They went inward on a rocky ledge, and passed a warm and foul river, and afterwards entered a chamber which reeked with loathsome vapour and was strewn with slime. Then did they behold Utgard-Loke[1]. He was bound to the

---

[1] This is evidently Loke, not the Utgard-Loki in the chapter "The City of Enchantments". Loke's place of torture was situated in the utmost part of Nifel hel.

rock with great fetters. So long had he lain there that
his hair and his beard had grown hard as elk horns.
Desiring to return homeward with proof of his achievement, Thorkill snatched out a single hair of Utgard-
Loke's beard, whereat a foul stench came forth. Then
flying serpents made attack upon the strangers, spouting
venom which caused limbs to wither and heads to be
struck off, so that but few men escaped to the galleys.

When Thorkill returned to Denmark he was so
greatly disfigured by the venom that his friends hardly
knew him. He went to the king and related all he had
seen and what had happened to him, and he showed the
horn-like hair of Loke's beard from which deadly fumes
escaped and suffocated several who were nigh. Gorm
was terror-stricken when he came to know of the horrors
of the foul dwelling of his favoured god, Loke, and he
fell back dead ere Thorkill had finished his tale.

Beyond the realms of torture are "the Glittering
Plains", where good men and women who have died
upon earth live ever in bliss and amidst scenes of beauty.
This part of the Other-world is also called Odainsaker,
"the acre of the not-dead", and Jord lifanda manna,
"the earth of living men".

Erik, a prince of Denmark, made a vow that he
would go thither, and another prince from Norway, who
was named Erik also, set forth with him and their followers towards the east, and they journeyed a great
distance beyond India, until they reached a dark forest,
in a land where the sun never shone and the stars were
beholden by day. Onward they went through perilous
places until there was light again. They came at length
to a river, which was spanned by a bridge of stone, and
on the other side was a green and level plain. A great
dragon stood upon the bridge, keeping constant guard,

and its jaws gaped wide, issuing forth flame and smoke. Erik of Denmark feared to go farther, and said they must needs return; but Erik of Norway drew his sword, and seizing the right hand of one of his followers rushed forward with him. In horror and anguish the others beheld the two men vanishing in the dragon's jaws, so they mourned for them greatly and returned home by the way they had come.

Many years passed by, and at length Erik of Norway and his companion appeared in their native land. They told that when they went nigh to the dragon they were blinded by smoke, but they pressed on. Soon the air was cleared, and they found that they had crossed the bridge and were travelling over a glittering plain which was covered with gleaming flowers that gave forth sweet odours. It was ever summer there and ever bright and warm, but there were no shadows cast by flowers or trees or living beings. They journeyed on until they saw a beauteous tower suspended in mid-air. A ladder hung from it, and they climbed towards the door. Fair was the room they entered. The carpet was of hushing velvet, and on a gleaming table, which was laden with rich dainties, stood dishes of silver and wine goblets of graven gold. Sumptuous beds were in the tower also, and the air was filled with faint perfume. Erik and his companion were made glad, because they deemed that they had at length come unto Odainsaker.

Now while Erik lay in soft slumber there appeared before him a shining youth, who was his guardian spirit,[1] and he asked the prince if he desired to remain there forever. But Erik said that it was his desire to return, so that he might relate the wonders he had beheld. Then the spirit told him he had reached not Odainsaker, which

[1] His Hamingje.

lay beyond, and was so very fair that the tower and the land over which it was suspended seemed dreary and unlovely in comparison. But no man who ever went thither could return again. It was the prince's choice, however, to seek his fatherland; and when he returned and told of the wondrous things he had beheld he was called Erik the Far-travelled.

Helge Thoreson also visited the Glittering Plains. In a great forest he met Gudmund and his twelve daughters, who were clad in scarlet robes, and rode upon stately steeds harnessed with gold. Ingeborg, the fairest of the maids, was moved with love towards Helge, who remained with her for three days. A great tent was erected and a feast prepared; rich were the dainties, and the dishes were of silver and gold. When Helge took his departure he received much treasure from Gudmund, and he returned with it to his sire, nor were men ever told whence it was obtained.

There came a great tempest on Yule-night, and in the midst of it two strange men entered the dwelling of Helge's sire, and took the young man away.

When a year had gone past Helge appeared again with the two men, and stood before King Olav Trygveson in his feasting hall. The strangers gave to the monarch two great drinking horns, which were decorated with gold, and said that they were sent to him by Gudmund. These were then filled with mead, and the bishop blessed them,[1] but when the horns were handed to the strangers they threw them away. Then the fire went out; every light was extinguished; there was clamour and confusion

---

[1] The blessing counteracts the evil influence of a spell. In the Highlands a child should be blessed ere its name is asked, and strangers should bless a house on entering it. The blessing is not only a proof of friendly intentions, but a preventive, for he who blesses is unable to practise black magic for the time being.

in the feasting hall and the guests were terror-stricken. Afterwards it was found that Helge and the strangers had vanished. Then were prayers offered up for Helge's return.

At next Yuletide the strangers came back with Helge unto the king, and immediately went away, leaving behind them the young man, who was stricken with blindness. He told that he had spent happy days with Gudmund, but he was forced to return because of the prayers which were offered up. Ere he parted from his spirit bride she made him blind, lest his eyes should ever gaze with love upon the daughters of men.

Now after Hadding, son of Halfdan, had slain the sea dragon[1] he had strange adventures. He rescued, from a great giant Ragnhild, the fair daughter of the King of Nitheri, and she became his bride. One evening, in midwinter, while they feasted together, a spirit woman rose up, and she bore with her a bunch of white cowbanes, freshly plucked, and she asked Hadding, who wondered greatly to see summer flowers at such a time, if he had desire to behold the place where they grew. The young king answered her that he would fain see it, whereat she flung her mantle over him and together they disappeared.

'Twas thus it came that Hadding set forth to journey towards Hela. He went through a dark land, and black were the mists about him, while the air was ice-cold. Then he came to a road which was daily trod by many feet, and he walked on until he reached a swiftly flowing river which was filled with sharp and pointed weapons. With his guide Hadding crossed the bridge, and came to a plain where two great armies contended in battle. Thus did many men who were sword-slain upon earth

[1] See Chapter "The Gods Reconciled".

choose to live in Hela, where they performed again their deeds of might and fell without fear.

At length the woman took Hadding towards a place which was surrounded by a high wall. He had already gazed from afar off, as he descended the hills, upon the beauties of the enclosure, where grew the flowers which were plucked in midwinter and stately beings in robes of purple had blissful dwelling.

The old woman tried to leap over the wall, but was unable to do so. She, however, showed Hadding that the place within was indeed the land of life. She seized a fowl which she carried with her, and flung its head, which he wrung off, over the wall. The head was speedily restored again, and the bird crowed loudly.

Hadding thereafter returned again unto his own land, and he endured many perils upon the way.

## Spenser's Mimer

Guyon finds Mammon in a delve
Sunning his treasure hoar,
Is by him tempted and led down
To see his secret store.

At last he came upon a gloomy glade,
Covered with boughs and shrubs from heaven's light,
Whereas he sitting found in secret shade
An uncouth, savage and uncivil wight,[1]
Of grisly hue and foul ill-favoured sight;
His face with smoke was tann'd and eyes were bleared,
His head and beard with soot were ill bedight,
His coal-black hands did seem to have been seared
In smith's fire-spitting forge, and nails like claws appeared.

[1] This is Spenser's Mammon. He resembles very closely Gudmund-Mimer, the chief of elfin smiths who in Norse mythology produce the vast stores of treasure accursed.

His iron coat, all overgrown with rust,
Was underneath envelopèd with gold;
Whose glittering gloss, darkened with filthy dust,
Well yet appearèd to have been of old
A work of rich entail and curious mould,
Woven with antiques and wild imag'ry:
And in his lap a mass of coin he told
And turnèd upside down, to feed his eye
And covetous desire with his huge treasury

.     .     .     .     .     .

And round about him lay on every side
Great heaps of gold that never could be spent;
Of which some were rude ore, not purified
Of Mulciber's devouring element;
Some others were new driven, and distent
Into great ingots and to wedges square;
Some in round plates withouten moniment[1];
But most were stampt, and in their metal bare
The antique shapes of Kings and Kesars strong and rare

.     .     .     .     .     .

"What secret place," quoth he,[2] "can safely hold
So huge a mass, and hide from heaven's eye?
Or where hast thou thy wonne[3], that so much gold
Thou canst preserve from wrong and robbery?"
"Come thou," quoth he, "and see." So by and by
Through that thick covert he him led, and found
A darksome way, which no man could descry,
That deep descended through the hollow ground,
And was with dread and horror compassèd around.

So soon as Mammon there[4] arrived, the door
To him did open and afforded way:
Him followed eke Sir Guyon evermore,
Ne darkness him ne danger might dismay.
Soon as he entered was, the door straightway

[1] Superscription, image.      [2] The Knight Guyon.
[3] Dwelling.      [4] The gate of hell.

Did shut, and from behind it forth there leapt
An ugly fiend, more foul than dismal day;
The which with monstrous stalk behind him stept;
And ever as he went due watch upon him kept.

. . . . . .

Both roof, and floor, and walls, were all of gold,
But overgrown with dust and old decay,
And hid in darkness, that none could behold
The hue thereof; for view of cheerful day
Did never in that house itself display,
But a faint shadow of uncertain light,
Such as a lamp, whose life does fade away;
Or as the moon, cloathèd with cloudy night,
Does shew to him that walks in fear and sad affright.

In all that room was nothing to be seen
But huge great iron chests, and coffers strong,
All barr'd with double bends, that none could weene
Them to enforce with violence or wrong;
On every side they placèd were along,
But all the ground with skulls was scatterèd
And dead men's bones, which round about were flung
Whose lives, it seemèd, whilome there were shed,
And their vile carcases now left unburièd

They forward pass; ne Guyon yet spoke word,
Till that they came unto an iron door
Which to them opened of its own accord,
And showed of riches such exceeding store,
As eye of man did never see before,
Ne ever could within one place be found,
Though all the wealth, which is or was of yore,
Could gathered be through all the world around,
And that above were added to that underground.

The charge thereof unto a covetous spright
Commanded was, who thereby did attend,
And warily awaited day and night,
From other covetous fiends it to defend,

Who it to rob and ransack did intend.
Then Mammon, turning to that warrior, said:
"Lo, here the worldès bless! lo, here the end
To which all men do aim, rich to be made!
Such grace now to be happy is before thee laid."

He brought him, through a darksome narrow strayt[1],
To a broad gate all built of beaten gold:
The gate was open; but therein did wait
A sturdy villain, striding stiff and bold,
As if the Highest God defy he would:
In his right hand an iron club he held
But he himself was all of golden mould,
Yet had both life and sense, and well could weld
That cursed weapon, when his cruel foes he quell'd.

.        .        .        .        .        .

He brought him in.   The room was large and wide,
As it some guild or solemn temple were;
Many great golden pillars did up-bear
The massy roof, and riches huge sustain;
And every pillar decked was full dear
With crowns and diadems, and titles vain,
Which mortal princes wore while they on earth did reign.

A route of people there assembled were,
Of every sort and nation under sky
Which with great uproar pressed to draw near
To th' upper part, where was advanced high
A stately siege[2] of sovran majesty;
And thereon sat a woman gorgeous gay,
And richly clad in robes of royalty,
That never earthly prince in such array
His glory did enhance, and pompous pride display.

Her face right wondrous fair did seem to be,
That her broad beauties beam great brightness threw
Through the dim shade, that all men might it see;
Yet was not that same her own native hue

---

[1] Street, narrow passage.        [2] Throne.

But wrought by art and counterfeited shew,
Thereby more lovers unto her to call;
Natheless most heavenly fair in deed and view
She by creation was, till she did fall;
Thenceforth she sought for helps to cloak her crime withal.

There, as in glist'ring glory she did sit,
She held a great gold chain y-linkèd well,
Whose upper end to highest heaven was knit,
And lower part did reach to lowest hell;
And all that press did round about her swell
To catchen hold of that long chain, thereby
To climb aloft, and others to excell:
That was Ambition, rash desire to sty[1],
And every link thereof a step of dignity.

Which whenas Guyon saw, he gan enquire,
What meant that press about that lady's throne,
And what she was that did so high aspire?
Him Mammon answerèd: "That goodly one
Whom all that folk with such contention
Do flock about, my dear, my daughter is;[2]
Honour and dignity from her alone
Derivèd are, and all this worldès bliss,
For which ye men do strive; few get, but many miss.

*From " The Faërie Queene", Book II, Canto VII.*

## The Garden of Hela

Him forth thence led
Through grisly shadows by a beaten path
Into a garden goodly garnishèd
With herbs and fruits, whose kinds mote not be redd[3]:
Not such as earth out of her fruitful womb
Throws forth to men, sweet and well savourèd,

---

[1] Ascend.        [2] Urd, goddess of fate, is Mimer's daughter.
[3] Must not be declared.

But direful deadly black, both leaf and bloom,
Fit to adorn the dead and deck the dreary tomb.

. . . . . .

The garden of Prosèrpina[1] this hight:
And in the midst thereof a silver seat,
With a thick arbour goodly over dight,
In which she often used from open heat
Herself to shroud, and pleasures to entreat:
Next thereunto did grow a goodly tree
With branches broad dispread and body great,
Cloathèd with leaves, that none the wood might see
And laden all with fruit as thick as it might be.

Their fruit were golden apples glist'ring bright
That goodly was their glory to behold;
On earth like never grew, no living wight
Like ever saw, but they from hence were sold. . . .

. . . . . .

The war-like elf much wondered at this tree[2],
So fair and great, that shadowed all the ground;
And his broad branches laden with rich fee
Did stretch themselves, without the utmost bound
Of this great garden, compassed with a mound. . . .

## The River of Torture

Which to behold he clomb up to the bank;
And, looking down, saw many damnèd wights
In those sad waves, which direful deadly stank,
Plongèd continually of cruel sprites,
That with their piteous cries and yelling shrightes[3],
They made the further shore resounden wide:
Amongst the rest of those same rueful sights
One cursèd creature he by chance espied
That drenchèd lay full deep under the garden side.

[1] In Saxo she is Urd.    [2] Like Ygdrasil.    [3] Shrieks.

Deep was he drenchèd to the upmost chin,
Yet gapèd still as coveting to drink
Of the cold liquor which he waded in;
And, stretching forth his hand, did often think
To reach the fruit which grew upon the brink;
But both the fruit from land, and flood from mouth,
Did fly a-back, and made him vainly swink;
The whiles he starved with hunger, and with drouth
He daily died, yet never throughly dyen couth[1].

He looked a little further and espied
Another wretch, whose carcas deep was drent[2]
Within the river which the same did hide.
But both his hands most filthy feculent[3]
Above the water were on high extent,
And feigned to wash themselves incessantly.
Yet nothing clearer were for such intent,
But rather fouler seemèd to the eye;
So lost his labour vain and idle industry.

## The Fruit of Forgetfulness

Infinite more tormented in like pain
He there beheld, too long here to be told;
Ne Mammon would there let him long remain,
For terror of the tortures manifold,
In which the damnèd souls he did behold,
But roughly him bespake, "Thou fearful fool
Why takest not of that same fruit of gold?
Ne sittest down on that same silver stool,
To rest thy weary person in the shadow cool?"

All which he did to do him deadly fall
In frail intemperance through sinful bait
To which if he inclinèd had at all
That dreadful fiend, which did behind him wait,

1 Could.　　2 Drenched.　　3 Muddy, foul.

Would him have rent in thousand pieces straight;
But he was wary wise in all his way
And well perceivèd his deceitful sleight,
Ne suffered lust his safety to betray;
So goodly did beguile the guiler of his prey.

And now he was so long remainèd there
That vital powers gan wax both weak and wan
For want of food and sleep, which two up-bear
Like mighty pillars, this frail life of man,
That none without the same enduren can:
For now three days of men were overwrought,
Since he this hardy enterprise began:
Forthy[1] great Mammon fairly he besought
Into the world to guide him back as he him brought.

The god, though loth, yet was constrained t' obey;
For longer time than that no living wight
Below the earth might suffered be to stay:
So back again him brought to living light.
But all so soon as his enfeebled spright
Gan suck this vital air into his breast,
As overcome with too exceeding might,
The life did flit away out of her nest,
And all his senses were with deadly fit oppressed.

# Hela in the Border Ballads

## The Three Roads

True Thomas lay on Huntlie bank;
  A ferlie he spied wi' his ee;
And there he saw a ladye bright,
  Come riding doon by the Eildon Tree.

   .    .    .    .    .    .

[1] Therefore.

" Harp and carp, Thomas," she said;
    " Harp and carp along wi' me;
And if ye dare to kiss my lips,
    Sure of your bodie I will be."

" Betide me weal, betide me woe,
    That weird[1] shall never daunton me."—
Syne he has kissed her rosy lips,
    All underneath the Eildon Tree.

.      .      .      .      .      .

She 's mounted on her milk-white steed;
    She 's taen true Thomas up behind:
And aye, whene'er her bridle rung,
    The steed flew swifter than the wind.

O they rade on, and farther on;
    The steed gaed swifter than the wind;
Until they reach'd a desert wide,
    And living land was left behind.

" Light down, light down, now, true Thomas,
    And lean your head upon my knee;
Abide and rest a little space
    And I will shew you ferlies three.

" O see ye not yon narrow road
    So thick beset with thorns and briers?
That is the path of righteousness,
    Though after it but few enquires.

" And see ye not that braid, braid road,
    That lies across that lily leven?
That is the path of wickedness,
    Though some call it the road to heaven.

" And see not ye that bonny road,
    That winds aboot the fernie brae?
That is the road to fair Elfland,
    Where thou and I this night maun gae.

[1] Urd—destiny.

"But, Thomas, ye maun hold your tongue,
  Whatever ye may hear or see;
For, if you speak word in Elfyn land,
  Ye 'll ne'er get back to your ain countrie."

O they rade on, and farther on,
  And they waded through rivers aboon the knee,
And they saw neither sun nor moon,
  But they heard the roaring o' the sea.

It was mirk, mirk night, and there was nae starn light,
  And they waded through red blood to the knee;
For a' the blood that 's shed on earth
  Rins through the springs o' that countrie.

Syne they came on to a garden green,
  And she pu'd an apple frae a tree—
"Take this for thy wages, true Thomas;
  It will gie thee the tongue that can never lee."

*Thomas The Rhymer.*


## The Mountains

"O where have you been, my long, long love,
  This long seven years and more?"—
"O I 'm come to seek my former vows
  Ye granted me before."—

  .     .     .     .     .     o

She has taken up her two little babes,
  Kissed them baith cheek and chin;
"O fare ye weel, my ain two babes,
  For I 'll ne'er see you again."

  .     .     .     .     .     .

She had not sailed a league, a league,
  A league but barely three,
When dismal grew his countenance,
  And drumlie grew his ee.

The masts that were like the beaten gold,
  Bent not on the heaving seas;
But the sails, that were o' the taffetie,
  Fill'd not in the east land breeze.

They had not sailed a league, a league,
  A league but barely three,
Until she espied his cloven foot,
  And she wept right bitterlie.

" O hold your tongue of your weeping," says he,
  " Of your weeping now let it be;
I will show you how the lilies grow
  On the banks of Italy."—

" O what hills are yon, yon pleasant hills,
  That the sun shines sweetly on?"—
" O yon are the hills of heaven," he said,
  " Where you will never win."—

" O whaten a mountain is yon," she said,
  " All so dreary wi' frost and snow?"—
" O yon is the mountain of hell," he cried,
  " Where you and I will go."

*The Demon Lover.*

## Demon Vengeance

Up then spake the Queen o' Fairies
  Out o' a bush o' broom—
" She that has borrowed young Tamlane
  Has gotten a stately groom."—

Up then spake the Queen o' Fairies
  Out o' a bush o' rye—
" She's taen awa' the bonniest Knight
  In a' my companie.

" But had I kenn'd, Tamlane," she says,
  " A lady wad borrowed thee,

I wad ta'en out thy twa grey een,
    Put in twa een o' tree.

" Had I kenn'd, Tamlane," she says,
    " Before ye came frae hame—
I wad ta'en out your heart o' flesh,
    Put in a heart o' stane."

" Had I but had the wit yestreen
    That I hae coft the day—
I 'd paid my kane seven times to hell
    Ere you 'd been won away."

                   *The Young Tamlane.*

## The Birk o' Paradise

There lived a wife at Usher's Well,
    And a wealthy wife was she,
She had three stout and stalwart sons,
    And sent them o'er the sea.

They hadna been a week from her,
    A week but barely ane,
When word came to the carline wife
    That her three sons were gane.

They hadna been a week from her,
    A week but barely three,
When word came to the carline wife,
    That her sons she 'd never see.

" I wish the wind may never cease,
    Nor fishes in the flood,
Till my three sons come hame to me,
    In earthly flesh and blood."[1]

---

[1] She had evidently power to work a spell and secure her wish.  Belief in wishing power is not yet quite extinct in Scotland.

It fell about the Martinmas,
  When nights are lang and mirk,
The carline wife's three sons came hame,
  And their hats were o' the birk.

It neither grew in syke or ditch,
  Nor yet in ony sheugh;
But at the gates of Paradise
  That birk grew fair eneugh.

## Gilly Flowers

  The fields aboot this city fair
    Were a' wi' roses set,
  Gilly flowers and carnations rare
    Which canker could not fret."
                    *Clerk Saunders*

## The Garden Fruit

She led him intil a fair herbere,
  There fruit groand was gret plenté,
Pears and apples, both ripe they were,
  The date and eke the damsyn tree,
  The fig and eke the wineberry.

    .     .     .     .     .

He pressed to pull the fruit with his hand,
  As man for food was nyhonde faint,
She said, "Thomas let that stand,
  Or else the fiend will thee attent.

"If thou pull them, sooth to say,
  Thy soul goes to the fire of Hell;
It comes not out till Domisday
  And there ever in pain to dwell."
                    *Thomas The Rhymer.*

# CHAPTER XXV

## The Doom of the Volsungs

The Swan Maidens—Weland Legend—Asa-god's Adventure—The Treasure Curse—Fafner becomes a Dragon—Regin the Wonder Smith—The Volsung Family—Odin brings the Magic Sword—Marriage of Signy—King Siggeir's Treachery—Volsung and his Sons are slain—The Survivor, Sigmund —Desire for Vengeance.

ERE the sons of Ivalde warred against the gods, they loved three swan maidens, whose songs in summer were sweet to hear. One morning the snow-white birds flew towards a lake in Wolfdales. The brothers followed them, and they beheld sitting on the shore three beauteous valkyries, who were singing and spinning flax. Beside them lay their swan coverings, and these the brothers captured. Then had they the swan maids in their power, and they took them to be their brides. Egil-Orvandel had Obrun, Slagfin-Gjuki had Swan-white, and Thjasse-Volund had All-white.

For seven years they all lived happily together. But in the eighth year the swan maids were seized with longing, and in the ninth they flew away in search of conflicts. Nor did they ever again return. In vain did Orvandel-Egil make swift pursuit on his skees, and in vain did Slagfin-Gjuki search for his lost bride. But Thjasse-Volund remained behind, and when the Winter War began to be waged, he retired to a deep mountain recess where he concealed his treasure, which he cursed with spells.

Then did Thjasse-Volund erect a smithy where he forged the magic Sword of Victory, so that he might wreak his vengeance upon the gods, and become chief ruler in Asgard. A wondrous serpent ring did he also fashion. It was given power to multiply without end, and when Mimer came suddenly upon the cunning artificer and bound him, he found within the smithy a chain of seven hundred rings which could fetter the wind.

In ancient England minstrels were wont to sing to Angles and Saxons of Volund, the wonder smith, whom they called Weland.[1] He was a prince of the fairies. In other lands and in other tongues was the "Lay of Volund" sung also. Mimer was named Nithud, and called "King of Sweden".

Now King Nithud desired greatly to possess the treasures of Weland. So he sent mounted warriors to Wolfdales to take the elf prince captive. In bright moonlight the men rode forth clad in shining armour. When they reached Weland's hall, they entered it boldly, for the smith, who was a skilled archer, was hunting afar. They beheld, hanging on the wall, a chain of seven hundred rings; they took it down, and one ring they kept. Then the men concealed themselves. In time Weland returned from the chase. Keen-eyed was he indeed, for he at once seized the rings and sat down on a bear's skin to count them. He found that one was missing, and he deemed fondly that his fairy wife had returned, because for her he had forged the ring. Musing thus a long time, he fell fast asleep.

[1] Beowulf had armour made by Weland. In Scott's *Kenilworth*, chap. xiii., he appears as "Wayland Smith", whose fame "haunts the Vale of the Whitehorse" in Berkshire. The legend is associated with the burial place of a Danish chief. "Wayland", like the Highland fairy, performs during the night work left for him to do. His fee is sixpence. This fairy smith was also known in France.

In sorrow he awoke; his hands were chained and his feet were fettered.

Then his captors bore him away, and they put him on an island to forge weapons and ornaments for the king. The heart of Weland was filled with wrath.

"On Nithud's belt," he cried, "I behold the sword which I fashioned with all my skill. I have lost for ever my shining blade. Bodvild, the queen, hath now the ring of my fairy bride. I shall ne'er be appeased."

In his secret heart Weland vowed to be avenged. He took no rest; he sat not by day nor slept at night. He kept striking with his hammer.

One day two young sons of the king entered the smithy. He slew them, and of their skulls made drinking-cups which he sent unto the king. Then unto him came also Bodvild, the queen, and she loved him because that she wore the magic ring. So by the wonder smith was she beguiled.

Weland ceased not to work until he had fashioned for himself eagle pinions. Then he flew away, leaving the queen to grieve bitterly for him because of the spell that was upon her, while Nithud lamented for his sons.

When Thjasse-Volund perished in Asgard, whither he had flown, and the other sons of Ivalde passed also, the curse remained upon the treasure, which was then guarded by a dwarf, or, as some tell, by a fiery dragon. In after days the curse fell upon each man who became possessed of the doomed hoard of the sons of Ivalde. And ever did the rings continue to multiply, and the chain to grow, ring following ring and linking one to the other, and each one like to the first that was forged by the wonder smith. The rings came down the Ages and the chain extended from land to land.

So grew also, link by link, the wondrous story chain

of Ivalde's sons and of the swan maidens whom they loved and lost. Their fame can never end nor their sorrows, nor can the doom of the treasure curse pass away while ring follows ring and the chain grows on.

Old is the ring tale of the Volsung's doom. By Iceland's skalds was it sung to harp music in other days, and warriors loved to hear it in the feasting hall as they drank mead, while the log fire reddened their faces and the night wind bellowed through the gloom.

For it was told that there was once a dwarf king named Hreidmar who possessed much treasure. He had three sons and three daughters. The first son was named Fafner, the second Ottar, and the third Regin. Fafner had great strength, and was fierce as he was surly : he claimed the possessions of the others for himself. Ottar was wont to fish in otter guise, and caught salmon in the river, which he laid out on the bank. Regin had neither the might of Fafner nor the cunning of Ottar, but he had skilful hands, and he became a wonder smith who shaped weapons of iron and ornaments of silver and gold.

One day Odin and Honer and Loke journeyed together, and it chanced that they drew nigh to the dwelling of Hreidmar. On the river bank they saw the otter : he had devoured a salmon and lay fast asleep. Loke, who was ever working evil, flung a sharp stone which smote the dwarf's son and killed him, and when he had done that, he took off the skin. Then the gods went towards the dwelling of Hreidmar and entered it.

Wroth indeed was the dwarf when he beheld the otter's skin, and he seized the gods and demanded ransom. So Loke had to go forth alone to obtain sufficient gold, while Odin and Honer were kept secure.

Now Loke knew that a great treasure hoard lay hidden in a dark mountain cavern ; it was guarded by a dwarf named Andvari, who had taken the guise of a pike, and ever concealed himself in a deep pool below a waterfall. Loke resolved to possess the gold, so that the gods might be set free. So he went to Ran, the sea-goddess, and when he had told her of the plight of the gods, he borrowed her wondrous net. Then he hastened to the pool below the waterfall and fished up Andvari the pike.

"What fish art thou?" he said. "Thou dost lack cunning to be thus taken unawares. Of thee I demand life ransom in water gold."

The pike answered: "My name is Andvari, and my sire is Oinn. By a Norn of evil fortune was I doomed to pass my days in cold waters."

But Andvari could deceive not Loke, and was forced to pay life ransom, unwilling as he might be. So changing his shape, he went to the mountain cavern to yield up the treasure of which he was guardian. In vain Andvari sought to keep back a single gold ring which had power to multiply. But Loke demanded it with the rest. Then was the dwarf moved to great anger.

"My treasure is accursed," he cried. "It shall bring death to two brothers, and cause strife among eight kings. No man shall ever be made glad by my gold."

Now Hreidmar had demanded of the gods that ne should receive as ransom for his son's death as much gold as would cover the otter skin. Loke laid upon the skin all the treasure he had obtained save the ring, which he sought to keep for himself. But Hreidmar perceived that a single whisker hair of the otter stood bare, and he demanded that it should be covered. Unwillingly did Loke lay the ring upon it. Then were the gods ransomed and set free.

Loke was angry as the dwarf had been, because he

had perforce to part with the magic ring, and ere he went his way he spoke fiercely to Hreidmar, saying:

"Thou hast received gold enough now, and my head is safe. But thou shalt never prosper, nor shall thy sons prosper after thee. Take thou with the gold the curse that follows it."

Then Fafner arose and demanded the entire treasure for himself. He fought with his sire, to whom he gave his deathwound.

Ere he died, Hreidmar besought his daughters to avenge him. But one, who was named Lyngheid, said that a sister could slay not her brother, whereat her sire foretold that she would have a daughter whose son would be his strong avenger.

Fafner drave forth his sisters and his brother Regin, and possessed himself of all the treasure. Heavily indeed did the curse fall upon him, and there was never again any joy in his heart. He went unto a lonely place, which was called "Glittering Heath", to be guardian of his ill-gotten gold, and he brooded over it there with anger and suspicion, until he became a wingless dragon which was feared and hated by all men.

Regin was thus made poor, and he went to a king whose wonder smith he became. He shaped strong weapons and many ornaments of gold and silver, for which he received great praise and royal honours. But in his heart he grieved because that he had been robbed by his brother of his just share of the treasure. Great was his desire that the dragon should be slain, so that he himself might become possessed of the wealth. But many years passed ere the avenger had birth, as Hreidmar had foretold, and Fafner was killed. The avenger was Sigurd, and his sire was Sigmund, son of Volsung. Noble was he and of great strength and battle power, like all his kin. Bright, too, were his days until the curse of the treasure fell upon him.

Now the sire of Volsung was Rerir, who was the son of Sige. The sire of Sige was Odin. It chanced that Sige went forth to hunt in wintertime through a snow-wreathed forest. With him went Brede, who was a servant to Skadi, and was skilful in the chase. At the day's end Sige was enraged because Brede had taken more game than him; so he slew the man and concealed his body in a snow wreath. But the crime was discovered and Sige was banished from the land of his folk.

Then did Odin come to his son's aid, and gave him war vessels and a force of brave war-men. Many victories were won by Sige. His fame in battle was spread far and near, and he conquered and ruled the land of the Huns. He achieved great glory in his prime, but his life's end was clouded by dissensions in the kingdom. Even the queen's brothers conspired against him. Then a great battle was fought and Sige was slain. His son Rerir reigned after him. His kinsmen he slew and put their army to flight. Thus did he avenge the death of his sire.

Rerir became a greater monarch than Sige. He took for wife a noble lady, but as the years went on they fell to mourning, because that no child was born to them. So they prayed to the gods, and Freyja heard them with compassion. Then was one of her maids, who was a daughter of the giant, Hrimner[1], sent to earth in crow guise bearing an apple for the queen. Thus was the queen's desire fulfilled. But soon afterwards the king sickened and died. The child was not born until he was seven years old, and he was named Volsung.

Now Volsung became the most powerful king of his

[1] Angerboda, the Hag of Ironwood, when she was a maid attendant to Freyja.

time. He was far famed as a warrior, and he ruled his people justly and well. A great house did he cause to be built. In the midst of it grew a mighty oak which was named Branstock, and its branches overhung the roof. It was told that Volsung had for wife the giant's daughter, Ljod, whom gentle Freyja had sent with the magic apple to his queen mother. They had two sons and one daughter, and the first-born were Sigmund and his twin sister, Signy. The lad was as strong and brave as the girl was comely and fair.

At that time Siggeir was King of the Gauts, and he sought to have Signy for his bride. So it came that they were wed in Volsung's hall. A great feast was given and the warriors of the Gauts were there, and they made merry with Volsung's nobles and his two sons.

When the feast was over, a tall, old man entered the hall. He wore a blue cloak, mottled with grey, a round hat which was drawn down over his face, and tight breeches of linen. He had but one eye, and his feet were bare. In his hand he carried a gleaming sword, and he plunged it into Branstock right up to the hilt. None spoke, but they all watched him with mute amaze. Then he spake gravely unto them.

"I gift this sword", he said, "unto the man who can draw it from Branstock. He shall find it a goodly blade indeed, for it hath no equal."

Then he vanished from before them. . . . He was Odin, but no man knew him.

Now the chief warriors who were there laid hands, one after the other, upon the sword. But in vain did they endeavour to draw it forth. It stuck deep in the tree, defying them as it tempted them. But at length Sigmund grasped the hilt in his strong right hand, and pulled out the blade, which he thus had for himself as a gift from Odin.

Ill pleased was King Siggeir, for he sought greatly to possess the shining blade for himself, and he made offer to purchase it with much treasure; but Sigmund refused to deliver it up even though the King of the Gauts gave unto him all the gold he possessed.

Siggeir answered not. He sat moodily apart, for he deemed that the young warrior had spoken scornfully. With anger in his heart he devised a treacherous scheme with purpose to gain his desire and to wreak vengeance upon the kinsfolk of his queen. So next morning he made ready to depart, although the wedding celebrations were not ended, and he invited Volsung and his sons to visit him after the space of three months. Volsung gave his word to do so, and took leave of Siggeir and Signy. Unwilling indeed was the fair bride to leave the land of her people, and she would have parted with her husband had her father permitted her.

When three moons had waxed and waned, Volsung and his sons with their followers voyaged in three ships to Gautland. Fair winds favoured them and they made speedy passage, and on a fragrant evening they reached a haven and went ashore. Then came Signy to them in secret to persuade them to return, because that her husband had collected together a great army to accomplish their fall. But Volsung disdained to go back.

"A hundred battles I have fought," he said, "and I was ever victorious. In my youth I feared not my foemen, and in my old age I shall flee not before them. A man can die but once, and he can escape not death at his appointed time. So we shall fare onward nor fear aught, and no man shall tell that Volsung ever fled from danger or sued for peace."

Signy desired to remain with her kin, but Volsung bade her return to Siggeir and stay with him.

Next morning brave Volsung and his two sons with all their followers went fully armed towards the hall of Siggeir. But a strong force came out against them, and after fierce and long fighting Volsung was slain with all his followers, and his two sons were taken captive. Siggeir then became possessed of Sigmund's sword, which was named Gram.

Earnestly did Signy entreat that her brothers should not be put to death, and although the cruel Gaut king relented somewhat, he caused them to be bound together to a felled tree in a deep forest. In the midst of the night a fierce she wolf came and devoured one of them. Secret messengers bore the sad tidings unto Signy and she grieved piteously. On the second night another son of Volsung was devoured; and so night after night one perished by the wolf until Sigmund alone remained alive.

Then Signy sent her messengers to smear Sigmund's body with honey, and they did according to her desire. In the darkness of night the wolf came to devour him. But when the monster smelt the sweet savour, she began to lick the young hero's face. At length she thrust her tongue into his mouth, and Sigmund seized it between his teeth and bit it off. As he struggled, he burst his fetters and the monster was slain.

Now the wolf was none other than King Siggeir's mother, who was skilled in witchcraft and had power to change her shape.

Sigmund found a safe retreat in the wood, where he made for himself a subterranean dwelling. In time Signy came to know that it fared well with him, but Siggeir knew not that Sigmund remained alive and awaited the hour of vengeance.

# CHAPTER XXVI

## How Sigmund was Avenged

The Forest Hut—Waiting the Day of Vengeance—Signy's Sons—Why they were slain—Sinfjotle, the Volsung—The Were-wolves—Attack on King Siggeir's Hall—Avengers buried alive—Their Escape—Siggeir's Fate—Signy's Tragic Farewell—Sigmund returns to his Kingdom—Usurper overthrown.

FOR long years, through summer's heat and winter cold, did Sigmund dwell in his forest hut, biding his time. Signy had two sons, and it was her heart's hope that their Volsung blood would stir them up to avenge her sire's death. She set at length to proving their worth. On their hands she put winter gloves, which she sewed through their flesh. But they cried out thereat, and she feared that they had more of Siggeir's nature than that of her kin.

When the eldest was ten years old she sent him unto Sigmund, so that it might be found whether he was fit to give service in the work of blood vengeance. Sigmund greeted the lad and took him within his hut. Then secretly he placed a venomous serpent in the meal sack, and having bidden Signy's son to bake bread, he went through the forest to gather firewood.

In time he returned, and he found that no bread had been baked, so he asked why it was not ready.

"I feared to place my hand in the meal sack," said the lad, "because something darted quickly in it."

Sigmund knew then that the lad lacked courage, and when he met with Signy he said her son was unworthy to be a Volsung.

"Then he is unworthy to live," his mother cried angrily. So Sigmund slew him.

Another winter came, and Signy sent her second son unto her brother; but he proved to be timorous like the first, and was put to death also.

Signy next conspired with a witch, and they changed shapes. The witch lived in Siggeir's hall as his queen. and Signy went through the forest towards Sigmund's secret dwelling. She begged for food and shelter, nor did her brother have knowledge of who she was. For three nights she dwelt in the underground hut and then returned to her home, where she again changed shapes with the witch.

In time Signy's third son was born, and he was indeed of Volsung blood. The name he received was Sinfjotle, and he grew up to pleasure his mother's heart, fair as her kin and strong and without fear. In secret she told him of her sire, and of how he died through Siggeir's treachery, and she told him of the wolf which devoured her fettered brothers. She filled his heart with the glory of the Volsungs and he took pride in their fame. One day she set to proving him, and she sewed gloves on his hands and wrists, piercing his flesh with the needle. But he twitched not a muscle, and her heart was gladdened. Then she tore off the gloves, and the raw flesh was laid bare.

"I have given thee sufficient pain," she said.

But the youth smiled. "Volsung", said he, "would shrink not from wounds so slight."

Soon afterwards Sinfjotle was sent by his mother unto Sigmund, and he was received as were the others, and set to bake bread.    A venomous serpent was again placed in the meal sack.

When Sigmund returned with firewood, he found that the bread was made ready.

"Found ye aught in the sack?" he asked the lad.

"Something darted quickly through the meal," Sinfjotle answered, "but I paused not to discover what it was, and it is baked in the bread."

Volsung's great son was well pleased with the lad, but he warned him not to partake of the bread, because he could resist not the poison.  But Sigmund ate of it himself, because he was of such great strength that the venom could harm him not.

Signy's son remained with Sigmund, who trained him in feats of strength.  Together they robbed and murdered men in the forest, and the lad proved his worth and grew speedily to full strength.  Sigmund thought sure he was a son of Siggeir, and he ever prompted him to avenge the death of Volsung, for he feared that the lad was but a Gaut at heart.  So he regarded the lad with suspicion, and was watchful lest he might prove treacherous like to Siggeir.

It chanced that on a darksome night they came together to a house in which robbers lay asleep. There they found two wolfskins, which gave those who wore them power to change their shapes.  These they took away, and when they put them on, Sigmund and Sinfjotle were transformed into were-wolves.  Then were they fierce indeed.  Between them they made a compact that one would call upon the other if confronted by seven men, and then they parted to prowl for their prey in the deep forest.

Ere long Sigmund had to fight against seven men. He set up the loud wolf howl, and Sinfjotle hastened to his aid, and between them they slew all the band. After that they parted, and then Sinfjotle had to contend against eleven men. But Signy's wolf son uttered no cry. He fought fiercely and alone, and slaughtered all his opponents. Then wearily he lay down to rest.

Sigmund came towards him soon afterwards, and when he found that Sinfjotle had surpassed him in valour he sprang upon the youth with wolf anger and did him grievous injury. But he speedily repented what he had done, and carried his companion to the underground dwelling, where he lay nigh unto death. In sore distress was Sigmund, and he vowed never again to go forth as a wolf. Then it chanced that he saw two weasels who fought together. One seized the other as he had done to Signy's son, but it ran speedily to find a herb which restored its companion to full strength again. He sought to find the healing herb, and a raven[1] flew towards him bearing a leaf in its beak, which it let fall at his feet. Perceiving that it was of the herb he desired to find, Sigmund hastened to his hut and laid the leaf upon Sinfjotle's wounds. The youth was at once healed and the affliction passed.

Together the heroes waited until they could regain their wonted shape again. Then they destroyed the wolfskins, lest the one should slay the other.

Sigmund perceived that the lad was his equal in strength, and deemed that the time had come when they could wreak Volsung vengeance against Siggeir, King of the Gauts. So they armed themselves and went forth. When they reached the hall they concealed themselves among the mead casks which stood along the entrance way. But ere night fell two of Siggeir's children, who played with a golden ball, cried out because

[1] One of Odin's ravens.

that they saw two grim warriors in shining armour crouching behind the casks. Sinfjotle sought to slay them, but Sigmund disdained to shed their blood. So the alarm was raised and Siggeir and his war-men issued forth to contend against the intruders. The avengers sprang up with drawn swords. They feared not the overwhelming force that clamoured for their blood. Sinfjotle first slew Siggeir's two children and then the fight raged fierce and fast. Many warriors fell. Sigmund and his companion made great slaughter, but their foemen were so numerous that in the end they were taken captive and bound.

Then did Siggeir and his nobles take counsel together to devise how the twain might be given the most cruel death, and it was decreed that they should be buried alive.

In the morning two stone grave chambers were made, one beside the other, and in these were Sigmund and Sinfjotle laid. Ere the slab and earth were placed over them, Signy came forth with flesh wrapped in straw and flung it into the graves. There was it allowed to remain, so that their torture might be prolonged. Then the barrows were covered over.

The buried heroes spake out one to another in the darkness, and Sigmund bethought him at length to partake of the flesh. So he cast aside the straw, and when he had done that he discovered that a sword was thrust through the flesh. He knew by the hilt that it was Gram, and his heart leapt within him.

With the wondrous sword the two men sawed through the great slab which covered the grave chambers, and when darkness fell they came forth.

It was the night of Volsung vengeance, long desired, long waited for. Sigmund and Sinfjotle hewed logs with

Gram, and heaped the wood splinters round the hall. Then they put fire to them, and soon the dwelling of King Siggeir was wrapped in flames.

The king woke up, and through the smoke he cried in anguish: "Who hath come against me with fire? Now death assaileth me!"

Sigmund heard him, and in triumph he answered: "Now dost thou know, O treacherous man, that a son of Volsung remains alive. I am Sigmund, and Sinfjotle, son of Signy, is here with me."

The flames spread. Death encompassed all that were in the hall. None could escape, because the avengers guarded the door. But Sigmund was loath that Signy should perish, and he called to her to make escape with all the treasure she could seize. The queen heard her brother's voice amidst the roar of flames, and she came to the door with empty hands.

"Full well thou knowest," she said unto Sigmund, "that I never forgot how Siggeir killed King Volsung. My very children I had slain because they were too weakly to avenge my sire's death. But behold! Sinfjotle is a mighty warrior indeed, for he is not only mine own son, but a son of a son of King Volsung also. For vengeance have I striven through long years, so that Siggeir might have his deathdue in the end. Now my labour is finished and my purpose is achieved. I have no need of longer days, nor do I desire to live now. By compulsion was my life spent with Siggeir; now that I have free choice I shall die gladly with him. . . . Fare thee well."

So saying she kissed Sigmund and Sinfjotle, and hastening back to her husband she perished with him in the flames. . . . Thus was the death of King Volsung avenged.

Sigmund was now free to return to his own land, and with his son he crossed the sea. A usurper sat upon Volsung's throne, but he was speedily overcome by the avenging heroes, and the glory that had departed from Hunaland was restored once again.

# CHAPTER XXVII
## Helgi Hundingsbane

Helgi's Youth—Hunding slain in Battle—Wooing of the Valkyrie Maid
—Hodbrod, the Rival—How Sigrun was won—Dag's Vengeance—Helgi is
slain—Sigrun's Curse—She sorrows for her Husband—Helgi's Ghost—Meeting
with Sigrun—The Love Song at the Grave—Lovers born again.

SIGMUND became a mighty ruler, and he made Borghild
his queen. In happiness they dwelt together, and they
had two sons who were named Helgi and Hamund. At
Helgi's birth norns came and foretold that he would
achieve great renown, as indeed he did, for while he
was yet a youth he became a far-famed warrior, strong-
armed and fierce, in battle prowess surpassing even his
sire.

In time Helgi was chosen to be chief leader of the
army, and so fiercely did he fight against King Hunding
that he was surnamed Hundingsbane.

Now Helgi in his boyhood had gone in disguise to
Hunding's hall, where he was reared and trained in feats
of strength. The day came when he was ready to wield
arms against his country's foe, so he took his departure.
As he left the Hall, he sent a message to King Hunding,
making known whom he had fostered. The king was
wroth, and he sent out warriors to slay the lad. But
Helgi disguised himself as a bondmaid, and when his
pursuers entered the house in which he had taken refuge
they saw a woman grinding corn.

"The bondmaid hath fierce eyes," they said. "She is not the daughter of a peasant. Her hands are more fitted for the sword."

So strong was Helgi, and so swiftly did he work, that the millstones were broken. It is not a warrior's task to grind corn.

In the war that followed a great battle was fought, and Helgi slew Hunding. Several of the king's sons fell by his sword in another battle, and those who survived vowed blood vengeance against him.

As Helgi left the battlefield he clad himself in a wolf-skin, and in a forest he met a fair princess who was named Sigrun. She rode on a white horse and her maidens rode behind her. King Hogni, against whom Helgi had fought, was her sire, and she was a valkyrie and a swan maid.

The young warrior was heart-stricken with love for the fair princess, and he besought her to be his bride. But she told him that her sire had already promised her to Hodbrod, son of King Granmar; whereat Helgi vowed that he would go against his rival in battle. Then did Sigrun promise to be his bride when he had slain the hated Hodbrod.

So it fell that Helgi Hundingsbane warred against Hodbrod and his allies, the kinsfolk of Sigrun. He crossed the seas with Sinfjotle and a strong army; but a great tempest broke forth, and the ships would have been foundered had not the valkyrie maid come to protect them. After enduring great tribulation Helgi reached the kingdom of Granmar, where he fought a great battle. Sigrun hovered in mid-air, and gave her lover sure protection, and he prevailed over Hodbrod and slew him. Then was Hogni slain also, and all his sons fell with him save Dag.

Sigrun hailed her lover and gave him praise because

that he had slain the mighty Hodbrod, yet did she mourn for her sire and her brothers.

Helgi comforted her, saying: "The norns have not given thee good fortune in all things. I have slain thy kindred. Thou couldst not choose otherwise, because it was thy doom from birth to be the cause of great bloodshed. For thy sake have warriors striven. Weep not, Sigrun; heroes must die at their appointed time."

Sigrun embraced her lover and said: "Although those who have fallen were still alive, I would love but Helgi."

Then Helgi reigned over the land which he had conquered, and Sigrun was his queen. With Dag he took vows of fellowship and spared his life; but Hogni's son deemed that the call of blood vengeance was stronger than the oaths he had taken, even although he had sworn by Hela's holy river, and he resolved in his heart to take Helgi's life.

Now it fell that Odin intervened. He gave to Dag his great spear Gungner, and as the youth went with the king through a forest grove, he drave the spear through Helgi's back, so that he fell dying upon the green sward. Thus was Hogni avenged.

But great was Sigrun's grief when Dag came to her with tidings that he had slain the world's best king. On his head she heaped curses, nor could she be consoled.

"May thine oaths smite thee," she cried: "all the oaths thou didst swear with Helgi by Hela's shining stream. May thy ship sink with thee, although fair winds prevail. May thy horse stumble when thou art pursued by thy foes. May thy sword in battle wound none but thyself. The death of Helgi must be avenged against thee, and thou shalt be a wolf in the forest. . . .

Be thy life empty of all thou dost desire.   May thy food
be the flesh of dead men."

"Wouldst thou call down such ill upon thy brother?"
Dag pleaded with her.   "The hand of Odin hath been
laid heavily on Helgi.   I shall give to thee golden rings,
and half of the kingdom for thyself and thy sons."

But Sigrun wailed in her grief: "Oh! never again can
I be glad, neither by day nor by night.   I love not life
any more, for I shall ne'er behold my shining hero who
was blithe in the hall and valorous in battle.   High was
Helgi above all other men as the ash tree is high above
shrubs. . . . Never again can I see him alive."

A grave mound was raised over Helgi's body, and
his spirit went to Valhal.   Odin made him chief ruler,
and he gave Hunding a bondsman's tasks, for he set
him to hew wood, to leash the hounds, and groom the
horses, and ere he went to sleep to give mash to the
swine.

But Helgi could not be happy even in Valhal, because that Sigrun cried ever for him; as bitterly and oft
as her tears fell his wounds bled afresh.   By nighttime
he rode to the grave mound with many followers.   There
was no rest for Helgi among the dead.

Sigrun's bondmaid beheld the ghastly warriors riding
round the mound, and she cried to them: "Why ride
ye forth, ye dead men?   Can slain warriors return home
again?   Or hath the world's end come at length?"

"The world's end hath come not yet," the slain war-
men made answer, "but dead heroes would fain return
home. . . . The wounds of Helgi bleed afresh because
of Sigrun's sorrow.   Bid her come hither to stay the
unceasing flow of anguish."

Then did the bondmaid go unto Sigrun.   "Hasten
thee to the grave mound," she cried.   "Dead men are

abroad, and thou mayest behold the king once more. Helgi is there; his wounds bleed ever because of thy tears, and he would fain that thou wouldst give him healing."

Sigrun's tears ceased falling awhile. "Glad am I to go forth even in darkness unto Helgi," she cried, "and may the dews never shine to the dawn. His cold lips shall I kiss; I shall embrace my dead hero."

So she hastened unto the grave mound, and there she beheld her lord. Wan and pale was he indeed, and sorrow-stricken and cold. Sigrun kissed him and embraced him, and cried:

"O Helgi, thy hair is white with rime; thou art drenched with the dews of death. Cold, cold are thy hands; they are dripping blood. How shall I heal thee, O my hero?"

Helgi made answer: "Bright flower of the south, thy tears have made me wet; thy sorrow hath drenched me with the dews of death. Ere thou dost sleep, O gold-decked maid, thou dost ever weep most bitter tears, and they fall upon my breast; as drops of blood they fall: they are cold and they pierce me: heavy are they and sharp as is thine anguish. . . . Grieve not although life and kingdom be lost; sing not the dirge of mourning although my wounds are deep, for know that dead men have brides and kings' dead daughters are with them."

Sigrun spread out a smooth grave bed for Helgi, and said to him, speaking low:

"A bed without pain I have made for thee, Helgi; in comfort thou shalt rest upon it, O son of the Volsungs. O my king, O my love, I shall lie in thy bosom. I shall take thee in mine arms as if thou wert still alive."

"White maid whom I loved," spake Helgi, "strange would it indeed be if the high-born daughter of King

Hogni were laid while yet alive in a dead man's arms.
. . . Now forth must I ride on the dawn-red road.  I
must climb, on my steed, the bridge of the gods, ere
the shining cock of Asgard awakens the heroes in
Valhal."

So they parted there at the grave mound, and Helgi,
mounting on his steed, vanished in mid-air.

But when the day passed, and the night fell, Sigrun
again returned to the grave mound of Helgi.  She wept
no tears and waited, but her hero came not nigh.  All
through the hours of darkness she waited, until the dawn
broke faintly through the trees.  Sitting there by her husband's grave mound, the love-lorn lady sang:

> Ah! would that he came
> For fain would I greet him;
> He would come if he knew
> That I wait here to meet him;
> He'd come were he hearing—
> Heart-hearing my call,
> The son of great Sigmund,
> From Odin's high hall.
>
> O Helgi, mine own,
> My fair one, my rare one—
> Helgi, mine own.
>
> Now waneth my hope
> Of Helgi's returning,
> For the eagles awake
> And the dawn fires are burning;
> My love hath not heard me,
> He comes not to-night. . . .
> All the elf folk and death folk
> To Dreamland take flight.
>
> O Helgi, mine own,
> My white one, my bright one—
> Helgi, mine own.

The bondswoman soothed Sigrun, and 'twas thus she
sang to her :—

Oh! hush thee.   Oh! hush . . . who maketh thy moan,
     White Queen of the Southland,
Fair Sigrun who waiteth in darkness alone,
     O loved one of Helgi;
Thy heart should be filled, not with hope, but with dread—
'T is well that dawn cometh and black night hath fled—
More fearsome and fierce are the warriors dead
     In darkness than day-shine.

But Sigrun would not be comforted, and she died of
sorrow.   Sad minstrels, singing to harp music in the
feasting hall, have told that Helgi and Sigrun were born
to life again.

## Clerk Saunders

Clerk Saunders and May Margaret
     Walked ower yon garden green;
And sad and heavy was the love
     That fell thir twa between.

.          .          .          .          .

It was about the midnight hour,
     When they asleep were laid,
When in came her seven brothers
     Wi' torches burning red.

.          .          .          .          .

Then up and gat the seventh o' them,
     And never a word spake he;
But he has striped his bright brown brand
     Out through Clerk Saunders' fair bodye.

Clerk Saunders he started and Margaret she turned
     Into his arms as asleep she lay;

And sad and silent was the night
  That was atween thir twae.

.     .     .     .     .

The clinking bell gaed through the town,
  To carry the dead corpse to the clay;
And Clerk Saunders stood at May Margaret's window
  I wot, an hour before the day.

"Are ye sleeping, Margaret?" he says,
  "Or are ye waking presentlie?
Give me my faith and troth again,
  I wot, true love, I gied to thee."

"Your faith and troth ye sall never get,
  Nor our true love sall never twin,
Until ye come within my bower
  And kiss me cheek and chin."

"My mouth it is full cold, Margaret,
  It smells now o' the ground;
And if I kiss thy comely mouth
  Thy days o' life will no' be lang.

"O, cocks are crowing a merry midnight,
  I wot the wild fowls are boding day;
Give me my faith and troth again,
  And let me fare me on my way."—

"Thy faith and troth thou sall na get,
  And our true love shall never twin,
Until ye tell what comes o' women,
  I wot, who die in strong traivelling?"

"Their beds are made in heaven high,
  Down at the foot of our good Lord's knee,
Weel set about wi' gilly flowers;
  I wot sweet company for to see.

"O, cocks are crowing at merry midnight,
  I wot the wild fowl are boding day;
The psalms of heaven will soon be sung,
  And I, ere now, will be miss'd away.

Then she has ta'en a crystal wand,
  And she has stroken her troth thereon;
She has given it him out at the shot-window,
  Wi' mony a sad sigh, and heavy groan.

"I thank ye, Marg'ret; I thank ye, Margaret;
  And aye I thank ye heartilie;
Gin ever the dead come for the quick,
  Be sure, Marg'ret, I'll come for thee."—

It 's hosen and shoon, and gown alone,
  She climb'd the wall, and followed him,
Until she came to the green forest,
  And there she lost the sight o' him.

"Is there ony room at your head, Saunders?
  Is there ony room at your feet?
Or ony room at your side, Saunders,
  Where fain, fain I would sleep?"—

"There 's nae room at my head, Marg'ret,
  There 's nae room at my feet;
My bed it is full lowly now:
  Amang the hungry worms I sleep.

"Cauld mould is my covering now,
  But and my winding-sheet;
The dew it falls nae sooner down
  Than my resting-place is weet.

"But plait a wand o' bonny birk,
  And lay it on my breast;
And shed a tear upon my grave,
  And wish my soul gude rest.

" And fair Marg'ret and rare Marg'ret,
　And Marg'ret o' veritie,
Gin e'er ye love another man,
　Ne'er love him as ye did me."—

Then up and crew the milk-white cock,
　And up and crew the grey;
Her lover vanish'd in the air,
　And she gaed weeping away

*—Scottish Border Ballad*

# CHAPTER XXVIII

## Sigurd the Dragon Slayer

Fate of Sinfjotle—Poisoned by the Queen—The Grey Ferryman—Sigmund woos Hjordis—Battle with King Lynge—Odin intervenes—The Heroes' Last Hours—How the Queen was rescued—Birth of Sigurd—Regin's Story—Sigurd avenges Sigmund's Death—Combat with the Dragon—The Language of Birds—Regin is slain.

WHEN Helgi won his kingdom and his bride, Sinfjotle returned again unto Hunaland. Thereafter he set to warring in distant realms, and he achieved widespread renown and won much treasure. Now it chanced that his eyes fell with love upon an alien maid of exceeding great beauty, and he sought to have her for himself. But she was also desired by the brother of Borghild, Sigmund's queen. So the two fought together, and Sinfjotle slew his rival and laid waste and plundered his land. Thereafter he returned home and brought tidings of his deeds.

Wrothful was Borghild, and she sought to drive her brother's slayer from the kingdom; but Sigmund would brook not such an evil doing. So he made offer of blood treasure to his queen, and she made pretence to be appeased, knowing well she could prevail not against the king's will. Yet in her secret heart she brooded over her brother's death and resolved to be avenged upon Sinfjotle. So she held a funeral feast, and went round with the mead horn among the war men who had gathered in the hall. When she asked Sinfjotle to drink, he feared to partake, and Sigmund seized the horn and emptied it. A second time was the horn filled by Borghild, and a second time Sigmund took it from his son. But the third time Sinfjotle must needs drain the horn himself, and when he did that he fell down and died, because the drink was poisoned. Thus did Borghild take vengeance on her brother's slayer.

Great was the grief of Sigmund when Sinfjotle was dead. The war-men in the hall feared that his sorrow would kill him. Loud mourning was heard there then at the funeral feast, and Sigmund, who had grown old, lamented long for his son. Then tenderly he took Signy's offspring in his arms—that Volsung of Volsungs—and bore him through the evening dusk towards the firth's grey beach with purpose to take him to the opposing shore.

He perceived a small boat. In it was a tall, old man, grave of aspect, grey bearded, and having but one eye. A round hat was drawn low on his forehead, and he wore a dim blue cloak mottled with grey. Men tell it was Odin, but Sigmund knew not who it was.

Unto him the grey ferryman spake, bidding him lay Sinfjotle's body in the boat; but he said there was no room for Sigmund, who must needs go round the firth end if he would reach the opposing shore. So Sigmund parted with him and hastened over the beach. Ere long he turned round to gaze upon the boat as it went over the waters. . . . Suddenly it vanished from his sight. . . . So passed Sinfjotle, son of Sigmund and Signy, whose grandsire was mighty Volsung of Odin's kin.

Sigmund turned homeward. He entered the hall sorrowing. He drave forth Borghild, remembering how Sinfjotle died, and she became an outcast, so that ere long she perished.

Then Sigmund sought another bride. Hjordis, daughter of King Eylime, was comely in his eyes, and he sent messengers to her sire beseeching her for wife. Now King Lynge, son of King Hunding whom Helgi had slain, desired also to have the fair princess. Her sire would favour neither Sigmund nor Lynge, and gave the maid her choice; and she vowed she would wed the Volsung. 'Twas thus it befell, and a great marriage feast was held. Then Sigmund returned to Hunaland with his bride, and King Eylime went with them.

Wroth was King Lynge. Tidings he sent unto Sigmund that he would war against him and shatter the power of the Volsungs. So he assembled a great army and set forth to wreak his vengeance and capture Hjordis.

Sigmund feared the issue of battle, for the stronger force was with Lynge. But his courage faltered not. Great treasures have warriors gained, but Odin gave Sigmund a sword. Although he had grown old, his faith in Gram was strong. Yet he deemed it best that Hjordis should be concealed, and with a bondmaid, and bearing much treasure, the queen was given safe retreat in a deep forest.

A great shore battle was fought. Sigmund contended fiercely against overwhelming odds. None could stand against him, and for a time it seemed that Lynge could not prevail. Sigmund's arms were red with blood of his foeman, nor got he a single wound.

Then entered the field through Lynge's war-men an old and one-eyed man. He wore a blue cloak, and his round hat was drawn low on his brow. In his hand was a great spear, and he went against Sigmund.

That was the Volsung's fateful hour. Odin desired his death. The god shook his great spear, and when Sigmund smote it the sword Gram broke in twain. Thereupon Lynge's war-men fell upon the hero and gave him his deathwound. King Eylime, who fought by Sigmund's side, was slain, and the Volsung army was scattered in flight. The shoreland was red with heroes' blood; numerous as dead leaves were the bodies of the slain.

King Lynge waited not on the battleground. He pressed onward with his army towards Sigmund's hall; but when he reached it he could find not Hjordis nor any treasure. So search was made through all the kingdom, and although Lynge found not the bride he sought, he was made glad because that the Volsung power was ended and the last of the line was slain. But he recked not of a hero unborn, and although he set an alien ruler over Hunaland the glory of the Volsungs was fated to return again in greater splendour.

Now when night fell, Hjordis went towards the battleground and found Sigmund where he lay grievously wounded and awaiting death.

She sought to give him healing, so that he might avenge her sire; but Sigmund told her that his wounds could heal not, for Odin desired his death, and his sword Gram was shattered.

"I have fought while Odin willed it," he said, "and now 'tis his desire that I should die."

Then he counselled Hjordis to keep the broken sword, so that it might be welded for her son unborn, and he foretold that the babe would grow up to achieve renown which would live through the ages.

"Now," said Sigmund faintly, "I am death-weary, and must go hence to be with my kin."

All night long Hjordis sat beside the dying king. She soothed him; she watched him tenderly, and when dawn was breaking golden in the east she closed his eyes in death, and wept over him.

Then seaward she gazed and beheld a fleet of viking ships coming nigh to the shore.   Hastily she bade her bondmaid change raiment with her, saying: "Henceforth thou shalt say that thy name is Hjordis."

The leader of the viking horde was Alv, son of King Hjaalprek of Denmark.   He came ashore with his warmen.   He spoke to Hjordis and her maid, and was told of the hidden treasure, and that he took speedily on board a war ship.   The queen he took also and her bondmaid.

Then Alv returned to Denmark, and ever he deemed that the bondmaid was Sigmund's queen, but Hjaalprek's spouse, when she beheld the two women, suspected that the bondmaid was the nobler of the two.

To the king she spoke secretly thereanent, and Hjaalprek fell to questioning the pair.   First he addressed her who pretended to be queen, and said:

"How knowest thou the hour of rising in wintertime when the stars are clouded over?"

The bondmaid answered him, saying: "It hath been my wont to drink heavily at dawn, and I awake athirst."

"A strange custom for a king's daughter," the king remarked.

Then Hjaalprek asked of Hjordis how she could tell when the hour of rising came, and she answered thus:—

"My sire gifted me a magic gold ring, and it turns ice-cold on my finger when the hour cometh to rise in the wintertime."

The king laughed.   "No bondmaid's sire giveth gold rings.   A king's daughter art thou.   Of this thou shouldst have told us heretofore."

Then Hjordis made confession that she was indeed Sigmund's queen, and thereafter she was honoured and well loved in the Hall of Hjaalprek.

When her son was born, the name he received was

Sigurd. A Volsung was he indeed. Bright were his eyes, and his face was kingly, and Hjaalprek took pride in him. He grew up to be strong and fearless; a warman's skill had he ever and Volsung pride, and he had great wisdom, and was eloquent of speech.

His foster father was Regin, the wonder smith, brother of the dragon Fafner, and he gave the lad instruction in many arts, and in the mystery of runes, and taught him many languages.

One day Regin asked the lad if he knew that his father had left great treasure, and that Hjaalprek guarded it; and Sigurd said it was guarded for him and he had faith in the king. Then Regin urged him to ask a horse from Hjaalprek, and when the lad did that the king bade him select the one he desired.

An old, grey-bearded man, with one eye, came to Sigurd, who knew not that he was Odin, and he chose for the lad a steed which was of Sleipner's race. Sigurd called it Grane because it was grey, nor was its equal to to be found in the world.

Now Alv took Hjordis for wife, and they lived happily together.

Then a day came when Regin, perceiving that the lad grew to manhood's strength and wisdom while he was yet young, bethought to tell him of the treasure over which the dragon Fafner kept constant guard. He urged Sigurd to slay the monster.

"I am scarce more than a child yet," Sigurd said; "why dost thou urge me to do this mighty deed?"

Then Regin told the story of the treasure, and how Loke had taken it from the dwarf Andvari; how it was given to his own sire, whom his brother Fafner slew so that he might have all the gold for himself.

Sigurd heard him in silence, and when Regin said:

"If thou shalt go forth to slay Fafner I shall forge a mighty sword for thee."

So the lad said: "Forge then a sword for me which shall be without an equal, for fain would I do mighty deeds."

Then Regin went to his smithy and made a sword; but the lad smote it on the anvil and it flew in pieces. A second sword he splintered also.[1]

Thereafter Sigurd went to his mother and asked for the broken pieces of his sire's great sword Gram. Then he bade Regin forge it anew, and the smith did that, although unwillingly. When it was made, the lad put the blade to test and clove the anvil in twain. Next he cut wool with it in the river, so keen was its edge. He was well pleased with Gram.

Regin then bade him promise to slay Fafner, and Sigurd said: "As I promised thee, so shall I do, but first I must set forth to avenge the death of my sire."

Stronger grew the lad, and he was of great stature,[2] and skilled in feats of arms. Ere he set forth to do deeds of valour he paid visit to Griper, his mother's brother, who had power to foretell what would come to pass. Sigurd desired to know what the norns had decreed regarding him, and although Griper was at first unwilling to tell him, he at last unfolded to the lad his whole future life.

---

[1] A similar story is told in the Highlands of Finn (Fingal), who shook sword after sword to pieces until the smith forged a matchless blade which had to be tempered with the blood of the first living thing that entered the smithy in the morning. Finn slew the smith. Both stories are probably of common origin.

[2] The Highland Finn was 60 feet high, and Garry was a dwarf because he was but 40 feet in height. Sigurd did not attain such godlike stature, but he was, according to Saga statistics, nearly 20 feet high; for when his sword was girt on, the end of it touched the ears of growing rye. The sword was seven spans in length. Finn also avenged his father's death, but he never slew a dragon nor sought great treasure. His ambitions were those of a huntsman.

Thereafter Sigurd went to the king and besought that he should get ships and war-men to go forth against the tribe of Hunding, and avenge upon King Lynge the death of Sigmund. Hjaalprek gave him according to his desire. A great storm broke forth as he crossed the seas, and as the ships came nigh a headland a man beckoned to Sigurd and desired to be taken aboard. The young hero commanded that this should be done. His name was Fjorner[1], and he carried out the behests of Urd. He sang strange runes regarding the battle that was to be. As he did so the storm passed away, and they drew nigh to the kingdom of King Lynge. Then Fjorner vanished.

Sigurd laid waste the country, and tidings were borne to King Lynge that fierce foemen had invaded the kingdom. A great army was collected to oppose them, but Sigurd was given victory, and he slew Lynge, and thus avenged his sire's death. With the sword Gram he clove the king in twain, and all the sons of Hunding who were there he slew also. So did Sigurd achieve great renown, and with the treasure he had captured he returned unto Hjaalprek.

Ere long Regin spake to him in secret, calling to mind his promise to slay the dragon Fafner.

"As I have promised," Sigurd said, "so shall I do."

Regin went forth towards the Glittering Heath with the young hero, whom he counselled to make a pit so that he might slay the dragon from beneath when it came out to drink.

"If the dragon's blood fills up the pit, how will it fare with me?" Sigurd exclaimed.

"Thou seem'st to be afraid," Regin said. "Unlike thy kin art thou."

---

[1] One of Odin's names.

Sigurd went towards the dragon's dwelling, but Regin waited at a distance. Then to the young hero came an old and grey-bearded man with one eye, and he gave counsel that he should dig many pits, so that the blood of the dragon might not drown him.[1] Sigurd knew not that the man was Odin, but he did as he was advised: he dug many pits, and in one of them he concealed himself and waited for the dragon to come forth.

In time Fafner crawled from his lair, roaring and spouting venom. The earth shook, and Regin trembled in his hiding place. But Sigurd was not afraid. He waited until the monster was over the pit in which he stood, then he plunged his sword Gram through the dragon right up to the hilt. He drew it forth again, and the blood reddened his arms, and ran into the pits.

Fafner tossed in fury, and destroyed all things that were nigh him, but soon he knew well that he was wounded unto death. As he lay helpless and weak he beheld Sigurd coming forth.

Fafner spake and asked him: " Who art thou that feared me not? What is thy name, and what is thy sire's name?"

Sigurd answered: "My folk are strangers among men. My name is Lordly Beast. I have nor sire nor mother, and hither came I alone."[2]

Fafner said: "Wilt thou lie to me in my hour of death, by saying that thou hast nor sire nor mother or other name than Lordly Beast?"

---

[1] It would appear that in making imperfect swords and advising the construction of only one pit, Regin desired to be rid of Sigurd when he had served his purpose.

[2] The reluctance shown by Sigurd is evidence of his belief in the magical power of names. He feared that the dragon could, by using his name, exercise an evil influence over him. Even at the present day certain peoples in these islands are charged with lack of courtesy because they refuse to give their names to strangers.

Sigurd thereupon said: "My name is Sigurd, and I am Sigmund's son."

"Brave was thy sire," said the dragon, "but didst thou never hear that I was feared among men? Name thou him who urged thee to slay me."

Sigurd told not of Regin, and the dragon warned him that the gold would be a curse to him.

But the young hero said: "We can but keep our gold till life's end, and a man dieth once only."

Fafner then said: "By Regin was I betrayed. Thee too would he betray; he desires my death and thine."

Soon afterwards the dragon died, whereupon Regin came forth from his hiding place. He came humbly towards the young hero and spake words of flattery to him. Then he said: "But, alas! thou hast slain my brother, nor am I myself without blame."

Sigurd said angrily: "When I performed this great deed thou didst crouch like a coward in a bush."

"It was I who forged the sword with which thou didst slay Fafner," said Regin.

Then Sigurd answered: "Better in battle is a brave heart than a strong sword."

Again Regin said: "Alas! thou hast slain my brother, nor am I myself without blame."

Sigurd cut out the dragon's heart, and Regin drank the blood. Then the wonder smith bade the young hero to roast the heart for him while he lay down to sleep. The lad thrust a rod through it and roasted it over a fire. When the heart frizzled he laid his finger on the spot, lest the blood should come forth, and then he thrust his finger in his mouth. When he did that he at once understood the language of birds.

---

[1] Here again we have strong resemblance to the story of Finn. Black Arky, who slew Finn's father, Coul, caught a certain salmon and asked the lad to roast it without

One bird sang: "Why dost thou sit roasting the dragon's heart for another when thou shouldst eat it thyself and obtain great wisdom?"

Another sang: "Regin lies there with purpose in his heart to betray Sigurd."

A third sang: "Sigurd should slay Regin and possess all the treasure for himself."

The first bird sang: "Regin hath drunk of the dragon's blood and will become a wolf. Sigurd would be wise if he thought of his own safety. He who hath a wolf's ears will soon have the teeth of a wolf."

Another bird sang: "Sigurd will be less wise than I deem him to be if he spares the man who desired his own brother's death."

Sigurd leapt up. "The day hath not come when Regin shall slay me," he said, and at once cut off the head of the wonder smith.

Then the young hero ate a portion of Fafner's heart,[1] and took the rest with him. Thereafter he went to the dragon's lair and took forth the treasure—the rings, the awesome helmet, the sword Hrotte, gold armour, and many ornaments. In two chests he placed the treasure, and these he put upon the back of his strong steed Grane.

The birds sang to him.

"There is a maid most fair if thou couldst possess her. . . ."

"Green roads twine to the hall of Giuki, and thither

raising a blister. Then he went to sleep. A blister rose, and Finn pressed it down, and having burnt his finger he thrust it into his mouth. He touched a tooth, and it became his "Tooth of Knowledge". He then knew who Arky was and slew him. In some Gaelic stories Finn bites his thumb when he desires to know anything. There are no birds in the Finn story.

[1] Because of the cannibalistic belief that by eating an enemy he would obtain from flesh and blood whatever strength or wisdom the other possessed in life.

is Sigurd led. The king hath a daughter and thou hast gold for her. . . ."

"On Hindarfell there is a high and gold-decked hall; it is girt around with fire. . . .

"There sleepeth on the fell a maid of war, a chosen of heroes; flames flash round her. Odin hath given her long and unbroken sleep, for she hath stricken down those whom he favoured. Brynhild's sleep is sure and lasting; thus have the norns decreed."

So Sigurd rode on. The birds sang to him and he heard with wonder. Nor rested he on the green-girt way until he came to Hindarfell, where Brynhild lay wrapped in a magic sleep.

## The Sleeping Beauty

Year after year unto her feet,
  She lying on a couch alone,
Across the purple coverlet,
  The maiden's jet-black hair has grown
On either side her trancèd form
  Forth streaming from a braid of pearl;
The slumbrous light is rich and warm,
  And moves not on the rounded curl.

The silk star-broidered coverlid
  Unto her limbs itself doth mould
Languidly ever; and, amid
  Her full black ringlets downward roll'd,
Glows forth each softly shadow'd arm
  With bracelets of the diamond bright;
Her constant beauty doth inform
  Stillness with love, and day with light.

She sleeps: her breathings are not heard
  In palace chambers far apart.

*Sigurd, the dragon slayer, from the painting by Nielsen.*

*Wood portals from a Norwegian church carved with scenes from the Volsung Saga.*

The fragrant tresses are not stirr'd
   That lie upon her charmed heart.
She sleeps: on either hand upswells
   The gold-fringed pillow lightly prest:
She sleeps, nor dreams, but ever dwells
   A perfect form in perfect rest.

.     .     .     .     .     .

He comes, scarce knowing what he seeks:
   He breaks the hedge: he enters there:
The colour flies into his cheeks:
   He trusts to light on something fair:
For all his life the charm did talk
   About his path, and hover near
With words of promise in his walk,
   And whispered voices at his ear.

*Tennyson.*

# CHAPTER XXIX
# Brynhild and Gudrun

Brynhild's Magic Sleep—Awakened by Sigurd—Lovers pledge their Troth—The Draught of Forgetfulness—Gudrun wins Sigurd—Gunnar's Wooing—How Brynhild was deceived—Quarrel with Gudrun—Sigurd is murdered—Gudrun's Sorrow—Brynhild dies on Sigurd's Pyre—Ride to Hela.

WHEN Sigurd came nigh to Hindarfell, in the land of the Franks, he beheld a blaze of light on the hill. Then he perceived that a stately castle was girt round with magic fire. Its roof was of shining gold. A banner on the highest tower floated in the wind.

He rode towards the castle. He went through the flames on the back of Grane. He dismounted and went within. There he beheld a beauteous battle maiden wrapped in magic sleep; golden was her hair, and she was clad in armour. . . . He went towards her and took off her gleaming helm, and her locks fell free. Yet her eyes opened not, so strong was the sleep spell that was upon her. . . . He drew his magic sword and cut through her armour so that it fell to pieces, whereat the maiden awoke. . . . Her wondrous eyes glowed upon him; her pale cheeks reddened and her lips opened.

"How long hast thou lain asleep?" asked Sigurd.

"Who art thou," the maiden sighed, "that hast shorn my armour asunder, and hath power to break the runes of sleep? . . . Art thou indeed Sigurd, the son of great Sigmund? Hast thou come at last with the helmet of darkness and the sword which slew Fafner?"

Sigurd answered: "I am even Sigurd, the son of Sigmund, and my sword hath shorn thine armour asunder."

"None but a Volsung could have done the deed," cried Brynhild, for indeed it was she — the beauteous valkyrie whom Odin had punished by laying her in a magic sleep because that she had caused to fall in battle those whom he favoured.

"A Volsung am I," Sigurd answered, "and I have come to thee because thou art so fair and full of wisdom. Fain would I learn of thee."

Then Brynhild smiled. She threw back her golden hair, and gazed forth upon the world once more. She saw the bright sun and the fresh green ways, and like a dawn-awakened bird she raised her voice in song.

> Long was my sleep, long was my sleep,
> Darkling 't was lone and dreamless and deep—
> Long as the evils that mankind endure,
>     As long and as sure;
> Helpless in sunshine and starshine I've lain,
> Wrapped by the runes that bind like a chain—
>     Helpless ye found me:
>     Odin had bound me—
> Bound me in sleep where I lay. . . .
>     Hail to the day!
>     Hail to the sons of the light!
>     All hail to the night!
> Hail and O hear, beholding us twain,
> And give what we hope now to gain. . . .
> Hail ye gods and ye goddesses dear,
>     And Earth, the mother of all!
> Give us of wisdom and tenderness here,
> Hands that shall heal and hearts without fear
>     Till death shall at length on us call. . . .

Then Brynhild told Sigurd how Odin had touched

her with the sleep thorn, and said that never again would she be a chooser of the slain, but would lie in slumber until a lover came.

"But I vowed a vow," she said, "that I would never wed a man who knew what it was to be afraid."

Sigurd said: "Fain would I hear of thy wisdom, for which thou art famed."

"With gratitude can I speak to thee," said Brynhild, "but let us first drink mead together. May thou profit by what I shall teach thee, and may thou in after time remember what I now speak unto thee."

She filled a golden goblet and gave to Sigurd to drink.

"The mead," she said, "is mixed with renown and songs merry and sad, and with wise thoughts and tender heart thoughts and valorous speech. . . . Thou shalt grave war runes on thy blade, and twice shall Tyr be named. Runes of ocean shalt thou carve on stern and rudder and oar; thou shalt have peaceful sea-ways. . . . Runes thou shalt learn to ward off blood vengeance and doom. . . . Runes thou shalt learn to call fairy help when a son cometh, and runes for wound healing which thou shalt carve on trees whose branches are bending towards the east. . . . I shall teach thee runes of high-heartedness and valour—the runes of the gods, the runes of the elves, and the runes of the wise Vans. . . . I shall give thee runes that shall aid thee in all things until life ends. . . . Now thou shalt choose what thou dost desire to be and to have. . . ."

Sigurd spake: "I was born to be without fear. I shall forget thee never, and in my heart shall I treasure what thou givest unto me."

Then Brynhild gave runes to Sigurd, and she counselled him to give friendship for friendship, and to have forbearance so that he might win fame among men.

"Take close account of what is evil," she said; "from a maiden's love and a man's own wife wrong may come. Give little heed to those who speak more harshly of others than they deem they do; take not advice from men of poor judgment. Ever be watchful of danger wherever thou farest; let not a woman enchant thee in the feasting hall. Heed not the unwise speech of a man who hath drunken deep. Keep the oaths thou dost swear. Trust not him whose kin thou hast slain. . . . I can read not of thy future right well, nor perceive clearly what shall befall thee, but may evil come not from thy wife's kindred."

Sigurd said: "None other but thee shall I have for my bride."

Brynhild made answer: "If it were given me to make choice among all the sons of men, thee alone would I desire to be mine."

Sigurd gave to the gold-haired maiden the magic ring which was in Fafner's hoard.

Then did they swear binding oaths together, vowing that they would ever be faithful one to another until life's last loop was spun.

Thereafter went Sigurd on his way, for he must needs travel unto the hall of King Giuki. Loving Brynhild, he went, but it was doomed that he should break his binding vows, and spurn the golden-haired maiden whom he had rescued from magic sleep. It was indeed fated that he should drink the draught of forgetfulness, so that new love might enter his heart, for he must needs suffer because of the treachery of another.

A warrior of noble seeming was Sigurd, and wondering eyes beheld him as he drew nigh to the dwelling of Giuki. Great was his height, and he had the shoulder-breadth of two men. Young was he, and very fair.

His eyes were blue, and of such brightness that men quailed before him; his nose was high-ridged, and bent like to an eagle's beak; broad was his face from cheek bone to cheek bone. His hair was copper-brown, and hung over his shoulder gleaming in sunshine, and his beard was short and fair. All beholders gazed with mute wonder upon his great sword Gram.

He was withal fearless and high-hearted, one who loved his friends and was unafraid of any foe. Ever ready was he to give aid to kinsmen and allies. Such eloquence of speech was his that men were drawn towards him.

Those who played games round Giuki's hall ceased when Sigurd came nigh. King Giuki greeted him with welcome to his dwelling, and the treasure chests were taken from Grane's back and borne within.

The king had for wife the crafty Grimhild, who was a sorceress, and they had a beauteous daughter who was named Gudrun. Their three sons were Gunnar, Hogne, and Guttorm.

Now, when Grimhild beheld Sigurd, she was taken with desire that he should have her daughter for his bride, and ill-pleased was she when she found that his heart was filled with love for Brynhild.

It chanced that the two maidens dreamed dreams. Brynhild had a vision of Gudrun coming towards her, and on the day that followed Gudrun indeed came in a gold-decked chariot with all her maidens, for Gudrun had also dreamt a dream and desired that the wise Brynhild should solve it.

Brynhild, who was King Budle's daughter, dwelt betimes at her castle, and betimes at the Hall of Heimar, who had for wife her sister Bænkhild. Her brother was King Atle the Mighty.

It was at Heimar's hall that Giuki's daughter found the fair battle maiden on that fateful day.

Gudrun told Brynhild of her dream. "It seemed," she said, "that we were together in a forest and saw a noble stag. Copper-coloured was its hair, and we both desired to possess it. But no one save myself alone could reach the stag, and I possessed it, and was made glad. Then thou didst come, Brynhild, and thou didst slay my stag, and I wept bitterly. Thereafter thou didst give me a young wolf which was red with the blood of my kin."

"Alas!" Brynhild sighed; "I can read thy dream. Thou shalt marry Sigurd, whom I desire for my lover. A magic drink he shall receive, and he shall turn from me. Then shall there be a feud, and he shall be slain, and thou shalt thereafter marry my brother King Atle the Mighty, whom thou shalt slay in the end."

Gudrun wept. "Terrible indeed it is," she said, "to have knowledge of these things."

So she left Brynhild and returned with her maidens to the hall of King Giuki, her sire.

Three years passed, and Sigurd remained with the king who had given him welcome. With Gunnar and Hogne he took oaths of fellowship, and they hunted together and made merry.

Ever did Queen Grimhild desire that Sigurd should take Gudrun for his bride, and at length she brewed a magic drink which would make him forget the battle maiden whom he had chosen for his bride.

A night came when they sat together in the feasting hall, and the queen rose and filled the drinking horn with the magic drink and gave it unto Sigurd, saying:

"It hath pleasured us to have thee abiding with us

here. Thou shalt receive from us all thou dost desire. Drink thou from this horn the mead which I have prepared for thee."

Sigurd drank as she desired, and he forgot Brynhild and the binding vows he had sworn with her. The love he had for her passed away, and he saw that Gudrun was very fair.

Then the queen said: "King Giuki shall be to thee a sire, and his sons are thy brethren."

To the king in secret Grimhild spake, as she embraced him: "Give thou our daughter for wife unto Sigurd. Great is his wealth, and it would be well that he should ever be with us."

Giuki disdained to offer his daughter even unto Sigurd, but the queen constrained her son Gunnar to counsel the young hero to have the beauteous maid for his bride.

So it fell that Sigurd and Gudrun were wed in the Hall, and they dwelt happily together. They had a son, and his name was Sigmund.

Queen Grimhild next desired that her son Gunnar should have Brynhild for wife, and she said: "Go thou and woo the battle maiden, and Sigurd shall go with thee."

"That will I do right willingly," Gunnar made answer, "for I would fain have golden-haired Brynhild for my bride."

Then he rode forth towards the hall of Heimar, and with him went Sigurd. Grimhild had wrought a spell so that Brynhild would know not her former lover.

Gunnar besought of Heimar that he should have the battle maiden for wife, but Heimar said: "Brynhild shall only wed him whom she herself doth choose. To her thou must go. She dwelleth in a castle beyond, which is girt about with magic fire, and thou must needs ride through the flames to win nigh unto her."

Then Gunnar rode towards the dwelling of Brynhild, and Sigurd went with him.   But when they came nigh to the fire-girt castle Gunnar's steed would go no farther, for it feared the flames.

Sigurd said: "To thee shall I give Grane, on whom to ride through the fire."

So he dismounted; but when Gunnar sat upon the back of Grane, the steed refused to move forward.   None save Sigurd could go unto Brynhild; none could ride through the flames save Sigmund's noble son.

Then took Sigurd the semblance of Gunnar, and Gunnar the semblance of Sigurd, as Queen Grimhild had given each of them power to do, and Sigurd leapt upon Grane's back and rode through the magic fire.

Brynhild saw Sigurd coming towards her and said: "Who art thou who hast come through the magic fire?"

Sigurd answered: "My name is Gunnar, son of Giuki.   Thee shall I have for my bride, because that thou didst vow to marry him who would reach thee through the flames."

"Thee shall I wed," Brynhild said, "if thou shalt promise to slay those who also desire to have me for wife."

"That shall I promise thee," answered Sigurd, and the battle maiden was well pleased.

Three nights he abode with Brynhild in the castle, and ere he left her she gave to him the ring that was once Andvari's, and had been taken by Sigurd from the hoard of Fafner — the ring of doom which was a bane to them both.

Through the flames once more went Sigmund's great

son. With Gunnar he again changed shapes, and together they returned unto the hall of Giuki.

In time fair Brynhild left her fire-girt castle and went unto the dwelling of Heimar, to whom she told how fate had served her.

"Fain was I," she said, "that it had happened as aforetime—that Sigurd had come through the flames towards me instead of Gunnar."

"As it hath chanced," said Heimar, "so must it be."

Now Brynhild had a daughter, whose name was Aslog. A Volsung was she by birth, for her sire was Sigurd, and it was fated that she would be the last of her race. The battle maiden gave the child to Heimar, so that she might be nourished and fostered and kept free from harm.

When Brynhild did that she went with King Budle, her father, to the hall of Giuki. There was a feast of splendour held, and Gunnar and the battle maiden were wed. They drank mead together and made merry.

But if joy came to the heart of Brynhild, it speedily vanished when she beheld Sigurd with another bride. In secret she bewailed her fate, because that her first love who had awakened her from magic sleep had been taken from her by treachery and sorcery. Nor could such sorrow have long endurance. The treasure curse was upon them all; the shadow of doom was already darkening their days.

Ere long the pent-up grief storm broke forth in lamentation and feud; ere long there was shedding of blood and the heart call of vengeance.

It chanced that Brynhild and Gudrun bathed together in the river, and the battle maiden perceived that Andvari's doom ring was worn by Sigurd's bride. They fell to quarrelling one with another. Thereafter Brynhild went home; pale was her face and anger burned in her eyes: her heart was in torment.

On the morn that followed Gudrun besought Brynhild to sorrow not.

"Thy heart is evil," the battle maiden said; "it giveth thee joy to see me grieve. But thou shalt escape not thy due, for no longer can I endure to see thee with Sigurd."

"Thou hast Gunnar, my brother," said Gudrun; "a worthier lord is he than thou dost deserve. Well mayest thou take joy in him."

"Happy would I indeed be with one more noble," Brynhild answered.

Then Gudrun taunted her, and told how Sigurd had gone through the flames in the guise of Gunnar so that she might be beguiled.

There was no joy in the heart of Brynhild thereafter. Her days and nights she spent in lamentations, so that she was heard by all. Nor would she speak unto anyone, not even her husband; for when she wailed not, she lay like to one who was dead; alone in her chamber she lay; her face was white as winter's snow, and ice-hard and cold.

At length Gunnar besought Sigurd to go unto her, for to none had she spoken for many days, nor had she eaten or drunken aught.

But Sigurd feared that he could quench not the flames of her grief, and knew well that she fostered ill against him with dire intent. Yet was he constrained to speak to her. So Sigurd entered her chamber.

"Arise, O Brynhild," he cried, "for lo! the sun is bright; grieve no more, and make merry in our midst."

Brynhild opened her eyes, as aforetime she had done when Sigurd awakened her from magic sleep.

"So," she spake, "thou art so bold as to come hither

—thou who hast among all the others been most treacherous unto me."

"Speak not thus," said Sigurd; "for what reason dost thou sorrow so deeply?"

"Because the sword is not red with thy heart's blood," Brynhild answered.

Then was Sigurd moved to grief also. To Brynhild he spake tenderly and low. "Thee did I love better than mine own life," he said; "but alas! I was given to drink of the mead of forgetfulness, so that a spell was cast over me and I knew thee not. Yet did I sorrow when I came to know that thou, my heart's desire, wert wife to another. . . . Now be my doom fulfilled, for I desire not to live any more."

"Too late! . . . too late!" cried Brynhild. "It is too late to speak of thy sorrow. Now will greater scorn be turned against me than heretofore. . . . Women shall mock; none shall pity me."

Then Sigurd said he would put away Gudrun and nave her for wife, but Brynhild would hearken not.

"All things have changed," said the woman of sorrow, "and I would fain die. . . . I have been deceived. . . . I desire thee not, and I desire no other."

In sore grief did Sigurd leave her; his head was bowed, his eyes were dimmed, and never again was there joy in his heart.

"I would fain die," Brynhild wailed. . . . "I have been deceived. . . . Sigurd hath deceived me and death is his due. . . . I will not have him live with her who taunts me with scorn. Even now he telleth her of what hath passed, and she mocketh me."

When Gunnar entered Brynhild's chamber she spake:

"Thou shalt live not another night if thou dost not slay Sigurd. . . ."

Nor aught else would she say unto him.

That was indeed a grievous speech to the ears of Gunnar — to be asked to slay one with whom he had taken binding vows. Yet did he love Brynhild more than Sigurd. So he went unto his brother Hogne and told him what had come to pass.

"If Sigurd is slain," Hogne said, "a noble warrior indeed shall be cut off, and doom and shame may be our dower."

So together they went unto Guttorm, who was young and had not sworn oaths with Sigurd, and he consented to do the will of Brynhild.

In the morning Guttorm entered the bedchamber where Sigurd and Gudrun lay fast asleep. He drew his sword. He thrust it through Sigurd's body and gave him his deathwound. Then he turned to make hasty escape.

Sigurd woke in his agony, and, seizing his sword Gram, he flung it at Guttorm and slew him.

Then Gudrun, who lay with her arms about her loved one, awoke to her sorrow; her body was wet with the blood that streamed from Sigurd's deathwound. Bitterly she moaned and wept.

"Grieve not too much," her husband sighed: "as the norns have decreed, so has it come to pass; my doom was hidden from me, and it has now fallen. . . . The hand of Brynhild is in this foul deed: she who loves me above all other men desireth that I should die. . . . Ah! had I not been stricken while I slept, many great men would have fallen ere I could be overcome. . . ."

Then Sigurd died. . . . Even while he spake he was taken from Gudrun, and she gave forth a loud and bitter cry that was heard throughout the Hall.

Brynhild laughed. . . .

Said Gunnar : "Thou dost not laugh for joy, O monstrous woman, for thy cheeks have grown grim and death-white. . . . How wouldst thou feel now if thine own brother Atle were slain before thine eyes ?"

"Vain is thy threat against Atle," Brynhild answered ; "there shall yet be much bloodshed, but thou thyself must fall ere he shall die."

Gudrun cried : "Sigurd is dead ; my kinsmen have slain him."

Nor other moan she made.

Brynhild sighed in secret : "One I loved, and no other, and he is laid in death."

All through the moonless night that followed the death day, Gudrun sat beside her husband's body. Her tears were dried ; her cheeks were pale ; she smote not her hands nor uttered any cry. Many sought to comfort her, but her heart was cold.

At length her sister came and drew the white sheet from off Sigurd's body, and said :

"Gudrun, turn thine eyes upon him thou lovest. Kiss his lips. Take him in thine arms as if he were still alive."

Gudrun looked in Sigurd's face. . . . His eyes were glazed in death ; his lips were cold ; pale were his cheeks, and his hair was red with blood.

She lay down beside Sigurd ; she kissed his lips and wept.

Then spake her sister : "Never knew I of love like to the love that Gudrun beareth for Sigurd."

Gudrun said : "Like to a sword-lily among grass blades was Sigurd among the sons of Giuki, my brothers. . . . I whom he raised up am now but a leaf cast to the winds. . . . Never more by day or by night shall I hear his voice most sweet. . . . Upon me have my brothers wrought this sorrow; my brothers have made me grieve with bitterness. Their oaths are broken, and they are brought to shame, and their kingdom shall be laid waste. Never shall they have joy in the treasure which they desire; it shall be their bane and drag them down to death."

Brynhild came and saw Sigurd's body. She stood apart and spake not, but her eyes burned with grief fire.

Then went she unto Gunnar and cursed him and all his kin, because that the vows of friendship were broken and he and they had conspired against Sigurd and her heart's desire.

"Together we plighted our troth," she cried, "and to the grave shall I follow him."

Gunnar desired not that Brynhild should die, but Hogne said: "She hath ever been a bane to us. 'Twere better that she died now."

Ere yet Brynhild sought death, she caused to be slain Sigmund, the son of Gudrun. But Gudrun could find not greater deeps of sorrow than she had already reached.

A great pyre was built, and on it were laid the bodies of Sigurd and his son. When it was set ablaze, Brynhild rode towards it upon her white steed, and cried:

"*Gudrun would have died with Sigurd had she a soul like to mine.*"

Then she leapt amidst the flames, and was burned with him she loved so well.

So Brynhild passed from the world of men, and she rode the darksome ways towards Hela to search for Sigurd.

At Hela bridge the giant maid, who keeps watch, stood before her and said:

"Thou shalt pass not by this way. O gold-haired maiden, thy hands are red with the blood of heroes. . . . On Giuki's hall thou hast brought sorrow and scaith."

"Blame me not," Brynhild answered; "my life was robbed of love; my vows were despised; by treachery was this evil done upon me, and I was mocked at and put to shame. . . . Sigurd was betrayed, and I was betrayed by Sigurd, whom I love, and now seek in death."

Then golden-haired Brynhild sang, swan-like and sweet, her death song on Hela bridge.

> Ah! but for battle never ending
> Are mortals made alive,
> Ah! but to live o'er long to sorrow—
> To sorrow and to strive;
> Yet Sigurd and I shall live in Hela,
> As fain we'd lived before—
> Our fame shall echo through the Ages
> Ever and evermore.

Spurring her white steed she cried: "Sink down, O giant maid!" and rode on to Hela's glittering plains.

## "Gudrun's Sorrow"[1]

> Home they brought her warrior dead:
> She nor swooned, nor utter'd cry;
> All her maidens, watching, said,
> "She must weep or she will die."
>
> Then they praised him, soft and low,
> Call'd him worthy to be loved,

---

[1] Although the Volsunga saga version of Sigurd's death is followed, a fragment of song pictures the tragedy in a grove from which the warrior's body was carried to Gudrun. Clerk Saunders was slain in bed also, and this ballad suggests the existence of an early version of the Volsung story ere the Helgi lays were introduced. Tennyson's beautiful poem appears to have been suggested by a version of the Gudrun story.

*Spenser's "Faërie Queene."*

*Brynhild, from the statue by Bissen.*

Truest friend and noblest foe;
  Yet she neither spoke nor moved.

Stole a maiden from her place,
  Lightly to the warrior stept,
Took the face-cloth from the face;
  Yet she neither moved nor wept.

Rose a nurse of ninety years
  Sat his child upon her knee—
Like summer tempest came her tears—
  "Sweet my child, I live for thee.

Tennyson.

# CHAPTER XXX

## The Last of the Volsungs

Brynhild's Daughter—Escape to Norway—Her Protector murdered—
Why she was called Krake—The Princess Thora—Her Dragon-like Serpents
—How Ragnar won his Bride—The Northern Cinderella—Wooed by the
Viking—The Slave becomes a Queen—Story of Svanhild—Wife of Jormunrek
(Ermenrich)—Bikki (Sibech) the Accuser—Fate of Gudrun's Daughter.

Now when Brynhild died, Heimer feared that Giuki's
vengeful sons would slay Aslog because that she was the
last of the Volsungs, and might rear up a son who would
come against them.   So he prepared to take flight.   He
made a harp, in which he concealed Brynhild's child with
certain of her treasures, and voyaged to Norway, where
he made pretence to be a minstrel.   He went to a house
in Spangerejd and dwelt in it.   He revealed not there the
secret of the child's concealment.   But one day the house-
wife perceived that there was treasure in the harp, for
the door of Aslog's harp-chamber was not closed, and
a portion of rich cloth protruded from it.   Then was
Heimer murdered in his sleep, and Aslog was taken forth
with the treasure that was hers.

The child grew up in the strange household, and her
foster-parents were not only poor but cruel and harsh;
the high-born girl was made a slave, and was set to work
at menial tasks.   As the years passed by her beauty
shone forth, and her captors, fearing that blame would
fall upon them for doing evil, kept her clad in rags, and

smeared her face with soot and tar, so that no eye might gaze upon her with wonder. Then was she nicknamed Krake, which signifies "the crow".

Thus did Aslog abide with harsh and strange folk until the coming of the great viking Ragnar Lodbrog, who had fame not only on the high seas for deeds of valour, but also because he had slain the venomous serpents which were the bane of King Heroth's kingdom.

It chanced that the king had gone hunting in the woods, where he found two young snakes; these he bore home with him to his daughter Thora, by whom they were fed until they grew so large that she dreaded to approach them. Each then began to devour an ox daily; and they both became so powerful that they laid waste the countryside, and killed men and beasts with their venomous breath.

King Heroth feared to contend against the serpents, but he offered his daughter in marriage to the man who would slay them. Now Thora was fair to behold, and many heroes went forth to fight the monsters; but they suffered death one after another, and the affliction grew greater, so that all people were in constant fear and peril.

The day came when Ragnar heard of Thora, whom he desired for wife, being set up as a reward for serpent-slaying, and he resolved to win her by mighty deeds. So he bade that a mantle and breeches of wool be fashioned for him, and when they were ready he gave King Heroth to know that he would make attack on the serpents.

It was the season of winter, and he dipped his woollen attire in a stream and it was soon frozen hard. Clad thus, he was protected against the venom, so he girt on his sword and took a spear in his right hand and a shield in his left and went forth to fight, so that Thora might be his bride.

A great serpent came against him, but he feared not, and prepared to combat with it. Then another great serpent hastened to the aid of the first, and he was soon in dire peril. They spouted venom upon Ragnar, but his frost-bound clothing protected him; and they smote him with their tails, but he stood firm. Terrible was the conflict which was waged, and the king and all who were with him were filled with alarm, and sought high and narrow hiding places, fearing that Ragnar would be overcome.

The serpents were enraged, and they made ferocious attack with monstrous jaws agape, but Ragnar raised his shield against them each time they sought to bite. He was indeed sore pressed and greatly wearied; but at length he cast his spear at them and it went through their hearts, so that they were both slain.

A great shout was raised by those who were in hiding, and the king came forth to honour Ragnar. He laughed to see the strange attire of the hero, and nicknamed him "Lodbrog", which signifies "shaggy-breeches".

Then was a great banquet given. Ragnar was attired in splendour, and he was given Thora for wife. But when she had borne him two sons she died, although young and fair, and her husband mourned for her.

Ragnar then plundered on the high seas and raided Scotland and Pictland. He set a new king over the Orkneys, and went against Norway.

It chanced that he came one day to Spangerejd, and there he sent men ashore to procure bread. When they returned with the food he was made angry because that it was burned. The men told him that they had gone to a house in which there was a beautiful maiden: they could refrain not from gazing upon her, and so the bread was burned.

Now Ragnar bethought him to have such a maiden for his bride, so that he might forget his grief for Thora. He sent to her a message bidding her to come unto him. Desiring to put her wisdom to test, he told his messengers to ask her to come not on foot nor yet driving; not attired and yet not naked; not feasting and yet not fasting; not with anyone and yet not alone.

Aslog, who was named Krake in her poor dwelling, came towards the great sea king neither driving nor on foot but riding upon a goat with her feet trailing upon the ground; she came without attire, but yet not naked, because her hair was so long and bountiful that it covered her body, and she drew a net about her; she came not feasting nor yet fasting, because she held an onion to her lips and tasted of it; she was not alone, because her dog walked by her side.[1]

Ragnar, who was now a great king, took beauteous Aslog, the daughter of Sigurd and Brynhild, for his bride, and their sons were named Ingvar and Ubbe.[2]

After Sigurd's death Gudrun had a daughter who was named Svanhild. She was given for wife to Jormunrek,[3]

---

[1] So did Grainne come to Diarmid in the Highland Fian tale. Grimm also gives a version of the story with numerous references to similar tales in other languages than Gaelic and German. In Saxo (Book 9) there is a more sordid account of Ragnar's wooing of "a certain young woman" who became the mother of Ubbe. Like Odin, when he wooed Rhind, Ragnar made use of female attire. Our version is from Ragnar's saga. The Volsunga saga drops Aslog at the point where she became Krake.

[2] Here we meet history. By one authority Ingvar and Ubbe are said to be the northmen who murdered King Eadmund of England. Others identify them as the avenging sons who carved an eagle on the back of King Ella in Yorkshire, because he had driven their half-brother Ivar from the throne. Krake is a northern Cinderella, sung of in Norway and Denmark. She was a link between Odin and the Norse kings, who prided themselves in their descent from the Asa-god.

[3] Ermenrich (Hermanric) of the Ostrogoths.

King of the Gauts.  Like to a sunbeam was she in the hall of Giuki, and there was great sorrow when she went forth with her bondmaids.  Much treasure was she given, but the curse of Andvari's gold followed her. It fell that she was falsely accused by Bikki of unfaithfulness with a prince, and so greatly enraged did the king become that he ordered that she should be put to death by being trampled under the hoofs of horses.

Then was Svanhild bound and left lying on a plain; but although the horses ran over her they injured her not, some say because of her surpassing beauty, and others because of the brightness of her Volsung eyes.

The king deemed that his fair bride was innocent, because she had escaped injury, but Bikki, her accuser, poisoned the king's ear, and persuaded him to command that Svanhild should be laid upon the ground with her face downward.  Then were the horses driven over her again, and she was trodden deep down into the earth by the multitudinous hoofs.  So perished Svanhild, daughter of Gudrun, while Aslog, daughter of Brynhild, reigned as Ragnar's queen in a northern land.  In Norway's royal line alone doth the blood of the Volsungs flow.

The young prince, who was Jormunrek's son, was condemned to death by his sire and was hanged.[1]

---

[1] Saxo gives an account of a sham execution, but in the Dietrich story he is actually put to death.  Bikki is Sibech.

# CHAPTER XXXI
## Gudrun's Vengeance

Gudrun's Flight—Grimhild follows her—The Reconciliation—Wooed by
King Atle—Doom Dreams—The Fafner Hoard—Coveted by Atle—Invitation
to Gudrun's Brothers—Fateful Journey—Treachery—A Fierce Conflict—How
Hogne died—Gunnar among Vipers—Queen slays Atle—Becomes Bride of
Jonaker—Her Sons—Svanhild is avenged.

WHEN Sigurd and his son were burned with Brynhild on
the pyre, Gudrun refused to be comforted, nor could she
abide to remain in the Hall of Giuki among the oath-
breakers, her brothers, who had brought her husband to
his death. So she went forth alone to wander in the
forest with desire that wolves should devour her. Five
days she journeyed in her sorrow, knowing not whither
she went, until she came to the Hall of King Alv. There
was she received with pity and tenderness, and she had
for companion Thora, daughter of Hakon, King of
Denmark. She was well loved, and with Thora she sat
and embroidered on fair tapestry the deeds of Sigurd and
Sigmund.

Three summers went past and four winters ere
Queen Grimhild came to know where Gudrun had her
dwelling. She desired that her daughter should return
again, because King Atle the Mighty, the brother of
Brynhild, sought her for his bride. So Grimhild gave
much treasure to her sons, and went forth with them to
appease Gudrun with gifts of gold, so that the blood

feud might have end. Five hundred war-men rode with Grimhild and Gunnar and Hogne, and they greeted Gudrun and made offer to her of the treasure which they bore with them. Then did Gunnar give to Gudrun a golden goblet filled with the drink of forgetfulness, which Grimhild had brewed, so that she might put past old sorrows and hate. Gudrun drank and her grief faded.

Thereafter Grimhild told her daughter that King Atle desired her for wife, and said that she would be given more treasure when she was wed to him.

"I desire not another husband," Gudrun said; "nor could I live happily with the brother of Brynhild."

"If thou wilt wed Atle," said Grimhild, "thou shalt have sons, and it shall seem to thee that Sigurd and Sigmund are again in life."

"I seek not nor hope for gladness any more while I live," Gudrun answered.

But her mother pleaded: "Atle is foremost among kings. A nobler husband thou canst not find. May thou never he wed to any man," she added, "if thou shalt spurn this mighty ruler."

"Alas!" sighed Gudrun; "bid me not wed the brother of Brynhild, for he will bring great evil upon our kin, and be the death-bane of Hogne and Gunnar. By my own hand must he fall in the end if I become his bride."

Grimhild wept, nor listened to what Gudrun said. "I shall give thee lands and many war-men," she told her daughter, "if thou wilt take Atle to be thy husband. Thou shalt have joy with him until thy life's end. Besides, by marrying him thou wilt bring great honour unto thy kin."

"Alas! I must then be wed to him," said Gudrun, "although my heart desireth him not. But there is no gladness in store for me, for he will be a bane to my kin."

Grimhild rejoiced because that she at length worked her will, and soon a great company set forth towards the kingdom of Atle the Mighty. They travelled for seven days by land, and then for seven days they voyaged over the sea, and thereafter they travelled by land again for seven days ere they came unto the Hall of the King. A great banquet was held, and King Atle and Gudrun were wed. But the bride's heart was sad within her, nor did she ever have joy in the Hall of Brynhild's brother.

One morning when Atle woke from sleep he was greatly troubled because of the dreams he had dreamed. He spoke to Gudrun, saying:

"It seemed that thou didst thrust a sword through my breast."

"To dream of iron," the queen said, "is to dream of fire."

"And I dreamt also," continued the king, "that two water-reeds grew up in my hall. By the roots were they pulled up, and they dripped red blood; of them was I asked to partake. . . . Then it seemed that two hungry hawks flew from my wrist, and they went to Hela. Hearts had they steeped in honey, and I ate them. . . . Thereafter I dreamt that two cubs gambolled at my feet; of these did I also partake."

"Thy dreams forebode much ill," Gudrun said; "verily, thy sons are nigh unto life's end. Black grief is at hand."

Weeks passed and then years, and the doom dreams faded from the king's memory. Yet was there more unhappiness between the ill-mated pair.

Then a time came when Atle spoke much of the accursed treasure which Sigurd had found when he slew Fafner. Well he knew that Gunnar and Hogne had kept from Gudrun the greater part, so that they could boast of immense riches. In his heart Atle coveted the hoard, and desired it for himself; so he took counsel with his nobles, and decided to invite Gunnar and Hogne to visit his Hall. A trusted messenger, whose name was Vinge, was sent forth with a company of war-men to make promises to the brothers and induce them to journey to Hunaland. Gudrun knew well that there was evil intent in her husband's heart, so she carved runes of warning upon a gold ring and gave it to Vinge as her gift to Hogne. But Atle's messenger changed the runes so that they seemed to convey a speedy welcome from the queen.

When Vinge reached the Hall of Giuki he made his mission known. The brothers consulted one with another, suspecting treachery and Atle's lust for gold; but Gudrun's ring reassured them, and after they had drunk mead with the messengers, they promised to go forth with them.

But Hogne's wife, Kostbera, made keen scrutiny of Gudrun's ring in her bedchamber, and she saw that the runes had been altered from warning to welcome. To her husband she spoke thereanent. She had also dreamt an ominous dream, in which she saw the Hall overthrown by a rising flood.

But Hogne chided her for thinking ill of Atle. He had given his promise to Vinge to fare forth with him, and scorned to break it.

Gunnar's wife had also dreams of warning. She saw her husband pierced by a sword, while wolves howled about him.

"Little dogs will bark at us," Gunnar said.

"Methought I also saw," his wife continued, "a

battle maiden of sad visage entering the hall. She seemed to be a valkyrie."

"A man must die at his appointed hour," Gunnar said; "besides, it is not good to live over long."

Now Gunnar, who was king, for Giuki had departed hence, was well loved by his people, and in the morning they clamoured about him, beseeching that he should not leave them.

But he bade them to feast with him. "We may never again drink mead together," he said, "but no man can escape his fate."

Gunnar's wife spake unto Vinge. "Methinks," she said, "that ill fortune will come to our kind from this journey."

But Vinge swore many oaths, saying that no evil was intended. "May I be hanged," he said, "if a sign of treachery is shown against Gunnar and Hogne in the kingdom of Atle."

There were tears and lamentations when the warrior sons of Giuki went forth never again to return to the kingdom of their sires, although great glory would be theirs by reason of valorous deeds and unflinching courage.

Gunnar's wife embraced her king, and Kostbera embraced Hogne, saying: "May days of gladness be thine."

"Forget not to make merry," Hogne said, "no matter what befalls us on our journey."

When they had voyaged over the sea, there were dumb foretellings of their doom. So swiftly and hard did the oarsmen ply their blades that rowing pins snapped and half the ship's keel was shorn off upon the beach. They leapt ashore and feared not. Gunnar and Hogne went inland towards Atle's stronghold with armour and full war gear and all their men. Two sons of Hogne were with them, and valorous Orkning, the brother of Kostbera, who had fame for mighty deeds.

They rode together through a dark wood, and when they approached the stronghold of Atle they perceived that the gate was closed against them. A great army was assembling to receive the guests.

Hogne raised his battleaxe and smote the gate asunder, for he must needs enter with dignity becoming his rank.

"Thou hast done wrong," Vinge snarled; "'twere more fitting that thou shouldst wait until I bring the gallows on which ye shall all hang. By smooth words have I induced ye all to come hither; ere long shall ye die together."

"Thy boasts affright me not," answered Hogne; "we shrink not from conflict, if conflict there must be. Yet hast thou wrought us ill, so take thy reward."

As he spake, Hogne swung his battleaxe and slew Vinge with a single blow.

Boldly rode the sons of Giuki until they came to the Hall of Atle. There was a strong army drawn up in line of battle.

King Atle came forth, and spake to the brothers.

"I bid ye welcome," he said, "but unto me must be now given up the great treasure which Sigurd won when he slew Fafner, and is now mine by right of Gudrun."

So fell the treasure curse upon them all in that hour of doom.

Gunnar spake. "Thou shalt never possess our riches," he said, "and if thou dost battle against us, we shall make of thee and thy kin a feast for the eagle and the wolf."

"Long have I desired," said Atle, "to punish ye

for the slaying of Sigurd. That indeed was a shameful doing, for his equal was found not among men."

Hogne spake boldly: "Long then hast thou brooded over that matter. A wonder it is that thou didst not sooner set thyself to the task."

Then began the battle, and against one another they cast their spears.

Tidings were borne unto Gudrun of hard fighting, and she hastened forth in great anger. She cast from her the royal robe, and rushing into the midst of the fray embraced her brothers and kissed them.

But in vain did she intervene. The time for peace was past, so she armed herself and fought beside Gunnar and Hogne against the war-men of Atle.

Bravely fought the brothers. The king's three brothers were slain, and Atle cried:

"Now am I the last of my kin, and by thee was Brynhild slain."

"Thou shalt have thy faring in time," answered Hogne; "the gods have decreed thy punishment."

Fiercer grew the conflict, for Atle rallied his war-men and urged them to battle. But he was driven back into his Hall, which soon streamed with blood. Great were the deeds of the valorous Giukings.

But at length Gunnar and Hogne were pressed hard and overpowered. Then were they bound in fetters.

Atle was wroth when he perceived that so many of his war-men were cut down, and he scowled upon Hogne.

"He hath cut down a host of my heroes," he said; "so let his heart be cut out."

"Do thy will," answered Hogne, "for I fear not. So grievously am I wounded that I may as well die."

But the king delayed taking vengeance. He desired

first to know where the Fafner treasure was concealed, so he had the brothers cast into separate dungeons.

Gunnar was first brought before him. "Thy life shall be spared," Atle said, "if thou wilt reveal where the treasure lies hidden."

Gunnar answered him. "Ere I speak," he said, "Hogne's heart must be brought unto me."

Then did Atle seek to practise deceit with much cunning. He had a thrall seized, so that his heart might be held up before Gunnar. The man screamed with anguish ere yet the knife touched him, for he desired not to miss constant fare and good, nor leave his well-loved swine.

The coward heart was cut out, and it trembled before Gunnar.

"That is not the valorous heart of my brother," he said, "but the heart of a thrall."

So Hogne had to be slain. He laughed when his enemies fell upon him, and they marvelled at his valour.

Then was the hero's heart plucked forth, and when Gunnar saw it he said :

"That indeed is the heart of great Hogne. See how it still beats without fear. I wavered while my brother was yet alive, but now can I die well satisfied, Atle, for thou shalt never know where the treasure lies hid. Yet thou, O King, shall escape not thy doom, and the Rhine river shall keep the secret of the gold."

Atle was wroth; his brow darkened and his eyes burned fire.

"Take hence the prisoner," he growled, and as he bade his men so did they do.[1]

---

[1] A similar legend regarding a secret is current in the Highlands. Neil Munro gives a spirited version in his picturesque tale "The Secret of the Heather Ale" in *The Lost Pibroch*.

Gunnar was bound and thrust into a loathsome dungeon which swarmed with vipers. But Gudrun sent unto him a harp, and he played upon it with his toes, making such sweet music that all the vipers were charmed into a magic sleep save one, which gnawed his breast until it reached his heart to suck his life's blood. Great torture did Gunnar suffer ere he died.

Men have told that the viper which killed the hero was the mother of Atle, who was a sorceress.

The king boasted before Gudrun, because that he had triumphed over her brothers.

"Gunnar and Hogne are indeed no more," the queen said, "and unto me is given a heritage of vengeance."

Atle liked not her speech, so he said: "Let peace be made between us. Thee shall I give much treasure as atonement for the loss of thy kin."

Gudrun would accept not of blood payment, but she desired that a funeral feast be held for Gunnar and Hogne.

The king gave ready consent, and then was the dread work of vengeance begun. Gudrun slew her two sons. Of their skulls she made drinking cups, and she had their hearts cooked in honey for the king. In his wine she mixed their blood.

When the feast was over, Atle desired that his sons should be brought before him.

"Thou hast given me dark sorrow," Gudrun said, "by slaying my brothers. Now hast thou thy reward. Thou didst eat the hearts of thy sons, and their blood hast thou drunken in thy wine from these their skull cups."

"Vengeful woman," cried Atle, "a great cruelty thou hast done by slaying thine own children."

"There shall be still greater cruelty yet," she answered him.

" Thou shalt be burned alive for this," Atle cried fiercely.

" Thine own death thou dost foretell," she said, " as well as mine."

Now a son of Hogne was left alive. He was a Niblung.[1] With him did Gudrun conspire. When Atle had drunken deep, and slumbered, his wife went with Hogne's son to his bedchamber, and she thrust a sword through him.

Atle woke up and cried: " Who hath given me my deathwound ? "

Gudrun made known herself, and said she had taken vengeance for her kin.

Atle pleaded that he would have stately burial, and the queen promised him a great pyre. When he died she set fire to the hall, and all that were within it were burned. In the darkness the war-men sprang one upon the other, and many fell fighting ere the end came.

Gudrun made escape, but she desired not to live any more. She hastened towards the shore and cast herself into the waves, so that her days might have end.

There are those who tell that she died thus, but others say that the waves bore her over the sea and cast her upon the beach nigh to the stronghold of King Jonaker.

A strong warrior was he. When he saw the queen's beauty he desired to have her for bride, and when she

---

[1] The Giukings were originally the Nibelungs (Hniflungs) who possessed the hoard guarded by Andvari (Alberich). That is why Hogne's son is called a "Niblung". The reference is a survival from one of the older versions of the legend. In the next chapter ths Nibelungs are dwarfs (elves) and the Giukings are the Burgundians. How myth and history commingled in endless variations is illustrated by the Dietrich stories. Similarly, myths which had a common and remote origin, and developed separately in various districts, were also fused by wandering minstrels.

was nourished and comforted the twain were married and they dwelt happily together.

Gudrun had three sons, and they were named Hamder, Sorle, and Erp. It is told that when they became full warriors she sent them forth against King Jormunrek to avenge the death of Svanhild. But Erp, it was deemed, was unwilling to go forth, so his brothers slew him.

Then Hamder and Sorle set forth. Their mother charmed their bodies against steel, and when they reached Jormunrek, Hamder cut off his hands and Sorle smote off his feet.

" If Erp were here," one said to the other, "he would have taken the king's head."

Many strong and well-skilled warriors fought against the sons of Gudrun, but without avail, for they could not wound them.

Then in the midst of the fray appeared a wise old man who had but one eye. He was Odin, but they knew it not. He counselled that the warriors should cast stones against the twain, who were protected by spells. As he advised, so was it done. Many stones were flung at Hamder and Sorle, and they were speedily slain.

So endeth the northern tale of the Volsungs and the Giukings.

# CHAPTER XXXII
## Siegfried and the Nibelungs

The Hero's Youth—His Service with Mimer—Wieland overcome—
Forging the Sword—The Dragon Regin—The Combat—How Siegfried became
invulnerable—Language of Birds—Mimer is slain—Prince journeys to Isenland—Queen Brunhild—Combat with Giants—The Dwarf Alberich—Cloak
of Obscurity—The Nibelung Hoard—Quest of Kriemhild.

SIEGFRIED[1] was a great and noble prince whose fame, by
reason of his mighty deeds, hath endurance through the
Ages. His sire was King Siegmund of the Netherlands
and his mother was named Sigelinde. Ere yet he had
reached the years that are mellowed by wisdom, Siegfried
was of proud and haughty spirit and brooked not restraint.
Great was his strength, and if his playfellows obeyed not
his will in all things, he smote them harshly, so that they
hated as much as they feared him. Wild and wilful was
the prince as a lad may be.

Of Siegfried's doings complaint was made unto the
king, who resolved to set him to work among strong
and skilful men. Accordingly the prince was sent unto

---

[1] Siegfried is the hero of the Nibelungenlied, the great Upper German poetic romance
(see Introduction). He is identical with the northern Sigurd of the Eddic poems and
Volsunga saga. The various versions of the popular tale developed from an older legend.
The Nibelungenlied is here introduced by a summary from Thidrek saga, a Norse poem
composed about the middle of the thirteenth century, which was based on the Lower
German version of the legend and the Dietrich poems. Our introduction gives a con-
secutive narrative. The Nibelungenlied opens abruptly by introducing Kriemhild, who
takes the place of the Norse Gudrun. Siegfried's early exploits are afterwards referred
to briefly.

Mimer, the wonder smith, who dwelt in a deep forest, so that he might acquire such knowledge of how weapons were made as would serve him well in aftertime. Mimer gave the lad heavy tasks to perform, and kept him working at anvil and bellows from morn till even. Skilful in time he became, and his strength increased beyond knowledge.

The years went past, and the lad endured the burden of servitude and the blows of his elders with humility. But one day he fell upon Wieland, the strongest and most cunning smith that was in Mimer's service, and dragged him by the locks through the smithy. Mimer was wroth, but Siegfried had discovered the full measure of his might and he commanded haughtily, as befits a prince, that a strong sword should be forged for him. The master smith realized that he must needs obey, however unwilling he might be; so he drew from the furnace a bar of glowing iron, and bade the lad to beat out for himself a worthy blade.

Siegfried swung high the great hammer and struck a blow which shook the smithy. The iron was splintered to pieces, the hammer snapped asunder, and the anvil was driven deep into the ground.

Mimer spake with anger, but Siegfried smote him heavily, and the other assistant he smote also.

Then the lad demanded to be given a sword equal to his strength. Mimer made promise to forge it for him. But in his heart he vowed to be avenged. First he went through the forest to the place where dwelt his brother Regin, who had been, by reason of his evil doings, transformed into a dragon. Mimer roused the monster to anger and bade him lie in wait for Siegfried. Thereafter he returned to the smithy and asked the lad to hasten through the forest unto the dwelling of the charcoal-burner, so that he might procure sufficient good fuel with which to forge the promised sword.

Siegfried seized his club and went forth. He came to a forest swamp which swarmed with venomous snakes and great lind-worms and toads; but he had more loathing than terror. When he reached the charcoal-burner he besought him for fire, so that he might destroy the reptiles.

"Alas, for thee!" the charcoal-burner exclaimed; "for if thou dost return again by the way thou didst come the dragon Regin will come forth to devour thee."

The prince scorned to be afraid, and snatching a fiery brand he returned through the forest and set in flames the trees and shrubbage of the swamp, so that all the loathsome reptiles were destroyed.

Then came forth the great dragon, bellowing loud and spouting venom. The earth trembled as he came. But Siegfried was not afraid. Thrice he smote the monster with his club and thus slew it.[1]

Perceiving that the dragon was dead, the prince cut it up, and a deep stream of blood issued forth. He dipped his finger into it, and marvelled to find that the skin had become hard as horn.

"Now shall I render myself invulnerable against battle wounds," he said.

So he cast off his clothing and plunged into the hot stream. His whole body was then made horn-hard, save a single spot between his shoulders, to which a gummy leaf had adhered.

Siegfried was well pleased. He clad himself and cooked pieces of the dragon's flesh, so that he might receive a meed of its strength. As he watched the flesh

---

[1] The necessity for more than one blow recalls Thor's conflicts with the Midgard serpent in Hymer's boat and at the Ragnarok battle.

broiling, he tasted a portion to discover if it were ready. When he did that the forest was filled with magic voices, for he could understand the language of birds.

Marvelling greatly, he listened to the birds as they sang:

> If Siegfried knew what we know,
>   What we know this day,
> He would seek, O, he would seek
>   The wonder smith to slay;
> For Mimer sent him to the wood
>   To be the Dragon's prey.

> Let Siegfried know what we know,
>   And ponder o'er our song . . .
> The wonder smith would fain, O fain,
>   Avenge his brother's wrong—
> Smite to live, or wait his blow
>   And live not long.

Siegfried heard with understanding, and his heart was hardened against the wonder smith. He cut off the dragon's head, and, hastening unto the smithy, he flung the trophy at Mimer's feet, bidding him to eat thereof. Wieland and his fellow fled, fearing greatly the prince's wrath, but Mimer sought to appease him with flattering words, and at length made offer, for life ransom, of the steed Grane, which was of Sleipner's race.

Siegfried accepted the gift, and then, remembering what the birds had sung, he smote Mimer with his club and slew him.

Then returned the young hero unto his sire, King Siegmund, who reproved him for killing the master smith, but he took pride in the lad because that he had slain the dragon.

Soon afterwards Siegfried was given arms and armour, and became a complete warrior. A banquet was held, and beakers were drained, when, with loud acclamations, the prince was hailed as heir to the kingdom of the Netherlands.

Thereafter Siegmund's strong son went forth to win renown in distant lands, and northward he bent his way towards Isenland. On the shore of the Netherlands a ship awaited him. A great gale blew, and the master mariner feared to go forth. But Siegfried would brook not delay, and crossed the stormy seas without fear, despite the peril he endured.

He landed in safety and journeyed towards the castle of Queen Brunhild. The gates were shut and bolted, but he broke them open. Then did the knights who were on guard rush against him, and they began to fight. But Brunhild came forth and bade that the combat should cease, and she gave the prince right courtly welcome.

Now Brunhild was very fair, and was a battle maiden of wondrous strength and prowess. Many wooed her, but no knight came nigh who was worthy her skill; those who encountered her were slain one by one. Maid attendants she had, too, and they were clad in armour and bravely were they wont to fight for their queen.

Siegfried saw that Brunhild had great beauty, but he had no desire to win her by combat against her knights or by vying with her in feats of strength.

"She whom I shall have for wife," he said, "must be gentle and womanly. I love not the battle maiden."

Yet he departed not without display of prowess, for he seized a boulder and flung it so great a distance that all who saw the feat performed wondered greatly.[1]

The prince then went on his way until he came to the land of the Nibelungs. It chanced that the king had died, and his two sons, Nibelung and Schilbung, disputed

---

[1] He resembles the boulder-flinging mountain giants.

over the treasure hoard. Unto Siegfried they made offer
of a wondrous sword, which had been forged by the
dwarfs, if he would make just division of their father's
riches. He did as they desired, but they sought to
repay him with treachery. For when he was given the
sword, which was named Balmung, they said that he had
kept back part of the treasure for himself. A quarrel
was stirred up, and it waxed fierce. Then the king's sons
called forth twelve giants, so that the prince might be
overcome and bound, and thereafterwards imprisoned in
the treasure cavern of the mountain.

But Siegfried feared not any foe. He fought bravely
against the giants.

Then spells were wrought, and a thick mist gathered
in the place of conflict; but the sword Balmung was
wielded by Siegfried to such good purpose that he prevailed. A thunderstorm raged;[1] the mountains resounded
with dread clamour and the earth trembled. Yet did the
prince fight on, until he had slain giant after giant and
none remained alive.

Thereafter the dwarf Alberich came forth against
him, seeking to be avenged. A cunning foeman was
he, and not easy to combat against, for he had power
to become invisible. He possessed a cloak of obscurity,
and when he put it on Siegfried must needs combat with
menacing nothingness. Long they fought, and in the
end the prince had the dwarf in his power.[2]

Although Siegfried put to death the two sons of the

---

[1] Thor is suggested here.

[2] There is a curious Banffshire story of two mountain fairies who fought for the
love of a fairy lady. One was dark and the other was white. The former had power
to render himself invisible, but when he did so in the duel a red spot remained. The
white fairy saw the red spot floating in the air, and shot an arrow through it. The
dark fairy was slain because the red spot was his heart. This story is not of a common
type, and is evidently very old. The fairies occupied opposing hills, as if they were
the usual Scottish mountain giants. Of course, giants and fairies have much in common.

king, he spared Alberich, from whom he won the Cloak of Obscurity, which could, when he wore it, render him invisible.  For he followed the dwarf as he fled towards the mountain cavern in which the treasure was concealed. Then did the masterful hero possess himself of the hoard, and he made Alberich the keeper of it when he vowed to obey his commands.

The Nibelung people acclaimed Siegfried as their king, but he tarried not long in their midst.  He took with him twelve bold war-men, and set sail again for the Netherlands.  His fame went speedily abroad, and his deeds were sung of by gleemen in many a hall.

A right valiant and noble prince did Siegfried become; all men honoured him, and by women was he loved.  Many a fair maiden sighed because he sought not to win one or another.  But he rejoiced in warlike feats and in games, and his heart was moved not with desire for any damsel.

There came a time, however, when gleemen sang of the beauty and grace of the Princess Kriemhild, the daughter of the King of Burgundy.  In the wide world there was none fairer, and Siegfried loved her in secret ere yet he beheld her, for he knew that she was his heart's desire, and he resolved that he would woo her right speedily.

He spake to his knights thereanent, and they told both king and queen of Siegfried's bold intent.  Siegmund and Sigelinde sought to repress his desire, but the prince would not be restrained.

The king warned his son that the warriors of Burgundy were fierce in war, and among them were Gunther and strong and vengeful Hagen.

"What I shall obtain not by fair request," Siegfried said, "I may win in battle."

His sire made offer of a great army, but the prince said he would go forth as one of twelve knights. He scorned to win Kriemhild by force, and vowed he would woo her by reason of brave deeds.

Then were preparations made for the journey, and the queen caused rich and gorgeous apparel to be fashioned for Siegfried and his men, and when they rode forth they were indeed of noble seeming.

Siegmund and Sigelinde sorrowed greatly when their son kissed them farewell.

"Grieve not," Siegfried said, "for no evil shall come nigh me."

Then rode he away, the noble prince, to share his meed of joy and meet his doom.

# CHAPTER XXXIII
## The Promise of Kriemhild

The Fair Princess—Her Dream and her Desire—Arrival of her Lover—
Hagen's Warning—The Year of Waiting—War declared—Siegfried's Great
Deeds—Two Kings taken captive—Lovers meet—A Vision of Beauty—The
Worthy Knight—The Kiss and the Vow—Gunther desires Brunhild—Sieg-
fried's Reward.

THE Princess Kriemhild was of great beauty, nor could
her equal be found in any land. Many a gallant knight
came to death seeking to win her. When her sire, the
King of Burgundy, died, she was guarded by her three
brothers, Gunther and Gernot and Giselher. The queen
mother, who was named Ute, had much wealth, and
dwelt with her three brave sons and fair daughter in a
splendid and stately palace at Worms.

Now it chanced that, ere Siegfried came, Kriemhild
dreamt a strange dream, and in the morning she spake
regarding it to her mother, saying:

"Methought that I did possess a falcon which was
strong and of noble seeming. It was faithful to my will,
but there came two fierce eagles and slew it before my
eyes. I wept; never did I endure greater sorrow."

The wise old queen said: "I can read thy dream, my
child. Thou shalt have a strong and noble husband, but
early shall he be taken from thee."

"Dear mother mine," pleaded the princess, "speak
not to me of a husband. I desire not the love of any

man. My heart's wish is to be ever fair, and to live with thee as I live now until death comes. I seek not the sorrow that love doth surely bring."

"If ever thou shalt have surpassing joy in this life," Ute said, "it shall be given thee by a husband's love. Ah, Kriemhild, thou wouldst indeed be a comely bride! May God send hither a knight who is worthy thee."

Kriemhild blushed. "Speak not again in such wise, mother mine," she said softly. "Full oft is it found by women that their bliss but leads to great sorrow. Neither shall I seek, so that I may avoid all misfortune."

But although the fair princess was long thus minded, the time came when she knew the love of a noble knight, to whom in the end she was wedded. But even as the falcon of her dream was slain, so was her husband. He fell by the hands of her own kinsmen, and so great was her desire for vengeance that many found death ere it was fulfilled.

Siegfried and his knights came riding towards the palace at Worms. Many marvelled greatly to behold them, so noble were they and so richly apparelled. Their raiment flashed with gold, and gold-decked were their bridles. In shining armour they came; high were their helms, and their shields were new and bright. On proudly stepping steeds they rode their stately way, with clink of sword and spear and clang of armour. Siegfried led them on. Nor ever was beheld a fairer knight; on his shield a crown was painted, and he wore the great and matchless blade Balmung, which men gazed upon with wonder.

Tidings were borne to the palace of the prince's approach. King Gunther wondered who he might be, so he bade Hagen to survey him from a window.

Hagen did so and said: "Never have I gazed upon

Siegfried, but methinks this noble knight is him and no other. Surely he cometh hither to seek some new enterprise. . . It was this same prince who overcame the Nibelungs and possessed himself of their treasure. For he fought against giants and slew them, and wrested from the dwarf Alberich the Cloak of Obscurity. Never was there a greater hero. He killed the dragon of the forest and bathed himself in its blood, so that no weapon can wound him. Let Siegfried be given welcome, O king. Worthy is he indeed of the friendship of brave men."

The king went forth from the palace. He welcomed the prince. Then he spoke to him saying:

"Why hast thou come hither unto Worms?"

Siegfried made bold answer. "The fame of thy brave knights," he said, "hath gone abroad. I would fain combat with them and with thee for all thy lands and thy strongholds."

But the king spoke words of peace, and sought to have the prince for his ally. In the end his will prevailed, and Siegfried and the knights drank wine together with Gunther.

Thereafter they held games, and Siegfried outshone all others by reason of his strength and skill, for there were none who could throw boulders or shoot arrows like to him. When the knights tilted in the courtyard the eyes of many fair maidens were turned upon the stranger knight.

Fair Kriemhild peered forth from a palace window. She was well content to watch the noble prince. Siegfried beheld her not, but he knew that his loved one was gazing upon him. Yet at heart was he sad, and he wondered how he could win her.

Next day the king and all his men went forth to

hunt. Siegfried went with them, and Kriemhild fretted alone. Heavy, too, was the heart of the prince.

The weeks went past and the months; the knights hunted oft and vied one with another at sports, but the lovers met not. Nor did Siegfried ever once behold the fair lady he sought for his bride. . . . So was a long year of waiting endured by the twain.

Now it chanced that two kings, who were brothers, desired to war against Gunther and invade his kingdom. Namely were they Ludger of the Saxons, and Ludgast of the Danes. They sent envoys to Worms to make demand of the tribute which was paid aforetime; but Gunther, having taken counsel of Siegfried and his knights, answered them "Nay", and called forth his war-men and made ready for conflict.

Ere long the armies met in battle array. The Danes and Saxons were in number forty thousand, and the strength of the Burgundians was not nigh so great. But great were the deeds of Siegfried, and on the field there was not his equal.

Ere the battle began the prince challenged King Ludgast to single combat, and fiercely did they fight one against the other. Hard were the blows that Siegfried dealt with his sword, Balmung, and in the end the king yielded and was taken prisoner. Ludgast's knights sought to rescue him, but the prince slew thirty, so that but one escaped.

Hagen guarded the royal prisoner, and Gernot rushed into the fray with but a thousand men. Bravely fought the Burgundians. But Siegfried was their strong arm that day. Thrice he drave through the mass of foemen, and the blood of slain men ran behind him like to the Rhine waters. At length he came nigh to Ludger, whom he sought. The Saxon king knew well that his brother of Denmark had been taken captive, and he was wroth thereat. He deemed that Gernot had done the deed. But soon he discovered the truth. Not long did he combat with the heroic prince when he beheld upon his shield a shining crown.

"Cease fighting," the king cried to his men, "for the devil hath sent against me bold Siegfried, the son of Siegmund."

So the Saxon banner was lowered, and King Ludger was Siegfried's prisoner. Five hundred valiant knights were taken captive also, and were led to Worms by Hagen and Gernot.

Now a trusty messenger bore unto Kriemhild secret tidings of the battle, and when she heard of Siegfried's mighty deeds her face reddened like to the rose, and her heart rejoiced not only because he had won great renown, but for reason that he had suffered no hurt in battle.

The two captive kings were brought before Gunther, and they made offer of much gold for life ransom.

Then did Gunther speak nobly. "Thou shalt go free," he said, "but first let there be a peace treaty betwixt us."

Readily did the royal prisoners pledge themselves, and they were honoured as guests. The wounded knights were tended with care, and those who sought not to depart from Worms ere they were healed, remained as friends. The war was ended and there was peace, and Siegfried prepared to return to the Netherlands; but Gunther pleaded with him to tarry yet awhile. That the prince consented to do because of the love he bore for Kriemhild.

A great banquet was held thereafter. From far and near brave knights assembled to rejoice because that

victory was given to their arms. All the high-born
ladies were bidden as guests, and Queen Ute came
with a hundred maidens. Many knights awaited the
coming of that fair company, hoping that their eyes
would be gladdened by sight of the beauteous princess.
Siegfried hoped and waited also.

Then appeared the fairest of the fair. Like to the
rose-red dawn beaming amidst murky clouds she came
before them all. . . .

Ended was then the trouble of one who had long
brooded over her; at last did he behold his heart's desire
in all her beauty. Many gems were sparkling on her
garments. Her cheeks were rose red and shining with
love. . . . None who was there did ever before gaze
upon such beauty. As the cloud-girt moon excelleth
the stars, so did Kriemhild surpass in splendour all the
women who were about her. . . . Gallant knights and
gay were stirred with reckless desire to display their
prowess before that fair lady.

The chamberlains made clear a path before her, yet
did the love-lorn war-men press eagerly to gaze upon
Kriemhild.

Siegfried was gladdened and made sorrowful. "How,
ah, how can I win thee!" he sighed. "Alas, my hope is
vain! I dare not draw nigh to thee. . . . Would I were
dead."

His cheeks by turns were red and white. . . . Peerless he stood apart, the great son of Siegmund; noble was
his bearing, and as fair was he to look upon as if he were
painted upon parchment by a cunning master. Truly
was it said that eye did never behold a lordlier warrior.

The busy chamberlains bade the knights to stand
aback, and they gazed with gladness upon the fair ladies,
richly robed, who came following Queen Ute.

Then Gernot besought King Gunther that Siegfried be presented unto fair Kriemhild, and the prince was brought before his heart's desire, so that she might greet him. His sadness was swept from him, like dew before sunlight.

Modestly did the maiden greet the brave prince, and her cheeks reddened when he was nigh to her.

"Sir Siegfried, I bid thee welcome," she said; "a valiant and noble knight art thou."

His heart rejoiced thereat; he no longer despaired when he heard her voice, and, bowing low, he kissed her white hand. Then met their eyes, which were filled with secret love. The prince pressed her hand softly, and their hearts did beat together.

Never again had Siegfried such gladness of soul as at that sweet moment, when he turned to walk by her side. . . . All eyes were upon them, and one to the other said that never was there a knight worthier such a prize.

They went before the king, who bade Kriemhild to kiss the noble prince. . . . Nor did Siegfried conceive ere then that life had such joy in store for him.

King Gunther said: "Thus is Siegfried greeted because that many valiant men have fallen by his sword. . . . God grant that he shall never take leave of us."

So was the ceremony ended ere the banquet began. Kriemhild parted a little while from her lover. She went forth in radiant beauty amidst all her fair maidens; there were none like to her—none.

Ere long the lovers met again. The prince waited not for mass; he sought his heart's desire. So they spoke one to another, and she praised him sweetly, thanking God the while for his valour in battle.

Siegfried bowed low and said : "Thee shall I serve all my days, because that I love thee so."

For twelve days did the rejoicings continue, and each day the prince walked beside Kriemhild. So was royal honour bestowed upon him. The guests made merry; they tilted in the courtyard, they feasted and drank wine together; but at length the time came for them to depart.

One by one they took leave of Ute and Kriemhild, as did also Siegfried, who was plunged thereat in despair.

"Never can I win her," he sighed. . . .

He went forth and called his men; his steed was quickly saddled, and he turned to ride homeward.

But Gunther, hearing of his sudden purpose, sent Giselher to plead with him to remain, saying: "Here thou canst ever see the fair maidens at will."

"Unsaddle the seeds , ' the prince commanded. "I thought to go forth but Giselher hath prevailed upon me to tarry yet a time."

Because of his love he remained there; nor could he have been happier elsewhere, for he spake to Kriemhild each day. . . . So time passed, but heavy was his heart with love. For love he tarried but to sorrow, and in the end he died for love.

Now it chanced that King Gunther desired greatly to have Brunhild for his bride. He spake with Siegfried thereanent. It was told that Brunhild had vowed to woo not any man who surpassed her not in feats. Great was her strength. First she flung a spear, and her wooer must needs excel her with his. Then cast she a stone, and leapt as far. The knight who failed in either trial was speedily slain. Many sought to woo her, and many died because of their boldness.

Gunther boasted that never was there a woman born whom he could not vanquish. But Siegfried warned him, saying:

"Thou knowest not Brunhild, who hath the strength of four men. Go not unto her if thou dost prize thy life."

"So great is her beauty," the king said, "that I must needs try to win her."

Hagen counselled that he should take Siegfried with him; whereat the king offered the prince reward of honour and service if he would aid him to win Brunhild.

Siegfried said: "If thou shalt give me Kriemhild for wife, thee shall I serve in this thy enterprise. Nor other reward do I seek."

Gunther said: "Thine shall Kriemhild be when I return unto my kingdom with Brunhild for wife."

So they took vows together, and made plans for their journey. The king desired to have an army with him, but the prince prevailed upon him to go forth with only the brothers Hagen and Dankwart and himself. Then Siegfried said that he would take with him the Cloak of Obscurity, which he had won from the dwarf Alberich.

To Kriemhild went Gunther and the prince, and besought her to have fashioned for the four knights raiment both rich and goodly, and the king said they must needs have three changes for four days.

The fair princess set her maids to work, and she herself did cut out each garment. Snow-white silk from Araby and Zazamanc, and silk, green as clover, did the princess bring forth, and silks also from Libya and Morocco. With rare gems was the rich attire adorned, and wrought also with embroideries of gleaming gold. The black-spotted ermine was spared not, and linings were made of bright fishes' skins.

When the king and his three brave knights were all apparelled, each one vowed that their equals were never before beheld.

Kriemhild pleaded with Gunther to go not forth upon his perilous enterprise, but he would not be changed in his intent. The princess wept when farewells were spoken, and to Siegfried she said:

"To thy care do I commend my brother, King Gunther."

Siegfried answered her: "Sorrow not, nor have any fear. If I die not, I shall bring him back again in safety to the Rhineland."

Kriemhild gave him thanks, and was comforted.

Then were their shields of gold and bright weapons and armour carried to the shore. They went aboard— Gunther, the king; Siegfried, Prince of the Netherlands, and the valiant brothers, Hagen and Dankwart.

The white sail was spread; a fair wind filled it, and the ship went down the Rhine.

Many fair maidens watched from windows. Kriemhild wept as the ship fared on.

# CHAPTER XXXIV

## How Brunhild and Kriemhild were won

Brunhild's Domain—The King and his Vassal—Wooing the Amazon—
Her Challenge—Misgivings—Siegfried aids Gunther—Spear and Boulder Con-
tests—Brunhild is won—Fears of Treachery—Siegfried's Secret Mission—Adventure in Nibelung—The Army—Return to Burgundy—Wedding Feast—
Brunhild's Jealousy—Struggle in Darkness—Invitation to Worms.

FOR the space of twelve days the ship voyaged across the
sea, and then drew nigh to a strange shore. Siegfried
had beheld it aforetime, and knew that it was Isenland,
but Gunther and his knights gazed with wonder on
the green lands and the many castles towering upon
the headlands.

"He who did cause these strongholds to be built,"
the king said, "must indeed be a mighty monarch."

"Thou dost now behold the many towers and the
fair domain of Queen Brunhild," said Siegfried. "Yonder
is the great castle of Isenland."

The ship was steered into a safe haven, and the prince
warned his fellows to have care of their doings in presence
of the queen. "Thou shalt say," he counselled them,
"that I am but a vassal to King Gunther."

They went ashore and mounted their steeds. Siegfried held the stirrup to the king; the twain were clad
in snow-white silken raiment which glittered with bright
jewels. Hagen and Dankwart were apparelled in black.

Tidings of their approach were borne unto Queen
Brunhild. A courtier spake unto her, saying:

"There cometh hither, O queen, four goodly knights, and one is like unto Siegfried. With him is one of less noble seeming, but he rideth in front, and must therefore be a mighty king indeed. The other two resemble not one another. The first is black-browed and sullen, and fierce are his eyes; his fellow is fair to look upon and is yet of fearless bearing."

A force of knights bade the strangers to deliver up their arms. Unwilling was Hagen to do so, but Siegfried said that such was the custom of the country. Ill at ease were Gunther and Hagen and Dankwart when they beheld the queen and all her maidens coming towards them in midst of five hundred knights with drawn swords.

Brunhild spake to Siegfried only. She bade him welcome to her kingdom.

Then she asked of him: "Why dost thou come hither now with these goodly knights?"

Siegfried made answer: "I thank thee, O Queen, for thy greeting. This noble knight whom I serve is King Gunther. I have followed him because such is his will, else I should not have come hither. He desireth with all his heart to have thee for his bride."

"If such is his desire," Brunhild answered coldly, "the king must needs contend against me in the lists. If he proves to be the stronger, I shall be his bride; but if he fails, then must he and those who are with him be put to death."

Hagen said: "The king shall for certain prevail, because he doth so greatly desire to wed thee."

Brunhild answered him, saying: "Then must he cast the stone and leap to the spot where it falls, as I shall do, and he must also contend with me at spear-throwing. Be not too certain of his success. Consider well my challenge."

Siegfried whispered to Gunther, saying: "Fear not, for I shall give thee mine aid."

Then the king spake boldly unto Brunhild. "For thy dear sake," he said, "I shall risk my life, contending against thee even as thou dost desire."

Brunhild was made angry, and so fierce was she of aspect when her armour was put on, that Hagen and Dankwart feared for the life of the king.

Meanwhile Siegfried had hastened towards the ship. He donned the Cloak of Obscurity, which gave to him the strength of twelve men. Then he returned to the lists unseen by any who were there.

A ring was made, and Brunhild's seven hundred knights stood round it fully armed with naked swords.

Then the great queen came forth. Four men carried her shield, and when Hagen beheld that he cried: "Alas! King Gunther, she is the devil's bride. We shall surely be slain."

Three men carried Brunhild's mighty spear. Gunther began to be afraid, and wished that he were back again in Burgundy.

"Not even the devil could escape her," said he.

Dankwart lamented that their arms were taken from them. "Had Hagen and I but our swords," he said, "Brunhild's war-men would be less arrogant." Hagen spake likewise, and the queen, who heard what was said, bade that their armour and weapons be returned to them.

Then was a boulder carried towards the queen by twelve knights. . . . The men of Burgundy were stricken with fear. . . . "Would indeed that the devil had her," groaned Hagen.

Brunhild made ready to cast the stone. Gunther watched her with mute amaze. His heart sunk within him. Then it was that Siegfried, wrapped in the Cloak of Obscurity, stole to his side and touched his arm. . . .

The king started. He looked behind him, but saw no man. "Who laid his hand upon my arm?" he asked hoarsely.

"Hush!" whispered Siegfried. "I have come to help thee; so be not afraid."

First Brunhild flung her great spear against Gunther. He would have perished then, but Siegfried warded off the blow, yet not without hurt to himself.

Without delay the prince hurled back the spear, so that the haft struck the queen, for he desired not to slay her. She was felled to the ground. . . . Angrily she arose, but she praised the king for this prowess.

Thereafter Brunhild seized the mighty boulder with both hands, and, having flung it a great distance, she leapt beyond the place where it fell.

Gunther then went towards the boulder with the invisible prince. By the king did it seem to be lifted and thrown, but the mighty deed was accomplished by Siegfried, who cast the stone farther than Brunhild, and leapt farther with Gunther in his arms.[1]

Wroth was the queen because that her feats were surpassed, but she spake to her knights, saying:

"Now is Gunther made king over ye all."

Her face was flushed; her heart thirsted for vengeance.

[1] The stone-throwing contest is reminiscent of the duels of Scottish hill giants and giantesses, who contend one against the other from height to height. Sometimes a battleaxe and sometimes a stone hammer, but most often a boulder, is thrown. In Wales a mountain giant flings a quoit. In Ross-shire a giantess contends against a giant and wounds him on the forehead. Giantesses are often island dwellers like Brunhild, whose northern origin is not disputed, even by German folklorists. The Queen of Isenland was evidently a Hag heroine of a people among whom Matriarchy lingered as late as it did in the Pictish areas of Scotland. The wooing of Scathach by Cuchulainn is of similar character to the wooing of Brunhild. In the subsequent duel between Cuchulainn and his son, the latter throws his spear blunt end foremost.

The warriors of Isenland came towards the King of Burgundy and laid their weapons at his feet. They deemed not that it was Siegfried who had accomplished the mighty deeds and saved Gunther's life.

Meanwhile the prince hastened from the field and returned to the ship, in which he concealed the Cloak of Obscurity. Thereafter he came towards the castle and spake to Gunther, asking him when the trial of feats would begin. So did he deceive Brunhild and her people.

The queen delayed her departure from Isenland, and began to assemble a mighty army. Fearing that she meant ill towards them, Siegfried spake to Gunther and said that he must needs hasten to the kingdom of the Nibelungs and bring back with him a thousand knights, who would be their sure defence. The king was made glad thereat.

Once again did Siegfried assume the Cloak of Obscurity. Then he entered a boat and made it sail swiftly over the waves. Many gazed seaward with wonder, thinking that the boat was driven by wind and tide, for they saw not the prince.

Night had fallen black when Siegfried reached the Nibelung kingdom. He went towards the door of the great mountain in which the treasure hoard was concealed. He knocked loudly, demanding admittance as a weary traveller. In a strange voice he spoke, and the giant porter, who was moved to anger, seizing his shield, opened the door.

"Darest thou with thine evil clamour to awake our people?" the porter growled, and then struck a savage blow. Siegfried parried, but the giant smote again. He came nigh to overcoming the prince, who was greatly alarmed, and yet at heart proud of his strong servant.

For a time they fought hard together, but at length Siegfried threw down the giant and bound him.

Then came against him Alberich, the dwarf, clad in full armour; he fought with a mace which had seven balls on chains. The prince was for a time in great peril, but he overcame the dwarf also, and bound him.

Alberich then cried: " Had I not already vowed to serve another knight, thy slave would I be. Who art thou ?"

Said the prince: " My name is Siegfried. Knowest thou me not?"

" Glad am I it is thee and no other," the dwarf said. " Worthy indeed art thou to be King of the Nibelungs."

Then Siegfried unbound the dwarf and the giant, and gave order that a thousand knights be brought forth to do him service. Alberich awakened the heroes who were within, and thirty thousand hastened to obey the ruler. He chose from among them a thousand, and they all sailed forth together in many fair ships towards Isenland, where Brunhild reigned as queen, and Gunther and Hagen and Dankwart awaited their coming.

When three days had passed, Brunhild and her maidens saw, looking from the castle windows, the white sails of many fair ships coming over the sea towards Isenland. The queen was stricken with alarm, fearing a sudden invasion, but Gunther told her that the vessels bore his vassal Siegfried and certain of his own warriors whom he had left behind.

Brunhild went to the beach, and the first she greeted as aforetime was Siegfried. He was clad in gorgeous raiment, and noble was his bearing. . . . Thus was Gunther rescued from peril once again by the Prince of the Netherlands.

The queen then realized she must needs depart from

Isenland, and, having chosen her mother's brother to be chief ruler, she sailed towards Burgundy with Gunther and his knights. But she refused to be wed until she had reached the palace at Worms.

A swift and easy voyage was made, and when they were nigh to home Siegfried was sent ahead as envoy to Worms, so that Queen Ute and the Princess Kriemhild might know how the king had prospered.

Giselher beheld first the prince's approach, and he told his mother and fair sister that Siegfried was nigh. . . . Their hearts were filled with dark forebodings, but soon did the prince make them to rejoice with his glad tidings.

Siegfried sat by Kriemhild's side. Her face was rose-red with love, and it was her heart's desire to kiss him. . . .

"Gunther entreats thee to come to the shore," the prince said, "so that thou mayest welcome Brunhild hither."

Kriemhild went gladly with all her maidens, and Giselher led forth a great force of war-men. Brunhild was well pleased because that Gunther was a mighty ruler, and Kriemhild and she kissed one another with love. Together then they all made their way towards the stately palace at Worms.

A great banquet was held, and Gunther and Brunhild were wed. Thereafter in secret did Siegfried speak unto the king, saying:

"Hast thou no memory of thy vow? Thou didst swear that when Brunhild came hither I would be given Kriemhild for wife. . . . Well have I served thee."

Gunther said: "I forswear not my oath. What I can do that shall I do now."

So the king called Kriemhild before him and said:

"Thee did I promise unto Siegfried, and if thou wilt have him now my heart's desire will be fulfilled."

The princess answered: "Him I shall wed with great joy."

Then were the oaths sworn betwixt them. Proud and happy was the noble prince; maidenly and demure was the beauteous princess.

They all sat down to feast together. Brunhild was at Gunther's side. Her face was pale and cold, and when she beheld Siegfried and Kriemhild together she began to weep bitterly.

The king spake to her and asked: "Why dost thou sorrow? 'Twere more seemly to make merry, for thou art now Queen of Burgundy."

"I weep," Brunhild said, "because that thy sister hath been wedded to thy vassal. . . . Great is my shame thereat."

Gunther told his queen then that Siegfried had lands and castles that were his own. "Great riches hath he," said Gunther, "and therefore am I glad that Kriemhild hath wedded with him."

But Brunhild still sorrowed, and refused to be comforted.

When the feast was over they all returned to their chambers, but Brunhild said she would not be as a wife to the king until he told her all concerning Siegfried and Kriemhild. Gunther was wroth, and answered not, seeking to appease her with caresses, but she laid hands upon him so that he was overpowered. Then, binding the king with her waist girdle, she hung him on the wall.

Next morning Gunther told Siegfried what had happened, and the prince promised once again to be his aid. So, when night fell, he assumed the Cloak of Obscurity and entered Gunther's bedchamber, where he wrestled with the queen. A fierce conflict it was, and Brunhild deemed that her opponent was none other than her husband. In the end Siegfried prevailed, and he took from her the silken waist girdle which she wore, and drew from her finger unawares a ring of fine gold.[1]

Thus was Brunhild subdued; after that hour she had but the strength of other women.

Siegfried gave unto Kriemhild the girdle and the ring which had caused many knights to die in the lists at the castle of Isenland.

When the rejoicings came to an end the guests went their ways. Siegfried returned unto his own land, and Siegmund and Sieglind kissed and embraced him and his beauteous bride.

"Henceforward," Siegmund said, "my son shall reign as king." So spake he unto his people, and they rejoiced because that Siegfried was a mighty warrior.

Ten years went past, and a son was born to Kriemhild. He was named Gunther. At the same time Brunhild had a child, and he was called Siegfried.

All went well until Brunhild, who thought of Kriemhild with jealous heart, prevailed upon Gunther to invite Siegfried and his queen to a feast at Worms.

Gary went forth with the king's message, and was received with gladness by Siegfried and Kriemhild, and they bade him tell unto Gunther that they would both attend the feast.

When Gary returned to Worms, Brunhild asked of him: "Is Kriemhild still as fair as she was aforetime?"

---

[1] Evidently her strength was due to the magic girdle. The dwarf Laurin, in *Der Kleine Rosengarten*, has a girdle which gives him the strength of twelve men. When Dietrich of Bern, wrestling with him, snatches it off, he has the dwarf in his power.

The envoy answered her " Yea," and she brooded over it.

Brunhild still regarded Siegfried as a vassal to King Gunther, and she was angry because that he did not make payment of yearly tribute nor visit Worms to do homage, as befitted a subject ruler.

# CHAPTER XXXV
## The Betrayal of Siegfried

The Rival Queens—Their Quarrel—Brunhild plots against Siegfried—Hagen's Vow—The Tragic Hunt—How Siegfried was deceived—The Death Wound—Last Words—A Sad Homecoming—Kriemhild's Sorrow—Scene in Church—Blood Testimony—Gunther pleads for Forgiveness—Treasure taken to Worms—Where Hagen concealed it.

SIEGFRIED and Kriemhild went riding with a gay company towards Worms. There was joy in every heart, but it was fated to end in heavy grief. Prince Gunther journeyed not with them; never again did he behold his sire or his mother.

The aged King Siegmund rode forth with his son; he had desire to meet with Gunther and his knights, but had he known what sorrow was in store for him he would have fared not from the Netherlands.

Gunther gave to all of them right hearty welcome. The queens greeted one another with affection, but from that hour Brunhild could forbear not watching Kriemhild with jealous eyes. . . . When she beheld the twelve hundred knights of Siegfried, she said: "Never was there a subject king who had greater wealth." . . . The queen, however, gave meet entertainment to her guests; but ere long jealousy overcame love; the heart of Brunhild grieved because that Siegfried and his queen were so rich and powerful.

It fell that on a day when the knights tilted in the courtyard Kriemhild lauded her husband's prowess.

"Siegfried," she said, "excelleth every other knight as the moon doth the diminishing stars. For good reason take I pride in him."

"Valiant he may be," answered Brunhild, "yet thy brother Gunther surpasseth him, for he is the greatest of all kings."

"My brother is indeed a noble knight," Kriemhild said, "yet is my husband his equal."

Said Brunhild: "Did not the king surpass me in feats of strength in Isenland, what time Siegfried remained in the ship? He is but my husband's vassal. From his own lips I heard him confess it.

"Were Siegfried but a vassal," Kriemhild retorted, "thinkest thou that my brother would have given me unto him for wife? I pray thee to repeat not what thou hast said."

"That indeed I shall," said Brunhild. "Siegfried is our subject, and his knights await to do us service when called upon."

Angry was Kriemhild. "No service canst thou claim," she said. "My husband is greater than thine. If he were not he would have to pay tribute, and never hath he done so. I pray thee to cease thine annoyance."

"Boast not with empty pride," Brunhild cried angrily; "I am honoured far above thee."

"Know now," retorted Siegfried's queen, "that my husband is no vassal to thine, and is indeed a greater monarch. The kingdom of the Nibelungs he won by his strong right arm, and he hath inherited the Netherlands from his sire. To no man doth he owe allegiance. I am indeed a free and a mighty queen. Dare not to chide me. Thou shalt see when I enter church in thy company that I shall not walk behind."

"If thou art not my subject, then shalt thou go by thyself, nor walk in my train," Brunhild said.

In anger did Kriemhild leave the Queen of Burgundy, and she bade her maidens to put on their richest attire.

Many wondered to behold the queens walking apart. . . . It was doomed that many should sorrow because of that in aftertime.

When they met before the church Kriemhild went forward to enter first, and Brunhild forbade her. "Thou art my vassal," she said; "walk not before me."

"'Twere better that thou shouldst hold thy peace," retorted Kriemhild; "how can a vassal's paramour walk before a queen?"

"What dost thou mean?" Brunhild asked angrily. "Whom dost thou call a paramour?"

"None other than thee," answered Kriemhild. "Did not my husband win thee for thine? Thou didst prefer him thou now callest a vassal, forsooth. . . . Speak not to me any longer. Thou knowest the truth now."

Then Kriemhild entered the church, and Brunhild followed her, weeping sore. There was deadly hate betwixt them, and for that reason many a goodly knight went to his grave.

When the service was over, Brunhild confronted Kriemhild, saying: "Thou didst call me a paramour. I demand thee now to prove thy words."

"'Twere easy to prove them," retorted Kriemhild proudly, showing her rival the ring and the girdle which Siegfried had taken from her.

"A paramour to Siegfried thou wert indeed," she said.

Brunhild bowed her head with shame, weeping bitterly; and when Gunther asked her why she sorrowed she told him what Kriemhild had said.

Then was Siegfried brought before Gunther, and in Brunhild's presence he swore that he had never uttered what Kriemhild had boasted of.

"I grieve that my wife hath made Brunhild to sorrow," he said.

The knights who were there spake one to another. "Would that women might cease their gossip," said one. "Forbid your wives to boast about ye, else there will be strife and shame among us all."

But Brunhild was not comforted. It chanced that Hagen came nigh to her and found her weeping. He asked her why she did grieve so, and when she told him what Kriemhild had said, he waxed wroth because he had sworn allegiance unto Brunhild and served her faithfully, guarding her honour and her life.

"For this insult," he said fiercely, "Siegfried shall pay with his heart's blood. I shall avenge thee, O queen, or die."

Hagen spake to Gunther and the other knights in like manner, and he roused them all to enmity against Siegfried, who recked not of their secret plotting.

Hagen first contrived that certain knights should visit Worms, making pretence that they came as envoys from King Ludgast declaring war against King Gunther. Siegfried made offer of his service, and Kriemhild was proud thereat, yet did she fear that ill would befall him because that he was reckless and overdaring in battle.

Hagen spake with her treacherously, and she told him that when her husband bathed his body in the dragon's blood a leaf covered a spot betwixt his shoulders, and that if he were wounded there he would surely die. Brunhild's knight rejoiced in secret, but he promised to defend Siegfried, and counselled Kriemhild that she should mark the spot by sewing a small red cross upon his clothing, so that he might know where to defend her loved one.

Then Hagen spake to the king, and Gunther arranged that they should go through the forest on a great hunt which would last many days.

"Go not forth," Kriemhild pleaded with her husband. "I dreamt that thou wert given chase by two wild boars, and I saw the forest flowers made red with blood."

"Fear not for me, my heart's love," Siegfried said; "I go not a-hunting with foemen, but with thine own kin."

Kriemhild wept bitterly. "Alas! I fear for thy life," she cried. "But yesternight I did dream that thou wert caught betwixt two hills, which fell upon thee, and thou wert lost to my sight. . . . Stay with me here, Siegfried, else I shall sorrow without end."

Siegfried kissed and embraced her with tenderness, and then hastened to join the hunt.

She watched him through her tears as he went from her. Never again did she behold her dear one in life.

There was none like to Siegfried at the hunt. Many wild animals he slew, and he caught a bear alive and bound it, and when he set it free they all gave chase, but it would have escaped but for his valour.

They afterwards sat down to feast together. Food there was in plenty but no wine. Siegfried made complaint thereat, for he was grievously athirst, and he vowed he would never again hunt with them. Little did he dream that a plot was laid to accomplish his death.

Hagen said that there was a clear spring near by, from which they could take refreshment, and he challenged Siegfried to race with him thither for a wager.

Hagen stripped off his clothing, but Siegfried ran in full armour, carrying his shield and spear and his bow and quiver, and yet he reached the spring first. But the hero drank not.   He cast off his armour, and laid his weapons on the grass to await the coming of Gunther, the king, so that he might have refreshment before any other.

Dearly did he pay for his courtesy.   When the king had taken his fill, and Siegfried stooped down to drink, Hagen drew away stealthily the sword and the bow, and then plunged the spear through the hero's back at the spot where Kriemhild had embroidered the cross.   He drew not forth the weapon, but made hurried escape. Never before did he run so swiftly from any man.   Siegfried sprang up in anger, the spear sticking fast in his back, and sought for bow or sword to take vengeance on Hagen.   But he found his shield only, and flung it after the traitor.   It smote him to the ground, and the forest echoed the blow.   Had Siegfried but his sword, in that hour Hagen would have been slain.

Snow-white grew the cheeks of that sore-wounded man, the lordly guest of Gunther: he sank to the ground; his strength went from him; death was in his face.   Alas!   many a fair woman wept tears for him in aftertime.

Among the flowers lay Kriemhild's noble husband, and they were made red with his life blood.

He spake faintly, bitterly reproaching those who had plotted treacherously against him.   He called them cowards all.   "I have served ye well," he said, "and thus am I repaid.   The children yet unborn shall suffer for this foul deed."

Gunther wept.   "Weep not for treachery, thou from whom treachery hast come," Siegfried said.

"Now is all danger past," cried Hagen; "I rejoice that he is brought low."

"Boast not, murderous man," Siegfried warned him; "in fair conflict I had naught to fear from thee. . . . Oh,

Kriemhild, Kriemhild, my deepest grief is for thee! . . . Would that our son had never been born, because he must bear from his enemies the bitter reproach that his kinsmen are murderers and traitors."

Gunther he reproached for his ingratitude. "I have saved thy life," he said; "I have been the guardian of thine honour. This foul deed is my payment. . . . If thou hast any honour left, protect my wife, thy sister. . . ."

He groaned, for his wound afflicted him sore. Again he spake saying: "In days to come ye shall suffer for this monstrous deed; yourselves have you slain when ye slew me."

He spake no more. Among the blood-steeped flowers he struggled with death. . . .

They laid his corpse upon a golden shield and bore it towards Worms, and in the darkness they left it at the door of Kriemhild's dwelling.

In the morning, when the fair queen was going forth to prayers, she saw the dead body of Siegfried.

"My husband is dead," she cried. "Brunhild hath desired that he should be slain, and by Hagen was he murdered." Heavy was her heart with grief unutterable, nor could she be comforted.

Old King Siegmund embraced his dead son and wept bitterly.

Tenderly was Siegfried's body lifted and borne within; his wounds were washed; in grave robes was he dressed and laid upon a bier.

After three days of mourning the body was borne to the church, and many assembled there to gaze with sorrow upon the dead hero.

Gunther came and said that Siegfried had been slain by robbers. "I sorrow because that he is dead," he told Kriemhild.

"If there was sorrow in thine heart," she answered him, "my husband would not now be laid in death. Would I were dead and he were still alive!"

When Hagen approached the body of Siegfried the spear wound bled afresh. Thus was it proved to all who were there that he was indeed the murderer.

Great was the mourning on the day of Siegfried's funeral. Many wept in the streets. Kriemhild went to the grave, and or ever the coffin was covered over she besought to gaze once again upon the face of her husband. Her desire was granted her, and she lifted up that fair head in her white hands and kissed the death-cold lips of Siegfried. Then fell she in a swoon, nor did she open her eyes again until next morning.

Siegmund departed soon afterwards and journeyed to his own land. But Kriemhild would not return with him, because she desired to be avenged for her husband's death. She was ever mourning, but Brunhild cared not in her pride.

At length Gunther sought her forgiveness, deeming that she had mourned overlong. Kriemhild said: "I shall forgive him with my lips but never with my heart." Yet was she at length constrained to pardon all who had plotted the death of Siegfried, save Hagen, whom she could not suffer to look upon.

Hagen spake to Gunther of the Nibelung treasure, which he could not but think over, and the king contrived that Kriemhild should send for it. So came it to pass that a strong army was sent unto Siegfried's kingdom.

The dwarf Alberich lamented the loss of the Cloak of Obscurity; yet did he deliver up the vast treasure, in the midst of which was a magic rod which would give to the one who possessed it anything that might be wished for. But none knew its virtues.

Thus was all the wealth of the Nibelungs brought unto Kriemhild. She distributed gold to rich and poor, and many adventurous knights paid visit to Worms to share of her bounty. Wages she gave to a great number, so that ere long she had a strong force of war-men at her service.

Hagen was greatly alarmed thereat, and spoke unto the king of Kriemhild's doings. He counselled that the treasure should be taken from her; but Gunther refused to do any harm unto his sister because of the vows he had sworn. Then did Hagen seize the hoard by force, and carried it away. He sank it in the Rhine at Lochheim, with hope to enrich himself in after-time.

So was Kriemhild's immediate hope of vengeance cut off. She took her departure from Worms and went to dwell with her mother at Lorsch. There she embroidered tapestry with pictures of Balder, who had by his brother been slain.

There she tarried for many years, biding the hour of vengeance. Tidings at length came from beyond the Rhine which brought nearer the fulfilment of Siegfried's dying words: "Yourselves have ye slain when ye slew me."

# CHAPTER XXXVI

## The Nibelungen Tragedy

Kriemhild weds Etzel—Her Desire for Vengeance—The Festival—Invitation to Gunther and his Knights—Hagen's Bravery—The Doom Journey—Dietrich and Hildebrand—How the Guests were received—Treachery of the Queen—Scene at Banquet—Its Tragic Ending—Dietrich intervenes—Hall in Flames—Unconquered Heroes—Gunther and Hagen overcome—Gladness ends in Grief.

It fell that thirteen years after Siegfried's death Queen Helche of the Huns died, and King Etzel[1], who was a heathen, sought another bride. Rudiger, the rich margrave, surnamed "The Good", was sent as envoy to Worms to win Kriemhild; whereat Gunther was made glad, because Etzel was a mighty monarch, but grim Hagen grew angry, fearing that the widow of Siegfried would stir up enmity against them. Kriemhild ceased not to grieve for him whom she had loved, but her brothers and Queen Ute urged her to be wed to the mighty monarch of the Huns, and at length she gave her consent. Then sent she to Hagen for the Nibelung treasure, which she desired to distribute among the Hun warriors; but he refused to give it up saying: " She shall not give it unto those who are my foemen."

Kriemhild was made wroth thereat. Yet had she a portion of the treasure left, and she gave great gifts to the knights who came with Rudiger.

The widowed bride had lost not her great beauty

[1] Attila, "the scourge of God".

despite her long and deep sorrow, and when she came to the Court of Etzel, the courtiers vowed that she was even more fair than was Queen Helche. She kissed the king, and when she was wed she was kissed by twelve noble knights, among whom was Blœdel, the brother of Etzel, and the great warrior king, Dietrich of Bern, who had taken refuge at Etzel's Court when his uncle, Ermenrich, had by treacherous doings possessed himself of the kingdom of the Amelungs. So it came that Kriemhild had friendship and service from many strong war-men. Great was her power. All the treasure that Hagen had left her she gave to the knights, and at length she said unto herself:

"Now am I made powerful, and can strike against the enemies of Siegfried, for whom my heart still calleth."

As the days went past, and the years, her desire for vengeance grew stronger. There was not a Hun knight who would not do her willing service. Yet none did conceive of her fierce intent.

A son was born to King Etzel, and his name was Ortlieb. Like was he in countenance to fair Kriemhild, and the king loved her more dearly because of her child. So at length when she craved of him a boon he said that he would grant it willingly; and the queen besought him that he should send envoys to Worms and invite, unto a festival at his Court, Gunther and all his knights. As she desired, so was it done. Kriemhild spoke in secret to the envoys and bade them not to leave Hagen behind.

Gunther received the message gladly, nor suspected aught of Kriemhild's evil desire; but Hagen warned the king in counsel with his knights, saying: "We dare not go from here unto the Court of Etzel. Our lives are in peril, for Kriemhild forgets not who slew her husband Siegfried. . . . Her memory is long."

Thereupon Gunther's brothers taunted Hagen. "Thou knowest thine own guilt," one said; "therefore thou hast need to protect thyself well. 'Twere better thou didst remain at Worms, while those who fear not sojourn among the Huns."

Hagen was made wroth. "No man among you feareth less to venture forth than I do, and with thee shall I go if ye are determined to visit the Court of Etzel."

So it was arranged that they should set out forthwith, and Hagen spake after that of their journey as "the death ride".

Queen Ute had great desire that her sons should tarry in the kingdom. "I have dreamt an evil dream," she said. "Methought that all the birds in fair Burgundy were slain."

"He who is led by dreams," said Hagen, "is without honour and no hero. Let us unto the festival of Kriemhild."

Many women wept when they set forth. With Gunther rode a thousand and sixty knights, and his army did number full nine thousand men. When they reached the Danube River they found it to be high and running swift. Hagen sought for the ferryman, who desired not to take them across unless he were given rich reward. While searching, he saw bathing in a brook certain water fairies. He went stealthily towards them and possessed himself of their vestments. They had need, therefore, to make known to the fierce knight how he and all who were with him would fare upon their journey. One did promise that they would prosper and win great honour, but another said: "'Twere better to turn back. . . . Ye are all doomed. Who rideth unto the Court of Etzel rideth to death. Nor shall one return again unto Worms save the priest."

Then Hagen met with the ferryman and slew him for his boldness. He seized the boat, and, returning unto Gunther, he ferried across the knights and all their followers. As he crossed with the last company of men he beheld the priest among them, and remembering the prophecy of the water fairy, he seized him there and flung him overboard. But, although the man could not swim, he was driven over the waves and reached the shore in safety. When Hagen saw that the priest could return unto Burgundy, he knew that the foretelling of the water fairy was true, and said unto himself: "These, our warriors, are all dead men."

When they landed, Hagen splintered the boat in pieces. He was resolute indeed, and made certain that no man should turn back. The Bavarians came against them to avenge the ferryman's death, but they were beaten back, and Gunther and his war-men marched forward until they came unto Bechlaren, where Rudiger the Good gave them generous and hospitable entertainment and many gifts.

Tidings of their approach were borne unto Kriemhild. "The day of reckoning is at hand," she said unto herself. "Fain would I now slay the man who did destroy my happiness. . . . He shall pay dearly because that he hath made me to sorrow."

Aged Hildebrand spake unto Dietrich of Bern of the coming of the Burgundians, and counselled that he should ride forth to greet them. Hagen was a dear war friend to Dietrich aforetime, and there was good will betwixt them. So the fierce knight of Burgundy gave his friend warm greetings.

Dietrich was made glad, yet did he inwardly grieve, when he beheld the warriors from Worms.

"Know ye not," he said, "that Kriemhild hath

ceased not to sorrow for Siegfried? . . . This very day I did hear her lamenting because that he was dead."

Gunther reasoned that Etzel had bidden them thither with right royal welcome, and that Kriemhild had also sent warm greetings, but Hagen knew well that sorrow awaited them.

The Hun king knew not that his queen plotted against his guests, and his welcome was hearty and frank; but Kriemhild was haughty and cold. She kissed but her brother Giselher, who had no part in Siegfried's death. Unto Hagen she spake, saying:

"Hast thou brought hither the hoard of the Nibelungs which thou didst rob from me?"

Hagen answered: "I have touched it not. It is hidden below the Rhine waters. There shall it lie until the Day of Judgment."

"So thou hast brought it not," she said coldly. "Many a day have I grieved for it, and for the noble knight whose possession it was."

"I have brought but my weapons and my armour," said Hagen defiantly.

"I need not gold," Kriemhild sighed; "but I would fain have recompense for murder and robbery."

Then were the Burgundians, at the queen's desire, asked to lay down their arms; but Hagen made refusal for himself and the others, saying that it was the custom of the Burgundians to be fully armed on the first three days of a festival.

It chanced that soon afterwards Kriemhild urged certain of her knights to slay Hagen; but they forbore, fearing as they did his dark brows and quick-flashing eyes.

When night fell the guests were conducted to their dwelling. Grim Hagen and Volker, the minstrel, fearing the treachery of Kriemhild, sought not to take rest.

They clad themselves in their bright armour. Then they took their swords and shields and stood outside the door to guard their companions. After a time Volker took his fiddle, and, sitting upon a stone within the porch, he played merry airs which gladdened the hearts of those who were within, and they forgot their anxieties. Then he gave them soothing music and sweet, so that they were lulled to sleep. Thereafter he took up his shield again and stood beside Hagen at the door to guard the Burgundians against Kriemhild's war-men.

In the midst of the night the fierce Huns made stealthy approach; but when they beheld the knights keeping guard they turned away. Volker desired to challenge them to combat, but Hagen forbade him, and Volker cried out to the followers of Kriemhild: "Cowards, would ye venture hither to slay men in their sleep?" They answered him not. Kriemhild grieved because that her plan had failed, but she ceased not to plot against the guests.

A tournament was held in Etzel's courtyard, and Volker slew a Hun warrior. But for the king, vengeance would have been taken for that cause. "He hath been slain without intent," Etzel said; "let my guests go forth unharmed."

Kriemhild then spake to Dietrich of Bern and old Hildebrand, beseeching their aid to encompass the death of Hagen.

Hildebrand answered: "One man is not sufficient to overcome him." And Dietrich, answering her, said: "Speak not of this again, O Queen, I pray thee. These, thy kinsmen, have never done aught against me. 'Twill bring thee shame if thou dost any hurt to them, because they are now thy guests. It is not for me to avenge the death of Siegfried."

Thereafter did Kriemhild plead with Blœdel, King Etzel's brother, making him promise of rich reward, and he promised to achieve her purpose. He went forth to attack Gunther's men with a thousand of his followers. Dankwart was in command when Blœdel fell upon them without warning, and fierce was the conflict.

Meanwhile Gunther and Hagen and other knights sat at feast with King Etzel. Kriemhild caused her son Ortlieb to enter and sit nigh to Hagen, and the king said: "Lo! here cometh my only son to be among his kinsmen."

Hagen loved not the lad. "He hath a weak face," he said. "I could never be a guest at his Court."

Suddenly Dankwart rushed into the feasting hall. He alone of all the war-men had escaped the sword of Blœdel, whom he slew; his body was red with the blood of foemen. "Why dost thou tarry thus, brother Hagen?" he cried; "our men are slaughtered in their dwelling."

"Guard the door," cried Hagen, and seizing his sword he smote off the head of Prince Ortlieb before his father's eyes. Then he slew the lad's tutor and cut off the right hand of a minstrel who had borne Kriemhild's message unto Worms. Volker drew his blade also and made slaughter. In vain did the three kings, Etzel and Gunther and Dietrich, make endeavour to subdue the fray. Many Hun knights were slain, for the Burgundians were seized with battle fury and sought dire vengeance. They cut their way up and down the hall, and there was none who could stand against them.

Then did Kriemhild plead with Dietrich of Bern, beseeching his aid, what time he watched, standing upon a bench, the doughty deeds of his old war comrade Hagen.

"Save me and King Etzel from this our dire peril," cried the queen.

"I can but try," Dietrich answered. "Not for many years have I beheld such fierce fighting."

Then he uttered forth a great shout, and his voice was like to the blast of a war horn." Gunther heard him, and called upon his men to pause in the fray. "Mayhap," he said, "we have slain knights of Dietrich."

"No harm have ye done me or mine," Dietrich said, "but I ask of thee that I and those with me may have thy permission to go forth in safety."

"Thy wish is granted," answered Gunther.

Then did Dietrich clasp the fainting Queen Kriemhild with one arm and took King Etzel's with the other. Thus did he leave the hall with six hundred of his knights. Rudiger went also with five hundred. Neither sought to take part in the fray.

Thereafter was the conflict waged again with great fury, nor did it pause until not a Hun was left alive in the hall.

The Burgundians rested awhile; then they threw out the bodies of their foemen. Kinsmen of the slain mourned greatly.

King Etzel seized his shield and desired them to combat against the stranger at the head of his men; but Kriemhild warned him that he could not withstand the blows of fierce Hagen. But his knights had to hold him back by force, and, seeing this, Hagen taunted the king.

"The darling of Siegfried and her new husband are faint-hearted," he cried. "Ha, Etzel! Siegfried had thy lady to wife before thee. I slew him. Why, then, shouldst thou be angry with me?"

Kriemhild heard with anger. "Much gold shall I give, and castles and land," said the queen, "unto the knight who shall slay Hagen."

Volker shouted defiantly: "Never before beheld I so

many timorous knights.   Cowards all! ye have taken of
the king's substance and in his hour of trial ye desert
him.   I cry shame upon ye all."

Many bold warriors rushed against the knights of
Burgundy.   Stranger knights who were there fought also.
The nimble Iring of Denmark struck mighty blows,
and in the end he wounded Hagen.   Queen Kriemhild
praised him when he returned weary from the fray, and
prompted him to return again.   When he renewed the
conflict, however, Hagen slew him.

So fell many brave men, and the long summer day
ended and darkness fell.   The tumult ceased.

Then the Burgundians besought King Etzel that they
should be permitted to leave the hall and fight in battle,
but Kriemhild forbade it.

Her brother Giselher spake to the vengeful queen
saying : "I deserve not death at thy hands.   I was ever
faithful unto thee.   I came hither because that I did bear
thee love and thou didst invite me.   Thou must needs
now show mercy unto us."

"Can I show mercy who hath never received it?"
she answered him.   "The vile Hagen slew my child, so
those who stand by him must suffer with him.   But
this I shall promise thee—if Hagen be now delivered up
a truce will be granted forthwith."

Gernot answered : "Never shall thy wish be granted.
Rather would we die than ransom our lives with a single
knight."

"Then must we die indeed like to brave men,"
Giselher said.

"My brother Hagen is not without friends," cried
Dankwart; "ye who have refused quarter shall not
receive it.   Not at our hands."

In the midst of the night Kriemhild bade her

followers to set fire to the hall. That they did right gladly. The flames raged furiously, and one of them within cried: "Woe is me! we are doomed to die. Rather would I have fallen in battle."

Great was the heat, and the knights were tortured with thirst. Then did Hagen bid one of them to drink the blood of the slain war-men. One who suffered much knelt beside a corpse and drank the blood. The draught made him strong again. "Better is it than wine," he said.

The others did likewise, and were all refreshed so that they were able to endure their sufferings amidst the flames. Burning faggots fell upon them, but they protected themselves with their shields. Terrible was the heat. Never again shall heroes suffer as did these that night.

"Stand close to the walls," Hagen commanded; "your armour shall protect ye; let the blood quench the flaming brands."

When morning broke, the Huns wondered greatly to behold Hagen and Volker again standing on guard at the hall door."

Fierce attack was again made by the Huns, but they were beaten back. Nor did the conflict have pause until the last of Etzel's great knights was slain.

Then did Kriemhild and the king make appeal to Rudiger to aid them, but he desired not to attack the brave Burgundians.

"Shall I slay those whom I did entertain in my own house?" he exclaimed. "I forget not past friendship."

Yet was he constrained to fight, and he mourned his lot with the Burgundians.

"Would that I had a strong shield like thee," Hagen said; "mine own is hewn and battered sore."

Rudiger gave Hagen his own shield ere he fought at Etzel's command with those whom he loved. Fierce was the conflict and long, and in the end Gernot and Rudiger slew one another.

Then did Wolfhart, the bold knight of Bern, lead on the followers of Dietrich to avenge the death of Rudiger. One by one they were cut down by Gunther's heroes, save Hildebrand, who slew Volker. But Hagen made vengeful attack and wounded him. The old warrior fled. He hastened unto Dietrich, and cried: "All our men are slain, and of the Burgundians but Gunther and Hagen remain alive."

Dietrich was wroth. He sorrowed for his brave knights. No longer could he withhold from the fray. So he put on his armour and went unto the Hall. He first bade Gunther and Hagen to surrender; but they defied him.

Dietrich drew his sword and fell upon Hagen, whom he speedily wounded.

"Battle-weary art thou," Dietrich cried; "I shall slay thee not."

As he spake thus he caught Hagen in his arms and overpowered him. So was the valiant hero taken captive.

Dietrich led him bound before Queen Kriemhild, and her heart rejoiced. "Now is all my sorrow requited," she said; "thee, Dietrich, shall I thank until my life hath end."

The Prince of Bern said: "Slay him not. He may yet serve thee, and thus make good the evil he hath done."

Hagen was cast into a dark dungeon, there to await his doom.

Dietrich then fought against Gunther, who was more

fierce than Hagen had been. Indeed he came nigh to slaying Dietrich. But he was at length borne down, and taken prisoner and bound.

When the King of Burgundy was taken before Kriemhild, she said: "I welcome thee, O Gunther."

He answered her: "If thy welcome were made with love, I would thank ye, but I know well that thou dost mock."

Dietrich pleaded with the queen that Gunther and Hagen should be spared, but his words fell upon ears that heard not.

Kriemhild went unto Hagen and demanded that he should return unto her the treasure he had stolen.

The knight answered her: "Vows I took not to reveal where the hoard is hidden so long as my king liveth."

Then did the queen command that her brother should be slain. With her own white hand she held high by the hair before Hagen the dripping head of Gunther.

"Now all thy brothers are dead," Hagen cried. "Where the treasure is concealed is known but to God and myself alone. . . . Thou devil, thou shalt never possess it!"

So wroth was Kriemhild that she seized a sword and smote off the head of Hagen.

"Alas," cried King Etzel, "the boldest knight who ever fought in battle hath fallen by a woman's hand!"

Old Hildebrand, recking not what would happen him, drew his sword and smote the queen. A loud cry broke from her lips, and ere long Kriemhild died.

So ended the festival of King Etzel, as gladness must ever end in grief.

What befell thereafter I can tell not. Knights and

soldiers, wives and maids, were seen weeping, and heard lamenting for their friends.

So ends the Nibelungenlied.

.      .      .      .      .      .

Minstrels, singing the sorrowful lay of the death of Siegfried, and the fall of the Nibelungs, have told that Queen Brunhild and Queen Ute sat side by side embroidering on tapestry the death of Balder.

Again and again did Brunhild say to the mother of Gunther: "Each time I picture Balder, his face grows like unto that of Siegfried."

Soon tidings were brought to them of the death of Gunther and all his men. Brunhild wept not. She went out into the darkness, nor ever returned again.

When search was made, she was found lying dead in the grave mound of Siegfried, whom she had loved.

# CHAPTER XXXVII
## Dietrich of Bern

Hildebrand's Pupil—Alberich the Dwarf—Grim and Hilde—The Magic Sword—Conflict in the Cavern—Giant and Hag are slain—Great Sigenot—Dietrich taken Prisoner—In the Dragon's Lair—Hildebrand put to Shame—Giant overcome—Heime's Challenge—Wieland's son Witege—Fierce Combat—Dietrich in Peril—Peace Terms.

DIETRICH was the son of great Dietmar, King of Bern, whose brother was the fierce King Ermenrich. He was but seven years old when there came to his father's Court the battle hero, Hildebrand, far famed for valorous deeds. Unto that great warrior was given the care of the young prince, so that he might gain manly wisdom and skill in feats of arms. Fast friends they became ere long, and faithful were they one to another in after years, until death did thrust them apart.

It chanced that when the lad grew strong, and had desire for daring adventure, a giant and a giantess, whose names were Grim and Hilde, ravaged the land with fire, and did slaughter many goodly subjects. Dietmar raised a mighty army and went out against them, but he could discover not the hiding place of the monsters, who ever came forth unawares to work their evil designs.

Now Dietrich had great desire to combat with the giant and giantess, for he was brave as he was strong, and he sought most of all to win a warrior's renown.

With Hildebrand he hunted one fair morning in a deep forest. They came to a green and open space, when suddenly a dwarf started up and ran to escape them. The lad gave speedy chase, and soon he had the little man in his power. His name was Alberich, and he had fame as a cunning robber and a wonder smith. Dietrich desired to slay him, but the dwarf cried out:

"Kill me not, O Prince of Bern, and thou shalt have for thyself the great sword which I forged for Grim and Hilde. It is called Naglering, nor is its equal to be found in the world. I shall also guide thee unto a cavern where much treasure lies hidden."

Dietrich promised to spare the life of the dwarf if his promise were fulfilled, and Alberich said: "Thou must needs combat with Grim, who hath the strength of twelve men, and also with Hilde, who is even more to be feared, ere thou canst possess thyself of the treasure."

Binding vows were then taken by Alberich, who promised to return at eventide with the wondrous sword. As the dwarf promised so did he do. He met Dietrich and Hildebrand close to a great mountain cliff, and delivered up the shining sword, Naglering. Proud was the lad of that wondrous weapon, which brought him, as it befell, great fame in after years.

The dwarf then vanished, and Hildebrand and Dietrich went towards the cliff. Ere long they found the secret door and opened it. The sunlight streamed within, and they beheld, lying beside a fire, gaunt Grim and Hilde, who both at once sprang up angrily and desired vengeful combat. The giant sought for his Naglering, but found it not. Cunningly indeed had the robber dwarf taken it from him.

The giant then seized a burning log and leapt at Dietrich. Fast and ferocious were his blows, and the lad would full surely have been slain but for the sword he wielded.

Hilde sprang at Hildebrand and wrestled with him. Long and fierce was the struggle, because the warrior had great strength, but the giantess held him tightly round the neck, until, gasping for breath, Hildebrand fell to the ground. So was he completely overcome, and the end of his days seemed to be very nigh.

In vain the old warrior called upon Dietrich, who waged desperate conflict with the giant. But at length the lad prevailed. Leaping aside to escape a mighty blow, he smote Grim with Naglering and cut off his head. So perished the ferocious giant, who had laid desolate a great part of the kingdom of Dietmar.

Hildebrand was meanwhile in sore distress. Hilde began to bind him, so that he might be put to death by torture, but Dietrich smote her so great a blow that he clave her body in twain. But she relaxed not thereat her ferocious embrace of the swooning warrior. Such was her power that she united her severed parts before the lad's eyes, and caused herself to be made whole again. So Dietrich smote her the second time right through the middle, and yet again she was joined together as before.

Hildebrand cried faintly: " Leap thou between the Hag's severed body when thou dost strike next, and turn thine eyes from her."

As the warrior bade, so did Dietrich do. He cut Hilde in twain, and immediately separated her body with his own, nor did he look round.

That was the end of Hilde.[1] No longer could she work her evil will. So she cried:

---

[1] When Hercules fought with the nine-headed Hydra, each head, save one, which could not be hurt, grew again as fast as it was cut off. Then his nephew assisted him by searing the wounds with a torch. See *Classic Myth and Legend*, page 103.

"If Grim had fought with Dietrich as well as I have fought with Hildebrand, we should ne'er have been overcome."

Then life went from her, and Hildebrand was set free. The old warrior embraced the prince, praising his valour and skill, and the glory of battle gleamed in the eyes of Dietrich.

Great was the treasure which was concealed in the cavern. Dietrich took for himself a wondrous shining helmet. It was named Hildegrim, after the giant and the giantess, and it gave more than a mortal's strength to the hero who wore it.

The prince put the helmet on his head. He triumphed in the power it gave him. Then with Hildebrand he returned unto his sire, King Dietmar, who rejoiced greatly because of the valorous deeds of his son, and he made him a full knight before all the people.

There lived among the mountains to the west a great giant whose name was Sigenot, and he vowed to be avenged upon Dietrich because that he slew Grim, his uncle, and Hilde, his aunt, and possessed himself of their treasure, and especially the helmet Hildegrim. One day Dietrich rode forth alone to hunt in the deep forest, and in the midst of it he found Sigenot lying fast asleep. Proud was the lad of his strength, and overconfident withal, and he desired greatly to combat with the giant. So he dismounted and went fearlessly towards him and kicked his body. Sigenot leapt up in anger.

"At last thou art come," he cried. "Long have I waited for thee, Prince of Bern, so that I might take vengeance for the slaying of my kinsman Grim.

The giant seized his great spear, and Dietrich drew his sword Naglering. But unequal was the combat.

The giant smote but a single blow with the spearhaft and felled the prince, whom he speedily bound. Then he bore Dietrich through the forest, and cast him into a dark, underground cavern, which was a dragon's lair. Snakes crept about and hissed in the darkness; the prince had need to combat with them.

Meanwhile Hildebrand went through the forest searching for the prince. He wondered because he could not hear his huntsman's horn, and when he found his horse bound to a tree, he feared greatly that Dietrich had been slain. Great was the grief of Hildebrand. . . .

Suddenly he heard heavy footsteps coming through the trees, and ere long the great Sigenot confronted him.

"Who art thou, and whom dost thou seek?" the giant bellowed.

"Hildebrand is my name," answered the bold warrior, "and I seek for Dietrich, Prince of Bern."

The giant thrust his spear at him, but Hildebrand fought fiercely with his sword. Ere long, despite his valour, the warrior was disarmed, and Sigenot caught him by the beard, and dragged him through the forest, bellowing the while:

"Follow me, Longbeard, follow me; now are Grim and Hilde avenged. Soon shalt thou find thy Prince of Bern."

Now never before had a foeman dared to lay hands upon Hildebrand's beard, and for that reason he was more wroth with than afraid of the giant. As the warrior was being thus ignobly dragged to the cave in which Dietrich lay bound, he saw the sword Naglering lying on the ground. Nimbly he clutched it ere his captor was aware, and, striking fiercely, he wounded the giant, who suddenly relaxed his hold so that the warrior

*Dietrich overcomes Hagen, from the painting by Schnorr von Carolsfeld.*

*Dietrich, from the statue in the Church of the Franciscans at Innsbruck.*

leapt free. Then did fearless Hildebrand smite Sigenot and slay him with a single blow. So perished the kinsman of Grim when he deemed proudly that his vengeance was complete.

Deep was the underground cavern in which Dietrich was kept captive. The prince heard the voice of Hildebrand calling to him, and entreated him to make haste.

" Many vipers still remain alive," he said, "although not a few have I slain and devoured."

Hildebrand cast off his clothing, and each garment did he tear in shreds; then he made a rope which he lowered into the dark, snake-infested cavern, so that the prince might have release from his torture and unceasing conflict.

Dietrich seized the rope; but when Hildebrand began to pull him up, it snapped asunder.

'Twas then that the dwarf Eggerich came nigh, rejoicing because that Sigenot was slain. He speedily procured a rope ladder, and it was lowered to Dietrich, who was thus given escape from the dragon's cave and the hissing snakes that swarmed there.

The prince embraced his rescuer, but Hildebrand did chide him much because that he had ventured forth in the forest alone.

Then they took leave of the dwarf Eggerich, and returned together unto Bern. When the people came to know that the giant Sigenot was slain, they rejoiced greatly, and acclaimed Hildebrand and the fearless son of Dietmar.

Now there was not in all the kingdom a young warrior who was Dietrich's equal. His fame went far and wide, and bold knights came riding to Bern so that they might win his favour with challenge to feats of arms. Those who were worthy and of high birth did the prince choose to be his followers. In time he had thus command of many valorous knights. Among these were Witege and Heime, who had great fierceness and daring, and were so gloomy and cruel of heart that in peace as in war they were dreaded and shunned. Men they smote and women they hated and scorned; many young warriors they slew in conflict. Churls were they both, and how they came to be honoured by Dietrich must now be told.

Heime came first unto Bern. Dwarfish was he in stature, but his heart was full of valour, and he had strength beyond his years. He feared not the prince, despite his mighty fame. Unto him did his sire Studas, who was a breeder of war steeds amidst the mountains, give a swift grey horse, which was named Rispa, and the sword Blutgang.

When he rode boldly into the courtyard of the castle at Bern, Heime challenged Dietrich to single combat. The prince was made angry thereat. Hastily did he put his armour on and the shining helmet Hildegrim; then with his spear in one hand, and in the other his great red shield on which was pictured a golden lion, he charged the bold and low-born stranger. Terrible was the shock. Heime's shield was pierced through, but Dietrich's horse stumbled so that he came nigh to being thrown. Both their spears were broken in twain.

Then did the young warriors, leaping to the ground, cast aside their spearshafts and draw their shining swords. Fiercely did they combat one against the other. But Blutgang rang faintly against Naglering. Heime had skill and valour, but ere long his sword was cloven and shattered so that he was placed at Dietrich's mercy. But the prince was drawn towards him by reason of his prowess, and slew him not. He honoured, in generous mood, the surly stranger, and gave him place among his knight followers.

Ere many days passed another young warrior, seeking adventure, challenged the son of Dietmar to combat. His name was Witege, and he did hie from Denmark. The prince was moved with wrath against him, for he grew weary of the conflicts with each bold stranger who sought to put his skill and valour to test. But in that fierce Dane he met a knight who was more than his equal.

Now Witege was the son of Wieland, the wonder smith, a cunning and far-famed worker in iron. Skilful was the lad with bow and arrows, as was Eigel, his uncle. He scorned to work at the forge, and desired to seek adventures, so that he might win renown as a warrior. Of the fame of Dietrich he heard one day, and he resolved to challenge him to single combat.

Wieland could not prevail upon him to remain at home, so he fashioned for Witege a suit of shining armour, a great helmet, dragon - mounted, a spear of much strength, and a white shield on which was painted a hammer and tongs. Unto the lad he also gave a wonder sword of great sharpness, named Mimung, which he had aforetime forged by compulsion for a tyrant king.

Witege then set out to journey towards Bern in the land of the Amelungs. On his way he met Hildebrand and Heime, who were also riding to Dietmar's Court with a stranger knight. Witege waited them not, for they sought to rest awhile.

Soon he drew nigh to a strong castle in which twelve robbers had their dwelling. These, when they did behold the young knight coming towards them, spake one to another, saying: "His shining armour shall we take from him, and his right hand shall we cut off, and then send him homeward."

So they sallied forth against Wieland's strong son. Two rode in front and bade the lad surrender; but Witege drew the sword Mimung and slew them right speedily. The others charged against him and waged fierce and unequal conflict.

'Twas then that Hildebrand and Heime and the strange knight came nigh. Hildebrand urged his companions to hasten to Witege's aid, but Heime said: "Help him not; his pride is great; now let his valour be put to proof."

But the old warrior would suffer not that the robbers should slay the youthful hero; so he rode forward and the others followed him. Against the fierce band did they all battle together, save Heime, who looked on, and ere long seven lay dead on the ground, and the others were making swift escape.

Witege gave thanks unto Hildebrand, and together they took vows of knightly fellowship to be ever brotherly and true in after-time.

"Whither goest thou, valorous youth?" asked the elder warrior.

"I ride towards Bern," the son of Wieland made answer, "for it is my desire to meet with Dietrich in single combat."

Hildebrand cared not to hear speech so bold from that valiant young hero. Indeed he feared for Dietrich's safety. So when night fell, and the Dane lay fast asleep, he drew from the lad's scabbard the sword Mimung and placed in it his own.

At morningtide Witege called upon Dietrich to display his valour. As the tale has been told, Dietmar's son waxed wroth, because that the Dane was of lowly birth, being, indeed, but the son of a smith.

In vain did Hildebrand warn him of the youth's prowess and skill at arms.

"The time is at hand," Dietrich said, "when peace must prevail in the kingdom. I shall allow no churlish stranger to challenge me to conflict. Heavily shall he pay for his boldness."

"It may be," Hildebrand said, "that thou shalt not prevail against this valorous youth."

"Him shall I have this day hanged outside the gates of Bern," answered the prince.

"Ere thou art able to accomplish that," Hildebrand said, "thou hast a fierce battle to fight. I bid thee success, but not without fear."

Never before did Dietrich meet a doughtier war-man. Strong and rapid were the blows which Witege gave. He smote the prince heavily on the head, but the helmet Hildegrim resisted the edge of Hildebrand's sword, and the Dane cursed his sire Wieland because that his sword was of so little avail.

"Had I but a sword worthy my strength," he cried, "victory would speedily be mine."

Dietrich pressed him hard. With both hands he grasped the sword Naglering, and made daring onslaught with purpose to smite off the head of Wieland's son. But Hildebrand went between the warrior youths and called a truce.

"Spare thou his life," he cried to Dietrich, "and thou shalt have still yet another brave knight amidst thy followers."

"The dog shall die this day," the prince made angry retort; "stand thou aside, so that his life may have end."

The old knight was angry. He drew from his scabbard the sword which Wieland fashioned, and gave it unto Witege, saying:

" Thine own sword Mimung I return unto thee. Now defend thyself as befits thy valour."

Glad thereat was the heart of Wieland's son. "Alas," he cried, "that I did curse my sire! Behold, O Dietrich, the sword Mimung; now have I as great desire for battle as a thirsty man hath for drink and a hungry dog for its food."

'Twas then the swords sang loud. Mimung clove armour and shield as they were but cloth. The son of Wieland indeed struck mighty blows, and in time he wounded Dietrich. Indeed, five wounds did he give unto the prince, so that he was forced to call upon Hildebrand to put end to the fray. But the old warrior was wroth with Dietrich, and did heed him not.

King Dietmar then called upon Wieland's son to cease fighting, and promised him great gifts and a noble bride; but Witege waxed in battle fury, and sought for naught else but the death of that arrogant prince. Blow after blow he gave, until at length he split asunder the helmet Hildegrim, so that Dietrich's golden hair appeared.

Hildebrand desired not the prince's death. His wrath was melted when he perceived he was in peril, and he leapt forward and ended the fray. Then besought he Witege, because of the vows they had taken one with another, to swear fellowship with Dietrich and become his knight.

As the old warrior desired him, so did Witege do. He sheathed his sword and took oath of service to the prince, and they became fast friends. Together they went into the castle and drank wine.

But ill-pleased was Dietrich because that he was not the victor as aforetime, and he made resolve to go forth to seek further daring adventure, so that his fame might not be sullied in the land of the Amelungs.

# CHAPTER XXXVIII
## The Land of Giants

Maidens of Jochgrimm—The Storm Giant Ecke—His Search for Dietrich
—Combat in Dark Forest—Giant slain—The Well Nymph—Maiden in Flight
—Ecke's Brother Fasold—Overcome by the Prince—The Beast—Arrival at
Castle—Giant's Treachery—The Knights who quarrelled—Heime becomes a
Robber.

DIETRICH rode along through the forest in thick darkness. He journeyed towards Jochgrimm mountain,
where dwelt the beauteous princesses who had heard of
his fame and desired greatly to behold him. The prince
dreamed not of their treachery, or of the perils that he
must needs pass through.

Now there were three young giants who wooed the
maidens. They were brothers, and their names were
Ecke and Fasold and Ebenrot. Ecke, which signifies
"The Terrifier", was but eighteen years old. He had
already won fame as a warrior in single combat; but
having slain one foeman he could find not another who
dared to contend against him. Oft had he heard of
Dietrich's valour and great deeds, and he vowed that he
would lay him low. Unto Ecke was promise made in the
land of giants that if he slew Dietrich he should have for
wife Seburg, the fairest of the three princesses in Jochgrimm.

Ecke had wondrous strength. Twice seven days and
twice seven nights he could fast and travel onwards, nor
ever feel faint; from hill to hill he could leap like a

leopard.  He required no steed, nor was there one that could carry him.

When the strong giant came to know that Dietrich was to ride forth from Bern, he prepared to go against him. . . .  The Princess Seburg clad her lover in bright armour and wished him well.  He made swift departure. . . .  When he entered the forest the birds fled terrified before him; branches were bowed down and rudely shaken as he passed; trees swayed and groaned, and those that he smote crashed down and were uprooted. . . .  So rushed Ecke upon his way until he reached Bern, where he was told that Dietrich had gone towards Jochgrimm by another way.

Without pause the giant followed after the valorous prince.  So swift was his pace that he came nigh to him ere night fell.  He beheld four knights lying on the ground.  But one alone was alive, and he was grievously wounded.

"Seek not the Knight of Bern," the wounded man said; "like to lightning is his sword stroke."

Ecke went onward; raging furiously he went.  He feared not Dietrich; his heart's desire was to combat against the arrogant hero.  Night fell as he went through the trees.

In the blackness he heard a horseman coming nigh.  "Who art thou," he cried, "that rideth through the darkened forest?"

A deep strong voice made answer: "Dietrich of Bern."

"Thou shalt fight with me," Ecke cried, for he was impatient to win renown.

But Dietrich desired not to combat with any foeman in the darkness, and rode on.

Ecke strode beside the Knight of Bern, and made boast of his armour.

"By Wieland, the wonder smith, was it fashioned,"
Ecke said; " nor can thy blade Naglering cleave it. Bright
and sharp is mine own sword Ecke-sax. 'Twas forged
by him who made Naglering; of gold is the hilt, and it is
inlaid with gold. Of fine gold is my girdle also. Much
booty will be thine if thou canst overcome me."

But Dietrich could not be tempted to fight for sword
nor treasure in the forest blackness.

Ecke was made angry. " Thee shall I proclaim as a
coward," he cried, " because thou art afraid. . . ."

"When day breaks," Dietrich said, " I shall combat
with thee. Here in the darkness we can behold not
one another."

But Ecke, confronting him, refused to wait. " Thou
shalt have the Princess Seburg for thy bride if thou art
ready now for combat. Fairest is she of all maidens
upon earth."

Dietrich leapt from his horse. " By the gods," he
cried, " I shall fight thee now, not for thy treasure nor
even thy sword, but for Seburg the fair one!"

On stones did they strike their swords. . . . The
firesparks flashed bright, and they beheld one another in
the blaze and began to fight. Nor was there darkness
then, for their swords glowed like flames as they smote
together and flashed in the blackness. The clamour of
battle roared like thunder through the forest; the heavens
heard the clash of their shields. . . . The night was
filled with terror; the trees were scorched about them;
the grass was trodden under the ground by their feet.

Long they fought, nor did one wound the other.
Then Ecke bounded against the prince with all his
strength; their shields were interlocked, and Dietrich
stumbled and fell. Ecke held him down and said:

"If thou wilt permit me to bind thee, thy life shall

I spare. Fain would I deliver thee thus unto Seburg with thine armour and thy steed."

"Death is better than shame," Dietrich made answer.

So they wrestled one with another in the darkness. In vain did Ecke strive to overcome the Knight of Bern, who at length clutched the giant's great throat, and sought to roll over him. Long and terrible was that fierce struggle. Nor would one make peace with the other although they were of equal strength.

In vain did the prince beseech Ecke to swear oaths of fellowship with him.

Dietrich's steed at length broke free. It heard his cries and ran towards him in the night. Falke was its name, and it loved the prince better than life. Now it came to his aid, and, rearing high, the bold steed leapt upon the body of Ecke and broke his back.

Dietrich leapt to his feet, and seizing the giant's great sword he struck fire, and in the sudden blaze he smote off his foeman's head. Then was there silence in the forest.

When dawn broke through the trees Dietrich clad himself in the giant's shining armour; he girded on the mighty sword Ecke-sax, then rode on his way with the head of Ecke dangling from his saddle bow.

He had no great joy in his victory, because he feared that he would be accused of killing Ecke in his sleep.[1]

Dietrich rode on until he came to a forest spring and beheld a water nymph lying beside it wrapped in soft slumber. He laid hands on her, and she awoke. Then

---

[1] This story was orginally a storm myth, in which Dietrich was Thunor (Thor), and Ecke a tempest. The three princesses are the giant maids of a Tyrolese folk tale, who brew storms on Jochgrimm mountain. A Highland hag is also a storm-brewer. She is associated with the first week of April which is called "Cailleach". At Cromarty an April hag causes the south-westerly gales and, according to a local saying, still current, "harries the crooks" (empties the pots) of the fisher-folk who can't go to sea.

did the nymph heal the prince's wounds, and he became
strong again.   She pointed out to him the path which
led unto Jochgrimm mountain, and gave warning of the
dangers which would beset him.   Then did Dietrich
mount his steed again and ride towards the land of the
giants.

As he went through the forest a beauteous maid
came running towards him.   Swift were her steps, and
her face was pale and terror-stricken, because that she
was pursued by the giant Fasold, Ecke's brother, and his
fierce hounds.[1]

Dietrich gave the maiden his protection, and went
against the giant who pursued her.   When Fasold beheld
the prince clad in Ecke's armour, he cried:

"Art thou my brother Ecke riding hither on a
steed?"

Dietrich made answer: "I am not thy brother; him
have I slain."

"Thou dog of death," bellowed Fasold, "thou hast
murdered Ecke whilst he lay in sleep, else would he
never have been overcome."

"I fling thee back thy falsehood," Dietrich answered.
"Thy brother challenged me to fight in darkness for the
sake of fair Seburg.   Had I known he was of such great
strength I should ne'er have crossed swords with him."

Wroth was Fasold, and he rushed against Dietrich.
Stronger was he than Ecke.   In combat he scorned to
strike more than one blow; never before was a second
required.   Fiercely he smote his brother's slayer, and
Dietrich fell from his horse and lay in a swoon.   The

---

[1] Another nature myth.  So do the maidens of the Boyne, Tay, Ness, and other
rivers flee before the outraged well demon, who may be a giant, a dragon, or a kelpie,
because they had neglected, when drawing water, a ceremonial observance, or had
committed a theft.  Probably the Severn story, as related by Geoffrey of Monmouth,
was originally of similar character.  There are also Greek parallels.

giant then turned away and went towards the castle. He deemed that the prince was slain.

Dietrich lay not long upon the ground. His strength returned to him; he rose up; he leapt upon his horse; he hastened after the giant, for he desired to be avenged.

Now Fasold had vowed never to combat with any foeman who survived his first blow, but Dietrich taunted him, saying: "Thou art afraid to stand against me. A coward is Fasold, else would he combat with his brother's slayer."

The giant turned fiercely, for no longer could he endure the prince's words. Swiftly were their swords drawn, and hot but not brief was the conflict. Thrice was Dietrich wounded, but five times had he wounded with Ecke-sax the giant Fasold, who at length cried out for mercy.

"If thou wilt but spare my life," Fasold said, "thee shall I serve, and ever be thy faithful henchman."

"Had I not slain thy brother," answered Dietrich, "I would have thee gladly for my knight; but I can claim not the service of one whose kin I have wronged. Yet shall I take oaths of fellowship with thee. Let us pledge ourselves now to help one another in time of need, and be like unto brothers before all men."

So they swore oaths of knightly brotherhood, and went together towards Jochgrimm mountain.

A great beast came out against them, and men say that it was like unto an elephant. Fasold would fain have let it pass, but Dietrich dismounted and made fierce attack with Ecke-sax. Yet, although he gave the monster many wounds, he could not slay it. The beast came nigh to treading him underfoot, but once again did his steed Falke come to his rescue; it broke free; it leapt against and kicked the monster, which turned from the prince a while. Then Dietrich crouched under its stomach and stabbed there with the keen sword Ecke, making nimble escape as the beast fell to die.[1]

Then Dietrich and Fasold went on their way. They next beheld a great dragon flying towards them. It was flying very low, and in its jaws it carried a knight, who called loudly for help.

Dietrich struck at the monster, but even Ecke-sax could not pierce it. Whereat the knight said: "By my sword alone can the dragon be slain, but it lies within the monster's mouth."

The Prince of Bern thrust his hand between the dragon's jaws. He pulled forth the sword.

"Wound me not when thou dost strike," the knight cried.

Dietrich smote the monster with the keen-edged sword and slew it, and the captive knight was drawn forth.

"Thy name and lineage?" the prince demanded of him.

"My name is Sintram," answered the knight, "and kinsman am I to Hildebrand at Bern. I was journeying towards Bern, so that I might become a follower of Prince Dietrich. The dragon came upon me while I slept, else would it not have carried me away."

Dietrich's heart was made glad, and he restored unto Sintram his wondrous sword, saying: "I am he whom you seek to serve, even Dietrich, Prince of Bern."

So they went together on their way with Fasold. Then, as they drew nigh unto Jochgrimm mountain, the giant forgot his vows, and sought to take flight. But

---

[1] So was the dragon in Beowulf and the Fafner dragon, which Sigurd stabbed, put to death. The underpart only can be mortally wounded.

Dietrich would not have him go free until he reached the castle in which the princesses had their dwelling.

Ere long they reached a great castle. Two giant statues stood on each side of the door, and Fasold led him in. But when the prince came between the statues their arms fell, and had he not made swift escape he would have been slain by their stone clubs.

Dietrich was made wroth. He turned upon Fasold forthwith, and slew him because of his treachery. Then he entered the hall, and the three princesses and their mother, the queen, came towards him, for they deemed he was Ecke.

" 'Twas your desire," the prince said, " to behold Dietrich of Bern. He now greets thee thus."

So saying, he flung at their feet the head of the giant Ecke, and then turned from them. . . . He hastened without, and, mounting his steed, rode with Sintram towards Bern.

Heime came forth to meet Dietrich and greeted him with such warmth that Dietrich gave unto him the sword Naglering, which Alberich[1] had forged for the giant Grim. Ecke-sax he did keep for himself.

Witege was ill-pleased because that his fellow knight was thus honoured.

" I forget not," he said unto Heime, " that when I was beset by robbers thy sword remained in its sheath."

" Evil is thy tongue, thou self-sufficient man. Fain would I have it silenced," Heime said.

Both knights drew their swords to combat one against the other. Dietrich was wroth and stepped between them. Then he spake to Heime saying:

" Rash knight, thou shalt now go hence. 'Twas

---

[1] Alberich was called in French legend Auberon. Spenser introduced him to this country as Oberon. Alberich signifies " elf King ".

unseemly that thou didst not aid thy fellow when robbers came against him. . . . When by thy deeds thou hast proved thyself a hero, thou mayest return again unto Bern."

"With the sword thou hast given me," Heime said, "I shall win more than any man can take away."

He went forth alone. He waged war against the robbers and slew them, and became chief of a robber band. Many a wayfarer fell by his sword, and he was dreaded by valiant knights. He returned not unto Dietrich again until he was possessed of much treasure by his evil doings.

Against many giants did the prince combat, but never was he in greater peril than when Laurin, the dwarf, had power over him and his knights and held them all in captivity.

# CHAPTER XXXIX
## The Wonderful Rose Garden

Dietleib the Dane—How he became a Knight—Kunhild stolen by the Dwarf King—Knights to the Rescue—The Garden laid waste—Laurin's Vengeance—Witege overcome—Combat with Prince—The Invisible Combatant—Laurin is spared—Visit to Mountain Dwelling—The Banquet—Knights made Prisoners—Dietrich's Fiery Breath—Battle with Dwarfs and Giants—The End of Strife.

FIRST be it told of the lady Kunhild's brother, Dietleib the Dane. He had fame in his own land for strength and prowess, and great and glorious were the deeds of his sire, the brave Yarl Biterolf. It chanced that when the three journeyed towards Bern they were set upon by Heime and his robber band in the midst of a forest. Boldly fought the Danes, and the robbers were all killed, save Heime alone, whom Dietleib, with his sword Welsung, wounded on the forehead and put to flight.

Thereafter the young Dane became a servant unto Dietrich, making pretence that his name was Ilmenrik. It chanced that the prince paid visit to the Court of Ermenrich, and there was his Danish servant taunted by Walter of Wasgenstein. Dietleib was wroth, and he challenged the arrogant knight, wagering life against life, to prevail against him in performing feats of strength. All the Court assembled to behold the sport, and the knight was boastful and proud. But great was the might of Dietleib the Dane. He could putt the stone and throw the hammer so that men marvelled to behold, nor could Walter of Wasgenstein prevail against him.

Then did King Ermenrich pay life ransom in money for the boastful knight, and the Dane gave a great feast to which his master did invite many valorous war men.

Proud was Dietrich of his servant, and he made him a knight. Heime, who had returned, was present at the feast, and Dietleib sat beside him, and ere long he spake, saying:

"On thy forehead is an evil scar, Heime. How came thou by it?"

Heime made answer: "I shall tell thee in secret, Ilmenrik. Wounded was I in combat with Dietleib the Dane. I shall rest not until my shame be wiped out with his life blood."

"Know then," the new knight whispered, "that I am he whom thou didst attack with thy robber band. Look in my face. . . . I am no other than Dietleib. Fast was thy horse, else thou hadst not escaped me. But I seek not now to denounce thee before Dietrich. Let this secret be kept between us."

It chanced upon a day thereafter that fair Kunhild, Dietleib's sister, danced with her maids upon a green meadow. She went towards a linden tree; then suddenly she vanished from sight. The King of Dwarfs, whose name was Laurin, had long loved her for her beauty, and desired to have her for his bride. So he came secretly towards the maiden, and below the linden tree he cast over her his Cloak of Obscurity; then did he carry fair Kunhild away towards his castle among the Tyrolese mountains.

The heart of Dietleib was filled with sorrow, because that he loved his sister very dearly. He hastened unto

Hildebrand, who dwelt in his castle at Garda, and besought his aid, saying:

"The castle of Laurin is in the midst of a Tyrol mountain, and in front of it he hath a wondrous Rose garden."

"Many a life may be lost ere Kunhild is rescued," Hildebrand said; "but let us unto Dietrich and his knights, so that we may take counsel with them."

When that the knights came to know that Kunhild was taken away by the dwarf king, Wolfhart spake boldly, as was his wont, and said:

"Alone shall I ride forth and rescue this fair maid."

Dietrich heard the boast, nor made answer. He spake to wise old Hildebrand, saying: "Knowest thou aught of Laurin's Rose garden?"

"'Tis told," Hildebrand said, "that it hath four gates of gold. But no wall shields it. Round the Rose garden is drawn a silken thread, and he who breaks it shall have his right hand and left foot cut off. Laurin, King of Dwarfs, ever keeps watch o'er his wondrous garden, which is of exceeding great beauty."

Witege spake: "Laurin can punish not an offender who entereth his garden until he doth prevail against him in single combat."

"Then shall we fare forth," Dietrich said. "We seek but Kunhild, and need not despoil the Rose garden."

So the Prince rode towards the Tyrol mountain in which Laurin, King of Dwarfs, had his dwelling. With him went Hildebrand, Heribrand's son; Witege, Wieland's son; Dietleib the Dane, and Wolfhart, Hildebrand's kinsman.

Dietrich and Witege rode in front, because that Hildebrand had taunted the prince, as was his wont, for he had been his master. "Were I not with thee," he said, "thou couldst not overcome the dwarf."

So it fell that Dietrich and Wieland's son were first to reach the wondrous Rose garden. Witege broke to pieces a golden gate, and they entered together. Fair were the roses, and of sweet and refreshing fragrance ; their beauty gladdened Dietrich's eyes, and he was loath to despoil them. But Witege sought to defy the dwarf, and he rode through the blossoming shrubs, trampling them ruthlessly underfoot. Soon was the fair garden made desolate as a wilderness.

Wroth was Laurin, King of the Dwarfs. He rode forth on his steed, clad in full armour ; his spear was in his hand. But three spans high was he, yet had he wondrous strength and skill in conflict.

"What evil have I done thee that thou shouldst thus destroy my roses?" he cried bitterly. "Thy right hand and thy left foot I now demand, and must needs obtain."

Witege defied the dwarf with laughter and scorn. He deemed not that he was endowed with magical power. Diamonds sparkled upon Laurin's armour ; these made it swordproof and spearproof. He also wore a girdle which gave him the strength of twelve men. On his head was a shining crown, and therein was his weakness. Golden birds sang forth from it as if they were alive.

Witege lowered his spear. Laurin charged fiercely, and at the first thrust swept him from the saddle. In great peril was Wieland's son, for the dwarf bound him; but Dietrich made offer of gold to atone the evil he had done.

"Thy roses," he told Laurin, "will bloom again in May."

The dwarf made answer that he possessed already gold in abundance, but that his roses could not be restored unto him.

Witege taunted Dietrich. "Fearest thou to tilt with him?" he said; "must I die because thou dost shrink from Laurin?"

The prince was wroth, and he challenged the dwarf king forthwith to single combat, taking upon himself the blame for the evil which his knight had accomplished.

'Twas well for Dietrich that old Hildebrand then rode up with Wolfhart, his kinsman, and Dietleib the Dane. The old warrior counselled the prince to tilt not with the dwarf. "Rather shouldst thou fight him on foot with sword against sword," he said. "His armour thou canst not pierce, for by reason of the diamonds it is charmed against all weapons. Smite thou him upon the head."

As Hildebrand counselled, so did Dietrich do. He leapt from the saddle and challenged Laurin to combat with swords. Fierce was the conflict. The prince smote upon the dwarf's head blow after blow, so that he was made faint. But Laurin drew round him his Cloak of Obscurity and fought then unbeholden by the Prince of Bern.

Many wounds did Dietrich receive; but he waxed in battle fury and suddenly took the unseen dwarf in his arms and wrestled with him. From the prince's mouth issued forth flames of fire, but without avail; he could not injure Laurin.

"Snatch off his waist girdle," Hildebrand cried.

Ere long Dietrich possessed himself of the magic girdle, which gave to the dwarf his great strength. Then the prince had him in his power. He cast the

little king on the ground and tore off the Cloak of
Obscurity.

Laurin feared that he would be put to death, so he
called upon Dietleib, Kunhild's brother, who pleaded for
his life, for the young Dane desired most of all to discover where his fair sister was held in captivity. Thus
did the dwarf king escape the vengeance of Dietrich.
He gave thanks unto Dietleib, and when he had sworn
oaths of brotherhood with him, he invited the prince and
all his knights into his mountain castle.

They went together over a pleasant plain, and
through a fair forest. A great linden tree was there,
and many fruit trees whose odours were sweet. Birds
sang merrily in the branches, and Dietrich was glad of
heart. He began to make answer to the birds; but old
Hildebrand warned him not to whistle until he had left
the wood. All the knights were lighthearted save
Witege. He had bitter memory of how the dwarf had
prevailed against him, and suspected treachery. Wolfhart taunted him, but Wieland's son rode in front. He
was first to reach the castle entrance. He saw there a
bright golden horn suspended on a chain. He blew a
loud blast upon it. When he did that the door opened
wide and they all went within. An iron door was
opened; it closed behind them. Then through a door of
shining gold they went; it was shut fast like to the other.

Soon Dietrich and his knights found themselves in
a bright and spacious hall. Hundreds of dwarfs were
there. They made merry; they danced and they held
tournaments. Delicious wine was given unto the
strangers, and even Witege forgot to be suspicious, and
made merry with the others. Then did Laurin begin to
work his evil designs. He cast a spell upon Dietrich
and his knights, so that they could behold not one

another. They saw but the merry dwarfs and the glories of the mountain dwelling.

At length fair Kunhild appeared. She had been made Laurin's queen, and wore a gleaming crown. Many maidens came with her, but she was fairest of them all. Dwarfs playing harps, and dancing and performing strange feats, skipped before her and around. In her crown shone a bright jewel. It dispelled the magic mist, and the warriors beheld one another again.

Then was a great feast held. Kunhild sat with Laurin, and Dietleib, whom she embraced tenderly, she took beside her. They spoke in low voices one to another. Great was her desire to leave all the splendour and wealth that was there, and return once again to her own kin.

The dwarf persuaded all the knights to lay down their arms. So merry were they that they did so without fear.

Evening came on, and Laurin led Dietleib to a chamber apart, where he made offer to him of rich treasure if he would desert Dietrich and his knights. But the young Dane refused resolutely to be a traitor, whereat the dwarf vanished and the door was locked securely. Dietleib was made blind.

Then were the strangers given wine, which caused them all to fall into a deep sleep. The vengeful king Laurin thus had them in his power. He caused them to be bound, and they were all cast together into a deep dungeon, so that vengeance might be wreaked upon them, because that the Rose garden had been despoiled. There they lay helpless and blind.

Kunhild wept for them. When the dwarfs were all asleep she stole in secret to her brother's chamber and gave to him a golden ring which dispelled his magic blindness. Then did the young Dane secure possession of his weapons and those of his fellow knights.

Meanwhile Dietrich woke up. Wroth was he when he found that he was fettered. The dwarf's girdle restored his sight, and flames issued from his mouth, which melted his bonds of iron, so that he rose up. He went towards each of his companions and set them free one by one.

Dietleib then came with all their weapons, and with the prince he fought fiercely against the dwarfs. At length Dietrich wrenched from one of them a golden ring. He gave it unto Hildebrand, and his sight was restored. Then did the old warrior enter the conflict. The dwarfs fell fast before them. Thousands were put to death, for there was none in Laurin's castle who could prevail against the three great warriors.

At length Laurin rushed without. He blew a great blast upon his horn, and five giants armed with clubs came to his aid.

Wolfhart and Witege were still blind, but they could rest not while the clamour of battle raged about them, so they rushed into the fray and fought bravely. Then gave Kunhild unto them jewelled rings, and their blindness was dispelled.

The five giants fought against the five knights, and long and terrible was the struggle which ensued; but one by one the monsters were slain, and Dietrich and his knights were truimphant. The heroes waded knee deep in blood, so great was the slaughter which they accomplished in the kingdom of Laurin.

Then was the dwarf king made prisoner and Kunhild set free. Dietrich and his knights possessed themselves of much treasure, and they returned unto Bern, taking with them Laurin and Dietleib's fair sister.

Laurin was laughed at and put to shame, and he brooded over his evil lot, desiring greatly to be avenged upon Dietrich and his victorious knights. So he sent a secret message unto his uncle, Walberan, who was king over the giants and dwarfs in the eastern Caucasus, and besought him to come to his rescue.

He spoke secretly thereanent unto Kunhild, whereat she made promise that if he swore oaths of friendship with Dietrich, she would return with him to his mountain dwelling and be his queen once again.

So she prevailed upon Laurin to do her will. " My Rose garden", he said, " I shall plant again that the roses may bloom fair and fragrant in the sunshine of May."

The dwarf king drank wine with the prince of Bern and made peace, vowing to be his lifelong comrade and helper.

As they sat together at the feast, a message was borne unto Dietrich from King Walberan, demanding all the treasure and all the weapons that were in Bern, and the right hand and left foot of every knight who had wrought destruction in the Rose garden. Defiantly did the prince make answer and prepared for battle.

Dietrich and Walberan challenged each other to single combat, and they fought with great fierceness. Numerous were their wounds, nor could one prevail over the other. It seemed as if they would both be slain.

Then did Laurin ride forth, and, embracing his uncle, he prevailed upon him to make peace. Hildebrand pleaded likewise with Dietrich, and the combat was brought to an end. Together they then sat down to feast and drink wine, and they vowed oaths of friendship, so that there might be lasting peace between them.

Kunhild returned with Laurin unto his mountain

dwelling. The Rose garden was planted once again, and it bloomed fair in the sunshine of May.

Herdsmen among the hills, and huntsmen who wend thither, have been wont to tell that they could behold on moonlight nights Laurin and fair Kunhild dancing together in the green forests and in the valleys below the Tyrolese mountains. Dietleib's sister hath still her dwelling in the bright castle as in other days. She is Queen of the Dwarfs and can never die.

The Rose garden blooms ever fair, but unbeholden by men, in the sunshine of May, and many have sought to find it in vain.

# CHAPTER XL

## Virginal, Queen of the Mountains

The Maid-devouring Giant—Hildebrand slays Orkise—Dietrich and the Giants—Night Battle—The Black Horseman—Slaughter of Monsters—Castle Muter—Prince taken Prisoner—The Rescue—Janibas surrounds Virginal's Castle—Magic Tablet—The Avalanches—A Peerless Queen—Dietrich wins his Bride.

TIDINGS came unto Dietrich at Bern that Virginal, Queen of the Mountains, was in sore distress because that a giant wasted her land and had perforce to obtain as tribute, at each new moon, a fair maiden, whom he did devour.

The prince set forth with old Hildebrand to give aid to the queen, who had great beauty, and ruled over those dwarfs and giants in the Tyrolese mountains that never sought to do injury unto mankind. Her oppressor was named Orkise, whose son was Janibas, an evil magician.

As the two heroes rode through the forest there came unto them a dwarf whose name was Bibung. He guided them towards Jeraspunt, where the queen had her dwelling, but when night came he vanished. Snow fell next morning, and the knights were parted one from another. Ere long Hildebrand heard bitter cries, and he beheld a fair maiden who had been taken to the forest so that the giant might obtain her for tribute. Fairest was she of Queen Virginal's maidens. The knight proffered his protection and vowed to rescue her, whereat her heart was filled with gratitude and her eyes with joy tears.

Soon the forest was shaken with dread clamour, for the giant was coming nigh with his dogs to possess himself of his prey. Hildebrand drew his sword; not slow was he to enter the conflict, and ere long he slew the giant and put to flight his evil son Janibas.

The maiden returned with glad heart unto the queen, and gave tidings of how the giant Orkise had been slain. There was great rejoicing in the castle, and eagerly did Virginal and all her people await the coming of the heroes.

Meanwhile Dietrich fought with many of the giant's followers. The clamour of battle resounded far and near, and when Hildebrand hastened to his aid the horde was overcome; many were slain and many made escape.

Together did they then go upon their way towards the palace of Jeraspunt. Darkness came on, and they rode to the gate of the castle of Orkise, deeming it theirs by right of conquest. But small hospitality were they shown. No sooner did they demand entrance than fierce giants issued forth against them. Heavy clubs they bore, and they smote fiercely, but soon they were overcome by the valorous heroes. Then appeared a black horseman. He spake in a strange tongue, and giants sprang up out of the earth to continue the fight. As they were cut down others took their place, and when all the giants were slain, hissing snakes and nameless reptiles issued forth against Dietrich and Hildebrand, so that they had to fight constantly throughout the night. The black horseman entered not the fray, and when dawn broke he vanished from sight. Then did the heroes enter the castle and set at liberty three of Queen Virginal's maidens whom they found there.

Now, during the night the heroes slew a fierce

dragon. It carried in its jaws a brave knight whose name was Rentwin, and with him did Dietrich and Hildebrand journey towards his father's castle. There did they remain until their wounds were healed.

Thereafter the prince and his veteran companion set forth with Rentwin and his sire towards Jeraspunt. Eager was Dietrich to behold the fair maiden queen Virginal. He spurred his steed; he rode in front, and ere long he was lost to his fellow knights. 'Twas ill for him that he waited not for them, because the way was strange and wild, and he wandered from the straight path. So it chanced that he came unto the castle of Duke Nitger, called Muter.

Now the duke had many giants, and when one of them issued forth, Dietrich asked of him to be guided unto the palace of Queen Virginal. Answer was given him according to his desire; but when he turned to ride away the giant smote the hero with his club so that he fell from his horse. Then was brave Dietrich seized and bound and thrown into a dark dungeon. The duke's sister treated him with kindness. But for her protection the prince would have been put to death.

When Hildebrand reached the palace of Virginal he received tidings that the prince had been taken captive. So he hastened back unto Bern, and rode forth with many brave knights, among whom were Wolfhart and Witege and Heime. They laid siege to Castle Muter and fought against twelve giants. While the battle waged fiercely, Dietrich made escape and entered the fray. Victory was then with the heroes of Bern, and all the giants were slain.

The knights sought to put Duke Nitger to death, but his sister pleaded for him, and his life was spared by Dietrich.

Then did they all set forth towards Jeraspunt. On their way they beheld a dwarf riding towards them. Unto Dietrich spake the little man, and he told that fierce Janibas had surrounded the palace of Queen Virginal with a great army, and made demand of all her maidens and the magic jewel in her crown which gave her power to rule over all her subjects.

So the heroes pressed onward. They climbed the mountains over ice and snow, and soon they heard the fierce clamour of battle. The howling of the great black dogs of Janibas was like the howling of wintry tempests; strange monsters fought there, and the queen's defenders were in sore straits. The voices of the giants were loud as thunder peals.

In the midst of the battle Dietrich saw the black horseman. He knew him to be Janibas. An iron tablet he held in his hand and wrought spells upon it. The prince sprang upon him. His sword flashed fire. He broke in pieces the iron tablet and slew the dread worker of evil. Then pealed the loud thunder amidst the Tyrolese mountains; the glaciers were sundered, and avalanches fell upon the evil army of Janibas, which suddenly vanished from sight. Soon was there silence and peace, and an end to that dread conflict.

Queen Virginal sat alone, high throned in her mountain palace, unmoved and beautiful; brightly gleamed the jewel in her crown. A glistening silver veil was drawn round her body, and her maidens crouched trembling at her feet.

When the battle was ended, Dietrich made approach, and she called him " hero ", and greeted him with love.

" No longer can I reign here in Elfland," she spake. " Thy great deeds have I beheld, and for thy sake I shall leave my home and my kingdom, and henceforth live among men; for I shall be thy bride, and love thee so long as life may last."

Then were Dietrich and Queen Virginal wedded there with pomp and ceremony, and elves and heroes feasted within the mountain palace, and drank wine and made merry. Ere long Dietrich and his bride and the brave knights journeyed together to Bern, where they were received with acclamations by the people.

Dietrich and Queen Virginal lived happily together, and when King Dietmar died, the prince reigned in his place. Then was there peace within the kingdom; but evil was being wrought in another land, and it was fated that King Dietrich must become a fugitive among men ere he could triumph completely over his evil foemen.

# CHAPTER XLI
## Dietrich in Exile

Ermenrich and Sibeche — Fate of the King's Sons — The Harlungs — Quarrel with Dietrich — Battle between Kinsmen — Convoy captured — Knights ransomed — Dietrich surrenders his Kingdom — At the Court of Etzel — Campaign against Ermenrich — Boy Warriors slain — Witege and the Mermaid — Sorrow in Hunaland — The Nibelung Tragedy — Vengeance of Hagen's Son — End of Exile.

KING ERMENRICH was a mighty monarch, and all the rulers of the Southland owned him as overlord, and paid yearly tribute. His nephew, Dietrich, helped in his wars, and gave to him at length his fierce knights Witege and Heime.

Now it chanced that Ermenrich had an evil counsellor. His name was Sibeche,[1] and his wife had been wronged by the king. Sibeche first thought to slay Ermenrich, but chose rather to cause the great monarch to murder his own children and wage war against his own kin. Terrible was the vengeance of Sibeche; by reason of it many brave knights went to their death, and for long years bitter warfare was waged.

Ermenrich had three sons. Sibeche bore false witness against one and the king's second bride, Svanhild. The prince was hanged and Gudrun's daughter was trodden to death by many steeds. Another was sent to Britain as an envoy in a leaky ship and was drowned. The third,

---

[1] Bikki of the Volsung tale.   Ermenrich is Jormunrek.

by Sibeche's advice, journeyed to Norway to demand tribute, and there was he slain. Evil charges were then made, reviling the king's nephews, the Harlungs; war was waged against them, and they were overcome and slaughtered in their Rhine-land stronghold.

Nor was Dietrich spared. Sibeche poisoned the mind of Ermenrich against the valiant King of the Amelungs.

"Thy nephew's kingdom grows greater year by year," said Sibeche to the jealous king; "ere long he shall wrest thine own from thee. Thou shouldst demand of him payment of yearly tribute."

Then was the knight Randolt sent unto Bern to demand tribute, but Dietrich gave scornful refusal, whereat Ermenrich was made wroth, so that he vowed he would have his nephew hanged as a traitor.

In vain did Witege and Heime plead with the king. He gave ear to Sibeche, and marched against Bern with a great army. Dietrich went forth and met his sire's brother in battle array, and in a fierce night attack achieved an overwhelming victory, so that Ermenrich was beaten back.

It chanced, however, that Dietrich lacked sufficient treasure to continue the war, and old Hildebrand made offer of all the gold he possessed, as did also Bertram of Pola. So the knights set forth with Wolfhart, Dietleib the Dane, and other heroes to guard a convoy of five hundred horses bearing treasure unto Bern. Ermenrich came to know of their mission, so he had the convoy taken in ambush. Thus were the bravest knights of Dietrich made prisoners and his war treasure captured. Dietleib alone escaped. He carried the mournful tidings of disaster unto his king.

Dietrich sent envoys unto Ermenrich and offered exchange of prisoners, so that his knights might be set free; but the fierce monarch made answer that he would have them all hanged unless Dietrich ransomed them with his kingdom.

Noble-hearted was Dietmar's great son. He could suffer not to reign as king if his faithful followers were put to death. His soul was sad, because that Queen Virginal had sickened and died, and he sent a message to Ermenrich saying that he would depart from the kingdom if the lives of Hildebrand and Wolfhart and his other knights were spared.

Then Ermenrich came unto Bern with his army, and Dietrich bade farewell to his own land amidst the lamentation of the people, who loved him well. His brother, Diether, who was but a child, went with him. Old Hildebrand left behind his wife Ute and his babe Hadubrand, and followed his king, as did also the other knights for whose sake he had given up his kingdom.

Dietrich took refuge in the Court of Etzel[1], King of the Huns. He was made welcome there and greatly honoured. He fought with Etzel against the King of Wilkina-land[2], and against the King of Russia and Poland, and achieved great conquests. Grateful was Etzel for the help which Dietrich and his knights gave him.

But ever did Dietrich mourn for his lost kingdom. Queen Helche pitied him, because that he was sorrowing continually, and gave him for wife her niece, the gentle Princess Herrad. Soon afterwards King Etzel made promise that he would raise for Dietrich in early spring a great army, so that he might wage war against Ermenrich, and win back the kingdom of the Amelungs.

Years had passed since Dietmar's son rode forth from Bern. His brother Diether had grown into early

---

[1] Attila.　　[2] Norway and Sweden.

manhood; a brave and bold young knight he was. Well loved was he by Etzel's sons, Erp and Ortwin, and when the great army assembled, the three young friends must needs go forth to battle together, for they desired greatly to win renown as valiant war-men.

Etzel's queen would fain have held them back. She had dreamed in an evil dream that a dragon had entered the castle, carried away the lads, and devoured them while she looked on. But they pleaded with the king, and he gave them their desire. Dietrich vowed that they would have sure protection from danger, and Etzel sent forth with them the Margrave Rudiger and his fearless knights. With Dietrich went Diether, and old Hildebrand, Wolfhart, and Dietleib the Dane, and the other heroes who shared with their king exile in the land of Huns.

Sibeche commanded the army of Ermenrich, who was stricken with sickness, and he waited for the invading army on the southern bank of the river, at Ravenna, nigh to the frontier of the kingdom of the Amelungs.

Dietrich pushed towards Bern, but when he reached the city of Istria he left his brother Diether and Etzel's sons, Erp and Ortwin, in the care of old Elsan, so that they might suffer no harm. He deemed them too young to risk the perils of war against battle-hardened heroes.

Ill-pleased were the lads with their lot. They made resolve to follow the army, and having deceived old Elsan they stole forth from the city and rode swiftly to the front. They rode to their doom.

On the night before the battle Dietrich's forces were drawn up on the north bank of the river, and old Hildebrand went out to scout. A knight came from the foemen's camp with similar intent. They met but fought not, for the knight was Reinald. They sorrowed together that friends were divided by war, and ere they parted they embraced and kissed one another.

In the morning Dietrich led his knights across the river at a ford which Hildebrand had found. They fell upon Sibeche's division of the army and put it to flight. Witege was with Sibeche, but he fled not. He rode on; he slew Dietrich's standard-bearer, but the tide of battle went past him, and soon he found himself alone.

'Twas then that Diether and Etzel's two sons reached the front. They saw Witege and called him a traitor. Ortwin went against him, but ere long he was cut down. Then did Erp seek vengeance; he rushed against the ferocious knight. In vain did Witege warn him to hold back lest he would share his brother's fate; but Erp was without fear—a great warrior would he have been had he lived. Brief was the conflict, for Witege drew his sword Mimung and smote the prince so that his head was taken off.

Diether sorrowed and was made wroth. He drew his sword and rode against Witege.

Wieland's son watched him drawing nigh, and he spake to the lad, saying:

"Say if thou art Diether, brother of Dietrich; if thou art, I desire not to combat with thee."

Diether said: "The brother of Dietrich I am indeed, as thou shalt know to thy loss ere long."

"Then combat against another," Witege said; "seek battle glory elsewhere. I desire not to be thy slayer."

"Thou hast slain both Erp and Ortwin," cried Diether, "but me thou shalt not escape. Thou dog and traitor, I would die rather than not slay thee."

Bold attack made he forthwith, but Witege feared him not. He but parried his blows. But at length

Diether smote off his horse's head, and he had perforce to leap to the ground.

"I call to witness the god Irmin," Witege cried, "that I fight now but to defend myself."

When he said that he smote at Diether with his sword Mimung and cut the young hero in twain.

Witege wept. Sad at heart was he because that he had slain the lad, and greatly, too, did he fear the wrath of Dietrich.

Elsan, who had followed the lads from Istria, had meanwhile found Dietrich, and he gave him tidings of their fate. Dietrich smote off his head, and hastened towards the place of sorrow. He found the dead bodies of the young heroes; he wept over them.

"Alas," he cried, "what grief is mine! What sin have I committed that I should be punished thus? My body bears not a battle scar. I have triumphed in the field, and yet is my brother taken from me, and the sons of Etzel laid in death. Never again can I return unto the land of the Huns."

He looked around him. He beheld Witege taking flight on Diether's horse across the heath, and his heart burned to be avenged. On his steed Falke he leapt at a bound and rode after the traitor knight. Flames issued from his mouth, so great was his fury.

As he drew nigh to Witege, he called: "Flee not before me, thou hell-hound! If thou art not as great a coward as thou art a traitor, stand now that I may avenge my brother's death."

Witege paused not. He cried in answer: "I had to fight for my life against Diether. 'Twas not my desire to combat against him."

Swiftly rode Witege until he came to the shore of the lake at the river mouth. Dietrich pressed on close behind him; his spear was in his hand; he hurled it against the traitor. . . .

But Witege paused not; he rode into the water, and his wrathful pursuer was but a horse-length behind him. . . .

Then suddenly there rose out of the lake the mermaid Waghild, his grandsire's mother. She seized Witege and his steed and drew them beneath the waves. . . . Dietrich rode out until his horse had to swim, but he sought in vain for his brother's slayer. . . . Never again was Witege beheld by human eyes, for the mermaid bore him unto her cave under the waters and guarded him there.

Dietrich returned to the battlefield, and the remnants of Sibeche's army were put to flight. But Dietmar's great son had no joy in the victory, nor could he press on farther with the army of Huns, because that Etzel's two sons were slain. He could hope not for aught save the vengeance of him who had given him help to win back his kingdom.

He mourned for Diether and for Erp and Ortwin, and when they were given burial he bade Rudiger to lead back the army unto the land of the Huns. So did the margrave do: he returned unto Etzel with his heroes; he stood before the king; he gave unto him the mournful tidings of the loss of the two princes.

The queen lamented aloud, but the king, whose heart was sorrow-stricken also, spake saying:

"So hath it happened as it ever doth in the fortunes of war. Each man must die at his appointed time."

Then asked he of Rudiger: "Where is Dietrich and Hildebrand? Why come they not into my presence?"

"They mourn apart," answered the Margrave; "loath

are they to approach thee because that Erp and Ortwin have been cut off."

Then sent Etzel two knights unto Dietrich, but he refused to go with them before the king; whereat the queen, who at first was wroth against him, rose up and did herself go unto the hero.

She spake to him, saying: "How fought my sons Erp and Ortwin? Were they fearless and bold in battle and worthy their kin?"

"Because they feared not," Dietrich answered, "they fought and fell one after another; nor would they be parted, so great was their love."

The queen kissed him while she wept, and then led him before King Etzel.

Then did Dietrich cast himself at the feet of his great ally, and made offer of his life because that the princes were slain. But Etzel raised him up; Dietrich he kissed, and they sat down together. So was their friendship made more enduring.

When two summers went past the queen died. But ere life was taken from her she warned the king to wed not a wife from the land of the Nibelungs. "Else," she said, "thou and the children she may have shall suffer evil beyond concept."

But the good queen's words were forgotten when Etzel sent envoys unto King Gunther, so that he might have Kriemhild for his bride.

Now Dietrich and old Hildebrand had aforetime been friends of King Gunther and Hagen, and when the conflict was waged at Etzel's Court, by reason of Kriemhild's evil doings, they did hold aloof, until impetuous Wolfhart was drawn into the fray. Then was old Hildebrand wounded, and all the knights of Dietrich were slain.

'Twas then, as hath been told, that Dietmar's great

son took arms against Hagen and Gunther and overcame them. But when they were put to death, Hildebrand slew Kriemhild, whom he called "a devil".

Etzel said: "A devil she hath been indeed. But for her many a noble knight would still be alive."

Now be it told of how King Etzel passed from before men. Aldrian, Hagen's son, vowed to avenge his sire's death. So he paid visit unto Etzel and spake to him regarding the Nibelung treasure.

"If thou wilt accompany me," he said, "I shall reveal to thee alone where the gold lies hidden."

Etzel went forth. Hagen's son led him to a secret cave which is below the Rhine water. There he beheld vast treasure and his eyes were gladdened. But Aldrian stepped back suddenly and said:

"Now mayest thou have full enjoyment of the gold which thou didst desire, and I shall have vengeance for my sire's death."

When he spake thus, Aldrian shut the door of the cave, and Etzel perished of hunger in that concealed and secure prison in the midst of all the treasure which he desired to obtain.

So time went past, and then tidings came to Dietrich that Ermenrich had been slain by two princes, who avenged the death of Svanhild, and that Sibeche desired to sit upon the throne. He raised an army to march into his own kingdom, and old Hildebrand went with him.

"Rather would I die in Bern," Dietrich said, "than remain any longer in exile even among the Huns."

# CHAPTER XLII

## The King's Homecoming

The Army of Huns—Hildebrand and Hadubrand—The Challenge—
Hildebrand identifies his Son—Hadubrand suspects Treachery—The Combat
—Tragic Ending—Dietrich's Victory—Triumphant Return to Bern—Sibeche
slain—The Aged King—A Deathless Hero—The Wild Huntsman.

Now the length of time which Dietrich passed in exile
was thirty and two years. He had never ceased to long
to return again unto Bern. Hildebrand, who shared with
him his sorrow, shared also his hope. He had waxed
aged, and men tell that he had grown a century old, yet
was he fierce in conflict as of yore, and wise as he was
brave.

When Dietrich, leading his army of Huns towards
Bern, drew nigh to the northern frontier of the land
of the Amelungs, Hadubrand came forth against him
with a strong band. Then were the opposing forces
drawn up in battle array. And it was fated that
Dietrich should return alone unto Bern.

Ere the battle began two brave knights rode forth
from either army, challenging one another to single
combat. Fearless and of noble seeming were they both.
One was old Hildebrand; the other was Hadubrand,
his own son, who was but a babe when his father fared
forth with Dietrich from Bern. Long had they been
parted; now, at last, were they met, but to fight as
foemen.

Son and father had adjusted their armour with care; they were clad in coats of mail; their swords were girded over their armour when they rode into the fight.

Hildebrand, Heribrand's son, spoke first when they drew nigh one to another. He was the older and the wiser man. Few were his words, but he asked:

"Who among men was thy sire? . . . Which generation's child art thou? If thou wilt give me the name of but one of thy kinsmen, I shall know the others; all the nobles of the kingdom are known unto me."

Hadubrand answered: "Wise old men who died long ago were wont to tell me that my sire's name was Hildebrand. . . . Mine own name is Hadubrand. In years past Hildebrand fled eastward with Dietrich and many of his men. He left behind him, helpless and alone, his wife and his child; he left his own people behind. Dietrich had lost his sire; he had become a friendless man, and my sire hated Ermenrich — that worthy hero! . . . Hildebrand was wont to be with Dietrich a leader of the people; he loved warfare; well known was he indeed unto valiant men. . . . I do not believe that he is still alive."

Hildebrand was deeply moved, and he spake, saying: "Now do I call to witness Irmin,[1] the god of my people, that I dare not combat with thee, because that thou art so near of kin."

As he spake the old hero took from his arm the twisted armlet of fine gold which Dietrich had given him. He held it towards his son, saying:

"This do I give unto thee for love's sake, Hadubrand."

The son advanced not to accept his father's proffered gift. He suspected treachery, so he spake, saying:

[1] Irmin's Way is the "Milky Way".

"A warrior must receive gifts with his spear—when lance is against lance. . . . Thou art an old and cunning hero. Fain wouldst thou entice me now with gentle speech. . . . Thou wilt throw thy spear at me betimes. . . . So old art thou grown and so cunning, that thou art become a hardened deceiver."

Mournfully did Hildebrand shake his head.

"Seafarers have told me," his son protested, "that they heard from the east of warfare above the Wendel-sea.[1] 'Twas told them: '*Hildebrand, Heribrand's son, is dead.*'"

"O ruling god! What fate is ours?" cried Hilde-brand. . . . "For thirty summers and thirty winters have I wandered as a fugitive. Ever went I into battle against the bowmen, nor would one of them give me my death. . . . Now my own child will hew me with his sword or throw me down with his spear. . . . or else I shall be his murderer. . . ."

In silence he gazed a moment upon his son; he regarded the noble form with sorrow and pride.

"Thou mayest easily win the fight with so old a man as I am," he said, "if thy strength is great. If thou dost triumph, thou shalt have my treasure for booty."

Hadubrand made answer with softer voice, for he had spoken harshly: "I can see from thine armour," he said, "that thou hast a good master; and methinks thou didst never become a fugitive by compulsion."

Pleasant were the words of Hadubrand in the ears of his sire. Hildebrand loved his son because that he was fearless and bold and thirsted for the fray. He could delay not meeting him any longer, lest he should be called a coward by friends and foemen alike. So he spake, saying:

[1] The Mediterranean.

" He who would deny thee combat now would be the worst of eastern men. Greatly dost thou covet glory! By common right of war this conflict should show forth to-day which of us can make boast among men."

Then began they to fight. They tilted with their spears one against the other, but the heavy thrusts were parried by their shields. . . . Ere long they drew their swords — their hard-edged splitters — and fearfully they hewed until, at length, their white shields were splintered and battered. . . . They cast aside their broken bucklers. . . . They fought then with their swords alone.

Silence fell upon the opposing armies. No man spake. Every eye was turned upon the brave warriors in fierce conflict. . . . Neither side was confident of the issue. . . . Never before was Hildebrand so well matched; never did Hadubrand combat against so powerful a foeman.

Long they fought, so that it seemed the conflict would never end. . . . Then fell the last swordstroke. Sudden was its fall like lightning, and as sure, and Hadubrand sank upon the ground, bleeding from his death-wound.

Hildebrand flung his blade from him. He knelt beside the fallen hero. The stern old warrior wept bitter tears.

" Alas," he cried, " I have slain mine own son!"

Hadubrand, enduring sharp agony, looked up with death-bright eyes.

" Thou art, indeed, my sire," he said; " no man save Hildebrand could have prevailed against me."

Hildebrand wound his arms about the dying hero. Deathly white was his face like that of his son. Fate had stricken him sore. . . . The battle began to be waged nigh unto him and went past. . . . He spake not to the nobles who came near at eventide. . . . The eyes of the fallen warrior were then glazed by death; his lips were cold; his armour was reddened by blood; Hadubrand had died of his wounds. Hildebrand, Heribrand's son, had died of grief. . . .

Victory was won by Dietrich. His enemies were scattered before him, and those who were not slain fled unto their homes.

But sad was Dietrich's heart when he rode in triumph into Bern because that old Hildebrand was dead. By the people he was received with great rejoicings; he went unto his palace; there did the nobles greet him and do him homage, laying at his feet gifts of gold and many gems. So was he acclaimed the rightful king.

Sibeche sought in vain to stem the tide of victory which thereafter fell to Dietrich's arms. He marched against the king with a great army; he fought but a single battle. By a brave knight was he challenged to single combat, and after fierce and prolonged fighting he was cleft in twain. Thereafter was his army defeated, and those who survived the vengeance of Dietrich laid down their arms and did him homage. Then was Dietmar's great son exalted among men, for he was crowned king over all the dominions which Ermenrich had held. When Etzel died he was made king of the Huns also. Thus did he become the greatest monarch of his time— he who had long been an exile from his own land.

Long was the reign of King Dietrich, and there was peace over all the wide dominions which he ruled, for it was given unto him to be wise as he was powerful.

To a great old age did he live. And minstrels, wandering from land to land to sing in the halls of heroes, have told that he never died. For it chanced that he went forth one day to hunt in a deep forest. Among

the huntsmen there was none who was his equal even
although he was burdened with years.  He bathed himself, after the chase was ended, in a small lake.  A dwarf
came nigh and cried out:

"O King, the greatest stag which man hath ever
looked upon is rushing past; it escapeth the huntsmen."

Dietrich left the water; he wrapped a rug about himself and called for his horse, but he was not heard.

Then there burst through the trees a noble and high-
stepping black steed.  No man rode it.  Dietrich sprang
into the saddle; he urged it on, and the black steed ran
faster than the wind.

The dwarf rode behind him: "Swiftly indeed thou
dost ride," he cried; "when wilt thou return, O King?"

Dietrich made answer: "I can hold not back this evil
steed, nor can I dismount from it.  Nor can I return
again until it is the will of God and the Holy Mary."

So Dietrich vanished from sight.  And nevermore
was he seen among men.  Yet when the wind is high,
and the world is tempest-stricken, the sound of hoofs are
heard in mid-air, and men know then that Dietrich, seated
on his black steed, is pursuing the stag as of old across
the heavens."[1]

---

[1] Like Odin, Charlemagne, King Arthur, &c., he is the Wild Huntsman in the
Raging Host.

# INDEX

Ægir or Æger (ā'jir), xxvii, 20, 65, 73, 98, 99, 100, 107, 152, 170, 171, 173, 175.

Æschere (esk'ha-ra), 202, 204.

Afghan "Seven Sleepers", xlv *n*.

Africa, "Long-heads" of, xlvii.

Alberich (al'ber-ik), the elf king, 352 *n*, 359, 360, 364, 370, 377, 389, 405, 422.

Aldrian (al'dre-an), son of Hagen, 447.

Alfheim (alf'hime), home of elves, 20, 44, 132.

All-father, xxxi, 1, 2, 12, 13, 25, 185.

Alv (alf), prince of Denmark, 313, 343.

Alveig (alf-eeg), 47, 77.

Amelhede (amel'heed-e), Hamlet's burial place, 243 *n*.

Amelungs (a'mil-oonks), 392, 411, 414, 440, 442.

Amleth (am'let). See *Hamlet*.

Amlode (am'lo-dee). See *Hamlet*.

Amlode's meal bin, 234 *n*.

Amsvartner (am-svart'ner). See *Gulf of Black Grief*.

Andvari (and'va-rē) the dwarf, 286, 329, 342, 352 *n*.

Angerboda (an-gur-bo'-dà), Hag of Ironwood, 73 *n*, 90, 98, 152, 171, 179, 203 *n*, 288. Also *Aurboda*.

Angles, xxvi; Beowulf story of, xxxix, xl.

Anglo-Saxon gloom, xxviii; name for Milky Way, xxxvii, 65 *n*.

Annar (an'nar), 8.

Arabia, "Seven Sleepers" of, xliv, xlv.

Archæology and mythology, xxiv.

Argus (ar'goos), xxix.

Arnold, Matthew, 10, 20, 163-4, 168 *n*, 186.

Arthur (Celtic, art'her), the sleeping, xlvii; hunting, 453 *n*.

Arvak (ar-wak) and Alsvid (al-svid), sun-steeds, 6.

Asa-clan gloom, xxvii.

Asa-gods (ā-sa), creation of, 3.

Asgard (as'gard), xxv, xxxi, xxxvi, 10, 11, 15, 16, 19, 22, 25, 26, 27, 28, 29, 30, 31, 34, 35, 36, 38, 44, 46, 52, 57, 58, 59, 60, 62, 63, 64, 65, 66, 70, 71, 72, 74, 76; fall of, 77, 78, 79, 82, 85, 86, 87; Odin returns to, 88, 89, 90, 91, 92, 93; Ægir visits, 99, 112, 121, 126, 127, 128, 131, 132, 138, 141, 149, 150, 151, 156, 157, 167, 169, 173; at Ragnarok, 179, 180, 183, 188, 284, 304.

Asia Minor, xliv.

Asiatic myths, xxvii.

Ask, first man, 9, 108, 187.

Aslog (a-sloug') (Krake), last of the Volsungs, 330, 338, 341, 342.

Asmegir (a'sme-gīr), 148, 151, 155.

Asmund (a'smoond), son of Svipdag, 82, 86, 87.

Atle (at'lē), king of the Huns, 326, 327, 334, 343, 344, 345, 347, 349, 350, 351. See also *Etzel* and *Attila*.

Attila (at'e-la), Emperor of Huns, xxxix, xlii, 391 *n*. Also see *Etzel* and *Atle*.

Aud (owd), 8.

Audhumla (ow-dum'la), chaos-cow, 3.

Aurboda (owr-bod'a), Hag of Ironwood, 30, 72, 73. Also *Angerboda*.

Avo (a'vo), the elfin archer, 45, 142.

455

Babylonian myths, xxviii.

Bænkhied (ben'kide), Brynhild's sister, 326.

Balder (bal'dir), xxv, xxvii, xxix, xxxvi, xxxvii, xxxviii, 10, 27, 28, 65, 66, 146; world vows, 147; fate foretold, 148–9; his death, 150–1; funeral, 152–4; in Hela, 155–6, 157; poem, 158–9; his avenger, 165, 166, 167, 168, 169, 170, 173; his return, 183, 184; in heroic story, 221–31, 390, 403.

Balder's spring, 227.

Balmung (bal'moong), Siegfried's sword, 359, 363, 365.

Balor (baul-or), Celtic night-god, xxix.

Bechlaren (bech'lar-en), 394.

Beli (bā-le), the giant, 39, 54, 62, 68.

Bel-Merodach, xxviii.

Beowulf, the elder, 189.

Beowulf (bā-ō-wulf), the hero, xxv; historical theory, xxxix; a thane, 191; his resolution, 192; arrives at Heorot, 193, 194, 195; fight with Grendel, 198, 199, 200; the feast, 201; fight with Grendel's mother, 202–6; triumph and return home, 207–9; dragon fight and death, 210–9; as Boe and Vale, 231 n, 283 n.

Beowulf poem, xx; its gloom, xxviii; the plot, xxxix; history of, xl, xli; narrative, 187–219.

Bergelmer (ber-gel'mer), 4, 10, 169.

Bern, Verona, xlii n.

Bertram (ber'tram) of Pola, 440.

Bestla (best'la), 4.

Beyla (bī-la), wife of Bygver, 96.

Bibung (bee-bung) the dwarf, 434.

Bifrost (bē-frest), xxxvii, 15, 16, 19, 20, 23, 33, 60, 69, 99, 147, 181.

Bikke (bik'kee), 80.

Bikki (Sibech), 342.

Bil, moon-maid, xxxvii, 6, 7, 22.

Billing (bil'ling), elf of twilight, 165, 166, 168.

Billing, sunset elf, 20.

Billingsgate, 165 n.

Bilrost (bil-rest) and Bifrost, xxxvii.

Biterolf (bi'te-rolf), 424.

Bjarmaland (b'yar'ma-land), 257.

Bjarmians, 225.

Bjorno-Hoder (b'yorno-hooder), 45.

Black Isle, xlv.

Blœdel (blœ'del), brother of Etzel, 392, 397.

Blutgang (blut'gang) sword, 410.

Boann (bo'an), the Irish river goddess, xxxi.

Bodvild (bod'veeld), Queen of Sweden, 284.

Boe (bo'e), Balder's avenger, 230, 231. Also Bous.

Bolverkin (bol'werk-in), "the evil-doer", Odin as, 24.

Bor (ber), son of Bure, 4, 9, 10.

Border Ballads, Hela in, 276–81; Clerk Saunders, 305–8, 336 n.

Borghild (borg'hild), wife of Sigmund, 299, 309, 310.

Bous (bō'us) as Beowulf and Vale, 219 n. Also Boe.

Boyne river myth, 419 n.

Brage (bra'gee), 28, 39, 99, 153, 171, 172.

Bran (brân), dog with "Seven Sleepers", xlv.

Branstock (bran-stock), the oak, 289.

Brian Boroimhe (bree'an bor'iv), xlvii.

Brimer (bri'mer), 184.

Britain, King of, in Hamlet, 236–8, 240, 241, 242.

Britons, early, xl.

"Broad-heads", xxviii, xlvii.

Brok (brock), elf smith, 35, 37, 38,

Brooke, Stopford, xxvi, xxxix, xl, 219 n.

Brunhild (broon'heelt), 358, 369, 370, 372, 373, 374, 375, 377, 378, 379, 380, 381, 383, 384, 385, 388, 403.

Brute (broo'tee), xxxiv.

Brynhild (bren-held), 320, 323, 324, 325, 326, 327, 328, 329, 330, 331, 332, 333, 334, 335, 336, 338, 341, 342, 343, 344, 345.

Budle (bud'le), father of Brynhild, 326.

Bure (bur'e), first Asa-god, 3, 4.
Burgundians (ber-gun'dians), 352 *n.*
Burial customs in legends, xxiv, xxv.
Bygver (bīg-ver), Frey's servant, 96.
Byrger (bīr-ger), 6.
Byrr, xxxvi.
Byzantium (bi-zan'tium), 231.

Cailleach (cal-yach), period in April, 418 *n.*
Cailleach Mor (cal'yach more), the Scottish hag, xxii.
Cat, the big grey ("Midgard Serpent"), 121, 124.
Celtic gloom, xxviii; fatalism, 168 *n.*
Celtic myths, xxix.
Charlemagne (shar'le-mān), 453 *n.*
Christianity, adopted in Northern Europe, xx.
Churl (kurl), 188.
Cock, Hela's Red Fire, 14, 178, 179.
Cock of the North. See *Goldcomb.*
Constantinople, xliii.
Corineus (kor'in-yes), Cornish giant-slayer, xxxii.
Cornwall, giants of, xxxii, xxxiv.
Creation, story of, 1.
Cremation, burial customs, xxiv–v.
Cromarty (crom'ar-tee), hag of, 418 *n.*
Cuchullin (koo'hool-in), 242 *n.*
Cuse (koo'see), King of the Finns, 225.
Cyclopean (ky-klo'pee-an) fairies, xxxv.
Cyclops (ky'klops), Odin as, xxxi.

Dag, son of King Hogni, 300, 301.
Dagda (dag'da), Celtic god, xxxi.
Dagr (dag-ir), xxx, 8, 20.
Danann (dan'an) (Irish) gods, xxxiv, xxxv.
Dankwart (dank'wart), 370, 371, 372, 373, 374, 377, 397.
Dawn gods. See *Delling* and *Lugh.*
Dawn myths, xxix, xxxvii *n.*
Day myth. See *Dagr.*
Decius (dā'kee-us), xliv.
Delling (del'ling), elf of dawn, xxx, 8, 148.

Demon brides, 259 *n.*
Denmark, Beowulf visits, 192.
Devil, Odin and Svipdag identified with, xxxviii.
Diether (deet'her), Dietrich's brother, 441, 442, 443, 444, 445.
Dietleib (deet'leep) the Dane, 424, 425, 429, 430, 431, 433, 440, 442.
Dietmar (deet'mar), 404, 406, 407, 409, 411, 412, 414, 438, 441, 445, 446.
Dietrich (deet'reech) of Bern, xxxii, xxxvii, xxxviii, xxxix, xl, xlii, 352 *n,* 380 *n,* 392, 394, 396, 397, 398, 401, 402, 404, 405, 406, 407, 408, 409, 410, 411, 413, 414, 415, 416, 417, 418, 419, 420, 421, 422, 423, 424, 425, 427, 428, 429, 431, 432, 434, 435, 436, 437, 438, 439, 440, 441, 442, 443, 444, 445, 446, 448, 449, 452, 453.
Dingwall (ding'wall), xx.
Dises (dis'ez) of fate, 15, 17.
Dragon in *Beowulf*, 210–8, 421 *n.*
Draupner (drowp'ner), Odin's magic ring, 37, 67, 68, 154, 155, 157.
Dromi (drō'me), the chain, 92.
Dvalin (dva'lin), Sindre as, 89.
Dwarfs, xxxv, xxxvi, 5, 12, 13, 39, 179.

Eadmund (ed'mund), King of England, 341 *n.*
Earnaness (ern'a-ness), 219 *n.*
Earthquakes caused by Loke, 176.
Ebenrot (eben'rot), 415.
Ecke (eck'a), 415, 416, 417, 418, 419, 421, 422.
Ecke-sax sword, 417, 418, 420, 421.
Edda (ed'da), Elder or Poetic, xvii, xix, xli.
Edda, origin of word, xxii.
Edda, Snorri's or Prose, xvii, xviii, xix.
Edward the Confessor, xlvi.
Eggerich (ek'ker-ich) the dwarf, 409.
Egil (ā'gil) the elf, xxxv, xxxvii, 39, 45, 47, 48, 55, 100, 112, 282, 411.

Egther (ek'ter), "sword guardian", Gymer as, 74.

Egypt, xliv.

Elan (el'an), 190.

Eldir (el'dir), 171.

Elf maids of Urd, 15.

Elf smiths, 12.

Elivagar (el-i-vag'ar), the rivers, 2, 22, 38, 57, 100, 112, 132, 133, 142.

Ella (el'la), the English King, 341 n.

Elle (el-lē) the hag "Old Age", 123, 124.

Elsan (el'san), 442, 444.

Elves, xxxv, xxxvi; at Ragnarok, 179.

Elvidner (el-vid'ner), home of Hel, 91.

Embla (em'bla), first woman, 9, 187.

Eormanric (er'men-reek), in Beowulf, 201.

Ephesus, Seven Sleepers, of xliv, xlvi.

Erik, the devil, xxxviii.

Erik (e'rik) of Denmark, 265, 266.

Erik of Norway, 265, 266, 267.

Ermenrich (er'men - reek), xlii, xliii, 341 n, 392, 404, 424, 425, 439, 440, 441, 442, 447, 449, 452.

Erp, son of Etzel, 442, 443, 445, 446.

Erp, son of Gudrun, 353.

Etzel (et'sel), King of Huns, 391, 393, 395, 396, 397, 399, 400, 401, 402, 441, 442, 443, 444, 445, 446, 447, 452. Also Attila.

Eylime (ey'lim-e) the King, 311, 312.

Faerie Queene, Spenser's, 219 - 20, 269–76.

Fafner (faf-ner), 285, 287, 314, 315, 316, 317, 318, 322, 329, 346, 349.

Fairies, Scottish, xxxv, 359 n.

Falke (fal'ke), Dietrich's horse, 420.

Fasold (fa'solt), 415, 419, 420, 421, 422.

Fates, Norns are, 15.

Feng, Hamlet's uncle, 232, 233, 234, 236, 237, 238, 239, 240.

Fenja (fen-ya), giant maid, 39, 44, 247, 248, 249.

Fenrer (fen'rer) the wolf, 90; in As-gard, 91; binding of, 92, 93; in Gulf of Black Grief, 93, 94; source of River Von, 95, 96, 132, 171, 175, 176, 179; at Ragnarok, 180, 181, 182, 183.

Fians (fee'ans) (Fingalians), xlv, xlvi.

Finn the King in Beowulf, 201.

Finn - mac - Coul (fin"mak'kool), the Scottish giant, xxxii, xxxviii, xxxix, xlv; links with Sigurd, 315 n, 319 n.

Finns, 225.

Fjalar (fyal-ar), Suttung as, 23, 47, 74, 179.

Fjorner (fyor-ner), Odin as, 316.

Flodden, xlvii.

Folk tales and mythologies, xxiii.

Fomors (fo'mors), xxxiii, xxxiv.

Forsete (for-set'e), son of Balder, 45.

Frey (frī) as elf king, xxxv, xxxvi; the Asa-god, 28, 35, 36, 37, 44, 49, 53; in captivity, 54, 55; set free, 62, 63; loves Gerd, 66, 67, 68, 69, 70, 71, 72, 74; in revolt, 77, 96, 153, 172; at Ragnarok, 182, 187; in heroic story, 227; as Frode, 246 n.

Frazer, Prof., xxxvi.

Frederick of Barbarossa, xlvii.

Frederick the Great, xlii.

Freke (frek'ē), Odin's wolf-dog, 26, 167.

Freyja (frī-ya), xxxvi, 28, 30, 31, 32, 33, 39, 49, 50, 53; in captivity, 54, 55, 56, 57, 60, 61, 62, 63, 71, 72, 73, 83, 84, 85, 86, 126, 127; Thrym desires, 126, 127, 128, 129; enter-tains Hrungner, 138, 153, 201 n, 288, 289.

Frigg (frig), Queen of Asgard, 28, 146, 147, 149, 150, 151; maids of, 153, 155, 157, 173.

Frisians (free'see-ans), 201.

Frode (frō'dē), King of Denmark, 246, 247, 248.

Frode's Mill, 246. Also World Mill.

Frost giants, xxxii, 3, 16, 30, 31, 38, 44, 47, 59, 69, 87, 112, 128, 142, 178.

Fulla (ful'a), sister of Frigg, 147, 153, 157.

Gaelic literature, xxviii.
Game of gods, 12, 184.
Gangraad (gang'raad), Odin as, 169.
Garden of Hela, 259; flowers from, 268; in Spenser's *Faerie Queene*, 273-4, 275-6, 280-1.
Garm, watch dog, 95, 178, 180.
Geats (gā-ats), 191.
Geirrod (gīr'rod), the giant, xxxiii–iv, xliv, 99; captures Loke, 131, 132, 133; Thor slays, 134; in Hela, 257, 260, 261, 263.
Gelder (gel'der), 25, 39.
Gelder, King of Saxony, 224, 226.
Gelga (gel'gya), chain binding Fenrer, 95.
Geoffrey of Monmouth, xx, xxxii, xxxiv, 165 n, 419 n.
Gerd, giant maid, 66; wooed for Frey, 67, 68, 69, 70, 74, 96, 172, 179.
Gere (ger'e), Odin's wolf-dog, 26, 167.
Gernot (ger'not), 362, 366, 368, 399, 401.
Gerutha (ger'oo-ta), Hamlet's mother, 232 n, 233, 235, 236.
Gewar (gev'ar), xxxvii, 221, 223, 224, 225, 226, 227, 230.
Giant lore of Europe, xxxii, xxxiii, xxxiv, xxxv, xxxix, xl.
Giant maids, 4, 39, 44. See *Fenja* and *Menja*.
Ginnunga-gap (gi-noon-ga-gap), 1.
Giptes (gip-tez), 15.
Giselher (gee'sel-hār), 362, 369, 378, 395, 399.
Giuki (gi'ook-e), 319, 325, 326, 328, 329, 334, 336, 338, 342, 343, 347, 348.
Giukings (gi'oo-kings) as Burgundians, 352 n.
Gjallar-horn (g'yal'lar), 16, 21, 89, 178, 187, 262 n.
Gjalp (g'yalp), giantess, 99, 133.
Gjoll (g'yel) River, 151, 155.

Gjoll rock, 95.
Glam, xxxix.
Gleipner (glīp-ner), the magic cord, 93.
Glencoe, xlv.
Glittering Heath, 287, 316.
Glittering Plains, 265, 267.
Gloom of Teutonic literature, xxvii; of Celtic, xxviii.
Goats of Thor, 100.
Gods, local and imported, xxvii.
Goemagot (goy'ma-got), Cornish giant, xxxii.
Goldcomb, 14, 61, 62, 178.
Golden Age of gods, 12, 29, 30, 187.
Gorm, King of Denmark, xliv, 254, 255, 258, 259, 260, 264, 265.
Gram, the Volsung sword, 291, 296, 297, 311, 312, 315, 316, 326.
Grane (gran'nā), Sigurd's steed, 314, 322, 329; Siegfried's, 357.
Granmar (gran'mar), sire of Hodbrod, 300.
Gray's *Descent of Odin*, 159–62.
Greece, xliv.
Greek mythology, xxix; river myths, 419 n.
Greip (grīp), the giantess, 39, 99.
Grendel (gren-del) in *Beowulf*, xxxix, xl, 190, 191, 194, 197, 198, 199, 200, 202, 206, 207, 213.
Grendel's mother, 202, 206.
Grep (grāp), 30, 39, 54, 55.
Greybeard the ferryman, Odin as, 143, 144, 145.
Grid (greed), the hag, xxxiv, 132, 133, 134.
Gridarvold (greed'ar-vold), magic wand, 132.
Grim (greem), xxxix, 404, 405, 406, 407, 408, 409, 422.
Grimhild (grim'hild) the queen, 326, 327, 328, 329, 343, 344, 345.
Grimm, 341 n.
Griper (gree'per), Sigurd's uncle, 315.
Grjottungard (gryot-toon'-gard), Hrungner's domain, 139.

Groa (grō'a), elf of growth, 47, 48, 49, 50, 53, 60, 77, 79, 142, 143; as Hamlet's mother, 232 n.

Gudhorm (gud-hōrm), son of Halfdan, 48, 77, 78, 79, 80.

Gudmund (gud'moond) as Mimer, 257, 258, 259, 263, 267, 268, 269 n.

Gudrun (goo'-droon), 326, 328, 330, 331, 332, 333, 334, 335, 336, 341, 342, 343, 344, 345, 346, 348, 349, 351, 352, 353, 354 n, 439.

Gulf of Black Grief (Amsvartner), 19, 93, 95, 96, 175, 176, 178.

Gullintani (gull'in-ta-nee)(Heimdal), 16.

Gulveig-Hoder (gul'vēg-hoo-der), the hag, 30, 39, 71, 90, 157.

Gungner (goong'ner), Odin's spear, 35, 37, 181.

Gunlad (goon'lad), wooed by Odin, 22, 23, 24.

Gunnar (gun'nar), 326, 327, 328, 329, 330, 331, 332, 333, 334, 335, 344, 346, 347, 348, 349, 350, 351.

Gunnhild (goon'heeld), Asmund's queen, 87.

Gunno (gun'no), 230.

Gunther (gunt'her), 360, 362, 363, 365, 366, 368, 369, 370, 371, 372, 373, 374, 375, 376, 377, 378, 379, 380, 381, 382, 383, 384, 387, 388, 389, 391, 392, 393, 394, 395, 397, 398, 401, 402, 446, 447.

Gustr (gust'er), xxxvi.

Guttorm (goot'torm), 326, 333.

Gymer (gee'mer), xxx, 65, 66, 67, 68, 69, 70, 71, 74, 96, 172, 179.

Hadding (hat'tink), 47, 77; in hiding, 78, 79, 80; fight with Hand, 81, 82; slays Svipdag dragon, 84, 86, 87; in Hela, 268-9.

Hades (ha'dez), xxiv.

Hadubrand (ha'du-brant), Hildebrand's son, 441, 448, 449, 450, 451.

Hadvanus (had'van-us) the king, 82.

Hag, Brunhild as, xxxv-vi.

Hag, mother of Scottish giants, xxii.

Hag, the Scottish, xxxiii; the British, xxxix.

Hag in Beowulf. See Grendel's mother.

Hag of Ironwood, xxx, 30, 34, 39, 63, 71, 72, 88, 90, 98, 157, 184, 187, 203 n, 288; as Ljod, wife of Volsung, 289. See also Aurboda, Angerboda, and Gulveig-Hoder.

Hagen (ha'gen), 360, 363, 366, 370, 371, 372, 373, 374, 377, 385, 386, 387, 388, 389, 390, 391, 393, 394, 395, 396, 397, 398, 399, 400, 401, 402, 446, 447.

Hakon (ha'kon), King of Denmark, 343.

Halfdan (Halv'dan), 46, 47, 48, 49, 50, 52, 53, 59, 77, 78, 79, 84, 232 n, 268.

Halfe (half'e), giant, 78, 80.

Halga (Hal-ga) the Good, 190.

Hall, Dr. Clark, xxviii, xl, xli.

Halogaland (ha'lo-ga-lant), 225, 255.

Hama (ham'a), 201.

Hamder (ham'der), son of Gudrun, 353.

Hamingjes (ham'ing-yez), 15-7, 266 n.

Hamlet (ham'let), xxi, xxxvii, xxxviii, 232-46. Also Amleth and Amlode.

Hamund (ha'mund), son of Sigmund, 299.

Hand, the Great Black, 81.

Hardgrep (hard'grep), giant maid, 79, 80; killed by Great Hand, 81.

Harlungs (har'loonks), 440.

Harold and Balder's mound, 229.

Hati (ha-tee), moon-wolf, 7, 95, 182, 203 n.

Healfdene (half-den) in Beowulf, 189.

Heardings, tribe of Hadding, 78.

Hebrides, xix.

Heimar (hīm-ar), 326, 327, 328, 330, 338.

Heimdal (hīm'dal), 16, 20; as Rati, 23, 24, 60, 69; as Lyfir, 81; as a seal, 85, 86, 89; sea mothers, 99, 128, 153, 174, 178; at Ragnarok, 180, 181, 185, 187, 188.

Heime (hai'me), 410, 411, 412, 422, 423, 424, 425, 436, 439, 440.

Heimskringla (hims'kring-la), xviii, 77 n.

Hel, xxx, 90, 91, 180.

Hela (hel'a), 10, 13, 14, 15, 16, 17, 18, 19, 20, 23, 46, 49, 51, 60, 62, 70, 77, 89, 147, 148, 151, 152, 157, 177, 178, 181, 254–69, 270–81, 301, 335, 336.

Helche (hel'che), Queen of Huns, 391, 392, 441.

Helge Thoreson (Hel'ge-Thor'sen), in Hela, 267, 268.

Helgi, King of Halogaland, 225, 226, 227.

Helgi Hundingsbane (Hel'ge Hun'-dings-bane), xxv, xlii, 299, 300, 301, 302, 303, 304, 305, 309. 311.

Helheim (hel-him), 91.

Hengest (heng'est), 25, 39, 201.

Henry, grandson of Svipdag, 86.

Heorot (heor-ot), the great hall, building of, 190; Beowulf reaches, 193, 196, 197; Grundel overcome in, 198–9; feast in, 201; hag visits, 202, 208, 213.

Hercules (her'koo-lez) and hydra, 406 n.

Heremod (her'mod), in Beowulf, 208.

Hermanric (her'man-reek). See Ermenerich.

Hermes (her'mes), xxix.

Hermod (her-mod), xli, 90, 93; visit to Hela, 152, 154, 155, 156, 157.

Hermutrude (her"me-tru'de), Scottish queen, 240, 241, 242, 243.

Herogar (he'ro-gar), 190.

Herrad (her'rad), princess of Huns, 441.

Highland giants, xxxii; Seven Sleepers, xlv.

Hilde (heel'de), xxxix, 404, 405, 406, 408.

Hildebrand (heel'de - brant), xxxvii, xliii, 394, 396, 401, 404, 405, 406, 407, 408, 409, 411, 412, 413, 414, 421, 426, 428, 431, 434, 435, 436, 441, 442, 443, 445, 446, 447, 448, 449, 450 451, 452.

Hildeburgh (heel'de-boorg), 201.

Hildegrim (heel'de-grim) sword, 407, 410, 413, 414.

Himinbjorg (him'in-byerg), 16.

Hindarfell (hind'ar-fel), 320, 322.

History in mythologies, xxxiv.

Hittite Thor, xliii n.

Hjaalprek (hyaal'prek), King of Denmark, 313, 314, 316.

Hjordis (hyor-dis), mother of Sigurd, 311, 312, 313, 314.

Hlebard (hle'bard), the elf smith, 150.

Hnaef, 201.

Hodbrodd (hod'brod), 221, 300.

Hoder or Hodur (Hoo - der), xxix, xxxviii, 45, 146, 148, 149, 150, 151, 166, 168, 183, 185, 231 n.

Hogne (heg-ne), son of Giuki, 326, 333, 344, 346, 347, 348, 349, 350, 351, 352.

Hogni, sire of Sigrun, 300, 301, 304.

Holmgang (holm'gang), xxxiii.

Honer (he'ner), 4, 28, 29, 30, 57, 76, 183, 285.

Horatio (hor'ā-she-o), Hamlet's friend, 233 n.

Horsens (her-sens), 227.

Horvendil. See Horwendil.

Horwendil (hor'wen-dil), Hamlet's father, 232, 233, 234 n, 239.

Hother (hoo'ter), xxxvii; Balder's rival and slayer, 221–31, 232.

Hraesvelgur (hrae-svelg-ur), 9.

Hreidmar (hrid-mar), 285, 286, 287.

Hrethel (hret'hel) the King, 213, 214, 228 n.

Hrimner (hrim'ner), sire of Angerboda, 288.

Hrimthursar (hreem - toors - ar). See Frost giants.

Hringhorn (hreng-horn), Balder's ship, 152.

Hronesness (hron'es-ness), Beowulf's grave on, 217, 219.

Hrothgar (hroth'gar) builds Heorot, 190; sorrow over Grendel, 191, 192; receives Beowulf, 194; praises him,

200; Grendel's mother, 202, 203, 204, 206, 207, 208.
Hrungner (hroong'ner), the stone giant, 134, 137, 138, 139, 140, 141, 142.
Hrunting (hrun'ting) sword, 204.
Hrym (hreem) at Ragnarok, 179.
Huge (hoo'ge), the dwarf "Thought", 119, 124.
Hugin (hoo'gin), Odin's raven, 26.
Hunaland (hoon'a-land), 298, 309, 311, 312, 346.
Hunding (hun'ding) the King, 299, 300, 302, 311, 316.
Hvergelmer (hver-gel'mer), 2, 5, 11, 13, 14, 22, 38, 51, 57.
Hygelac (he'je-lak), 193, 194, 209, 210, 214.
Hymer (hee-mer), the giant, 97, 98, 100, 101, 102, 103, 104, 105, 106, 107, 110, 125.
Hyrrokin (heer'ro-kin) the hag, 152.
Hyuki (hyuk'e), 6, 7, 22, 25, 39.

Iceland, colonizatio᠎ of, xix; Hamlet of, xxxvii.
Ida (ē-da), 186.
Idavoll (eedā-vol), 12.
Idun (ee'doon), 28, 39, 57; stolen from Asgard, 58, 59, 67, 100, 153.
Illyria (il-lee'ree-a), xlii.
Ilmenrik (eel'men-reek), 424.
Ing (ēng), Svipdag as, 82.
Ingvar (ēng-var), son of Krake, 341.
Innsbruck (ins'bryk), xliii.
Inverness (in'ver-ness), giants of, xxxiii; Seven Sleepers of, xxxv, xlv.
Ireland, xxxvii n.
Irish giants, xxxiv.
Irmin (er'min), 444, 449.
Irmin's way, the Milky Way, xxxvii, 449 n.
Ironwood (Iarnvid — yarn - wid), home of Hag, xxx, 73, 87; at Ragnarok, 179, 180, 203 n. See Hag of Iron-wood.
Isenland (ee'sin-lant), 372.
Italy, xliii, xliv.

Ivalde (ee'vald-e), xxxvi, xxxvii, xxxviii, 12; as Svigdur, 22, 24, 25, 26, 28, 34, 36, 37, 38, 39, 44, 45, 52; as Vate, 65, 100, 131, 132, 133, 141, 223n, 234n, 282, 284.

"Jack and Jill", 6 n.
"Jack the giant-killer", 170 n.
Jalk (yalk), name of Odin, 170.
James IV of Scotland, xlvii.
Janibas (ya'nee-bas) the magician, 434, 435, 437.
Jarl (yarl), 188.
Jarnsaxa (yarn-sax-a), 99; mother of Thor's son Magni, 141.
Jeraspunt (yā'ris-poont), 434, 435, 436, 437.
Jochgrimm (yoch-grim) mountain, 415, 418 n, 419, 420.
Jörd (yerd), 8, 27.
Jormungand (yer'mun-gand). See Midgard Serpent.
Jormunrek (yer'mun-reek), Ermenrich, 341, 342.
Jotunheim (yē'toon-hime), 9, 12, 20, 30, 32, 39, 46, 48, 49, 53, 59, 62, 78, 88, 112, 126, 127, 128, 129, 132, 137, 138, 139, 169, 173, 179.
Jotuns (yē'toons), xxxiv, 4. See Frost giants and Mountain giants.
Jubainville on Greek and Celtic myths, xxix.
Jupiter, xxxii.
Jutland (yoot'lant), 227, 232, 238, 243.

Kerlogar (ker'lowg-er) rivers, 155.
Kingu, husband of Tiawath, xxx.
Koll, King of Norway, 232.
Kormet and Ormet rivers, 154.
Kostbera (kost'be-ra), wife of Hogne, 346, 347.
Krake (kra'ke), last of the Volsungs. See Aslog.
Kratim, Arabian dog with Seven Sleepers, xlv.
Kriemhild (kreem-heelt), 360, 361, 362, 363, 364, 365, 366, 367, 368, 369,

370, 371, 378, 379, 380, 382, 383, 384, 385, 386, 387, 388, 389, 390, 391, 392, 393, 394, 395, 396, 397, 398, 399, 401, 402, 446, 447.

Kunhild (koon'heelt), 424, 425, 426, 429, 430, 431, 432, 433.

Kvasir (kva'sir), son of Njord, 174.

Laurin (law'reen) the dwarf, 380 n, 423, 425, 426, 427, 428, 429, 430, 431, 432, 433.

Leding (lā-ding), the iron chain, 92.

Leifner's (līf-ner) flames, 78.

Leipter (līp'ter), holy river, 144, 155.

Lif and Lifthraser (lif'thra-ser), 148, 184.

Light hero, Svipdag as, xxxvii, xxxix.

Littur (lit'ur) the dwarf, 154.

Ljod (lyōd), wife of Volsung, 289.

Loch Maree (ma'ree), xx.

Lodbrog (lod-brog). See *Ragnar Lodbrog.*

Lodur (loo'dūr), 4, 29.

Loge (lō'ge), contest with Loke, 118, 119, 124.

Loke (lō'kē), Asa god, xxix, xxx, xxxvi, 4, 29, 30, 31, 32, 34, 36, 37, 38, 57, 58, 59, 64, 71, 73, 76, 78, 79, 80, 85, 89, 90, 95; with Thor in Jotunheim, 112; at Orvandel's dwelling, 113; at Utgard Loke's castle, 117, 118, 124; Thrym adventure, 126, 127, 128, 129, 130; Geirrod adventure and plot, 131, 132, 133; Balder plot, 146, 149, 157, 169; quarrel with gods, 170–3; pursuit of and punishment, 173–6; set free, 179; at Ragnarok, 180, 263–5, 285–6, 314.

Loki. See *Utgard Loke.*

Longfellow, poems by, 43, 108, 136, 158.

"Long-heads", xlvii.

Loptsson, Jon, xviii.

Ludgast (lūd'gast), King of Danes, 365, 385.

Ludger (lūd-ger), King of Saxons, 365, 366.

Lugh (loo), Celtic dawn god, xxix; Milky Way his "chain", xxxvii n.

Lynge (lin'ge), son of Hunding, 311, 312, 316.

Lyngheid (lyng'hide), daughter of Hreidmar, 287.

Macdonald, General Sir Hector, xlvii.

Magic swords, xxxvii, xxxix. Also *Balmung, Blutgang, Eckesax, Gram, Hildegrim, Hrunting, Mimung, Sword of Victory,* and *Welsung.*

Magic wands, xxxiv, 132. Also *Gridarvold.*

Magni (mag'nē), son of Thor, 141, 182, 183.

Mahomet, xliv.

Mammon, Spenser's as Mimer, 220 n, 269–76.

Manchuria (man'koor-ia), xlvii.

Mani (man'e) of the moon, 6, 22,

Mannus (man'nus), Halfdan as, 46.

Matriarchal tribe, xxii, xxxix, 375 n.

Mead, song or skaldic, 7.

Menja (men-ya), giant maid, 39, 44, 247–9.

Midgard (mid'gard), 9, 10, 12, 13, 15, 16, 19, 28, 47; winter spell in, 59, 63; conflicts in, 77, 83; peace in, 88, 129, 173; earthquakes in, 176; at Ragnarok, 179, 182, 187.

Midgard Serpent, xxx, 90; Thor's fight with, 97–111; as a cat, 124, 125; at Ragnarok, 179, 181, 356 n.

Milky Way, xxxvii; Odin rides over, 33; is "Watling Street", 65 n.

Mill of storms in Saxo's "Hamlet", 234, 246. See *World Mill.*

Mimer (mē'mer), xxx, xxxii, xliv, 3, 4, 8, 13, 18, 20, 21, 22, 34, 35, 45, 51, 57; is slain, 76, 89; sons of, 178, 181, 183, 184, 187, 220 n, 223 n; as Gudmund, 257 n; as Mammon, 269 n, 276, 283; the wonder-smith, 355, 357.

Mimer's grove, 13, 50, 59, 89.

Mimer's well, xxxi, 7, 21, 27.

Miming (mē'meng), son of Mimer, 223, 224. Also *Mimingus.*
Mimingus, 51. Also *Miming.*
Mimung sword, 411, 412, 414, 443.
Modgud (med'gud), 155.
Modsognir (med-seg-nir), 13.
Mokker-Kalfi (moo'ker-kyalf-ee) giant, 140, 141.
Moon, origin of, 5.
Moon myth, xxxvii, xxxviii.
Morn (mern), torture demon, 69.
Mountain giants, 16, 31, 87, 107, 178, 359 *n.*
Mundilfore (moon'dil-fer-ee), 4, 6.
Munin (moo'nin), Odin's raven, 26.
Munro, Neil, 350 *n.*
Muse, Edda as, xxii.
Muspelheim (mus'pel-hime), xxvii, 2, 6, 20.
Muter Castle (moo'ter), 436.
Mysinger (mee'sing-er), the sea rover, 248, 249.
Mythology, origin of, xxiii; tribal aspect of, xxiv, xxxiv.

Naastrand (naa'strand), 184.
Nagelfare (nag'el-fär-e), 8.
Naglefar (nag'el-fär), the "nail" ship, 19, 179, 180.
Naglering (nag'el-ring) sword, 405, 406, 407, 408, 410, 413, 417, 422.
Nanna (nan'na), xxxvii, xxxviii, 146, 153, 156, 157, 222, 225, 226, 227.
Napoleon, xlvii.
Narve (nar'va), Mimer as, 8, 45.
Narvi (nar've), son of Loke, 175.
Nat (nótt), night goddess, xxx, 8, 20, 28, 65.
Nature myth tragedies, xxix.
Ness river myth, 419 *n.*
Nibelungenlied (nee'be-lung-en-leed), xxviii, xxxv, xxxviii, xli, 354–403.
Nibelungs (nee'be'lungz), 352 *n*, 376, 383, 389, 391, 446.
Nidhog (nee'dhoog), 14, 15, 18, 182.
Nifelheim (nīfel'hime), xxvii, 1, 2, 5, 10, 13, 14, 20, 46, 100.

Nifel-hel (nīfel'hel), 17, 18, 19, 20, 5( 69, 91, 93, 147, 154, 264 *n.*
Night deities. See *Nat, Balor,* an *Argus.*
Nik, Odin as, xxxviii.
Nitger (net'ger) of Castle Muter, 436.
Nithud (nee'tood), King of Sweden 283, 284.
Njord (nyerd), xxxv, 28, 39, 44, 45 62; weds Skade, 65, 66, 74; de serted by Skade, 75; attacks Asgard 76, 98, 146, 153, 172, 179.
Noatun (nō'a-toon) ruled by Njord, 65 75, 98.
Norns, 14, 15, 20, 46, 49, 59.
Norway, xviii, xix.

Oak, Thor and, xliii.
Odainsaker (ō'den-sak-er), 265, 266 See *Hela.*
Oddi (od'di), xviii, xix.
Odin (ō'din), xxvi, xxxi, xxxvi, xxxvii xxxviii, xliv, 4, 6, 8, 10, 11, 12, 13 15, 19, 21, 22, 23, 24, 25, 26, 27, 29 30, 33, 34, 35, 36, 37, 48, 57, 60, 61 65, 66, 69, 71, 74, 75, 76, 77, 78, 79 81, 83, 84, 86, 87, 88, 90, 91, 92, 93 94, 96, 97, 98, 100, 137, 138, 141 143, 144, 145, 146, 147, 148, 149 151, 152, 153, 154, 155, 156, 157 159–63, 165–8, 169–70, 172, 174 177, 178, 180, 181, 182, 183, 184 186, 187, 226, 285, 288, 289, 290 295, 301, 302, 304, 310, 311, 312 314, 323, 341 *n*, 343, 453 *n.*
Odoacer (ō'do-ak-er), xliii.
Odur (ō'dur), Svipdag as, 83, 231 *n.*
Offotes (of-fo'tes), the giant, 154.
Olaf (ō'laf), history of, xviii.
Oller (ol'ler) as Ull, 231.
Olympians, xxxiv–v.
Onela (on'ela), 215.
Ope (op'e), torture demon, 70.
Orion (o-ri'on), Orvandel identified with 65 *n*, 142.
Orkise (or'kis-e), the giant, 434, 435.
Orkney (ork'ney), 340.

Orkning (ork'ning), brother of Kostbera, 348.

Ortlieb (ort'leeb), son of Etzel, 392, 397.

Ortwin (ort'win), son of Etzel, 442, 443, 445, 446.

Orvandel (ôr-van'del), 39, 45, 47, 48, 49, 55, 56; as Orion, 65 n; Thor's friend, 100, 112, 113, 131, 133, 134, 140, 141, 142, 143; as Hamlet's father, 232, 234 n, 282.

Orvandil. See *Orvandel*.

Ossian (osh'yan), 168 n.

Ossian's (osh'yanz) Cave, xlv.

Ostrogoths (os'tro-goths), xlii, 341 n.

Ottar (ot'tar), 285.

Paradise, xlv.

Patroklos (pa-trok'los), xxiv.

Pictish marriage customs, 242 n.

Polar star, 5.

Polonius (pol'on-i-us), 234 n.

Powell, Frederick York, xxi.

Proserpine (pros'er-pēn), 229.

Rafnagud (raf'na-gud), "raven god", Odin as, 26.

Ragnar Lodbrog (rag'nar lod'brog), 339; fight with serpents, 340; weds Krake, 341.

Ragnarok (rag'na-rok), xxvii, xxx, xliv, 16, 19, 71, 88, 89, 132, 148, 168, 176, 177–82, 262 n.

Ragnar's saga, 341 n.

Ragnhild (ragn'hild) the giant, 268.

Ran, wife of Aegir, nine daughters of, 99, 187, 219 n, 286.

Randolt (ran'dolt), 440.

Ratatosk (ra'ta-tosk), the squirrel gossip, 15.

Rati (ra-tee), Heimdal as, 23, 24.

Ravenna (ra'venn-a), xliii, 442.

Red Cock of Hela. See *Cock*.

Regin (rā'gen), 285, 287, 314, 315, 316, 317, 318, 319, 355.

Reinald (rī'nald), 443.

Rentwin (rent'win), 436.

Rerir (rā'rer), father of Volsung, 288.

Reykjaholt (reyk'ya-holt), xviii.

Rhind (reend), wooed by Odin, 165, 166, 167, 168, 219 n. 341 n. Also *Rinda*.

Rig-veda, xxx.

Rinda (rin'da), the Ruthenian princess, 230, 231.

River deities, 419 n.

River of Torture. See *Slid*.

Romulus Augustulus, xliii.

Rorik (ro'rik), son of Hother, 231, 232, 233, 236, 243.

Rose garden, the wonderful, 424–33.

Roskva (ros'kva), Orvandel's daughter, 113, 117.

Rowan, magic wand of, 132; "Thor's salvation", 134.

Rudiger (rood'e-ger) "The Good", 391, 394, 398, 400, 401, 442, 445.

Runes (roons), 27, 76.

Russia, xlvii.

Rydberg, xxi, xxii, xxxvii, xliv, 208 n, 219 n.

Saemund (sä'mund) the Wise, xviii, xix, xx.

Saga (sa'ga), a maiden, xxii, 26.

St. Swithin's Day, xlvi, 89 n.

Saxo, Danish historian, xx, xxi, xxii, xxvii, xxxviii, 219 n, 232 n, 258 n.

Saxons, xxvi, 25.

Scandinavian literature, xvii.

Scedeland (skade'land), 188.

Scotland, giant lore of, xxxiii, 375 n.

Scotland, Hamlet in, 241, 242.

Scottish queen in "Hamlet". See *Hermutrude*.

Scyld (skylt), xli, 188, 189.

Scyldings (skyl'tings), 189, 193.

Sea-dragon, Svipdag as, 83, 84.

Sea-hags, xxxiii.

Seburg (sä'burch), mountain maiden, 415, 417, 418, 419.

Seven Sleepers, xxxviii, xliv, 89.

Severn river myth, 419 n.

Shakespeare, xxi; Hamlet extract, 243–5.

Ship of Death. See *Naglefar.*

Shylock, 38 *n.*

Sibech (sē'bik), 342 *n.* See *Sibeche.*

Sibeche (sē'bek-e), 342, 439, 440, 442, 443, 445, 447.

Siegfried (seeg'freed), xxxii, xxxv, xxxviii, xlii, 354, 355, 356, 357, 358, 359, 360, 361, 263, 364, 365, 367, 368, 369, 370, 371, 372, 373, 374, 375, 376, 377, 378, 379, 380, 381, 382, 383, 384, 385, 386, 387, 388, 389, 390, 391, 392, 395, 396, 398, 403.

Siegmund (seeg'moont), sire of Siegfried, 354, 358, 361, 366, 367, 380, 382, 388.

Sif, harvest goddess, 34, 35, 138, 144.

Sigbrygg (sig'brig), sire of Groa, 47.

Sige (sig'e), son of Odin, 288.

Sigemund in *Beowulf*, 200.

Sigenot (si'ge-not) the giant, 407, 408, 409.

Siggeir (sig'gīr), King of the Gauts, 289, 290, 291, 292, 293, 295, 296, 297.

Sigmund (seeg'mund), sire of Sigurd, xxv, xli, 287, 289, 291, 292, 293, 294, 295, 296, 297, 298, 299, 304, 309, 310, 311, 312, 316, 318, 322, 323, 328, 329.

Signe (sig'ne), 47, 77.

Signy (sig'ne), daughter of Volsung, 289, 290-1, 292, 293, 294, 295, 296, 297, 310.

Sigrun (sig'roon), wife of Helgi Hundingsbane, 300, 302, 303, 304, 305.

Sigurd (see'goord), xxv, xxxviii, xlii, 287, 314, 315, 316, 317, 318, 319, 320, 322, 323, 324, 325, 327, 328, 329, 330, 331, 332, 333, 334, 335, 336, 341, 343, 348, 349, 354 *n.*

Sigyn (sē'geen), wife of Loke, 176.

Sindre (sin'dree), 6, 12, 35, 36, 37, 38, 45, 52, 59, 89.

Sinfjotle (sen-fyē-ot'le), 293, 294, 295, 296, 297, 300, 309, 310.

Sintram (sint'ram), 421, 422.

Sirius, Thjasse identified with, 65 *n.*

Sith, 49, 53, 55, 56, 62, 66, 77, 153.

Skade (skä'dee), xxxv, 64; selects husband, 65, 66; leaves Njord, 75, 98; punishes Loke, 175.

Skee-runners (shee-), mythical, xxxvii, 56.

Skidbladner (skid-blad'ner), Frey's ship, 35.

Skirner (skeer'ner), Svipdag as, 66; visits Gerd for Frey, 67, 68, 69, 70.

Skobeleff (ske'bel-eff), xlvii.

Skoll (skel), 7, 182.

Skrymer (skrim'er), the giant, 114, 115, 116, 117, 173.

Skuld (skoold), 15.

Skye, Seven Sleepers of, xlv.

Slagfin (slag'fin), 25, 282.

Sleipner (slipe'ner), Odin's steed, 33, 34, 37, 67, 76, 77, 87, 88, 93, 137, 138, 147, 148, 152, 154, 155, 314, 357.

Slid, river of torture, 19, 51, 154; in Spenser, 274-5.

Snorri Sturlason (snor're stoor'lä-sen), xviii, xx.

Sol, sun maid, 6, 39, 165, 184.

Solar myth theory, xl.

Sorle (ser'le), son of Gudrun, 353.

Spenser's *Faerie Queene*, 219-20, 269-76.

Star deities, xxxvi; Thjasse and Orvandel as, 65 *n.*

Stars, origin of, 5.

Stigande (sti-gan'de), Heimdal as, 188.

Stone Age myths, xxviii, xlvii.

Sun, origin of, 5.

Surtur (soort'er), xxxii, xxxv, 20, 22, 23, 24, 71, 87, 132, 168, 177, 180, 182.

Suttung (sut'toong), son of Surtur, 22, 23, 24, 47, 74, 88, 100, 178, 179, 180.

Svadilfare (sva'dil-far-e), horse of giant artisan, 31, 32, 33.

Svanhild (svon - hild), daughter of Gudrun, 341, 342, 343, 439, 447.

Svarin's mound, 47.

Svasud (sva'sood), 8.

Svigdur (svig'dur), 22, 23, 24, 25.

Svipdag (swip'dag), xxxv, xxxvii, xxxviii, xlii, 46, 48, 49, 50, 51, 52, 53, 54, 55, 56, 57; in Asgard, 61, 63; as Skirner, 66, 77, 78, 80; as Ing, 82; as Odur, 83; as sea-dragon, 84, 85, 179, 204n, 208 n, 223 n; as Hother and Hoder, 231 n; as Hamlet, 232 n.

Swan maids, xxxv, xxxvii, xxxviii, 282.

Sword of Victory, xxxv, 45, 51, 52, 57, 59, 60, 62, 63, 67, 69, 70, 71, 75, 77, 96, 179, 180, 207 n, 223 n, 262 n, 283.

Tarku (tar-ku) and Teshup (tesh-up), Hittite Thor, xliii n.

Tay river myth, 419 n.

Tell, William, xlvii; saga myth of, 48 n.

Tennyson, 320–1, 336–7.

Teutonic gloom, xxvii.

Theodoric (toyd'rik), xl, xlii, xliii. See Dietrich.

Theodosius (tā-o-do'se-us), xliv.

Theudemir (toyd'em-ir), xlii, xliii.

Thidrek (tēd'rik) saga, 354 n.

Thingsteads (ting'steds) of Asa-gods, 12, 13, 15, 16, 17, 33, 73, 77, 89, 128, 155, 179.

Thjalfe (te'älf'e), Orvandel's son, 113, 117, 119, 124, 140, 141.

Thjasse (te'äs-se), xxxvi, 39, 45, 46, 51, 52, 57; carries off Loke, 58, 59, 62, 64; as star Sirius, 65 n, 74, 75, 100, 179, 208 n, 262 n, 282–3, 284.

Thomas the Rhymer, xxxv, xlv, 278, 281.

Thor (thôr' or tôr), xxvi, xxxii, xxxiii, xxxvi, xxxviii, xliii, 8, 15, 16, 27, 33, 34, 36, 38, 45, 46, 47, 52, 73, 75, 76, 77, 78, 86, 88, 90; in Hymer's realm, 97, 98, 100, 101, 102, 103, 104, 105, 106, 107, 108–11, 113; adventures with Skrymer, 114–7;

with Utgard-Loke, 118–25; with Thrym, 126–31; with Geirrod, 132–4; poem, 135–6; fighting Trolls, 137; conflict with Hrungner, 138–41; Groa's incantation over, 142, 143; baffled by Greybeard, 143–5; at Balder's pyre, 152, 153, 154; taunted by Loke, 173; captures Loke, 175; at Ragnarok, 181, 182; in heroic story, 226, 356 n.

Thora (thôr'a), daughter of Cuse, 225, 227.

Thora, princess of Denmark, 343.

Thora, wife of Ragnar Lodbrog, 339, 341.

Thorkill (thôr'kel), xliv, 255, 256, 257–65.

Thrall, 188.

Thrym (thrim) the giant, 126, 127, 128, 129, 130, 131.

Thrymheim (thrim'hime), Skade's home, 65, 74, 75.

Thunder deities. See Thor, Dietrich as Thunor, and Hags of Scotland.

Thunor (thoon'er), xxxii, xliii, 418 n.

Thviti (thvee-te), Fenrer boulder, 95.

Tiawath, xxviii, xxx. Also rendered Tiamat and Tauthé.

Titans (tī'tans), xxxiv.

Tope (tô'pe), torture demon, 70.

Tree worship, xxxi, xxxvii.

Trolls, 13, 69, 90, 137.

Trygveson (trig've-sen), King Olav, 267.

Tyr (teer), xxvi, 28, 76, 92, 94; hand lost, 95; as Saxnot, 96, 97; in Hymer's realm, 98, 100, 101, 105, 106, 107, 153, 172; at Ragnarok, 180, 182, 324.

Tyrol, xli, 418 n.

Ubbe (oob'e), son of Aslog, 341.

Uist (oo'isht), Seven Sleepers of, xlvi.

Ull (ool), 49, 53, 54, 55, 62; rules in Asgard, 77, 88. Also Oller (ool'er).

Upsala (up-sa'la), 227.

Urd (oord), Queen of Hela, xxx, 4, 13, 15, 18, 20, 46, 60; Balder with, 151,

152, 156; at Ragnarok, 177, 200 *n*, 201 *n*, 229 *n*.
Urd's fount, 14, 59.
Uta (oot'a), Queen of Burgundy, 362, 367, 369, 378, 391, 393, 403.
Ute (oot'e), Hildebrand's wife, 441.
Utgard (oot'gard) Lokè, xxxii; Thor visits, 117–25, 171; Thorkill visits, 263–5.

Vafthrudner (vaf-throod'ner) the giant, 169, 170.
Vagnhofde (vag-en'hof-dee), the giant, 78, 80, 87.
Vala (vä'la), prophetess, 148, 177, 183, 185.
Vale (vä'le), son of Odin and Rhind, 149, 167, 168, 182. See *Boe*.
Valfather (val'father), Odin as, 25.
Valhal (val'hal), 19, 25; Hag burned in, 73, 89, 138, 167, 182, 302, 304.
Vali (va'li), son of Loke, 175.
Valkyries (val'keer-ez), as elves and swan-maids, xxxv, 19; as "Northern Lights", 48, 89; as wish-maidens, 97, 153, 155; as wood-maidens, 222, 228; Brynhild one of the, 328.
Vana (vän'a), gods, xxvii, xxxiv, xxxv, 3.
Vana-heim (vän'a-hime), 20, 28.
Varns, 7, 20, 165, 166.
Vasud (va'sood), 8.
Ve (vä), 4.
Vedfolner (ved-fol'ner), 14.
Vegtam (veg'tam), name of Odin, 148, 149.
Venom-dale, 19.
Verdande (ver-dan'dee), 15.
Verona as Bern, xlii *n*.
Vidar (vē'dar), son of Odin and Grid, 132, 180, 181, 182.
Vidfinner (ved-fen'ner), 6, 22.
Vigrid (veg-red), 180.
Viking Age, xxvi.
Vikings (Vik'ing), xix, xxxiv.
Vile (ve'le), 4.
Vimur (ve'mer), river, 133.
Vindsval (vind'sval), 8.

Vinge (vin'ge), 346, 347, 348.
Vingolf (vin'golf), 12.
Virginal (vir'gin-al), Queen of the Mountains, 434, 435, 436, 437, 438, 441.
Volker (fol'ker), 395, 396, 398, 400, 401.
Volsung (vol'soong), 285, 287, 288, 289, 290, 291, 293, 294, 295, 297, 298, 310.
Volsunga-saga, xxxviii, xli, 336 *n*, 341 *n*, 354 *n*.
Volund (Ve'loond), xxxvi, xxxvii, 39, 45, 46, 51, 52, 57, 58, 59, 62, 64, 74, 75, 179, 207 *n*, 262 *n*, 283, 284.
Von river, Fenrer source of, 95, 96.

Waghild (wag'heeld) the mermaid, 445.
Walamer (va'la-mer), xlii.
Walberan (val'bran), king of giants and dwarfs, 432.
Wales, giants of, xxxiv.
Walter of Wasgenstein (Val'ter of Vas'-gen-stein), 424, 425.
Wate (va'te), Ivalde as, 65 *n*.
Watling Street, xxxvii, 65 *n*.
Wayland Smith, 283 *n*.
Wealtitheow (wealt'etheow), Hrothgar's queen, 201.
Weders (we'ders), 193.
Weland (wel'and), xxxvi, 283, 284, 355, 411, 412, 413, 414, 417, 427, 429, 443.
Well worship, xxxi, xxxvii, 229 *n*.
Welsung (wel'sung) sword, 424.
Westminster, xlvi.
"Why the Sea is Salt" story, 249–53.
Widemer (wi'dem-er), xlii.
Wieland. See *Weland*.
Wiglaf (wig-laf), 215, 216, 217, 218.
Wiglek (wig'lek), Hamlet's slayer, 243.
Wild Huntsman in Raging Host, xxxi, 453 *n*.
Wind god, Odin as, xxxi; Thjasse as, xxxvi.

Wind hags, xxxiii.

Witches, xxxiii.

Witege (wi'te-ge), son of Weland, 410, 411, 412, 413, 414, 426, 427, 428, 429, 436, 439, 440, 443, 444, 445.

Wolfdales (wolf-dals), 46, 282, 283.

Wolfhart (wolf'hart), 401, 426, 428, 429, 436, 440, 441, 442, 446.

World Mill, xxxvii, 4, 5, 44, 69; giant maids of, 99, 147, 170; in Hamlet, 234 n.

World Tree, Ygdrasil, xxx, xxxi, 11, 13, 14, 15, 16, 18, 20, 27, 30, 59, 61, 62, 73, 89, 134, 178, 182, 183.

Worms, 362, 363, 364, 378, 380, 382, 390, 393.

Wyrd (wērd), 201, 214, 215.

Ygdrasil (ig'dra-sel). See World Tree.

Ymer (ee'mer), the chaos giant, xxviii, xxxvi, 2, 3, 5, 9, 10, 99, 169, 207.

Ynglinga (ing'ling-a) saga, xviii.

Zeno, xliii.